Dillard's Presents

Southern Living
Christmas
Cookbook

benefiting
Ronald McDonald House Charities

RONALD McDONALD
HOUSE CHARITIES

RONALD McDONALD
HOUSE CHARITIES

Merry Christmas from all of us at Dillard's!

We are proud to support the

Ronald McDonald House.

The purchase of this book helps families of seriously ill
children have a comfortable haven near their child.

Thank you!

May your family have a Happy New Year
and a prosperous 2009.

©2005 by Oxmoor House, Inc.
Book Division of Southern Progress Corporation
P.O. Box 2262, Birmingham, Alabama 35201-2262

Southern Living® is a federally registered trademark belonging to Southern Living, Inc.

ISBN-10: 0-8487-3267-7
ISBN-13: 978-0-8487-3267-7
Printed in the United States of America
First Printing 2005

Editor in Chief: Nancy Fitzpatrick Wyatt
Executive Editor: Susan Carlisle Payne
Art Director: Cynthia Rose Cooper
Copy Chief: Allison Long Lowery

Southern Living® Christmas Cookbook
Editor: Rebecca Brennan
Copy Editor: L. Amanda Owens
Editorial Assistants: Julie Boston, Brigette Gaucher, Jessica Dorsey Kohls, Terri Laschober
Senior Designer: Melissa Jones Clark
Senior Photographer: Jim Bathie
Senior Photo Stylist: Kay E. Clarke
Director, Test Kitchens: Elizabeth Tyler Luckett
Assistant Director, Test Kitchens: Julie Christopher
Test Kitchens Staff: Kristi Carter, Nicole Lee Faber, Kathleen Royal Phillips,
    Elise Weis, Kelley Self Wilton
Publishing Systems Administrator: Rick Tucker
Director of Production: Laura Lockhart
Books Production Manager: Greg A. Amason
Production Assistant: Faye Porter Bonner

Contributors
Consulting Editor: Jean Wickstrom Liles
Indexer: Mary Ann Laurens
Interns: Marian Cairns, Mary Catherine Shamblin

Cover: Turkey with Oyster Stuffing, page 29. Back cover: Santa Claus Cupcakes, page 240.

To order additional publications, call 1-800-765-6400.
For more books to enrich your life, visit **oxmoorhouse.com**

Tuscan Pork Roast
(page 109)

Hot Burgundy Cider
(page 54)

Tortellini Tapas
with Spicy Ranch
Dip (page 42)

Cinnamon Loaves
(page 156)

Santa Claus Cupcakes
(page 240)

contents

menus *for family & friends*

festive family feasts

A Blessed Thanksgiving

Roast Turkey with Pear-and-Hazelnut Stuffing

cranberry sauce

mashed potatoes   steamed broccoli   Marmalade Candied Carrots   bakery rolls

White Chocolate Tart with Pecan Crust   Sweet Potato Pie with Gingersnap Streusel

serves 8

menu prep plan

3 days ahead:
• Place turkey in refrigerator to thaw, if frozen.

1 day ahead:
• Prepare White Chocolate Tart with Pecan Crust.
• Cut and chill broccoli and carrots.

morning of:
• Prepare Sweet Potato Pie with Gingersnap Streusel.

5 hours ahead:
• Prepare Pear-and-Hazelnut Stuffing; stuff and bake turkey.

2 hours ahead:
• Microwave potatoes; mash potatoes, and set aside.

1 hour ahead:
• Prepare Marmalade Candied Carrots.
• Steam broccoli.
• Spoon cranberry sauce into serving dish.

last minute:
• Reheat veggies in microwave, if needed.
• Heat rolls.

Roast Turkey with Pear-and-Hazelnut Stuffing

prep: 18 min.   cook: 3 hrs., 40 min.   other: 15 min.

1   (12-pound) turkey *
Fresh sage leaves (optional)
Pear-and-Hazelnut Stuffing (page 12)
⅓   cup butter or margarine, melted
⅓   cup all-purpose flour
1½   cups turkey or chicken broth, divided
1   teaspoon freshly ground pepper
¾   teaspoon poultry seasoning
½   teaspoon salt
Garnish: fresh sage leaves

Remove giblets and neck, and rinse turkey thoroughly with cold water; pat dry. Tuck several fresh sage leaves under skin of bird, if desired. Lightly pack 1½ cups Pear-and-Hazelnut Stuffing into neck cavity of turkey. Lightly pack 5 cups stuffing into body cavity. Tuck legs under flap of skin around tail, or close cavity with skewers, and truss. Tie ends of legs to tail with cord. Lift wingtips up and over back, and tuck under turkey.

Place turkey in a lightly greased roasting pan, breast side up; brush entire bird with melted butter. Bake at 325° for 3 to 3½ hours or until meat thermometer registers 180° in meaty part of thigh and 165° in stuffing. Baste turkey frequently with remaining melted butter and pan juices. If turkey starts to brown too much, cover with aluminum foil. When turkey is two-thirds done, cut the cord or band of skin holding the drumstick ends to the tail; this will ensure that the insides of the thighs are cooked. Turkey is done when drumsticks are easy to move up and down. Transfer turkey to a serving platter. Let turkey stand 15 minutes before carving.

Combine flour and ½ cup broth; stir until smooth. Add to drippings in roasting pan. Bring to a boil over medium heat, stirring constantly. (Place pan over 2 burners, if necessary.) Stir in remaining broth, pepper, poultry seasoning, and salt. Reduce heat, and simmer 5 minutes or until gravy is thickened, stirring frequently.

Serve turkey with Pear-and-Hazelnut Stuffing and gravy. Garnish, if desired. Yield: 12 servings.

* If you purchase a frozen turkey, allow 3 days for it to thaw in refrigerator.

Roast Turkey with Pear-and-Hazelnut Stuffing, cranberry sauce, mashed potatoes, steamed broccoli, Marmalade Candied Carrots (page 12)

Pear-and-Hazelnut Stuffing

prep: 20 min.   cook: 1 hr.

1   pound ground pork sausage
4   celery ribs, sliced
1   large onion, chopped
½   cup butter or margarine, melted
2   large red pears, chopped
4   garlic cloves, minced
1   (16-ounce) day-old French bread
       loaf, cubed
1   cup toasted, chopped hazelnuts
3   tablespoons chopped fresh sage or
       1 tablespoon rubbed sage
2   teaspoons coarsely ground pepper
1½ cups turkey or chicken broth

Brown pork sausage in a large skillet, stirring until it crumbles. Drain sausage on paper towels. Discard drippings.

Sauté celery and onion in butter in large skillet over medium-high heat just until crisp-tender. Add chopped pear and garlic; sauté until pear is tender. Remove sautéed mixture from heat.

Place French bread cubes in a large bowl. Stir in sausage, celery mixture, hazelnuts, sage, and pepper. Pour broth over stuffing, stirring gently. Stuff turkey, using 6½ cups stuffing.

Place remaining stuffing in a lightly greased 8-inch square pan. Bake, uncovered, at 325° during the last hour the turkey bakes. Yield: 11 cups.

Marmalade Candied Carrots

prep: 11 min.   cook: 16 min.

2   pounds carrots, scraped and sliced
       diagonally
⅔   cup orange marmalade
2   tablespoons brown sugar
2   tablespoons butter or margarine
3   tablespoons spiced rum
½   cup coarsely chopped pecans, toasted

Arrange carrots in a vegetable steamer over boiling water. Cover and steam 10 minutes or until crisp-tender.

Transfer carrots to a serving bowl. Gently stir marmalade into carrots until marmalade melts.

Combine next 3 ingredients in a small saucepan. Cook over medium heat until butter and brown sugar melt. Remove from heat; stir in pecans. Pour over carrot mixture in bowl. Toss gently. Yield: 8 servings.

White Chocolate Tart with Pecan Crust

editor's favorite

prep: 32 min.   cook: 18 min.
other: 9 hrs., 30 min.

18   pecan shortbread cookies, crushed
¾   cup finely chopped pecans
¼   cup butter or margarine, melted
2   (1-ounce) semisweet chocolate
       baking squares
1   tablespoon shortening
16   pecan halves
½   cup whipping cream
9   ounces premium white chocolate,
       finely chopped
1½ cups (12 ounces) mascarpone cheese
3   tablespoons Frangelico liqueur
1¼ cups whipping cream

Combine cookie crumbs, chopped pecans, and melted butter; stir well. Press mixture in bottom and up sides of an 11-inch tart pan with removable bottom. Bake at 375° for 8 minutes. Cool.

Combine semisweet chocolate and shortening in top of a double boiler; bring water to a boil. Reduce heat to low; cook until chocolate melts. Dip 8 pecan halves halfway into chocolate mixture. Let harden on a wire rack. Brush remaining chocolate mixture over prepared crust. Cool completely.

Place ½ cup whipping cream in top of a double boiler over hot, not simmering, water. Heat whipping cream thoroughly. Gradually add white chocolate, and stir constantly with a spatula until white chocolate melts. Remove from heat. Cool to room temperature. Dip remaining 8 pecan halves halfway into white chocolate mixture. Let harden on wire rack. Dip again, if desired. Cool remaining white chocolate mixture completely.

Position knife blade in food processor bowl; add mascarpone cheese and Frangelico. Process 10 seconds (mixture may look curdled). Add white chocolate mixture; process 30 seconds or until smooth. Slowly pour 1¼ cups whipping cream through food chute with processor running, blending 2 to 3 minutes or until mixture is very smooth, scraping down sides of bowl occasionally.

Spoon mixture into prepared crust. Cover and chill 8 hours. Top with dipped pecan halves. Let stand at room temperature 5 minutes before serving. Yield: 1 (11-inch) tart.

Plan ahead as much as possible for the big Thanksgiving feast so you can focus on enjoying the company of friends and family on the big day.

• Set the table, arrange the centerpiece, and select the serving dishes the day before so on the day of the meal you can attend to the food.
• Clean out your refrigerator and freezer to make room for all the pre-meal goodies and post-meal leftovers.
• Start the day with an empty dishwasher, and you'll find the task of cleaning more manageable.
• Designate an area for coffee, cider, tea, and other beverages. Your guests can serve themselves and create an instant opportunity to feel at home.

Sweet Potato Pie with Gingersnap Streusel

**prep: 19 min.   cook: 1 hr., 8 min.
other: 30 min.**

2   cups gingersnap crumbs
⅓   cup butter or margarine, melted
1   (29-ounce) can sweet potatoes, drained and mashed
1¼   cups evaporated milk
¾   cup firmly packed brown sugar
3   large eggs, beaten
1¼   teaspoons ground cinnamon
1   teaspoon ground allspice
⅔   cup coarsely crushed gingersnaps
⅓   cup firmly packed brown sugar
3   tablespoons all-purpose flour
2   tablespoons butter, cut up
Garnish: sweetened whipped cream

Combine 2 cups gingersnap crumbs and ⅓ cup melted butter; stir well. Firmly press crumb mixture over bottom and up sides of a 9½-inch deep-dish pieplate. Bake at 350° for 6 to 8 minutes. Cool.

Stir together sweet potatoes and next 5 ingredients; pour into prepared crust. Bake at 350° for 20 minutes.

Combine ⅔ cup crushed gingersnaps, ⅓ cup brown sugar, and flour; cut in 2 tablespoons butter with a pastry blender until mixture is crumbly. Sprinkle streusel over pie, and bake 15 more minutes. Cover pie with aluminum foil, and bake 25 more minutes or until set. Cool on a wire rack. Garnish, if desired. Yield: 1 (9½-inch) deep-dish pie.

Sweet Potato Pie with Gingersnap Streusel

As this pie bakes, the spicy aroma of cinnamon and allspice fills your kitchen and delights your senses.

Holiday Dinner for Two

tossed green salad
Tenderloin for Two with Peppercorn Cream
hot cooked rice   Green Beans with Crispy Shallots
Fudge Pie with Peanut Butter Sauce
serves 2

menu prep plan

morning of:
• Prepare Fudge Pie, and make Peanut Butter Sauce.

1 hour ahead:
• Thaw beans.
• Prepare green salad (do not add dressing).

40 minutes ahead:
• Cook rice.
• Cook tenderloin fillets and make Peppercorn Cream sauce.
• Prepare Green Beans with Crispy Shallots.

last minute:
• Toss green salad with dressing.

Tenderloin for Two with Peppercorn Cream

prep: 9 min.   cook: 25 min.

1   tablespoon olive oil
2   (6-ounce) beef tenderloin fillets
Salt and pepper to taste
¼   cup brandy
1   large garlic clove, minced
1   teaspoon multicolored peppercorns, crushed
½   teaspoon dried oregano
⅛   teaspoon salt
⅔   cup whipping cream
1½ tablespoons sour cream
Hot cooked rice
Garnish: fresh oregano sprigs

Heat oil in a medium skillet until hot. Sprinkle fillets with salt and pepper. Sear on both sides in skillet. Remove from skillet, and place on a rack in a broiler pan.

Broil 5½ inches from heat 5 minutes on each side or until meat thermometer registers 145° (medium-rare).

Add brandy to drippings in skillet; bring to a boil, stirring to loosen particles from bottom. Add minced garlic and next 3 ingredients; cook 1 minute. Add whipping cream; bring to a boil, and cook 6 minutes or until sauce is reduced by half. Remove from heat. Whisk in sour cream, and spoon over fillets. Serve with rice. Garnish, if desired. Yield: 2 servings.

Green Beans with Crispy Shallots

prep: 9 min.   cook: 8 min.

1   shallot
1   (9-ounce) package frozen French-cut green beans, thawed
3   tablespoons boiling water
1   tablespoon butter or margarine
1   tablespoon sliced pimiento
2   teaspoons balsamic vinegar
¼   teaspoon salt
¼   teaspoon sugar
¼   teaspoon pepper
1   tablespoon butter or margarine

Slice shallot lengthwise into very thin slivers. Place beans in a skillet. Add boiling water; cover and cook 2 minutes over medium heat. Uncover and stir in 1 tablespoon butter, pimiento, vinegar, salt, sugar, and pepper. Sauté 1 minute.

Transfer bean mixture to a small serving plate. Add 1 tablespoon butter to skillet. Add slivered shallot, and cook over medium-high heat until crisp and browned. Remove with a slotted spoon, and drain on paper towels. Sprinkle browned shallot over beans, and serve immediately. Yield: 2 servings.

Fudge Pie with Peanut Butter Sauce

prep: 13 min.   cook: 36 min.

1¼ cups chocolate wafer crumbs
⅓   cup butter or margarine, melted
½   cup butter or margarine, softened
½   cup firmly packed brown sugar
3   large eggs
1   (12-ounce) package semisweet
       chocolate morsels, melted
1   teaspoon vanilla extract
½   cup all-purpose flour
¾   cup chopped unsalted peanuts
Peanut Butter Sauce
Frozen whipped topping, thawed
Toasted, chopped peanuts

Combine chocolate wafer crumbs and ⅓ cup melted butter; press mixture firmly on bottom and up sides of a 9-inch pieplate. Bake at 350° for 6 to 8 minutes.

Beat ½ cup butter at medium speed with an electric mixer until creamy. Gradually add sugar, beating mixture until blended. Add eggs, 1 at a time, beating after each addition. Stir in melted chocolate morsels and vanilla. Add flour, beating at low speed just until blended. Stir in ¾ cup peanuts. Pour into prepared crust. Bake at 350° for 28 minutes; cool on a wire rack.

To serve, top with Peanut Butter Sauce, whipped topping, and additional chopped peanuts. Yield: 1 (9-inch) pie.

Peanut Butter Sauce

prep: 5 min.   cook: 9 min.

¼   cup firmly packed brown sugar
3   tablespoons butter or margarine
2   tablespoons light corn syrup
½   cup crunchy peanut butter
⅓   cup whipping cream
1   large egg, slightly beaten
2   teaspoons vanilla extract

Tenderloin for Two with Peppercorn Cream, hot cooked rice, Green Beans with Crispy Shallots

A cream sauce seasoned with crushed peppercorns adds a pungent flavor to these tenderloin fillets.

Combine first 3 ingredients in a small heavy saucepan. Bring to a boil, stirring frequently.

Stir in peanut butter and whipping cream, and cook 2 minutes. Gradually add one-fourth of hot mixture to egg, stirring constantly. Add to remaining hot mixture.

Cook, stirring constantly, 1 minute or until mixture reaches 160°. Remove from heat, and add vanilla. Cool. Yield: 1⅓ cups.

Busy Mom's Super-Quick Supper

Praline Chicken
Rosemary Roasted Potatoes   steamed green beans
Coconut-Pecan Chess Pie
serves 6

menu prep plan

morning of:
- Prepare Coconut-Pecan Chess Pie.

1 hour ahead:
- Prepare Rosemary Roasted Potatoes; keep warm.
- Steam green beans; keep warm.

20 minutes ahead:
- Prepare Praline Chicken.

Praline Chicken

prep: 5 min.   cook: 15 min.

2   teaspoons Creole seasoning
6   skinned and boned chicken breasts
¼   cup butter, melted
1   tablespoon vegetable oil
⅓   cup maple syrup
2   tablespoons brown sugar
1   cup chopped pecans, toasted

Sprinkle seasoning on both sides of chicken. Cook chicken in butter and oil in a skillet over medium heat 5 minutes on each side or until done. Remove chicken, reserving drippings in skillet. Place chicken on a serving platter; keep warm.

Add syrup and sugar to drippings in skillet; bring to a boil. Stir in pecans; cook 1 minute or until heated. Spoon mixture over chicken. Yield: 6 servings.

Rosemary Roasted Potatoes

prep: 10 min.   cook: 40 min.

2   pounds round red potatoes, unpeeled and quartered
2   garlic cloves, minced
¼   teaspoon salt
½   teaspoon dried thyme
1   tablespoon olive oil
2   teaspoons chopped fresh rosemary
⅛   teaspoon pepper

Combine all ingredients in a large zip-top freezer bag. Seal bag, and shake well to coat. Arrange potato in a well-greased 13- x 9-inch baking dish.

Bake, uncovered, at 450° for 40 minutes or until potato is tender, stirring occasionally. Yield: 6 servings.

Coconut-Pecan Chess Pie

prep: 8 min.   cook: 40 min.

3   large eggs, lightly beaten
1   cup sugar
⅓   cup buttermilk
2   tablespoons butter or margarine, melted
1   tablespoon cornmeal
½   teaspoon coconut flavoring
¾   cup flaked coconut
¼   cup chopped pecans
1   unbaked 9-inch pastry shell

Combine first 6 ingredients; stir in coconut and pecans. Pour filling into pastry shell.

Bake at 400° for 10 minutes. Reduce heat to 350°, and bake 30 more minutes. Cool on a wire rack. Yield: 1 (9-inch) pie.

Praline Chicken, steamed green beans, Rosemary Roasted Potatoes

Make-Ahead Comfort Food Dinner

mixed green salad

Make-Ahead Company Beef Stew   Mashed Potato Bowls

bakery rolls

Cookies 'n' Cream Dessert

serves 6

menu prep plan

up to 1 month ahead:
• Cook bacon, and prepare Make-Ahead Company Beef Stew; freeze separately.
• Prepare Mashed Potato Bowls; freeze.

up to 1 week ahead:
• Prepare Sugar-and-Spice Pecans (page 98); store in an airtight container.

1 day ahead:
• Bake sugar cookies; decorate goblets with melted candy coating for Cookies 'n' Cream Dessert.
• Scoop ice cream balls; freeze.
• Place stew and bacon in refrigerator to thaw.

30 minutes ahead:
• Prepare mixed green salad.
• Heat stew; keep warm.
• Bake frozen Mashed Potato Bowls; keep warm.

last minute:
• Heat rolls.
• Assemble dessert just before serving.

Make-Ahead Company Beef Stew

Warmth and hospitality come straight from the freezer with this hearty stew.

prep: 21 min.   cook: 2 hrs., 12 min.
other: 9 hrs., 30 min.

1   (3-pound) boneless chuck roast, cut into 1-inch cubes
1   large onion, sliced
1   garlic clove, minced
1   tablespoon dried parsley flakes
½   teaspoon salt
½   teaspoon pepper
½   teaspoon dried thyme
1   bay leaf
1   cup dry red wine
2   tablespoons olive oil
4   bacon slices, cut crosswise into ¼-inch pieces
3   tablespoons all-purpose flour
1½ cups beef broth
½   pound baby carrots
1   (16-ounce) package frozen pearl onions
2   tablespoons butter or margarine
1   (8-ounce) package fresh mushrooms
Mashed Potato Bowls
Garnishes: fresh thyme sprigs, fresh chives

Combine first 8 ingredients in a shallow dish or zip-top freezer bag. Combine wine and oil; pour over meat mixture. Cover or seal; chill 1 hour. Drain well, reserving marinade.

Cook bacon in an ovenproof Dutch oven until crisp; remove bacon, reserving drippings in Dutch oven. Drain bacon on paper towels. Place in a zip-top freezer bag; seal and freeze.

Brown beef in reserved bacon drippings. Drain and return to Dutch oven; sprinkle with flour, and cook, stirring constantly, 1 to 2 minutes. Add reserved marinade and broth; bring to a boil.

Bake, covered, at 300° for 1 hour and 30 minutes or until tender. Add carrots and pearl onions; bake 30 more minutes.

Melt butter in a large skillet. Add mushrooms; sauté until tender. Add to beef mixture. Cool and spoon into a freezer container; cover and freeze up to 1 month.

Remove bacon and stew from freezer; thaw in refrigerator overnight. Place stew in a Dutch oven; cook over medium heat, stirring occasionally. Discard bay leaf. Serve in Mashed Potato Bowls. Sprinkle with bacon; garnish, if desired. Yield: 6 cups.

Mashed Potato Bowls

**prep: 16 min.   cook: 48 min.
other: 2 hrs., 30 min.**

4   large potatoes (3 pounds)
2   teaspoons salt, divided
1   (8-ounce) package cream cheese,
       softened
1   large egg, lightly beaten
2   tablespoons all-purpose flour
¼   teaspoon baking powder
1   tablespoon butter, melted
¼   teaspoon paprika

Cook potatoes, 1 teaspoon salt, and boiling water to cover in a Dutch oven 25
minutes or until tender. Drain and cool
to touch.

Peel potatoes; mash in a large bowl,
using a potato masher. Stir in remaining
salt, cream cheese, and next 3 ingredients until blended.

Spoon mixture into 6 large mounds
on a baking sheet. Shape each mound
into a 4-inch bowl, using the back of a
large serving spoon; cover and freeze
until firm. Place frozen bowls in zip-top
freezer bags; freeze up to 1 month.

Remove bowls from freezer; place
frozen bowls on a lightly greased baking
sheet. Brush with melted butter, and
sprinkle with paprika.

Bake frozen bowls at 450° for 15 minutes or until thoroughly heated and
lightly browned. Yield: 6 potato bowls.

Make-Ahead Company Beef Stew,
Mashed Potato Bowls, bakery rolls,
mixed green salad

Cookies 'n' Cream Dessert

prep: 12 min.   cook: 7 min. per batch

½   gallon vanilla ice cream
8   ounces chocolate bark coating, melted
½   cup finely chopped Sugar-and-
       Spice Pecans (page 98)
½   teaspoon edible gold-leaf powder
24   star-shaped sugar cookies *

Scoop ice cream into 12 balls onto a
baking sheet; place in freezer.

Place melted bark coating in a small
zip-top freezer bag. Snip a small hole
in 1 corner of bag; drizzle inside of
12 goblets to decorate. Set goblets aside
in a cool, dry place. (Do not store in
refrigerator.)

Place an ice cream ball in each glass.
Sprinkle ice cream with Sugar-and-Spice

Pecans and gold-leaf powder; top with
cookies. Yield: 12 servings.

* For cookies, roll a 20-ounce package of
refrigerated sugar cookie dough to ⅛-inch
thickness on a lightly floured surface.
Cut into star shapes, using star-shaped
cookie cutters that have been dipped in
flour. Bake on greased baking sheets at
350° for 7 minutes. Yield: 5 dozen.

Cozy Christmas Eve Entertaining

Orange-Ginger Hens with Cranberry Salsa
basmati rice pilaf   steamed baby carrots
Black-and-White Crème Brûlée
serves 4

menu prep plan

1 day ahead:
• Prepare Cranberry Salsa: chill.
• Trim carrots. if needed.
• Prepare Black-and-White Crème Brûlée; remove from water pan. and chill.

1 to 2 hours ahead:
• Prepare Orange-Ginger Hens.
• Prepare basmati rice pilaf; keep warm.

30 minutes ahead:
• Steam carrots.
• Complete preparation of Black-and-White Crème Brûlée.

Black-and-White Crème Brûlée

Orange-Ginger Hens with Cranberry Salsa

prep: 12 min.   cook: 1 hr., 6 min.

4   (1½-pound) Cornish hens
1   teaspoon salt
½   teaspoon pepper
¼   cup butter or margarine
¼   cup lemon juice
1   tablespoon grated orange rind
¾   cup fresh orange juice
4   garlic cloves. minced
1   tablespoon grated fresh ginger
1   tablespoon Dijon mustard
1   teaspoon prepared horseradish
Cranberry Salsa
Hot cooked basmati rice pilaf (optional)

Rub hens with salt and pepper; tie ends of legs together. if desired. Place. breast side up. on a rack in a roasting pan. Bring butter and next 7 ingredients to a boil in a saucepan: pour over hens. Bake at 375° for 1 hour or until done. basting often with butter mixture. Serve with Cranberry Salsa and. if desired. pilaf. Yield: 4 servings.

Cranberry Salsa

prep: 14 min.   other: 1 hr., 30 min.

1   cup dried cranberries
½   cup fresh orange juice
½   cup peeled. seeded. and diced cucumber
½   cup diced red onion
¼   cup chopped fresh cilantro
1   garlic clove. minced
1   jalapeño pepper. seeded and diced
¼   cup fresh lime juice
½   teaspoon ground cumin
½   teaspoon salt

Soak cranberries in orange juice in a bowl 30 minutes. Stir in cucumber and remaining ingredients. Cover and chill. Yield: 3 cups.

Black-and-White Crème Brûlée

editor's favorite
prep: 15 min.   cook: 57 min.
other: 9 hrs., 5 min.

2½ cups whipping cream. divided
5   (1-ounce) semisweet chocolate baking squares
6   egg yolks
½   cup granulated sugar
1   teaspoon vanilla extract
6   tablespoons light brown sugar

Orange-Ginger Hens with Cranberry Salsa, basmati rice pilaf, steamed baby carrots

Cook ½ cup whipping cream and chocolate in a heavy saucepan over low heat, stirring constantly, until chocolate melts and mixture is smooth. Pour into a large bowl.

Whisk together remaining 2 cups whipping cream, yolks, granulated sugar, and vanilla until sugar dissolves and mixture is smooth.

Whisk 1 cup egg mixture into chocolate mixture until smooth. Cover and chill remaining egg mixture.

Pour chocolate mixture evenly into 6 (6- or 8-ounce) baking cups; place cups in a 13- x 9-inch pan. Add hot water to pan to depth of ½ inch.

Bake at 325° for 30 minutes or until almost set. (Center will be soft.) Slowly pour remaining yolk mixture evenly over custards. Bake 20 to 25 more minutes or until set. Cool custards in water in pan on a wire rack. Remove from pan; cover and chill at least 8 hours.

Sprinkle each custard with 1 table-spoon brown sugar; place custards in a pan.

Broil 5½ inches from heat until sugar melts (about 2 minutes). Let stand 5 minutes to allow sugar to harden. Yield: 6 servings.

Christmas Morning Brunch

French Toast Sticks   sausage or bacon

Favorite Ambrosia   White Christmas Tree

serves 4 to 6

menu prep plan

1 day ahead:
• Peel and section oranges and grapefruit for Favorite Ambrosia; chill.
• Insert picks into cone for White Christmas Tree.

2 hours ahead:
• Assemble White Christmas Tree.

1½ hours ahead:
• Cook sausage or bacon; cover and keep warm.
• Prepare Favorite Ambrosia; chill.

30 minutes ahead:
• Prepare French Toast Sticks.

Children enjoy "decorating" this doughnut hole Christmas tree—you might want to buy a few extra doughnut holes in case some "disappear."

French Toast Sticks

prep: 7 min.   cook: 16 min.

8   (1-inch-thick) slices French bread
1   cup refrigerated eggnog
½   teaspoon ground nutmeg
¼   cup butter or margarine, divided
Sifted powdered sugar

Cut French bread slices into 1-inch-wide strips. Combine eggnog and nutmeg in a shallow bowl. Preheat griddle to 350°; melt 2 tablespoons butter.

Dip bread strips in eggnog mixture. Cook, a few at a time, 2 to 4 minutes on each side or until golden, adding additional 2 tablespoons butter as needed.

Sprinkle toast with powdered sugar. Serve with syrup. Yield: 4 to 6 servings.

Favorite Ambrosia

prep: 20 min.

3   oranges
2   grapefruit
1   large banana, sliced
½   cup coarsely chopped maraschino
        cherries
2   tablespoons mayonnaise
1   tablespoon powdered sugar
¼   teaspoon grated orange rind
¾   cup frozen whipped topping,
        thawed
¼   cup flaked coconut, toasted
Garnish: maraschino cherries with stems

Peel and section oranges and grapefruit, catching juice in a bowl. Toss banana slices in juice; remove with a slotted spoon. Place grapefruit sections in a small glass bowl. Layer orange sections, chopped cherries, and banana slices over grapefruit. Pour juice over fruit.

Combine mayonnaise, powdered sugar, and orange rind; fold in whipped topping. Spoon over fruit; sprinkle with coconut. Garnish, if desired. Yield: 4 to 6 servings.

White Christmas Tree

prep: 11 min.

1   (10-inch) plastic foam cone
3   dozen powdered sugar-coated
        doughnut holes or small
        doughnuts
Fresh cranberries
Fresh mint sprigs (optional)

Position foam cone on a pedestal or serving plate covered with a white doily. Insert wooden picks into cone about 1 inch apart. Place a doughnut on each wooden pick, covering entire cone.

Place cranberries on wooden picks, and insert into cone between doughnuts. Decorate tree with fresh mint sprigs, if desired. Display cone as an edible centerpiece. Yield: 1 doughnut tree.

French Toast Sticks, sausage or bacon, Favorite Ambrosia, White Christmas Tree

A Southern-Style Holiday Feast

Cranberry Ham

Honey-and-Nut Rice   steamed broccoli spears

Sweet Potato Biscuits

serves 8 to 10

menu prep plan

1 day ahead:
• Cut and chill broccoli spears.

morning of:
• Bake Sweet Potato Biscuits.

3 hours ahead:
• Prepare Cranberry Ham.

1 hour ahead:
• Prepare Honey-and-Nut Rice; keep warm.
• Carve ham; keep warm.

last minute:
• Steam broccoli.
• Reheat biscuits.

Cranberry Ham

prep: 20 min.   cook: 2 hrs., 4 min.

1   (5- to 7-pound) smoked fully cooked ham half
Whole cloves
1   (8-ounce) can jellied cranberry sauce
¼   cup firmly packed brown sugar
3   tablespoons cider vinegar
1   tablespoon commercial steak sauce
½   teaspoon dry mustard
¼   teaspoon ground allspice
¼   teaspoon ground cloves
2   tablespoons orange juice
1   bunch red grapes
Garnish: salad savoy

Remove and discard skin from ham. Make ¼-inch-deep cuts in fat on ham in a diamond design with a sharp knife; stud with whole cloves. Place ham, fat side up, on a rack in a shallow roasting pan. Insert meat thermometer, making sure it does not touch fat or bone.

Combine cranberry sauce and next 6 ingredients, stirring well. Baste ham lightly with cranberry mixture. Cover and bake at 325° for 1 hour. Uncover and baste ham. Bake, uncovered, 1 more hour or until meat thermometer registers 140°, basting every 15 minutes.

Combine orange juice and remaining cranberry mixture in a skillet. Trim grapes to make several small clusters.

Add grapes to orange juice mixture; toss gently. Cook over low heat just until juices bubble and grapes are glazed.

Transfer ham to a serving platter. Add glazed grapes. Garnish, if desired. Yield: 10 to 14 servings.

Idea for Leftovers: Chop leftover Cranberry Ham, and toss with any leftover Honey-and-Nut Rice. Cover and chill. Serve as a main-dish salad in Bibb lettuce cups.

Honey-and-Nut Rice

prep: 13 min.   cook: 6 min.

1   cup sliced celery
¾   cup chopped onion
2   tablespoons butter or margarine
3½   cups cooked long-grain rice
1   cup coarsely chopped walnuts, toasted
⅓   cup raisins
⅓   cup golden raisins
3   tablespoons honey
3   tablespoons lime juice
1   tablespoon olive oil
¼   teaspoon salt
¼   teaspoon ground cinnamon
¼   teaspoon pepper
Garnish: celery leaves

Sauté celery and onion in butter in a Dutch oven until vegetables are tender.

Cranberry Ham,
steamed broccoli spears,
Sweet Potato Biscuits

*Clusters of glazed grapes
adorn Cranberry Ham
and provide a tasty
garnish.*

Remove from heat. Add rice, walnuts, and raisins, stirring well.

Combine honey and next 5 ingredients in a small bowl; stir well. Drizzle honey mixture over rice. Toss gently. Spoon into a serving bowl. Garnish, if desired. Yield: 8 to 10 servings.

Sweet Potato Biscuits

prep: 12 min.   cook: 12 min.

2	cups self-rising flour
3	tablespoons brown sugar
¼	teaspoon ground allspice
¼	cup butter or margarine
3	tablespoons butter-flavored shortening
1	cup cooked, mashed sweet potato
¼	cup plus 2 tablespoons milk
2	tablespoons butter or margarine, melted

Combine first 3 ingredients in a bowl. Cut in ¼ cup butter and shortening with a pastry blender until mixture is crumbly. Add sweet potato and milk, stirring just until dry ingredients are moistened. Turn dough out onto a floured surface; knead 3 or 4 times.

Roll dough to ½-inch thickness; cut with a 2-inch round cutter. Place biscuits on an ungreased baking sheet. Brush with melted butter. Bake at 400° for 12 minutes. Yield: 1½ dozen.

Christmas Dinner with All the Trimmings

Wild Rice Soup

Turkey with Oyster Stuffing

Green Beans Supreme   buttered carrots   whole-berry cranberry sauce

Easy Buttery Crescent Rolls

Simple Ambrosia   Chocolate-Caramel-Pecan Pie

serves 10 to 12

menu prep plan

3 days ahead:

• Place turkey in refrigerator to thaw. if frozen.

• Make Easy Buttery Crescent Rolls dough; chill.

1 day ahead:

• Prepare Chocolate-Caramel-Pecan Pie; chill.

• Prepare Simple Ambrosia; chill.

• Prepare Wild Rice Soup; chill.

6 hours ahead:

• Prepare Turkey with Oyster Stuffing.

• Bake Easy Buttery Crescent Rolls.

1 hour ahead:

• Assemble Green Beans Supreme.

• Bake Oyster Stuffing (baking dish).

30 minutes ahead:

• Bake Green Beans Supreme.

• Reheat Wild Rice Soup.

• Carve turkey.

• Reheat rolls.

• Spoon cranberry sauce into serving dish.

Wild Rice Soup

Mild-flavored chervil adds distinctive flavor to this special-occasion soup.

prep: 12 min.   cook: 1 hr., 6 min.

1	(6-ounce) package wild rice
1	cup finely chopped onion
1	teaspoon salt
1	teaspoon dried chervil
1	teaspoon curry powder
½	teaspoon dry mustard
½	teaspoon pepper
¼	cup butter or margarine, melted
1	(8-ounce) package sliced fresh mushrooms
½	cup thinly sliced celery
½	cup all-purpose flour
6	cups chicken broth
2	cups half-and-half
⅔	cup dry sherry

Garnish: fresh chives

Cook wild rice according to package directions.

Meanwhile, cook onion and next 5 ingredients in butter in a large Dutch oven over medium-high heat, stirring constantly, until onion is tender.

Add mushrooms and celery; cook, stirring constantly, until mushrooms are tender. Reduce heat to low. Add flour, stirring until blended. Cook 1 minute, stirring constantly.

Gradually add chicken broth; cook over medium heat, stirring constantly, until slightly thickened.

Stir in cooked rice, half-and-half, and sherry; cook until thoroughly heated. To serve, ladle soup into individual soup bowls. Garnish, if desired. Yield: 12 cups.

Beginning the meal with an appetizer soup is an elegant start to a holiday dinner.

Wild Rice Soup

Turkey with Oyster Stuffing, whole-berry cranberry sauce, Green Beans Supreme (page 30), Easy Buttery Crescent Rolls (page 30)

Turkey with Oyster Stuffing

prep: 1 hr., 4 min.   cook: 4 hrs., 20 min.

- 4   large onions, chopped (about 4½ cups) and divided
- 2   medium carrots, scraped and chopped (about 1 cup)
- 1   celery rib, chopped (about ½ cup)
- 12 sprigs fresh parsley
- 3   sprigs fresh celery leaves
- 2   sprigs fresh thyme or ½ teaspoon dried thyme
- 2   bay leaves
- 2   whole cloves, crushed
- 1   (10- to 12-pound) turkey
- 1½ cups finely chopped fresh celery leaves
- 2   tablespoons chopped green bell pepper
- 2   tablespoons chopped fresh parsley
- 1   teaspoon rubbed sage
- ½   teaspoon salt
- ½   teaspoon black pepper
- ½   teaspoon dried thyme
- ½   teaspoon ground mace
- ½   teaspoon ground cloves
- 1   cup butter or margarine, melted
- 12 cups soft breadcrumbs (fresh)
- 2   (12-ounce) containers Standard oysters, well drained and chopped
- 6   slices bacon
- 1   to 2 cups chicken broth
- 3   tablespoons all-purpose flour

Place 1½ cups chopped onion and next 7 ingredients in bottom of a large roasting pan; set aside.

Remove giblets and neck from turkey; reserve for another use. Rinse turkey thoroughly with cold water; pat dry. Place turkey, breast side up, on a rack in prepared pan. Set aside.

Cook remaining chopped onion, chopped fresh celery leaves, and next 8 ingredients in butter in a large skillet over medium-high heat, stirring constantly, until tender. Combine onion mixture, breadcrumbs, and oysters in a large bowl. Set aside.

Cook bacon in a large skillet until crisp; remove bacon, reserving ¼ cup drippings. Reserve bacon for another use.

Spoon 2 cups oyster mixture into body cavity of turkey. Spoon remaining oyster mixture into a lightly greased 11- x 7-inch baking dish, and refrigerate. Tie ends of legs together with string. Lift wingtips up and over back, and tuck under bird. Rub entire surface of turkey with bacon drippings.

Cover pan with heavy-duty aluminum foil, being careful not to let foil touch turkey. Bake at 325° for 2½ to 3 hours. Uncover and bake 1 more hour or until a meat thermometer inserted in meaty portion of thigh registers 180° and stuffing registers 165°.

Bake oyster mixture in baking dish at 325°, uncovered, for 45 minutes or until golden.

Transfer turkey to a large serving platter, reserving drippings in pan. Pour drippings through a wire-mesh strainer into a glass measuring cup, discarding solids. Skim fat from drippings. Add enough broth to drippings to measure 2 cups.

Combine 2 cups drippings and flour in a medium saucepan, stirring with a wire whisk until mixture is smooth. Cook over medium heat, stirring constantly, until mixture thickens slightly. Serve gravy with turkey. Yield: 10 to 12 servings.

Stuffing Note: Stuff the bird just before you put it in the oven, never ahead. Bake until stuffing temperature reaches 165°. Immediately remove and refrigerate any stuffing left over from the turkey cavity. Reheat until hot and steaming (165°).

Green Beans Supreme

prep: 12 min.   cook: 55 min.

3   (16-ounce) bags frozen cut green
      beans
1   cup sliced onion
2   tablespoons minced fresh parsley
¼   cup butter, melted and divided
¼   cup all-purpose flour
2   teaspoons salt
½   teaspoon pepper
1   (16-ounce) carton sour cream
2   cups (8 ounces) shredded processed
      American cheese
1   cup fine, dry breadcrumbs
      (commercial)

Cook green beans according to package
directions; drain well.

Cook onion and parsley in 2 tablespoons butter in a large skillet over
medium-high heat, stirring constantly,
until tender. Reduce heat to medium-low.
Stir in flour, salt, and pepper. Add sour
cream, stirring well. Add green beans;
cook until thoroughly heated, stirring
occasionally.

Spoon mixture into an ungreased
13- x 9-inch baking dish; sprinkle with
cheese. Combine breadcrumbs and
remaining butter; sprinkle over cheese.
Bake at 325° for 25 minutes or until
cheese melts and breadcrumbs are
browned. Yield: 12 servings.

---

cranberry sauce savvy

If you'd like to fresh up the color of a can of
whole-berry cranberry sauce, stir in a handful
of fresh cranberries. Cover loosely with heavy-
duty plastic wrap, and microwave on HIGH for
3 minutes or until mixture is bubbly but berries
have not quite begun to pop; stir gently.

Easy Buttery Crescent Rolls

*These rolls bake up extra light and
buttery. You can chill this dough up to
three days, and cut and shape as much
as you need when you need it.*

make-ahead
prep: 17 min.   cook: 16 min.
other: 3 hrs., 35 min.

1   (¼-ounce) envelope active dry yeast
1   cup warm water (100° to 110°),
      divided
1   teaspoon sugar
1   cup butter or margarine, softened
½   cup sugar
½   teaspoon salt
2   large eggs
4   to 4½ cups all-purpose flour

Combine yeast, ¼ cup water, and 1 teaspoon sugar in a 1-cup glass measuring
cup; let stand 5 minutes.

Combine yeast mixture, remaining
warm water, butter, and next 3 ingredients in a large mixing bowl; beat at
medium speed with an electric mixer
until well blended. Gradually stir in
enough flour to make a soft dough. Place
dough in a well-greased bowl, turning
to grease top. Cover and chill at least
3 hours or up to 3 days.

Turn dough out onto a heavily floured
surface, and knead lightly 4 or 5 times.
Divide dough into fourths; shape each
portion into a ball. Roll each ball into an
11-inch circle on a lightly floured surface. Cut each circle into 8 wedges; roll
up each wedge, beginning at the wide
end. Place on ungreased baking sheets,
point sides down. Cover and let rise in a
warm place (85°), free from drafts, 30
minutes or until doubled in bulk. Bake
at 375° for 14 to 16 minutes or until
golden. Yield: 32 rolls.

Simple Ambrosia

*Oranges, pineapple, and coconut make
a versatile fruit dish to serve as a side
dish or light dessert.*

prep: 32 min.   other: 1 hr.

18   small oranges
2   (15¼-ounce) cans crushed
       pineapple, undrained
3   cups grated fresh, canned, or frozen
       coconut
1   cup chopped walnuts, toasted
Whipped cream (optional)
Garnish: maraschino cherries with
       stems

Peel and section oranges, catching juice
in a large nonmetal bowl. Add orange
sections, pineapple, and coconut to juice;
toss gently. Cover and chill thoroughly.

To serve, stir in toasted walnuts, and
spoon fruit mixture into individual
dishes; top each serving with a dollop
of whipped cream, if desired. Garnish,
if desired. Yield: 10 to 12 servings.

Chocolate-Caramel-Pecan Pie

*For this menu, prepare two pies to
serve 12.*

prep: 29 min.   cook: 32 min.
other: 2 hrs., 30 min.

2   cups finely chopped pecans
¼   cup granulated sugar
¼   cup butter or margarine, melted
1   (14-ounce) package caramels
¼   cup milk
1   cup chopped pecans
8   (1-ounce) semisweet chocolate
       baking squares
⅓   cup milk
¼   cup sifted powdered sugar
½   teaspoon vanilla extract

Chocolate-Caramel-Pecan Pie

Combine pecans, granulated sugar, and melted butter in a small bowl; stir well. Firmly press mixture in bottom and up sides of a 9-inch pieplate. Bake at 350° for 12 minutes. Cool completely on a wire rack.

Unwrap caramels, and place in a medium saucepan. Add ¼ cup milk; cook over low heat until caramels melt, stirring often. Remove from heat, and pour over prepared crust. Sprinkle 1 cup chopped pecans over caramel mixture.

Combine chocolate, ⅓ cup milk, powdered sugar, and vanilla in a heavy saucepan. Cook over low heat until chocolate melts, stirring constantly. Drizzle evenly over pecans. Cover and chill 2 hours. Yield: 1 (9-inch) pie.

Simple Day-After-Christmas Supper

leftover roasted chicken, smoked turkey breast, or honey-glazed ham

Broccoli Parmesan   Sweet Cornbread Dressing

cranberry sauce   bakery rolls

Lemon Pie (page 205)

serves 6

menu prep plan

morning of:

• Bake corn muffin mixes for Sweet Cornbread Dressing; set aside.

1 to 2 hours ahead:

• Prepare Lemon Pie.
• Prepare Sweet Cornbread Dressing; keep warm.
• Prepare sauce for Broccoli Parmesan.

30 minutes ahead:

• Arrange chicken, turkey, or ham on platter.
• Steam broccoli; pour sauce over broccoli.
• Spoon cranberry sauce into serving dish.
• Heat rolls.

Broccoli Parmesan

prep: 7 min.   cook: 11 min.

1   (16-ounce) package fresh broccoli florets
2   tablespoons butter or margarine
3   tablespoons chopped onion
2   tablespoons all-purpose flour
1   teaspoon chicken bouillon granules
1¾ cups milk
½   cup freshly grated Parmesan cheese
½   teaspoon salt
½   teaspoon pepper
½   teaspoon dry mustard
¼   teaspoon ground marjoram
Additional grated Parmesan cheese (optional)

Arrange broccoli in a steamer basket over boiling water. Cover and steam 5 minutes or until crisp-tender. Keep warm.

Melt butter in a heavy saucepan; add onion, and sauté until tender. Add flour and bouillon granules, stirring until blended.

Cook, stirring constantly, 1 minute. Gradually add milk; cook over medium heat, stirring constantly, until thickened and bubbly. Stir in cheese and next 4 ingredients; pour over broccoli in serving bowl. Sprinkle with additional cheese, if desired. Yield: 6 servings.

Sweet Cornbread Dressing

prep: 17 min.   cook: 1 hr., 26 min.

other: 20 min.

2   (8½-ounce) packages corn muffin mix
2   celery ribs, chopped
1   medium onion, chopped
2   tablespoons vegetable oil
1   (10¾-ounce) can cream of chicken soup, undiluted
1   (14-ounce) can chicken broth
1½ teaspoons rubbed sage
½   teaspoon pepper
¼   teaspoon celery salt
2   hard-cooked eggs, chopped

Prepare corn muffin mixes according to package directions; pour all batter into a lightly greased 8-inch square pan. Bake at 400° for 25 to 28 minutes or until golden; cool in pan on wire racks. Crumble cornbread into a large bowl.

Sauté celery and onion in hot oil in a large skillet until tender. Add soup and next 4 ingredients to skillet, stirring mixture until blended; bring to a boil. Pour over cornbread, stirring until moistened. Stir in chopped egg. Spoon into a lightly greased 8-inch square baking dish. Bake at 350° for 40 to 45 minutes or until lightly browned. Yield: 6 to 8 servings.

leftover roasted chicken, cranberry sauce,
Broccoli Parmesan, Sweet Cornbread
Dressing, bakery rolls

New Year's Eve Dinner

Jalapeño-Black-Eyed Pea Dip
Golden Glazed Ham
Spinach-Vegetable Couscous
Orange Blossom Cheesecake
Champagne
serves 12

menu prep plan

1 day ahead:

• Prepare Orange Blossom Cheesecake; chill.

• Make Jalapeño-Black-Eyed Pea Dip; chill. (Do not prepare orange slices.)

• Chill Champagne.

morning of:

• Prepare orange slices for Orange Blossom Cheesecake. Let dry as directed.

2 hours ahead:

• Prepare Golden Glazed Ham.

• Arrange orange slices on cheesecake.

1 hour ahead:

• Prepare Spinach-Vegetable Couscous.

Jalapeño-Black-Eyed Pea Dip

If you'd like to lighten this dip, substitute a fat-free Italian dressing for the regular dressing.

prep: 18 min.   other: 2 hrs.

2   (15-ounce) cans black-eyed peas, rinsed and drained

1   (15-ounce) can black-eyed peas with jalapeño peppers, rinsed and drained

2   medium tomatoes, seeded and chopped

1   cup Italian dressing

¾   cup chopped onion

½   cup chopped yellow bell pepper

½   cup chopped green bell pepper

¼   to ¾ cup seeded, chopped jalapeño pepper

1   (2-ounce) jar diced pimiento, drained

1½ teaspoons minced garlic

½   teaspoon ground cumin

½   teaspoon black pepper

Combine all ingredients in a large bowl, stirring well. Cover and chill at least 2 hours. Serve dip with large corn chips or tortilla chips. Yield: 8 cups.

Golden Glazed Ham

Leftovers from this recipe are yummy straight from the fridge.

prep: 7 min.   cook: 1 hr., 36 min.
other: 10 min.

1   (7-pound) fully cooked ham half

2   cups firmly packed brown sugar, divided

2   (12-ounce) cans beer

2   tablespoons honey

2   tablespoons Dijon mustard

½   cup bourbon

Place ham, fat side up, in a deep roasting pan. Press 1 cup brown sugar onto all sides of ham. Pour beer into pan. Insert meat thermometer into ham, making sure it does not touch fat or bone. Cover and bake at 325° for 30 minutes. Remove 2 cups drippings from pan.

Combine remaining 1 cup brown sugar, honey, mustard, and bourbon in a saucepan; cook over medium heat, stirring constantly, until sugar melts. Baste ham with sugar mixture. Return ham to oven; bake, uncovered, 1 hour or until meat thermometer registers 140°, basting with reserved drippings and sugar mixture every 10 minutes. Let stand 10 minutes before slicing. Yield: 14 servings.

Spinach-Vegetable Couscous

prep: 29 min.   cook: 7 min.   other: 15 min.

¼   cup olive oil
1½ teaspoons ground ginger
1½ teaspoons ground turmeric
1½ teaspoons ground cinnamon
2   (14-ounce) cans chicken broth
1⅓ cups couscous, uncooked (about
      8 ounces)
½   cup golden raisins
½   cup pitted dates, diced
½   cup blanched almonds, toasted
3   medium carrots, scraped and diced
1   large tomato, diced
1   small yellow squash, diced
1   small zucchini, diced
1   small red onion, chopped
3   cups spinach leaves, rolled and
      sliced (about 2½ ounces)
½   cup olive oil
¼   cup lemon juice
¼   teaspoon salt

Combine first 5 ingredients in a Dutch
oven; bring to a boil. Add couscous;
cook 2 minutes or until most of liquid
is absorbed, stirring often. Remove from
heat; stir in raisins and dates. Cover and
let stand 15 minutes.

Combine almonds and next 6 ingredients in a large bowl. Combine ½ cup oil,
lemon juice, and salt in a jar; cover
tightly, and shake vigorously. Pour oil
mixture over almond mixture; toss well.
Add couscous mixture; toss well. Serve
immediately, or chill slightly. Yield:
12 servings.

Orange Blossom Cheesecake

To make slicing this cheesecake easier,
cut the oranges for decorating the top
into the thinnest slices possible.

prep: 30 min.   cook: 3 hrs., 39 min.
other: 14 hrs.

3   cups gingersnap crumbs
⅓   cup butter or margarine, melted
2   teaspoons grated orange rind
1½ cups fresh orange juice
⅓   cup unpeeled and thinly sliced fresh
      ginger
4   (8-ounce) packages cream cheese,
      softened
⅔   cup sugar
1   (6-ounce) package white chocolate
      baking bar, melted
4   large eggs
2   tablespoons grated orange rind
1   tablespoon vanilla extract
3   cups water
1½ cups sugar
2   oranges, unpeeled and cut into very
      thin slices

Combine first 3 ingredients in a bowl;
stir well. Firmly press crumb mixture on
bottom and up sides of a 9-inch springform pan. Chill.

Combine orange juice and ginger in a
saucepan; bring to a boil. Reduce heat,
and simmer 20 to 30 minutes or until
reduced to 3 tablespoons. Pour mixture
through a wire-mesh strainer into a
small bowl, discarding ginger.

Beat cream cheese at medium speed
with an electric mixer until creamy. Add
⅔ cup sugar, beating well. Add strained
orange juice mixture, and beat well.
With mixer running, add chocolate in a
steady stream, beating until blended.
Add eggs, 1 at a time, beating after each
addition. Stir in 2 tablespoons orange

Orange Blossom Cheesecake

rind and vanilla. Pour batter into prepared pan.

Bake at 300° for 1 hour and 25 minutes. Turn oven off, and leave cheesecake
in oven 4 hours. (Do not open oven door.)
Cool to room temperature in pan on a
wire rack; cover and chill at least 8 hours.

Cover a wire rack with wax paper.
Combine water and 1½ cups sugar in
a large skillet; cook over medium heat
until sugar dissolves, stirring often.
Reduce heat to medium-low; simmer 3
minutes. Add orange slices, 1 at a time,
and simmer 45 minutes. Turn orange
slices, and simmer 45 more minutes or
until tender and translucent. Arrange
orange slices in a single layer on prepared rack. Let dry 1 hour.

Carefully remove sides of springform
pan. Overlap orange slices in a decorative pattern on top of cheesecake. Yield:
12 servings.

holiday entertaining

Autumn Celebration

Brussels Sprouts with Parmesan Soufflés
Wild Rice-Stuffed Turkey Breast *or* Molasses-Grilled Pork Tenderloin (page 110)
Roasted Winter Vegetables   Buttered Asparagus Spears
bakery rolls
Double-Chocolate Bombe *or* Apple Dumplings with Maple-Cider Sauce (page 209)
serves 8

menu prep plan

1 day ahead:
• Bake cake and make mousse for Double-Chocolate Bombe. Assemble bombe in bowl; chill.
• Cut and cook vegetables for Roasted Winter Vegetables; chill.
• Cook asparagus spears; chill.

4 to 5 hours ahead:
• Prepare Chocolate Ganache, and complete Double-Chocolate Bombe.
• Prepare Parmesan Soufflés up to chilling stage; chill.
• Prepare Wild Rice-Stuffed Turkey Breast.

30 minutes ahead:
• Cook Brussels sprouts, and complete Brussels Sprouts with Parmesan Soufflés.

1 hour ahead:
• Bake Roasted Winter Vegetables.
• Carve turkey breast.

last minute:
• Complete preparation of asparagus.
• Heat rolls.

Brussels Sprouts with Parmesan Soufflés

editor's favorite

prep: 18 min.   cook: 8 min.

1   pound Brussels sprouts, each cut in half lengthwise
8   bacon slices
¼   teaspoon salt
¼   teaspoon freshly ground pepper
Parmesan Soufflés (page 39)

Cook Brussels sprouts in boiling water to cover 1 minute; drain. Plunge into ice water to stop the cooking process; drain. Separate leaves; discard cores.

Cook bacon in a large skillet until crisp; remove bacon, reserving 1 tablespoon drippings in skillet. Crumble bacon. Sauté sprout leaves, salt, and pepper in bacon drippings 1 minute. Arrange on serving plates. Top with Parmesan Soufflés; sprinkle with bacon. Serve immediately. Yield: 8 servings.

Brussels Sprouts with Parmesan Soufflés

Wild Rice-Stuffed Turkey Breast (page 39),
Roasted Winter Vegetables (page 39)

Wild Rice-Stuffed Turkey Breast,
Roasted Winter Vegetables, bakery rolls,
Buttered Asparagus Spears (page 40)

Parmesan Soufflés

prep: 29 min.   cook: 36 min.

4   frozen phyllo pastry sheets,
     thawed
½   cup butter, melted and divided
¼   cup all-purpose flour
⅛   teaspoon dry mustard
Pinch of ground nutmeg
1   cup milk
1   cup grated Parmesan cheese,
     divided
4   large eggs, separated
½   teaspoon salt
¼   teaspoon freshly ground pepper

Cut 32 (7-inch) squares from pastry
sheets. Brush squares with ¼ cup melted
butter, and arrange into 8 stacks, stag-
gering corners; fit stacks into 6-ounce
custard cups, allowing corners to overhang edges.

Whisk together remaining ¼ cup butter, flour, mustard, and nutmeg in a
saucepan until smooth; cook over low
heat, whisking constantly, 1 minute.
Gradually add milk, and cook over
medium heat, whisking constantly, until
thickened and bubbly. Pour into a large
bowl; gradually add ⅔ cup cheese.
Whisk in yolks, salt, and pepper; cool
to lukewarm.

Beat egg whites until stiff peaks form;
fold into cheese mixture in 2 batches.
Spoon into custard cups; place in a large
roasting pan. Add hot water to pan to
a depth of 1 inch. Bake at 350° for
20 minutes or until slightly firm to
touch; cool in water on a wire rack. Lift
soufflés gently from cups; place on a
greased baking sheet. Sprinkle with
remaining cheese. Chill up to 4 hours, if
desired.

Bake at 375° for 10 minutes or until
thoroughly heated. Serve immediately.
Yield: 8 servings.

Wild Rice-Stuffed Turkey Breast

**prep: 28 min.   cook: 2 hrs., 24 min.
other: 1 hr.**

1   (3-ounce) package dried cherries
1½ cups port wine
3½ cups chicken broth, divided
½   cup uncooked wild rice
½   cup uncooked long-grain rice
1   teaspoon freshly ground pepper
1   small onion, chopped
½   cup diced celery
2   cups soft whole wheat breadcrumbs
1   (4½- to 5-pound) skinned and
     boned turkey breast
2   teaspoons chopped fresh rosemary
2   garlic cloves, minced
1   tablespoon kosher salt
1   tablespoon freshly ground pepper
2   tablespoons butter or margarine
¼   cup all-purpose flour

Combine cherries and wine; let stand
1 hour. Drain, reserving wine.

Meanwhile, bring 2 cups broth and next
5 ingredients to a boil in a medium
saucepan; cover, reduce heat, and simmer
30 minutes or until liquid is absorbed and
rice is tender. Cool; stir in cherries and
breadcrumbs.

Place turkey between 2 sheets of heavy-
duty plastic wrap; flatten to 1-inch thickness, using a meat mallet or rolling pin.

Rub skinless side of turkey with rosemary and garlic; spread evenly with rice
mixture. Starting at a long side, tightly
roll up breast, jellyroll fashion; secure at
2-inch intervals with kitchen string.

Sprinkle the turkey with salt and
1 tablespoon pepper; place on a lightly
greased rack in a roasting pan.

Bake at 375° for 1 hour and 45 minutes
or until a meat thermometer inserted into
thickest portion registers 170°. Remove

from pan, reserving any drippings in pan;
let turkey stand 10 minutes before slicing.

Melt butter in a heavy saucepan over
low heat; stir in reserved drippings. Whisk
flour into butter until mixture is smooth.
Cook, whisking constantly, 1 minute.
Gradually add reserved wine and remaining 1½ cups broth; cook over medium
heat, whisking occasionally, 5 minutes or
until thickened. Serve with sliced stuffed
turkey. Yield: 8 to 10 servings.

Roasted Winter Vegetables

prep: 21 min.   cook: 54 min.   other: 28 min.

4   parsnips, peeled
4   turnips, peeled
½   medium rutabaga, peeled
½   medium butternut squash, peeled
2   quarts water
2   tablespoons kosher salt, divided
¼   cup all-purpose flour
1   teaspoon freshly ground pepper
⅓   cup butter or margarine, melted

Cut parsnips into 1-inch slices; cut
turnips, rutabaga, and squash into 1-inch
cubes. Bring parsnip, turnip, rutabaga, 2
quarts water, and 1 tablespoon salt to a
boil in a Dutch oven; boil, stirring occasionally, 5 minutes. Add squash; cook 7
to 10 minutes or until squash is slightly
tender. Drain vegetables, and cool. Cover
and chill up to 8 hours, if desired.

Combine remaining salt, flour, and
pepper in a zip-top freezer bag; add
one-third of vegetables. Seal; shake until
coated. Place vegetables in a single layer
in a large greased roasting pan. Repeat
procedure with remaining vegetables and
flour mixture. Drizzle vegetables with
melted butter, tossing gently. Bake at
375° for 30 minutes or until golden.
Serve immediately. Yield: 8 servings.

Buttered Asparagus Spears

quick & easy

prep: 2 min.   cook: 19 min.

3   pounds fresh asparagus *
2   quarts water
¼   cup butter or margarine
½   teaspoon salt
½   teaspoon freshly ground pepper

Snap off tough ends of asparagus. Bring 2 quarts water to a boil in a Dutch oven. Add asparagus: cook 3 to 5 minutes or until crisp-tender. Rinse with cold water; drain. Cover and chill, if desired.

Melt butter in a large skillet: add asparagus, salt, and pepper. Sauté until thoroughly heated. Serve immediately. Yield: 8 servings.

* 3 pounds fresh green beans can be substituted for asparagus, if desired.

Double-Chocolate Bombe

editor's favorite

prep: 26 min.   cook: 20 min.
other: 10 hrs., 10 min.

½   cup pecan pieces, toasted
¼   cup butter, softened
¼   cup shortening
1   cup sugar
1½   teaspoons vanilla extract
3   large eggs, separated
1   cup all-purpose flour
½   teaspoon baking soda
½   cup buttermilk
Chocolate Mousse
White Chocolate Mousse
Chocolate Ganache
Garnish: chocolate curls

Process pecans in a food processor until ground: set aside.

Beat butter and shortening at medium speed with an electric mixer until creamy: gradually add sugar, beating well. Add vanilla, beating until blended. Add egg yolks, 1 at a time, beating until blended after each addition.

Combine flour, soda, and ground pecans: add to creamed mixture alternately with buttermilk, beginning and ending with flour mixture. Beat at low speed until blended after each addition.

Beat egg whites until stiff peaks form: fold into batter. Pour mixture into a well-greased and floured 15- x 10-inch jelly-roll pan.

Bake at 350° for 20 minutes or until a wooden pick inserted in center comes out clean. Cool in pan on a wire rack 10 minutes: remove from pan, and cool completely on wire rack.

Line a 3-quart mixing bowl (8½ inches across) with plastic wrap. Cut cake lengthwise into 2-inch strips; line prepared bowl with cake strips, reserving remaining strips. Spread Chocolate Mousse over cake in bowl: cover and chill 1 hour.

Pour White Chocolate Mousse into bowl over chocolate layer. Cover and chill 1 more hour. Cover with remaining cake strips. Cover and chill at least 8 hours.

Invert bombe onto a large cake plate: spread Chocolate Ganache over bombe. Garnish, if desired. Yield: 8 to 10 servings.

Chocolate Mousse

prep: 6 min.   cook: 5 min.   other: 45 min.

1   cup whipping cream, divided
1   (8-ounce) package semisweet
        chocolate baking squares
¼   cup light corn syrup
¼   cup butter
2   tablespoons powdered sugar
½   teaspoon vanilla extract

Cook ¼ cup whipping cream and next 3 ingredients in a heavy saucepan over low heat, stirring constantly, until chocolate melts. Cool.

Beat remaining ¾ cup whipping cream, powdered sugar, and vanilla at high speed with an electric mixer until stiff peaks form: fold into chocolate mixture. Cover and chill at least 30 minutes. Yield: 2½ cups.

White Chocolate Mousse

prep: 5 min.   cook: 5 min.   other: 20 min.

½   cup whipping cream, divided
3   (1-ounce) white chocolate baking
        squares
2   tablespoons light corn syrup
2   tablespoons butter
1   tablespoon powdered sugar
¼   teaspoon vanilla extract

Cook 2 tablespoons whipping cream and next 3 ingredients in a heavy saucepan over low heat, stirring constantly, until smooth. Cool.

Beat remaining whipping cream, powdered sugar, and vanilla at high speed with an electric mixer until stiff peaks form; fold into white chocolate mixture. Yield: 1¼ cups.

Chocolate Ganache

prep: 2 min.   cook: 4 min.

1   (8-ounce) package semisweet
        chocolate baking squares
¼   cup whipping cream

Cook chocolate and whipping cream in a heavy saucepan over low heat, stirring constantly, until chocolate melts. Yield: ¾ cup.

Double-Chocolate Bombe

Tree-Trimming Chili Dinner

Tortellini Tapas with Spicy Ranch Dip
White Christmas Chili
Spicy Candy Cane Breadsticks
Banana Pudding Trifle
serves 6

menu prep plan

1 day ahead or morning of:
- Prepare Banana Pudding Trifle.
- Prepare White Christmas Chili; chill.
- Prepare Spicy Ranch Dip.

2 to 3 hours ahead:
- Prepare Tortellini Tapas (keep warm up to 2 hours).

40 minutes ahead:
- Reheat White Christmas Chili.
- Bake Spicy Candy Cane Breadsticks.

Tortellini Tapas with
Spicy Ranch Dip

Tortellini Tapas with Spicy Ranch Dip

The breadcrumb coating is the key to keeping the tortellini tender.

make-ahead

prep: 8 min.   cook: 25 min.   other: 1 hr., 40 min.

1   (9-ounce) package refrigerated cheese-filled tortellini
1   (16-ounce) bottle Ranch-style dressing with peppercorns, divided *
2   large eggs
2   cups fine, dry breadcrumbs (commercial)
¾   cup mild chunky salsa
¼   cup chopped fresh cilantro
2   cups vegetable oil
Garnish: fresh cilantro sprigs

Cook tortellini according to package directions; drain and cool. Whisk together 1 cup dressing and eggs in a large bowl until blended.

Add tortellini, and let stand 10 minutes. Drain and dredge in breadcrumbs; place on a baking sheet. Cover and chill at least 1 hour. Stir together remaining dressing, salsa, and chopped cilantro; cover dip, and chill.

Pour oil into a Dutch oven; heat to 375°. Fry tortellini, in batches, until golden on both sides. Drain on paper towels. Garnish, if desired. Serve with dip. Yield: 8 appetizer servings.

* 1 (16-ounce) bottle Ranch-style dressing plus ½ teaspoon cracked black pepper may be substituted, if desired.

Make-Ahead Note: Fry tortellini according to directions; drain and place on a baking sheet. Keep warm in a 200° oven up to 2 hours.

White Christmas Chili (page 44)

White Christmas Chili

prep: 18 min.   cook: 45 min.

8   skinned and boned chicken breasts
2   medium onions, chopped
2   garlic cloves, minced
1   tablespoon vegetable oil
2   (14-ounce) cans chicken broth
4   (15.5-ounce) cans cannellini beans
        or other white beans, rinsed and
        drained
1   (15.5-ounce) can cannellini beans
        or other white beans, rinsed,
        drained, and mashed
2   (4.5-ounce) cans chopped green
        chiles, undrained
1   teaspoon salt
1   teaspoon ground cumin
¾   teaspoon dried oregano
½   teaspoon chili powder
½   teaspoon ground black pepper
⅛   teaspoon ground cloves
⅛   teaspoon ground red pepper
Toppings: shredded Monterey Jack
        cheese with jalapeño peppers,
        salsa, sour cream, chopped fresh
        cilantro

Cut chicken into bite-size pieces.

Sauté chicken, onion, and garlic in hot oil in a Dutch oven over medium-high heat 10 minutes or until chicken is done.

Stir in broth and next 10 ingredients; bring to a boil. Reduce heat, and simmer, uncovered, 30 minutes. Serve with desired toppings. Yield: 15 cups.

Spicy Candy Cane Breadsticks

These are perfect companions for gumbo, stew, or chili. They're shaped like candy canes, but they're spicy hot rather than sweet!

prep: 26 min.   cook: 12 min.

1   (11-ounce) can refrigerated
        breadsticks
1   large egg, lightly beaten
2   tablespoons paprika
2   tablespoons seasoned pepper blend *
        (we tested with McCormick)

Separate breadsticks; working with 2 at a time, roll each breadstick into a 20-inch rope. Brush ropes with egg. Twist ropes together, pinching ends to seal.

Combine paprika and pepper blend; spread mixture on a paper plate. Roll breadsticks in pepper mixture, pressing gently to coat. (Wash hands between rolling each breadstick, if necessary.)

Place breadsticks on a greased baking sheet, curving top of each breadstick to form a candy cane shape. Bake at 375° for 10 to 12 minutes or until golden. Yield: 6 servings.

* If you can't find seasoned pepper blend, combine equal portions of cracked black pepper, red bell pepper flakes, and salt.

Spicy Candy Cane
Breadsticks

Banana Pudding Trifle

editor's favorite

prep: 27 min.   cook: 10 min.   other: 3 hrs.

1⅓ cups granulated sugar

¾   cup all-purpose flour

½   teaspoon salt

4   cups milk

8   egg yolks

1   tablespoon vanilla extract

1   (12-ounce) package vanilla wafers

¼   cup bourbon

2   tablespoons rum

6   ripe bananas, sliced

6   (1.4-ounce) chocolate-covered
     toffee candy bars, crushed

2   cups whipping cream

2   tablespoons sifted powdered sugar

Combine first 3 ingredients in a large heavy saucepan; whisk in milk. Bring to a boil over medium heat, whisking constantly. Remove from heat.

Beat egg yolks until thick and pale. Gradually stir one-fourth of hot mixture into yolks; add to remaining hot mixture, stirring constantly. Cook, stirring constantly, 1 minute. Stir in vanilla.

Layer one-third of wafers in a 16-cup trifle bowl or 4-quart baking dish. Combine bourbon and rum; brush over wafers. Top with one-third of banana.

Spoon one-third of custard over banana, and sprinkle with ⅓ cup crushed candy bar. Repeat layers twice.

Beat cream at medium speed with an electric mixer until foamy; gradually add powdered sugar, beating until soft peaks form. Spread over trifle; sprinkle with remaining crushed candy. Cover; chill 3 hours. Yield: 10 to 12 servings.

Caroling Party

Sautéed Shrimp and Pasta
mixed salad greens with Garlic Dressing
Parmesan Breadsticks
Chocolate-Raisin Bread Pudding
serves 8

menu prep plan

morning of:
- Peel and devein shrimp; chill.
- Prepare Parmesan Breadsticks.
- Prepare Crème Anglaise for pudding; chill.
- Tear salad greens; chill.

2 hours ahead:
- Prepare bread pudding and dressing.

30 minutes ahead:
- Cook pasta; keep warm.

15 minutes ahead:
- Prepare Sautéed Shrimp.
- Reheat Parmesan Breadsticks.
- Toss green salad with Garlic Dressing.

Sautéed Shrimp and Pasta

prep: 25 min.   cook: 5 min.

3   pounds unpeeled, large fresh shrimp
½   cup butter or margarine
2   (0.7-ounce) envelopes Italian
        dressing mix
Hot cooked pasta

Peel shrimp, and devein, if desired.
    Melt butter in a large skillet over medium heat; stir in dressing mix. Add shrimp; cook, stirring constantly, 3 to 5 minutes or until shrimp turn pink. Serve over pasta. Yield: 8 servings.

Sautéed Shrimp and Pasta,
Parmesan Breadsticks

Garlic Dressing

If any dressing is left over, use it as a marinade for meats or as a topping for baked potatoes or veggies.

prep: 4 min.

2   tablespoons fresh lemon juice
2   elephant garlic cloves
½   cup grated Parmesan cheese
¼   cup olive oil
3   tablespoons mayonnaise
1   teaspoon salt
½   teaspoon freshly ground pepper

Position knife blade in food processor bowl; add lemon juice and garlic. Process until garlic is finely chopped. Place garlic mixture in a small bowl; stir in cheese and remaining ingredients. Yield: 1 cup.

Parmesan Breadsticks

prep: 26 min.   cook: 13 min.   other: 30 min.

2   (¼-ounce) envelopes active dry yeast
1½   cups warm water (100° to 110°)
4   cups all-purpose flour, divided
2   teaspoons salt
1½   tablespoons honey
1   large egg
½   cup butter or margarine
2   tablespoons grated Parmesan cheese
½   teaspoon garlic powder
½   teaspoon dried parsley flakes

Combine yeast and ½ cup warm water in a 1-cup glass measuring cup; let stand 5 minutes. Combine 2 cups flour and salt; set aside.

Combine yeast mixture, remaining 1 cup warm water, honey, and egg in a large bowl; beat at medium speed with an electric mixer until blended. Gradually add flour mixture, beating until blended.

Gradually stir in enough of remaining 2 cups flour to make a soft dough.

Turn dough out onto a floured surface; knead until smooth and elastic (6 to 8 minutes). Place in a greased bowl, turning to grease top. Cover and let rise in a warm place (85°), free from drafts, 15 minutes.

Combine butter and remaining 3 ingredients in a small saucepan; cook over medium heat until butter melts, stirring occasionally. Set aside.

Punch dough down; turn out onto a lightly floured surface. Roll dough into a 21- x 6½-inch rectangle. Cut dough crosswise into 21 (1-inch) strips. Twist each strip 2 times (dough will be soft). Place strips on a lightly greased baking sheet; brush with half of butter mixture. Cover and let rise in a warm place, free from drafts, 10 minutes. Bake at 400° for 12 minutes. Brush with remaining butter mixture. Yield: 21 breadsticks.

Chocolate-Raisin Bread Pudding

prep: 19 min.   cook: 50 min.   other: 35 min.

1   (1-pound) loaf cinnamon-raisin bread
4   large eggs, lightly beaten
1½   cups milk
½   cup whipping cream
½   cup firmly packed brown sugar
⅓   cup Irish cream liqueur
¼   cup dark rum
1   (4-ounce) semisweet chocolate baking bar, chopped
½   cup raisins
1   tablespoon grated orange rind
1   tablespoon vanilla extract
Crème Anglaise

Remove crust from bread; reserve crust for other uses. Cut bread into cubes, and place in a large bowl.

Combine eggs and next 5 ingredients in a medium bowl; stir in chocolate and next 3 ingredients. Pour over bread; stir well. Cover and chill 30 minutes.

Pour into a greased 9-inch springform pan. Bake, uncovered, at 350° for 50 minutes or until a knife inserted in center comes out clean. Cool in pan 5 minutes. Carefully remove sides of pan; cut pudding into wedges. Serve warm with Crème Anglaise. Yield: 8 servings.

Crème Anglaise

prep: 16 min.   cook: 8 min.   other: 30 min.

1   vanilla bean
1⅓   cups whipping cream
⅔   cup milk
4   egg yolks
½   cup sugar
½   cup Irish cream liqueur

Cut a 2-inch piece of vanilla bean, reserving remaining bean for other uses. Split bean lengthwise. Combine bean, cream, and milk in a heavy saucepan. Cook over medium heat, stirring constantly, until mixture reaches 185°.

Whisk together yolks and sugar in a bowl. Gradually stir about one-fourth of hot mixture into yolks; add to remaining hot mixture, stirring constantly. Cook over low heat, stirring constantly, 6 minutes or until thickened. Discard vanilla bean, and stir in liqueur. Cover and chill. Yield: 2⅔ cups.

Festive Brunch for a Crowd

Biscuits 'n' Sausage Gravy

scrambled eggs   Garlic-Cheese Grits

fresh fruit   bakery sweet rolls

serves 12

menu prep plan

1 day ahead:
- Cut and chill fresh fruit.
- Prepare and bake biscuits. Store in zip-top plastic bag at room temperature.
- Prepare Sausage Gravy; cover and chill.

45 minutes ahead:
- Prepare Garlic-Cheese Grits.
- Scramble eggs; cover and keep warm.

last minute:
- Reheat Biscuits 'n' Sausage Gravy.
- Heat sweet rolls, and place on serving tray.

Here's a versatile menu for a crowd of 12, 24, or 36. The grits serve 36, but you can easily halve the recipe. The biscuits and gravy serve 12, so double or triple as needed.

Biscuits 'n' Sausage Gravy

prep: 10 min.   cook: 12 min.

3   cups self-rising soft wheat flour
¼   teaspoon baking soda
1   teaspoon sugar
½   cup butter-flavored shortening
1¼   cups buttermilk
Butter or margarine, melted
Sausage Gravy

Stir together first 3 ingredients in a large bowl; cut in shortening with a pastry blender until mixture is crumbly. Add buttermilk, stirring just until dry ingredients are moistened. Turn out onto a floured surface; knead 4 or 5 times.

Roll dough to ¾-inch thickness; cut with a 2½-inch round cutter. Place on a lightly greased baking sheet. Bake at 425° for 12 minutes or until golden. Brush tops with melted butter. Split biscuits open; serve with Sausage Gravy. Yield: 12 servings.

Sausage Gravy

prep: 4 min.   cook: 14 min.

½   pound ground pork sausage
¼   cup butter or margarine
⅓   cup all-purpose flour
3¼   cups 1% low-fat or whole milk
½   teaspoon salt
½   teaspoon pepper
⅛   teaspoon dried Italian seasoning

Brown sausage in a skillet, stirring until it crumbles. Drain, reserving 1 tablespoon drippings in skillet. Set sausage aside.

Add butter to drippings; heat over low heat until butter melts. Add flour, stirring until smooth. Cook 1 minute, whisking constantly. Gradually whisk in milk; cook over medium heat, whisking constantly, until thickened and bubbly. Stir in seasonings and sausage. Cook, whisking constantly, until thoroughly heated. Yield: 3¾ cups.

Garlic-Cheese Grits

prep: 5 min.   cook: 20 min.

3½   quarts water
1½   tablespoons salt
4   cups quick-cooking grits, uncooked
5   garlic cloves, minced
1   (2-pound) loaf pasteurized prepared cheese product, cubed
1   cup half-and-half
⅔   cup butter or margarine

Bring water and salt to a boil in a large Dutch oven; gradually stir in grits and garlic. Cover, reduce heat, and simmer 10 minutes, stirring occasionally.

Add cheese, half-and-half, and butter; simmer, stirring constantly, until cheese and butter melt. Yield: 36 servings.

Biscuits 'n' Sausage Gravy,
Garlic-Cheese Grits, fresh fruit

Appetizer Party

Garlic-Pepper Parmesan Crisps

Prosciutto-Wrapped Shrimp   Crab-Stuffed Peppers   BLT Dippers

Colorful Christmas Pâté with assorted crackers and baguette slices

Cranberry-Raspberry Sangría

serves 12

menu prep plan

1 day ahead:

• Prepare Garlic-Pepper Parmesan Crisps; store in airtight container.
• Prepare Cranberry-Raspberry Sangría up to club soda; chill.
• Prepare crabmeat mixture and cut peppers for Crab-Stuffed Peppers; chill.
• Cook and crumble bacon for BLT Dippers; chill.
• Prepare Colorful Christmas Pâté; chill.
• Peel and devein shrimp; chill.

3 hours ahead:

• Marinate shrimp 1 hour; assemble Prosciutto-Wrapped Shrimp, and chill.
• Assemble Crab-Stuffed Peppers; chill.

1 hour ahead:

• Unmold Colorful Christmas Pâté; arrange with crackers on tray.
• Assemble BLT Dippers.

last minute:

• Stir club soda into Cranberry-Raspberry Sangría.
• Broil Prosciutto-Wrapped Shrimp.

Garlic-Pepper Parmesan Crisps

prep: 24 min.   cook: 50 min.

12 ounces freshly grated Parmigiano-Reggiano cheese
2   teaspoons minced fresh garlic
1   teaspoon freshly ground pepper

Combine all ingredients in a small bowl, stirring well. Sprinkle cheese mixture into a 1½-inch round cutter on a nonstick baking sheet. Repeat procedure with cheese mixture, placing 16 circles on each sheet. Bake at 350° for 9 to 10 minutes or until golden. Cool slightly on baking sheets; remove to wire racks to cool completely. Repeat procedure 5 times with remaining cheese mixture. Yield: 8 dozen.

Prosciutto-Wrapped Shrimp

Be careful not to marinate the shrimp too long. It makes them tough.

prep: 24 min.   cook: 9 min.   other: 1 hr.

16 unpeeled, jumbo fresh shrimp
½   cup olive oil
¼   cup vermouth
2   teaspoons dried oregano
1   teaspoon freshly ground pepper
6   garlic cloves, minced
16 (8- x 1-inch) slices prosciutto

Peel and devein shrimp. Combine oil and next 4 ingredients in a large zip-top freezer bag. Add shrimp; seal bag, and marinate in refrigerator 1 hour, turning once.

Soak 8 (6-inch) wooden skewers in water to cover at least 30 minutes.

Remove shrimp from marinade, discarding marinade. Wrap 1 piece prosciutto around each shrimp. Thread 2 shrimp onto each skewer. Place skewers on rack of a lightly greased broiler pan. Broil 5½ inches from heat 7 to 9 minutes or until shrimp turn pink, turning once. Yield: 8 appetizers.

Prosciutto-Wrapped Shrimp,
BLT Dippers (page 52)

Crab-Stuffed Peppers

make-ahead

prep: 19 min.   other: 30 min.

½ pound fresh crabmeat, drained and
    flaked (about 2 cups)
2 green onions, finely chopped
    (about ¼ cup)
1 plum tomato, seeded and finely
    chopped
1 tablespoon minced fresh basil or
    parsley
½ cup mayonnaise
2 teaspoons lemon juice
½ teaspoon hot sauce
3 large red or green bell peppers
Fresh basil, sliced into thin strips

Combine first 4 ingredients in a medium
bowl; stir in mayonnaise, lemon juice,
and hot sauce. Cover and chill.

Meanwhile, cut bell peppers into 1½-
inch strips. (For bite-size pieces, cut
strips in half crosswise.) Spoon crab filling onto pepper strips, and top with
basil strips. Yield: 16 appetizer servings.

Make-Ahead Note: Cut bell peppers
into strips, and store in zip-top plastic
bags. Prepare crabmeat mixture 12
hours ahead. For a twist, top baguette
slices with the crab mixture.

BLT Dippers

*The bacon filling also makes a chunky
dressing for a salad.*

quick & easy

prep: 20 min.

1 cup mayonnaise
1 (8-ounce) carton sour cream
1 pound bacon, cooked and crumbled
2 large tomatoes, chopped
Belgian endive leaves

Combine mayonnaise and sour cream in
a medium bowl, stirring well with a wire
whisk; stir in bacon and tomato. Spoon
1 tablespoon onto individual Belgian
endive leaves, or serve with Melba toast
rounds. Yield: 4 cups.

Colorful Christmas Pâté

prep: 25 min.   other: 4 hrs.

1 (8-ounce) package cream cheese,
    softened
1 (4-ounce) package feta cheese
1 cup loosely packed fresh basil leaves
1 cup loosely packed fresh parsley
    sprigs
¼ cup pine nuts, toasted
3 tablespoons olive oil
3 garlic cloves, divided
¾ cup dried tomatoes in oil, drained

Line a 2½-cup mold or bowl with plastic wrap, leaving a 1-inch overhang
around edges. Set aside.

Beat cheeses at medium speed with an
electric mixer until creamy; set aside.
Process basil and next 3 ingredients
in a blender. Add 2 garlic cloves, and
process until smooth, stopping once
to scrape down sides. Remove from
blender, and set aside.

Process tomatoes and remaining garlic
clove in a blender until smooth.

Spoon one-third of cream cheese
mixture into prepared mold, spreading
evenly; spread with basil mixture. Spoon
one-third of cream cheese mixture over
basil mixture, spreading evenly; spread
with tomato mixture. Spread remaining
cream cheese mixture over tomato
mixture. Cover and chill at least 4 hours.

Unmold pâté onto a serving platter;
peel off plastic wrap. Serve with
baguette slices or assorted crackers.
Yield: 2 cups.

Cranberry-Raspberry Sangría

*If you like a sweeter drink, add a little
more sugar to suit your taste.*

prep: 7 min.   other: 8 hrs.

1 (48-ounce) bottle cranberry-
    raspberry juice cocktail
1 (750-milliliter) bottle dry, full-
    bodied Spanish red wine
2 tablespoons Grand Marnier or
    orange juice
¼ cup sugar
1 orange, thinly sliced
1 lemon, thinly sliced
1 cup fresh cranberries or fresh
    raspberries
2 cups club soda, chilled
Garnish: citrus rind curls

Combine first 4 ingredients in a large
pitcher, stirring until sugar dissolves.
Add fruit slices and cranberries; cover
and chill at least 8 hours. Stir in club
soda just before serving. Serve over ice.
Garnish, if desired. Yield: 12½ cups.

Cranberry-Raspberry Sangría

Holiday Open House

Hot Burgundy Cider
Curried Butternut-Shrimp Soup   Crunchy Parmesan Toasts
Praline-Mustard Glazed Ham and Raisin Butter
Old-Fashioned Sweet Potato Biscuits   Hopping John Salad
Honey-Apple Cake, vanilla ice cream, and Honey Sauce
serves 12

menu prep plan

1 day ahead:

• Prepare Curried Butternut-Shrimp Soup through processing squash in blender; chill mixture and shrimp.
• Prepare Raisin Butter; chill.
• Bake Honey-Apple Cake, and prepare Honey Sauce; chill reserved sauce.
• Scoop ice cream balls; freeze.
• Prepare Hopping John Salad (do not add bacon); chill.
• Prepare Old-Fashioned Sweet Potato Biscuits. Store at room temperature in airtight container.

3 hours ahead:

• Bake Praline-Mustard Glazed Ham.

1 hour ahead:

• Complete preparation of Curried Butternut-Shrimp Soup; keep warm.
• Prepare Hot Burgundy Cider; keep warm.
• Carve ham.

30 minutes ahead:

• Add bacon to Hopping John Salad.
• Prepare Crunchy Parmesan Toasts.
• Reheat Honey Sauce and Old-Fashioned Sweet Potato Biscuits.

Hot Burgundy Cider

prep: 15 min.   cook: 20 min.   other: 5 min.

2   cups water
2   family size tea bags
3   quarts apple cider
½   cup lemon juice
1   cup sugar
6   whole allspice
6   whole cloves
6   (3-inch) cinnamon sticks
1   liter Burgundy or dry red wine
Garnishes: kumquats, whole cloves

Bring water to a boil in a large Dutch oven; remove from heat, and add tea bags. Cover, and let stand 5 minutes; remove tea bags, squeezing gently, and discard.

Add cider and next 5 ingredients to Dutch oven. Bring to a boil; reduce heat, and simmer 10 minutes. Remove and discard spices; stir in wine, and cook just until thoroughly heated. Ladle into mugs; garnish, if desired. Yield: about 12 servings.

Hot Burgundy Cider

Praline-Mustard Glazed Ham
(page 57)

Curried Butternut-Shrimp Soup

This recipe can be prepared up to one day ahead. Complete all steps through processing butternut squash mixture in blender. Cover and refrigerate along with shrimp until you are ready to finish cooking.

make-ahead

prep: 30 min.   cook: 1 hr.

1   pound unpeeled, medium-size fresh
        shrimp
3   (14-ounce) cans chicken broth
½   cup dry white wine
1   carrot, chopped
1   fresh thyme sprig
6   to 8 whole peppercorns
2   medium yellow onions, chopped
        and divided
1   (3½-pound) butternut squash,
        peeled, seeded, and cut into
        ½-inch cubes
1   cup whipping cream
2   teaspoons curry powder
1   teaspoon dried thyme
¼   teaspoon salt
¼   teaspoon ground red pepper
Crunchy Parmesan Toasts
Garnishes: whipping cream,
        paprika, steamed shrimp

Peel shrimp, reserving shells; devein, if desired. Set aside.

Bring shrimp shells, chicken broth, next 4 ingredients, and 1 chopped onion to a boil in a Dutch oven; reduce heat and simmer 30 minutes. Pour mixture through a wire-mesh strainer into a bowl, discarding shells; return broth mixture to Dutch oven.

Add squash and remaining onion to Dutch oven. Bring to a boil; reduce heat, and simmer 20 minutes or until squash is tender.

Curried Butternut-Shrimp Soup

Process squash mixture in blender, in batches, until smooth; return mixture to Dutch oven. Stir in cream and next 4 ingredients. Bring to a simmer over medium-low heat; add shrimp, and cook 3 minutes or just until shrimp turn pink. Serve with Crunchy Parmesan Toasts. Garnish, if desired. Yield: about 12 cups.

Crunchy Parmesan Toasts

prep: 8 min.   cook: 10 min.

Brush 1 (5-ounce) package Melba toast rounds evenly with ¼ cup olive oil; sprinkle with ½ cup shredded Parmesan cheese and ¼ teaspoon freshly ground pepper. Bake at 350° for 8 minutes or until cheese melts. Yield: 24 servings.

Praline-Mustard Glazed Ham

The popularity of serving spiral-sliced hams during the holidays can make them hard to find. Shop early, or special order your ham to be sure you get what you want. You can purchase them at supermarkets and at specialty meat stores.

prep: 5 min.   cook: 2 hrs., 30 min.
other: 10 min.

1   (7- to 8-pound) bone-in smoked spiral-cut ham half
¾   cup firmly packed brown sugar
¾   cup Dijon mustard
1   cup maple syrup
⅓   cup apple juice
Raisin Butter

Place ham in a lightly greased 13- x 9-inch pan.

Stir together brown sugar and mustard; spread over ham. Stir together maple syrup and apple juice, and pour into pan. Cover with aluminum foil.

Bake at 350° on lower oven rack 2 hours. Remove foil, and bake 30 more minutes, basting every 10 minutes with pan drippings until meat thermometer inserted into thickest portion registers 140°. Let stand 10 minutes. Remove from pan, and serve with Raisin Butter. Yield: 12 servings.

Raisin Butter

prep: 15 min.   cook: 10 min.   other: 1 hr., 30 min.

½   cup golden raisins
¼   cup apple juice
½   cup butter, softened

Bring raisins and apple juice to a boil in a small saucepan; reduce heat, and simmer 10 minutes or until raisins plump. Cool.

Process mixture in blender until finely chopped. Add butter; process until well blended, stopping to scrape down sides. Cover; chill 1 hour. Yield: about 1 cup.

Old-Fashioned Sweet Potato Biscuits

prep: 15 min.   cook: 15 min.

4   cups all-purpose flour
2   tablespoons baking powder
2   teaspoons salt
1   cup butter or margarine, cut up
1   cup cooked, mashed sweet potato
1½   cups buttermilk
3   tablespoons butter, melted

Combine flour, baking powder, and salt in a large bowl. Cut in butter with a pastry blender until mixture is crumbly. Stir together sweet potato and buttermilk; add to dry ingredients, stirring just until moistened.

Turn dough out onto a lightly floured surface, and knead 3 to 4 times. Pat or roll to ½-inch thickness.

Cut dough with a 2-inch round cutter, and place biscuits on lightly greased baking sheet.

Bake at 425° for 10 to 15 minutes or until golden. Brush with melted butter. Yield: 18 (2-inch) biscuits.

Old-Fashioned
Sweet Potato Biscuits

Hopping John Salad

Hopping John Salad

This recipe will make 12 generous ½-cup servings. If your party will be held around dinnertime, double the recipe to allow guests to take larger portions.

prep: 20 min.   other: 4 hrs.

½   cup red wine vinegar
2   tablespoons balsamic vinegar
¼   cup olive oil
2   celery ribs, diced
1   yellow bell pepper, seeded and diced
1   red bell pepper, seeded and diced
½   medium onion, diced
4   (15-ounce) cans black-eyed peas, rinsed and drained
2   jalapeño peppers, seeded and diced
2   tablespoons chopped fresh parsley
1   garlic clove, minced
1   teaspoon salt
1   teaspoon freshly ground black pepper
½   teaspoon ground cumin
4   bacon slices, cooked and crumbled
Garnishes: lettuce leaves, chopped fresh parsley

Combine vinegars in a large bowl; add oil in a slow, steady stream, whisking until blended. Add celery and next 10 ingredients, gently tossing to coat. Cover and chill 3 to 4 hours.

Stir in bacon. Serve over lettuce and sprinkle with parsley, if desired. Yield: 7 cups.

Honey-Apple Cake

When served with vanilla ice cream, this moist cake is delightfully over the top. See "ice cream on ice" for how-to information on scooping ice cream balls prior to your party.

editor's favorite

prep: 15 min.   cook: 1 hr., 5 min.
other: 15 min.

1   cup pecans, finely chopped and divided
2   cups sugar
1   cup vegetable oil
¼   cup honey
3   large eggs
3   cups all-purpose flour
1   teaspoon baking soda
1   teaspoon salt
1   teaspoon ground cinnamon
¼   teaspoon ground nutmeg
1   teaspoon vanilla extract
3   cups peeled and diced Golden Delicious apples (about 3 apples, or 1 pound)
Honey Sauce
Vanilla ice cream (optional)

Grease and flour 10-cup Bundt pan; sprinkle bottom of pan with ¼ cup pecans. Set aside.

Beat sugar, oil, and honey at medium speed with an electric mixer until well blended. Add eggs, 1 at a time, beating just until blended.

Combine flour and next 4 ingredients. Gradually add to sugar mixture, beating at low speed just until blended. Stir in vanilla, remaining ¾ cup pecans, and apples. Spoon into prepared pan.

Bake at 350° for 1 hour and 5 minutes or until a wooden pick inserted in center comes out clean. Cool in pan on a wire rack 15 minutes; remove from pan, and place on a wire rack covered with wax paper. Pour ½ cup Honey Sauce over warm cake. Cool. Serve with remaining warm sauce and, if desired, ice cream. Yield: 1 (10-inch) cake.

Honey Sauce

prep: 5 min.   cook: 5 min.

1   cup firmly packed light brown sugar
½   cup butter or margarine
¼   cup milk
¼   cup honey

Bring all ingredients to a boil in a medium saucepan over medium-high heat, stirring constantly; boil, stirring constantly, 2 minutes. Keep warm. Yield: 1½ cups.

ice cream on ice

Honey-Apple Cake is even better with a scoop of ice cream. Here's how to make the ice cream balls beforehand to serve to a group.

• Chill a metal jellyroll pan in the freezer; this helps the ice cream balls keep their shape.

• Scoop ice cream, placing balls directly onto the cold pan. If the balls begin to melt during this process, place them in the freezer on the pan for about 15 minutes or until hardened. Return the ice cream carton to freezer during this time. When balls have hardened, resume process until you've made the desired number of balls.

• Freeze the balls, uncovered, several hours or until hard. Transfer to zip-top freezer bags for longer storage.

• For buffet service, place a bowl of ice cream balls inside a larger ice-filled bowl.

Vanilla Ice Cream,
Honey-Apple Cake

Casual Meal for Entertaining

Smoked Gouda Pork Chops

Best-Ever Potatoes   Spinach-Apple Salad

Sweet Potato-Praline Pie

serves 8

menu prep plan

morning of:
• Prepare Sweet Potato-Praline Pie.

2 to 3 hours ahead:
• Prepare dressing for Spinach-Apple Salad.

• Prepare Best-Ever Potatoes, but do not bake.

1½ hours ahead:
• Prepare Smoked Gouda Pork Chops; keep warm.

• Combine ingredients for Spinach-Apple Salad except apples and dressing; chill.

45 minutes ahead:
• Bake Best-Ever Potatoes.

last minute:
• Add apples and dressing to Spinach-Apple Salad.

Smoked Gouda Pork Chops, Best-Ever Potatoes, Spinach-Apple Salad

Smoked Gouda Pork Chops

prep: 14 min.   cook: 1 hr., 24 min.

1   cup all-purpose flour
1   teaspoon salt
1   teaspoon pepper
8   (1-inch-thick) rib pork chops
9   tablespoons vegetable oil, divided
1   teaspoon sweet Hungarian paprika
4   large onions, sliced
1   teaspoon sugar
4   teaspoons minced garlic

1   tablespoon sweet Hungarian paprika
2   cups beef broth
¾   cup (3 ounces) shredded smoked Gouda cheese
3   tablespoons butter or margarine
5   tablespoons all-purpose flour
¼   teaspoon salt
¼   teaspoon pepper

Combine 1 cup flour, 1 teaspoon salt, and 1 teaspoon pepper in a large zip-top freezer bag. Add chops; seal bag, and shake to coat.

Heat 3 tablespoons oil in a heavy skillet over medium-high heat until hot; add 4 chops. Cook 3 minutes on each side or until browned. Transfer to a 15- x 10-inch baking dish. Repeat procedure.

Sprinkle chops with 1 teaspoon paprika. Wipe skillet with a paper towel.

Heat 3 tablespoons oil in skillet until hot. Add onion; sprinkle with sugar. Cook, stirring constantly, 20 minutes or until tender and golden. Add garlic; cook 1 minute. Remove from heat. Add 1 tablespoon paprika; stir well. Spoon mixture over chops. Pour broth over onion mixture. Cover and bake at 350° for 45 minutes. Remove from oven; transfer chops to a serving platter. Pour onion mixture through a wire-mesh strainer into a 4-cup glass measuring cup. Add enough water to broth mixture to measure 2½ cups, if necessary. Set aside. Return solids in strainer to baking dish; top with chops. Sprinkle with cheese. Bake 5 more minutes or until cheese melts. Set aside, and keep warm.

Melt butter in a heavy saucepan over low heat; add 5 tablespoons flour, stirring until smooth. Cook 1 minute, stirring constantly. Gradually add reserved broth mixture; cook over medium heat, stirring constantly, until thickened and bubbly. Stir in ¼ teaspoon salt and ¼ teaspoon pepper. Serve chops and onion with sauce. Yield: 8 servings.

Best-Ever Potatoes

prep: 15 min.   cook: 1 hr., 44 min.

3   pounds baking potatoes, peeled
2½ quarts chicken broth
4   small carrots, scraped and cut into
      ½-inch pieces
1   small onion, chopped
¼   cup butter or margarine
1   teaspoon dried dillweed
1½ cups sour cream
3   tablespoons chopped fresh parsley
1   teaspoon salt
¼   teaspoon pepper
1   tablespoon butter or margarine

Combine potatoes and broth in a Dutch oven; bring to a boil. Reduce heat, and simmer 15 minutes. Add carrot and onion, and simmer 20 minutes or until potatoes are tender; drain.

Combine cooked vegetables, ¼ cup butter, and dillweed in a large bowl; mash. Add sour cream and next 3 ingredients, stirring well. Spoon potato mixture into a greased 11- x 7-inch baking dish; dot with 1 tablespoon butter. Cover and bake at 350° for 35 minutes. Yield: 8 servings.

Spinach-Apple Salad

prep: 15 min.   other: 2 hrs.

⅔   cup vegetable oil
½   cup white vinegar
1   tablespoon chutney
1   teaspoon salt
1   teaspoon curry powder
1   teaspoon dry mustard
10 cups tightly packed torn fresh
      spinach
4   Red Delicious apples, diced
⅔   cup salted dry-roasted peanuts
⅔   cup raisins
½   cup sliced green onions
3   tablespoons sesame seeds, toasted

Whisk together first 6 ingredients. Cover; let stand 2 hours.

Combine spinach and remaining 5 ingredients in a bowl; toss well. Pour dressing over spinach mixture, and toss gently. Yield: 8 servings.

Sweet Potato-Praline Pie

prep: 23 min.   cook: 55 min.   other: 1 hr.

1⅓ cups all-purpose flour
½   teaspoon salt
½   cup shortening
3   to 4 tablespoons cold water
3   tablespoons butter, softened
⅓   cup firmly packed dark brown sugar
⅓   cup chopped pecans
3   large eggs, lightly beaten
1   cup evaporated milk
1½ cups cooked, mashed sweet potatoes
½   cup granulated sugar
½   cup firmly packed dark brown sugar
1   teaspoon salt
1   teaspoon ground cinnamon
¼   teaspoon ground cloves
¼   teaspoon ground nutmeg

Combine flour and ½ teaspoon salt; cut in shortening with pastry blender until crumbly. Sprinkle cold water, 1 tablespoon at a time, over surface; stir with a fork until dry ingredients are moistened. Shape into a ball; cover and chill.

Roll dough into a 12-inch circle on a lightly floured surface. Place in a 10-inch pieplate; trim off excess pastry along edges. Fold edges under; crimp.

Combine butter and ⅓ cup brown sugar; stir in pecans. Press mixture over pastry shell. Bake at 425° for 5 minutes. Cool on a wire rack. Reduce oven temperature to 350°. Combine eggs and remaining 8 ingredients in a mixing bowl; beat at medium speed with an electric mixer until blended. Pour over praline layer in pastry. Bake at 350° for 50 minutes or until set. Cool on wire rack. Yield: 1 (10-inch) pie.

Christmas Candlelight Dinner

Beef Tenderloin Fillets with Balsamic Sauce

Garlic-Gruyère Mashed Potatoes   Roasted Asparagus with Red Pepper Sauce

bakery rolls

Ultimate Cheesecake

serves 6

menu prep plan

1 day ahead:

• Prepare Ultimate Cheesecake and Apricot Glaze; chill.

1 hour ahead:

• Prepare Garlic-Gruyère Mashed Potatoes; keep warm.

• Prepare Roasted Asparagus with Red Pepper Sauce.

30 minutes ahead:

• Prepare Beef Tenderloin Fillets with Balsamic Sauce.

last minute:

• Heat rolls.

Beef Tenderloin Fillets with Balsamic Sauce

prep: 5 min.   cook: 21 min.

4   (6-ounce) beef tenderloin fillets
2   tablespoons coarse sea salt or
        1 tablespoon regular salt
1   tablespoon coarsely ground pepper
2   tablespoons olive oil
Balsamic Sauce
Garnish: fresh thyme sprigs

Rub fillets with sea salt and pepper. Cook fillets in hot oil in a large ovenproof skillet over high heat 2 to 3 minutes on each side.

Bake at 350° for 8 to 15 minutes or until medium-rare or desired degree of doneness. Serve with Balsamic Sauce. Garnish, if desired. Yield: 4 servings.

Balsamic Sauce

prep: 8 min.   cook: 8 min.

¼   cup dry red wine
¼   cup dry sherry
3   tablespoons balsamic vinegar
2   garlic cloves, chopped
1   shallot, chopped
2   egg yolks
⅓   cup unsalted butter, melted

Bring first 5 ingredients to a boil in a small saucepan; cook 2 minutes. Cool.

Whisk yolks into wine mixture; cook over low heat, whisking constantly, until thickened. Slowly whisk in melted butter until blended. Serve sauce immediately. Yield: ½ cup.

Garlic-Gruyère Mashed Potatoes

prep: 11 min.   cook: 20 min.

6   medium potatoes (3½ pounds)
¾   cup hot milk
½   cup sour cream
¼   cup butter or margarine, softened
½   teaspoon salt
⅛   teaspoon ground red pepper
1   garlic clove, minced
¼   cup (1 ounce) shredded Gruyère
        cheese *
2   green onions, thinly sliced
⅓   cup chopped baked ham (optional)
Garnish: sliced green onions

Peel potatoes; cut into 1-inch cubes. Cook in boiling water to cover 15 minutes or until tender. Drain.

Mash potato with a potato masher; stir in milk and next 5 ingredients until blended. Stir in Gruyère cheese, thinly sliced green onions, and, if desired, ham. Garnish, if desired. Yield: 6 to 8 servings.

* ½ cup shredded Swiss cheese may be substituted for Gruyère cheese, if desired.

Beef Tenderloin Fillets with Balsamic Sauce,
Roasted Asparagus with Red Pepper Sauce,
Garlic-Gruyère Mashed Potatoes

Ultimate Cheesecake

prep: 14 min.   cook: 1 hr., 20 min.
other: 12 hrs., 10 min.

2   cups graham cracker crumbs
¼   cup sugar
½   cup butter or margarine, melted
7   large eggs
4   (8-ounce) packages cream cheese,
      softened
1¾ cups sugar
2⅛ teaspoons vanilla extract, divided
1   (16-ounce) container sour cream
½   cup sugar
Apricot Glaze

Stir together first 3 ingredients; press
into bottom and 1 inch up sides of a
10-inch springform pan. Chill 1 hour.
   Beat eggs with an electric mixer. Add
cream cheese; beat until blended. Add
1¾ cups sugar, beating well. Stir in 2
teaspoons vanilla. Pour into chilled crust.
   Bake at 350° for 1 hour and 15 minutes. Cool on a wire rack 10 minutes.
Increase oven temperature to 425°.
   Stir together sour cream, ½ cup sugar,
and remaining vanilla; spread over cheesecake. Bake at 425° for 5 minutes. Cool on
a wire rack 1 hour. Cover; chill at least 10
hours. Remove sides of pan. Serve with
Apricot Glaze. Yield: 12 servings.

Apricot Glaze

prep: 4 min.   cook: 4 min.   other: 1 hr.

1   (10-ounce) jar apricot jam
¼   cup sugar
¼   cup water
1   tablespoon rum or brandy

Combine first 3 ingredients in a saucepan;
cook over low heat, stirring often, until
consistency of syrup. Stir in rum; pour
through a wire-mesh strainer into a bowl,
discarding solids. Cool. Yield: 1½ cups.

Roasted Asparagus with Red Pepper Sauce

prep: 9 min.   cook: 35 min.

3   tablespoons olive oil
2   tablespoons balsamic vinegar
1   tablespoon teriyaki sauce
1   tablespoon dried basil
½   teaspoon salt
½   teaspoon pepper
¼   teaspoon dry mustard
¼   teaspoon ground nutmeg
1½   pounds fresh asparagus, trimmed
Red Pepper Sauce

Stir together first 8 ingredients in an
11- x 7-inch baking dish. Add asparagus, and toss to coat.
   Bake, covered, at 375° for 35 minutes,
turning asparagus once. Remove with a
slotted spoon; serve with Red Pepper
Sauce. Yield: 6 servings.

Red Pepper Sauce

prep: 11 min.   cook: 7 min.

1   (7.25-ounce) jar roasted red bell
      peppers, drained and sliced
½   small onion, chopped
1   garlic clove, minced
2   tablespoons olive oil
1   tablespoon balsamic vinegar
1   tablespoon orange marmalade
1   tablespoon teriyaki sauce
¼   teaspoon dry mustard
¼   teaspoon ground nutmeg
⅛   teaspoon dried crushed red
      pepper
¼   cup mayonnaise

Sauté first 3 ingredients in hot oil in a
large skillet over medium-high heat
2 minutes. Add vinegar and next 5
ingredients; cook 3 minutes. Remove
from heat; stir in mayonnaise. Yield:
1¼ cups.

Elegant Dinner Party

Carrot-Butternut Squash Soup

Pistachio Risotto with Saffron

Beef Tenderloin with Five-Onion Sauce   Oven-Roasted Potatoes, Green Beans, and Onions

Chocolate-Almond Torte *or* Mom's Pecan Pie

serves 8

menu prep plan

1 day ahead:

• Prepare Carrot-Butternut Squash Soup; chill.

• Make bread triangles for soup; store in an airtight container.

• Prepare Chocolate-Almond Torte or Mom's Pecan Pie; cover and chill torte or cover pie and store at room temperature.

1½ hours ahead:

• Prepare Beef Tenderloin with Five-Onion Sauce.

• While tenderloin bakes, prepare Pistachio Risotto with Saffron.

• Prepare Oven-Roasted Potatoes, Green Beans, and Onions.

• Whip cream for Chocolate-Almond Torte; chill.

last minute:

• Reheat soup, and slice tenderloin.

Carrot-Butternut Squash Soup

prep: 30 min.   cook: 32 min.

2   garlic cloves, minced
1   medium onion, chopped
2   tablespoons olive oil, divided
1   pound carrots, shredded
1   butternut squash, peeled and
      shredded
2   (14-ounce) cans chicken broth
½   cup cooked long-grain rice
8   (½-inch-thick) French bread slices
1½ cups fat-free milk
1   tablespoon grated orange rind
½   teaspoon salt
¼   teaspoon pepper
¼   cup chopped fresh parsley

Sauté garlic and onion in 1 tablespoon hot oil in a large Dutch oven 2 minutes or until tender. Add carrot and squash; sauté 5 minutes or until tender.

Add broth; bring to a boil. Reduce heat, and simmer 20 minutes. Stir in rice. Remove from heat; cool slightly.

Cut bread slices into 1-inch triangles; brush with remaining 1 tablespoon oil. Arrange on a baking sheet. Bake at 350° for 10 minutes or until lightly toasted.

Process vegetable mixture, in batches, in a blender until smooth, stopping once to scrape down sides; return to Dutch oven. Stir in milk, and simmer until thoroughly heated. Stir in orange rind, salt, and pepper.

Dip 1 point of each bread triangle in soup, and coat with parsley. Serve croutons on soup. Yield: 8 cups.

Pistachio Risotto with Saffron

prep: 6 min.   cook: 56 min.

¼   cup unsalted butter
1   medium-size yellow onion, chopped
1   teaspoon saffron threads
1¾ cups uncooked Arborio rice
1   cup dry white vermouth or chicken
      broth
5   cups chicken broth, divided
1   cup grated Parmesan cheese
¼   cup coarsely chopped red pistachios
Garnish: chopped red pistachios

Melt butter in a skillet over medium-high heat; add onion. Sauté 5 minutes. Add saffron; sauté 1 minute. Add rice; cook, stirring constantly, 2 minutes.

Reduce heat to medium; add vermouth and 2 cups broth. Cook, stirring constantly, until liquid is absorbed.

Repeat procedure with remaining 3 cups broth, ½ cup at a time. (Cooking time is 30 to 45 minutes.) Remove from heat; stir in cheese and ¼ cup pistachios. Garnish, if desired. Yield: 8 cups.

Beef Tenderloin with Five-Onion Sauce (page 66);
Pistachio Risotto with Saffron;
Oven-Roasted Potatoes, Green Beans, and Onions (page 66)

Beef Tenderloin with Five-Onion Sauce

prep: 44 min.   cook: 1 hr.   other: 10 min.

1   (3½-pound) trimmed beef
        tenderloin
1½   teaspoons salt, divided
1   teaspoon pepper, divided
2   tablespoons canola oil
3   tablespoons butter or margarine
2   large yellow onions, sliced and
        separated into rings
2   large red onions, sliced and
        separated into rings
2   bunches green onions, chopped
12   shallots, chopped
5   garlic cloves, minced
½   cup cognac or beef broth
½   cup beef broth

Sprinkle tenderloin with ½ teaspoon salt and ½ teaspoon pepper. Secure with string at 1-inch intervals. Brown meat on all sides in hot oil in a heavy roasting pan or ovenproof Dutch oven. Remove meat, reserving drippings in pan. Add butter to drippings, and cook over medium-high heat until melted. Add yellow and red onion rings; sauté 5 minutes.

Add green onions, shallots, and garlic; sauté 10 minutes. Stir in cognac and broth; cook over high heat, stirring constantly, until liquid evaporates (about 5 minutes). Place meat on top.

Bake, covered, at 450° for 35 minutes or until a meat thermometer inserted into thickest portion of tenderloin registers 145° (medium-rare).

Remove meat from roasting pan, reserving onion mixture in pan; cover meat loosely, and let stand at room temperature 10 minutes before slicing.

Cook onion mixture over medium heat, stirring constantly, 5 minutes or until liquid evaporates. Stir in remaining 1 teaspoon salt and remaining ½ teaspoon pepper. Serve sauce with sliced meat. Yield: 8 servings.

Oven-Roasted Potatoes, Green Beans, and Onions

prep: 11 min.   cook: 45 min.

¼   cup olive oil
1   garlic clove, crushed
½   teaspoon salt
½   teaspoon freshly ground black
        pepper
3   medium onions, quartered
2   pounds small round red potatoes,
        cut into ¼-inch-thick slices
1½   pounds fresh green beans,
        untrimmed

Stir together first 4 ingredients; set aside 1 tablespoon oil mixture. Place onion wedges and potato slices in a greased roasting pan, and drizzle with remaining oil mixture, stirring gently.

Roast at 450° on top rack of oven 20 to 25 minutes, stirring occasionally.

Add green beans to pan; drizzle reserved 1 tablespoon oil mixture over beans, stirring gently. Roast 15 to 20 more minutes or until vegetables are tender, stirring occasionally. Yield: 8 servings.

Chocolate-Almond Torte

editor's favorite

prep: 29 min.   cook: 39 min.
other: 9 hrs., 45 min.

1   cup whole almonds, toasted
2   tablespoons sugar
2   tablespoons vegetable oil
¾   cup butter or margarine
½   cup whipping cream
4   (4-ounce) bittersweet or semisweet
        chocolate baking bars, finely
        chopped
6   large eggs, separated
⅓   cup sugar
1   cup whipping cream
2   tablespoons sugar
3   tablespoons almond liqueur
        (optional)
Garnish: toasted sliced almonds

Butter and flour a 9-inch springform pan. Line with wax paper; butter paper.

Process ½ cup whole almonds and 2 tablespoons sugar in a food processor until ground. Spoon into a bowl. Process remaining ½ cup whole almonds and oil in food processor 3 minutes or until a thick paste forms, stopping often to scrape down sides.

Bring butter and ½ cup whipping cream to a boil in a heavy saucepan over medium heat. Remove from heat, and whisk in chocolate until smooth. Stir in almond mixtures; cool slightly.

Beat egg whites at high speed with an electric mixer until foamy. Add ⅓ cup sugar, 1 tablespoon at a time, beating until stiff peaks form and sugar dissolves (2 to 4 minutes). Beat egg yolks until thick and pale. Gradually add chocolate mixture to yolks, beating until blended. Fold in one-third of egg whites. Gradually fold in remaining whites. Pour batter into prepared pan.

Mom's Pecan Pie

Bake at 350° for 35 minutes or until almost set. Cool on a wire rack. Cover and chill up to 3 days. Run a sharp knife around edges to loosen. Remove sides of pan.

Beat 1 cup whipping cream at medium speed with an electric mixer until foamy; gradually add 2 tablespoons sugar, beating until soft peaks form. Stir in liqueur. Serve over torte. Garnish, if desired. Yield: 1 (9-inch) torte.

Mom's Pecan Pie

prep: 14 min.   cook: 50 min.

½ (15-ounce) package refrigerated
    piecrusts
4   large eggs
1   cup dark corn syrup
¾   cup sugar
⅓   cup butter or margarine, melted
Pinch of salt
1   teaspoon vanilla extract
1   cup chopped pecans
¾   cup pecan halves

Fit piecrust into a 9-inch pieplate according to package directions; fold edges under, and crimp.

Beat eggs and next 5 ingredients at medium speed with an electric mixer until smooth. Stir in chopped pecans; pour into crust. Arrange pecan halves on top of pie.

Bake at 350° for 50 minutes, shielding edges with aluminum foil after 30 minutes to prevent excessive browning. Yield: 1 (9-inch) pie.

New Year's Eve Appetizer Buffet

Cheese Terrine

Black-Eyed Caviar   Mushroom-Port Phyllo Purses   Tortellini Toss

Kahlúa Truffle Sticks   Champagne

serves 16

menu prep plan

1 day ahead:

• Prepare Cheese Terrine; chill.
• Prepare Black-Eyed Caviar; chill.
• Prepare Kahlúa Truffle Sticks; chill.
• Chill Champagne.

2 hours ahead:

• Prepare Mushroom-Port Phyllo Purses.
• Prepare Tortellini Toss.

1 hour ahead:

• Invert Cheese Terrine on serving platter; slice Italian bread.
• Place Kahlúa Truffle Sticks on serving plate.
• Arrange Black-Eyed Caviar and Mushroom-Port Phyllo Purses in serving dishes.

Cheese Terrine

prep: 25 min.   other: 8 hrs.

¼   cup dry white wine
1   pound provolone cheese, cut into
      $\frac{1}{16}$-inch-thick slices
Pesto Filling
Walnut-Goat Cheese Filling
Sun-Dried Tomato Filling
1   (15-ounce) jar marinara sauce
Italian bread
Garnishes: fresh basil, walnut halves

Cut a single piece of cheesecloth to fit into a 4-cup ring mold; dampen with wine, gently squeezing out excess moisture. Line mold with cheesecloth, allowing excess to extend over rim.

Cut cheese slices in half. Line bottom and sides of mold with half of cheese. Divide remaining cheese into thirds.

Spoon Pesto Filling over cheese in ring mold. Top with one-third of remaining cheese. Spoon Walnut-Goat Cheese Filling over cheese; layer another one-third cheese on top. Spoon Sun-Dried Tomato Filling over cheese, spreading to edges; top with remaining cheese. Fold cheesecloth over top; press lightly. Cover and chill 8 hours.

Unfold cheesecloth, and invert terrine onto a serving platter. Discard cheesecloth.

To serve, cut terrine into 1-inch slices. Serve with marinara sauce on Italian bread slices. Garnish, if desired. Yield: 16 appetizer servings.

Pesto Filling

prep: 6 min.

1   cup firmly packed fresh basil leaves
1   cup freshly grated Parmesan cheese
½   cup olive oil
2   garlic cloves, sliced

Process all ingredients in a blender until almost smooth, stopping to scrape down sides of container occasionally. Yield: 1 cup.

Walnut-Goat Cheese Filling

prep: 4 min.

1   cup crumbled goat cheese
⅔   cup toasted, chopped walnuts
¼   cup sour cream
1   garlic clove, sliced

Process all ingredients in a blender until almost smooth, stopping to scrape down sides of container occasionally. Yield: 1¼ cups.

Sun-Dried Tomato Filling

prep: 4 min.

1   (7-ounce) jar dried tomatoes
      packed in oil, undrained
1   cup freshly grated Parmesan cheese
2   teaspoons lemon juice

Process all ingredients in a blender until almost smooth, stopping to scrape down sides of container occasionally. Yield: 1¼ cups.

Cheese Terrine,
Tortellini Toss (page 71)

Black-Eyed Caviar

This appetizer provides a rainbow of color and, of course, that traditional dose of good luck.

quick & easy

prep: 16 min.   other: 2 hrs.

2   (15-ounce) cans black-eyed peas, drained
1   yellow or green bell pepper, finely chopped
½   cup roasted red bell pepper packed in oil, drained and finely chopped
½   cup minced red onion
½   cup minced fresh cilantro or parsley
¼   cup olive oil
2   garlic cloves, minced
2   tablespoons white wine vinegar
1   teaspoon ground cumin
2   teaspoons coarse grained mustard
¼   teaspoon salt

Combine all ingredients in a medium-size bowl; stir well. Cover and chill several hours. Serve at room temperature with pita chips. Yield: 4½ cups.

Mushroom-Port Phyllo Purses

prep: 29 min.   cook: 50 min.   other: 30 min.

1   (⅞-ounce) package dried shiitake mushrooms (¾ cup)
1   cup port wine
½   pound fresh mushrooms, chopped
¼   cup butter or margarine, melted
½   teaspoon dried thyme
½   cup soft cream cheese
¼   cup minced fresh chives
12   sheets frozen phyllo pastry, thawed
⅓   cup butter or margarine, melted
Freshly ground pepper
Blanched whole chives (optional)

Black-Eyed Caviar

Combine dried mushrooms and wine in a small saucepan; bring to a boil. Cover, remove from heat, and let mushroom mixture stand 25 minutes. Drain mushrooms, reserving wine; finely chop mushrooms. Strain wine through a coffee filter into a small bowl; reserve strained liquid and mushrooms.

Meanwhile, combine fresh mushrooms, ¼ cup butter, and thyme in a large skillet. Cook over medium-high heat 20 minutes or until liquid is absorbed, stirring frequently. Add reserved liquid and rehydrated mushrooms; simmer, uncovered, for 10 minutes, or until liquid is absorbed. Remove from heat; cool and stir in cream cheese and chives.

Place 1 sheet of phyllo on wax paper.

Brush lightly with melted butter. Layer 2 more sheets of phyllo on top, brushing each lightly with melted butter. Using kitchen scissors, cut layers into 9 rectangles. Place 1 level tablespoon of mushroom mixture in center of each phyllo rectangle. Sprinkle lightly with pepper.

Gather corners of phyllo over filling, and gently twist to close pastry. Lightly spray outside with cooking spray. Place on an ungreased baking sheet. Repeat procedure with remaining phyllo sheets and mushroom mixture.

Bake at 350° for 12 to 15 minutes or until golden. Tie a blanched chive around top of each purse, if desired. Serve hot or at room temperature. Yield: 3 dozen.

Tortellini Toss

prep: 23 min. cook: 10 min. other: 15 min.

2   teaspoons cumin seeds
1   tablespoon fennel seeds
½   pound unsliced pepperoni, cut into
       ¾-inch cubes
1   (7-ounce) jar dried tomatoes
       packed in oil
3   tablespoons Dijon mustard
3   large garlic cloves, sliced
½   cup olive oil
½   cup slivered almonds, toasted
1½ tablespoons lemon juice
2   pounds fresh cheese-filled regular
       or spinach tortellini
1   large yellow or red bell pepper,
       cut into 1-inch pieces
1   (6-ounce) can whole pitted ripe
       olives, drained
1   pint cherry tomatoes, halved

Place cumin and fennel seeds in a skillet; place over medium heat, shaking skillet often, until seeds are lightly browned and fragrant. Remove from heat, and cool.

Position knife blade in food processor bowl; add seeds, half of pepperoni, and next 3 ingredients. Cover and process until smooth. With processor running, pour olive oil through food chute in a slow, steady stream. Add almonds and lemon juice; process until almonds are finely chopped and mixture is blended.

Cook tortellini according to package directions; drain. Combine tortellini, remaining pepperoni, bell pepper, and olives in a large serving bowl. Add pepperoni sauce, and toss well. Gently stir in halved tomatoes. To serve, provide long wooden skewers for spearing. Yield: 16 appetizer servings.

Tortellini Toss

Kahlúa Truffle Sticks

prep: 25 min. cook: 29 min.
other: 3 hrs., 20 min.

2   tablespoons sugar
1   (3.5-ounce) bar Swiss dark
       chocolate, chopped
3   (1-ounce) unsweetened chocolate
       baking squares, chopped
¼   cup plus 2 tablespoons butter or
       margarine, softened and divided
¾   cup sugar
2   large eggs
⅔   cup all-purpose flour
¼   teaspoon salt
⅓   cup Kahlúa
½   cup semisweet chocolate mini-morsels

Line a greased 8-inch square pan with foil, allowing foil to extend over edges. Butter foil; sprinkle 2 tablespoons sugar onto foil.

Combine chopped chocolate and 2 tablespoons butter in a heavy saucepan. Cook over low heat until chocolate and butter melt. Remove from heat, and cool.

Beat remaining butter at medium speed with an electric mixer 2 minutes. Gradually add ¾ cup sugar, beating at medium speed 5 minutes. Add eggs, 1 at a time, beating until blended.

Combine flour and salt; add to butter mixture alternately with melted chocolate mixture and Kahlúa, beginning and ending with flour mixture. Mix at low speed just until blended. Stir in mini-morsels.

Spoon batter into prepared pan. Bake at 350° for 18 minutes (do not overbake). Cool completely. Cover and chill at least 2 hours. Invert uncut brownies in foil onto a cutting board. Peel off foil. Invert brownies again. Using a sharp knife, cut into 2- x 1-inch sticks. Yield: 32 brownies.

holiday recipes

breakfast anytime

Start the celebration early with a table full of taste-tempting breakfast breads and casseroles. In this section, make-ahead tips abound, making your Christmas morning meal even sweeter.

Banana-Coconut Muffins

prep: 9 min.   cook: 20 min.   other: 5 min.

2   cups all-purpose flour
1   tablespoon baking powder
½   teaspoon salt
⅓   cup sugar
1   large egg, lightly beaten
1   cup mashed ripe banana
⅔   cup milk
½   cup butter, melted and cooled
1   teaspoon vanilla extract
1   cup flaked coconut, lightly toasted

Combine first 4 ingredients in a medium bowl; make a well in center of mixture. Combine egg and next 4 ingredients; stir well. Add coconut; stir just until blended. Add banana mixture to dry ingredients, stirring just until dry ingredients are moistened.

Spoon batter into greased muffin pans, filling two-thirds full. Bake at 400° for 20 minutes or until muffins are golden. Cool on a wire rack 5 minutes, and remove from pans. Yield: 1 dozen.

Pumpkin Muffins

These versatile spiced muffins take you through the holiday season with finesse. Pop any remaining muffins in the freezer for up to three months.

freezer-friendly • quick & easy
prep: 9 min.   cook: 20 min.

4   cups all-purpose flour
1¾   teaspoons baking soda
½   teaspoon baking powder
1   teaspoon salt
2¾   cups sugar
1¼   cups raisins
¾   cup chopped walnuts
1   tablespoon ground cinnamon
1   tablespoon ground nutmeg
1   tablespoon ground cloves
4   large eggs, lightly beaten
2½   cups canned pumpkin
1   cup vegetable oil
1   cup water

Combine first 10 ingredients in a large bowl; make a well in center of mixture. Combine eggs and remaining 3 ingredients; add to dry ingredients, stirring just until moistened.

Spoon batter into paper-lined muffin pans, filling two-thirds full. Bake at 375° for 20 minutes or until a wooden pick inserted in center comes out clean. Remove from pans immediately. Yield: 3½ dozen.

Country Morning Muffins

Laden with grated carrot, raisins, apples, and nuts, this slightly sweet batter bakes enough muffins to give to several friends.

great gift
prep: 11 min.   cook: 25 min.

4   cups all-purpose flour
2½   cups sugar
4   teaspoons baking soda
4   teaspoons ground cinnamon
1   teaspoon salt
4   cups grated carrot (about 8 carrots)
1   cup raisins
1   cup chopped pecans
½   cup sweetened flaked coconut
2   Granny Smith apples, peeled and grated
6   large eggs
1¼   cups vegetable oil
2   teaspoons vanilla extract

Combine flour, sugar, baking soda, cinnamon, and salt in a large bowl; add carrot and next 4 ingredients, and stir well. Combine eggs, oil, and vanilla; stir well. Add to flour mixture, stirring just until moistened.

Spoon batter into greased muffin pans, filling two-thirds full.

Bake at 375° for 20 to 25 minutes or until golden. Yield: 4 dozen.

Blueberry-Almond Streusel Muffins

muffin magic

For perfectly rounded muffins, a lumpy batter is desirable. Stir gently just until dry ingredients are moistened. Don't overstir the batter, or the muffins will peak and have air tunnels throughout.

Pecan-Orange Muffins

editor's favorite

prep: 11 min.   cook: 20 min.

½   cup butter or margarine, softened
1   cup sugar
2   large eggs
2   cups all-purpose flour
1   teaspoon baking soda
1   (8-ounce) container plain yogurt
¾   cup chopped pecans, toasted
1   teaspoon grated orange rind
¼   cup orange juice
1   tablespoon sugar

Beat butter at medium speed with an electric mixer until creamy; gradually add 1 cup sugar, beating well. Add eggs, 1 at a time, beating until blended after each addition.

Combine flour and baking soda; add to butter mixture alternately with yogurt, beginning and ending with flour mixture. Beat at low speed just until blended after each addition. Stir in pecans and orange rind.

Place paper baking cups in muffin pans, and lightly coat with cooking spray; spoon batter into cups, filling almost full.

Bake at 375° for 18 to 20 minutes or until lightly browned. Brush orange juice over hot muffins, and sprinkle evenly with 1 tablespoon sugar. Yield: 1 dozen.

Blueberry-Almond Streusel Muffins

prep: 13 min.   cook: 20 min.

¼   cup all-purpose flour
¼   cup sugar
2   tablespoons butter, cut into pieces
⅓   cup chopped almonds
2   cups all-purpose flour
1   tablespoon baking powder
½   teaspoon salt
⅔   cup sugar
2   teaspoons grated lemon rind
1½ cups fresh or frozen blueberries
2   large eggs, lightly beaten
½   cup milk
½   cup butter, melted and cooled

Combine ¼ cup flour and ¼ cup sugar in a medium bowl. Cut in 2 tablespoons butter with a pastry blender until mixture is crumbly. Stir in chopped almonds. Set aside.

Combine 2 cups flour and next 4 ingredients in a large bowl. Add blueberries; toss gently to combine. Make a well in center of mixture.

Combine eggs, milk, and ½ cup butter; add to dry ingredients, stirring just until dry ingredients are moistened.

Spoon batter into greased muffin pans, filling two-thirds full. Sprinkle evenly with almond mixture.

Bake at 400° for 15 to 20 minutes or until muffins are golden. Remove from pans immediately. Yield: 16 muffins.

Cloud Biscuits

Cloud Biscuits

These large biscuits get their name from their light texture.

quick & easy

prep: 10 min. cook: 12 min.

2¼ cups self-rising flour
1   tablespoon sugar
½   cup butter-flavored shortening or
     regular shortening
1   large egg, lightly beaten
½   cup milk
1   tablespoon butter, melted

Combine flour and sugar in a medium bowl; stir well. Cut in shortening with a pastry blender until mixture is crumbly.

Combine egg and milk; add to flour mixture, stirring just until dry ingredients are moistened. Turn dough out onto a lightly floured surface, and knead 3 or 4 times.

Roll dough to ½-inch thickness; cut with a 3-inch round cutter. Place on an ungreased baking sheet.

Bake at 450° for 10 to 12 minutes or until golden. Remove from oven; brush melted butter over hot biscuits. Yield: 6 biscuits.

Sweet Little Biscuits

This recipe has just enough sugar to qualify it as a dessert. Top off the biscuits with a drizzle of honey or syrup.

quick & easy

prep: 11 min. cook: 15 min.

3   cups all-purpose flour
1   tablespoon baking powder
½   teaspoon baking soda
½   teaspoon salt
⅓   cup sugar
¾   cup butter or margarine
1   cup buttermilk
Milk

Combine first 5 ingredients, stirring well; cut in butter with a pastry blender until mixture is crumbly. Add buttermilk, stirring until dry ingredients are moistened. Shape into a ball; knead 4 or 5 times.

Roll dough to ½-inch thickness on a lightly floured surface. Cut with a 1¾-inch round cutter, and place biscuits on ungreased baking sheets. Brush biscuits lightly with milk.

Bake at 400° for 12 to 15 minutes or until lightly browned. Yield: 3 dozen.

Snappy Cheese Biscuits

Red pepper packs a little punch into these flaky cheese biscuits.

quick & easy

prep: 13 min. cook: 10 min.

1½ cups all-purpose flour
1   tablespoon baking powder
1   tablespoon sugar
½   teaspoon salt
⅛   teaspoon ground red pepper
1   cup (4 ounces) shredded sharp
     Cheddar cheese
⅓   cup shortening
½   cup milk

Stir together first 5 ingredients in a bowl; cut in cheese and shortening with a pastry blender until mixture is crumbly. Add milk, stirring just until dry ingredients are moistened.

Turn dough out onto a lightly floured surface; shape into a ball. Pat to ½-inch thickness; cut with a 2-inch round cutter. Place on an ungreased baking sheet.

Bake at 425° for 10 minutes or until golden. Yield: 15 biscuits.

the best biscuits

The art of making biscuits is easy to master when you follow these tips.

• Butter should be cold when you cut it into dry ingredients. This helps produce tender, flaky biscuits.

• If you don't own a pastry blender, use a fork and knife or two knives. You'll get the same results.

• Once you've added liquid ingredients to dry ones, keep the stirring to a minimum. You want a soft dough. Overstirring toughens biscuits.

• Use minimal flour on the work surface when you're rolling and cutting dough. Using too much flour in the dough makes dry biscuits.

• If you've misplaced your biscuit cutter, just use the rim of a drinking glass.

Whether you're an old-fashioned traditionalist or an inventive gourmet—or you just love great flavor but have little time to cook—we have a cinnamon roll for you. These three recipes span time and technique options but share sensational flavor.

Old-Fashioned Cinnamon Rolls

prep: 31 min. cook: 20 min. other: 2 hrs.

⅓ cup milk
⅓ cup butter or margarine
¼ cup firmly packed brown sugar
1 teaspoon salt
1 (¼-ounce) envelope active dry yeast
½ cup warm water (100° to 110°)
½ cup egg substitute
3½ cups bread flour, divided
¾ cup quick-cooking oats, uncooked
¼ cup butter or margarine, softened
¾ cup firmly packed brown sugar
¼ cup raisins
2 teaspoons ground cinnamon
1 cup sifted powdered sugar
2 tablespoons milk

Old-Fashioned Cinnamon Rolls

Combine first 4 ingredients in a saucepan; cook over low heat until butter melts, stirring occasionally. Cool to 110°.

Combine yeast and warm water in a 1-cup glass measuring cup; let stand 5 minutes.

Combine milk mixture, yeast mixture, egg substitute, 1 cup bread flour, and oats in a large mixing bowl; beat at medium speed with an electric mixer until blended. Gradually stir in enough remaining flour to make a soft dough.

Turn dough out onto a lightly floured surface; knead until smooth and elastic (about 8 minutes). Place dough in a large bowl coated with cooking spray, turning to coat top.

Cover and let rise in a warm place (85°), free from drafts, 1 hour or until doubled in bulk. Punch dough down; cover and let rest 10 minutes.

Divide dough in half; roll each portion into a 12-inch square. Spread each square with 2 tablespoons butter.

Combine ¾ cup brown sugar, raisins, and cinnamon; sprinkle mixture over each square. Roll up, jellyroll fashion; pinch seam to seal (do not seal ends).

Cut each roll into 1-inch slices, and place in 2 lightly greased 8-inch square pans.

Cover and let rise in a warm place, free from drafts, about 30 minutes or until almost doubled in bulk.

Bake at 375° for 15 to 20 minutes or until golden.

Combine powdered sugar and 2 tablespoons milk; drizzle over warm rolls. Yield: 2 dozen.

Christmas Morning Sticky Buns

Prepare this dough and chill it over-night, and all you'll have to do Christmas morning is pop it in the oven.

make-ahead

prep: 9 min.   cook: 30 min.   other: 8 hrs.

½   cup chopped pecans or walnuts
1   (25-ounce) package frozen roll dough, thawed
1   (3.4-ounce) package butterscotch instant pudding mix
½   cup butter or margarine, melted
½   cup firmly packed brown sugar
¾   teaspoon ground cinnamon

Sprinkle pecans in the bottom of a buttered 12-cup Bundt pan.

Arrange dough in pan; sprinkle with dry pudding mix.

Stir together butter, brown sugar, and cinnamon; pour over rolls (mixture will not cover all of dry mix). Cover and chill 8 hours.

Bake, uncovered, at 350° for 30 minutes or until golden brown. Invert onto a serving plate, and serve immediately. Yield: 8 servings.

Tiny Cinnamon Rolls

Transform canned crescent rolls into these dainty, sweet spirals.

quick & easy

prep: 11 min.   cook: 15 min.

1   (8-ounce) can refrigerated crescent rolls
1   tablespoon granulated sugar
1   teaspoon ground cinnamon
⅔   cup sifted powdered sugar
2   teaspoons milk
2   drops of vanilla extract

Tiny Cinnamon Rolls

Unroll crescent roll dough, and separate into 4 rectangles; pinch perforations within rectangles to seal. Stir together granulated sugar and cinnamon; sprinkle mixture evenly over rectangles.

Roll up, jellyroll fashion, starting with a long side; pinch edges to seal. Gently cut each log into 5 slices, and place, cut sides down, in a lightly greased 8- or 9-inch round cakepan.

Bake at 375° for 15 minutes or until rolls begin to brown.

Combine powdered sugar, milk, and vanilla, stirring until smooth; drizzle over warm cinnamon rolls. Yield: 20 rolls.

Gingerbread Scones

In this recipe, four spices mix with molasses to fill your kitchen with heart-warming holiday aromas.

prep: 10 min.   cook: 10 min.

2¼ cups all-purpose flour
1   teaspoon baking powder
¼   teaspoon baking soda
1   teaspoon ground cinnamon
½   teaspoon ground ginger
¼   teaspoon ground allspice
¼   teaspoon ground nutmeg
½   cup butter or margarine
½   cup currants
⅓   cup molasses
¾   cup whipping cream
Lemon Butter

Combine first 7 ingredients; cut in butter with a pastry blender until mixture is crumbly. Stir in currants. Add molasses and whipping cream, stirring just until dry ingredients are moistened. Turn dough out onto a lightly floured surface, and knead 4 or 5 times.

Roll dough to ½-inch thickness on a lightly floured surface; cut with a 2-inch round cutter. Place on lightly greased baking sheet.

Bake at 425° for 8 to 10 minutes or until lightly browned. Serve with Lemon Butter. Yield: 2 dozen.

Lemon Butter

prep: 3 min.

¼   cup butter or margarine, softened
¼   cup sifted powdered sugar
1   teaspoon grated lemon rind
1   tablespoon lemon juice

Combine all ingredients, stirring until blended. Yield: ⅓ cup.

---

the scoop on scones

• Scones resemble biscuits in texture but are usually sweeter and richer. Traditionally they were wedge-shaped, but they can also be round or square.

• The rules about minimal stirring, handling, and additional flour that apply to biscuits apply to scones, too.

• Scone dough is typically a bit sticky. Just pat the dough into a rough mound for baking.

Maple-Pecan Scones with Cinnamon Butter

prep: 9 min.   cook: 12 min.

¾   cup chopped pecans
2¼ cups all-purpose flour
1   teaspoon baking powder
¼   teaspoon baking soda
¼   teaspoon salt
⅓   cup maple-flavored syrup
¾   cup whipping cream
Cinnamon Butter

Spread pecans in a shallow pan. Bake at 350° for 5 minutes.

Position knife blade in food processor bowl; add ⅓ cup pecans. Process pecans until ground (about 5 seconds).

Combine ground pecans, remaining chopped pecans, flour, and next 3 ingredients. Add syrup and cream, stirring until dry ingredients are moistened.

Turn dough out onto a lightly floured surface, and knead 4 or 5 times. Pat dough into a 10-inch circle on a greased baking sheet. Using a sharp knife, make 8 shallow cuts in dough, forming wedges.

Bake at 425° for 10 to 12 minutes or until lightly browned. Serve warm with Cinnamon Butter. Yield: 8 servings.

Cinnamon Butter

prep: 5 min.

⅓   cup butter, softened
¼   cup maple-flavored syrup
¼   teaspoon ground cinnamon

Beat butter at medium speed with an electric mixer until fluffy; gradually beat in syrup and cinnamon. Yield: about ½ cup.

Hazelnut Scones

editor's favorite
prep: 14 min.   cook: 15 min.

2   cups all-purpose flour
2   teaspoons baking powder
¼   teaspoon salt
½   cup sugar
⅓   cup butter
½   cup chopped blanched hazelnuts
2   large eggs, lightly beaten
½   cup whipping cream
1½ tablespoons hazelnut-flavored
       liqueur or whipping cream
1   tablespoon sugar
18   whole hazelnuts

Combine first 4 ingredients in a bowl; cut in butter with pastry blender until mixture is crumbly. Stir in chopped hazelnuts; make a well in center of mixture.

Combine eggs, whipping cream, and liqueur; add to dry ingredients, stirring just until moistened.

Roll dough to ¾-inch thickness on a lightly floured surface. Cut with a 2½-inch round cutter, and place on lightly greased baking sheets. Sprinkle tops evenly with 1 tablespoon sugar, and place a hazelnut in each center.

Bake at 350° for 15 minutes or until lightly browned. Serve with honey, butter, or strawberry jam. Yield: 1½ dozen.

Whipping Cream Waffles

prep: 15 min. cook: 10 min.

2   large eggs, separated
1   cup whipping cream, whipped
1   tablespoon butter or margarine, melted
⅔   cup all-purpose flour
1   teaspoon baking powder
⅛   teaspoon salt
⅓   cup sugar
Cranberry Butter
Applesauce Cream

Beat egg yolks in a bowl until thick and pale; fold in whipped cream and butter. Combine ⅔ cup flour and next 3 ingredients; fold into whipped cream mixture.

Beat egg whites at high speed with an electric mixer until stiff peaks form; fold into batter (batter will be thick). Spoon half of batter onto a preheated, oiled waffle iron, spreading to edges.

Bake until lightly browned and crisp. Repeat procedure. Serve with Cranberry Butter, Applesauce Cream, syrup, or honey. Yield: 2 (8-inch) waffles.

Cranberry Butter

prep: 5 min.

½   cup butter, softened
¼   cup powdered sugar
2   tablespoons whole-berry cranberry sauce

Combine butter and powdered sugar; beat at medium speed with an electric mixer until blended. Stir in cranberry sauce. Spoon mixture into a butter crock; cover and chill. Yield: ⅔ cup.

Applesauce Cream

prep: 5 min.

½   cup whipping cream
½   cup applesauce
¼   cup sifted powdered sugar
1   tablespoon lemon juice

Beat whipping cream at medium speed with an electric mixer until soft peaks form; fold in applesauce, powdered sugar, and lemon juice. Cover and chill. Yield: 1½ cups.

Pumpkin Pancakes

Create a new morning sensation with these spiced pumpkin pancakes.

prep: 18 min. cook: 20 min.

2   cups all-purpose flour
1   tablespoon plus 1 teaspoon baking powder
1   teaspoon salt
2   tablespoons sugar
1   teaspoon ground cinnamon or pumpkin pie spice
4   large eggs, separated
1½   cups milk
1   cup canned pumpkin
½   cup butter or margarine, melted

Combine first 5 ingredients in a large bowl; make a well in center of mixture.

Combine egg yolks, milk, pumpkin, and butter; add to flour mixture, stirring just until dry ingredients are moistened.

Beat egg whites at high speed with an electric mixer until stiff peaks form. Gently fold into pumpkin mixture.

Pour about ¼ cup batter for each pancake onto a hot, lightly greased griddle. Cook pancakes until tops are covered with bubbles and edges look cooked; turn and cook other side. Yield: 24 (4-inch) pancakes.

Eggnog Pancakes

Start a new tradition by serving these eggnog-laced pancakes on Christmas morning. A hint of nutmeg and cloves permeates each tender bite.

freezer-friendly
prep: 15 min. cook: 10 min.

1⅓   cups all-purpose flour
¼   cup sugar
1   teaspoon baking soda
½   teaspoon salt
¼   teaspoon ground nutmeg
⅛   teaspoon ground cloves
1½   cups refrigerated eggnog
1   large egg, lightly beaten
1   tablespoon vegetable oil

Combine first 6 ingredients in a large bowl. Combine eggnog, egg, and oil; add to flour mixture, stirring just until dry ingredients are moistened.

Pour about ¼ cup batter for each pancake onto a hot, lightly greased griddle or skillet. Cook pancakes until tops are covered with bubbles and edges look cooked; turn and cook other side. Yield: 12 (4-inch) pancakes.

Freezing Note: These pancakes freeze and reheat with great results. Simply stack the cooked pancakes between sheets of wax paper, place in an airtight container, and freeze up to 1 month. To reheat, place the frozen pancakes in a single layer on a baking sheet. Bake at 325° for 10 minutes.

Cinnamon French Toast with Fruit and Pecans

prep: 8 min.   cook: 26 min.

2   cups all-purpose baking mix
1½ cups water
1   teaspoon vanilla extract
¼   teaspoon ground cinnamon
2   tablespoons butter or margarine
2   tablespoons vegetable oil
8   cinnamon bread slices
2   bananas, sliced
Fresh strawberries
¼   cup chopped pecans, toasted
Syrup

Whisk together first 4 ingredients.

Melt ½ tablespoon butter in ½ table-spoon oil in a large skillet over medium heat. Dip 2 bread slices in batter, and place in skillet. Cook 2 to 3 minutes on each side or until golden. Repeat procedure with remaining butter, oil, batter, and bread slices.

Top French toast with fruit and pecans. Serve with your favorite syrup. Yield: 4 servings.

Praline French Toast

As a shortcut, combine the melted butter, brown sugar, maple syrup, and pecans, and microwave at HIGH for 30 seconds.

prep: 7 min.   cook: 37 min.   other: 8 hrs.

8   large eggs, beaten
1½ cups half-and-half
1   tablespoon brown sugar
2   teaspoons vanilla extract
8   (1-inch-thick) slices French bread
½   cup butter or margarine
¾   cup firmly packed brown sugar
½   cup maple syrup
¾   cup chopped pecans, toasted

Cinnamon French Toast with Fruit and Pecans

Greet Christmas morning with a warm and hearty helping of Cinnamon French Toast topped with fresh fruit and nuts.

Combine first 4 ingredients in a large bowl, stirring with a wire whisk until blended. Pour 1 cup egg mixture into a greased 13- x 9-inch baking dish. Place bread in dish; pour remaining egg mixture over bread. Cover and chill 8 hours.

The next morning, melt butter in a saucepan over medium heat; add brown sugar and maple syrup, stirring until smooth. Bring to a boil; reduce heat, and simmer 1 minute, stirring constantly. Stir in pecans. Pour over French bread slices in baking dish.

Bake, uncovered, at 350° for 30 minutes or until set and golden. Yield: 8 servings.

Sausage-Stuffed French Loaf

For a bold flavor, use spicy sausage.

prep: 9 min.   cook: 31 min.

1   (16-ounce) loaf French bread
1   pound ground pork sausage
1   medium onion, chopped
1   cup (4 ounces) shredded mozzarella
     cheese
¼   cup chopped fresh parsley
1   teaspoon Dijon mustard
¼   teaspoon fennel seeds
¼   teaspoon salt
¼   teaspoon pepper
1   large egg, lightly beaten
2   tablespoons butter or margarine
1   garlic clove, minced

Cut off ends of French bread loaf, and set ends aside. Hollow out center of loaf with a long serrated bread knife, leaving a ½-inch-thick shell. Position knife blade in food processor bowl; add bread removed from inside loaf. Process to make coarse crumbs. Set bread shell and crumbs aside.

Cook sausage and onion in a skillet until sausage is browned, stirring until it crumbles; drain well. Stir in 1 cup reserved breadcrumbs, cheese, and next 6 ingredients. Spoon sausage mixture into bread shell, and replace loaf ends, securing with wooden picks.

Melt butter in a small saucepan; add garlic, and cook about 1 minute. Brush over loaf. Wrap loaf in aluminum foil, leaving open slightly on top.

Bake at 400° for 20 minutes or until cheese thoroughly melts. Yield: 4 servings.

Sausage-Filled Crêpes

Sausage-Filled Crêpes

freezer-friendly • make-ahead
prep: 12 min.   cook: 28 min.

1   pound ground pork sausage
1   small onion, diced
2   cups (8 ounces) shredded Cheddar
     cheese, divided
1   (3-ounce) package cream cheese
½   teaspoon dried marjoram
Basic Crêpes
½   cup sour cream
¼   cup butter or margarine, softened
¼   cup chopped fresh parsley

Cook sausage and onion in a skillet over medium heat, stirring until sausage crumbles and is no longer pink; drain. Return to skillet. Add 1 cup Cheddar cheese, cream cheese, and marjoram, stirring until cheeses melt. Spoon 3 tablespoons filling down center of each crêpe.

Roll up crêpes; place, seam sides down, in a greased 13- x 9-inch baking dish.

Bake, covered, at 350° for 15 minutes. Combine sour cream and butter; spoon over crêpes. Bake 5 minutes. Sprinkle with remaining 1 cup Cheddar cheese and parsley. Serve with sliced tomato, if desired. Yield: 6 to 8 servings.

Basic Crêpes

prep: 4 min.   cook: 20 min.   other: 1 hr.

3   large eggs
1   cup milk
1   tablespoon vegetable oil
1   cup all-purpose flour
½   teaspoon salt

Beat first 3 ingredients at medium speed with an electric mixer until blended. Gradually add flour and salt, beating until smooth. Cover and chill 1 hour.

Coat bottom of a 7-inch nonstick skillet with cooking spray; place over medium heat until hot. Pour 3 tablespoons batter into skillet; quickly tilt pan in all directions so that batter covers bottom of pan.

Cook 1 minute or until crêpe can be shaken loose from skillet. Turn crêpe, and cook about 30 seconds. Place on a dish towel to cool. Repeat procedure with remaining batter. Stack crêpes between sheets of wax paper and place in an airtight container, if desired. Chill up to 2 days, or freeze up to 3 months. Yield: 12 (7-inch) crêpes.

Make-Ahead Note: Assemble Sausage-Filled Crêpes ahead, if desired, and freeze. To reheat, remove from freezer; let stand 30 minutes at room temperature. Bake, covered, at 350° for 40 minutes or until thoroughly heated. Proceed as directed, adding sour cream topping and remaining ingredients.

Southwestern Soufflé Roll

Southwestern Soufflé Roll

prep: 23 min. cook: 53 min. other: 5 min.

2   tablespoons butter or margarine
1½   cups peeled, diced potato
2   green bell peppers, chopped
2   jalapeño peppers, seeded and minced
1   onion, chopped
4   garlic cloves, minced
4   ounces ham, diced (⅔ cup)
½   cup chopped fresh cilantro
½   teaspoon salt
¼   teaspoon black pepper
¼   cup butter or margarine, melted
2   tablespoons all-purpose flour
¼   teaspoon salt
1   cup milk
12   large eggs, separated
1   cup (4 ounces) shredded Monterey
     Jack cheese with peppers
Salsa

Melt 2 tablespoons butter in a skillet; add potato and next 4 ingredients. Sauté 20 minutes or until tender. Stir in ham and next 3 ingredients; set aside.

Whisk together ¼ cup melted butter, flour, and ¼ teaspoon salt in a heavy saucepan over low heat until smooth; cook, whisking constantly, 3 minutes or until bubbly. Gradually add milk, and cook over medium heat, whisking constantly, until thickened and bubbly. Remove from heat.

Beat egg yolks until thick and pale. Gradually stir about one-fourth of milk mixture into yolks; add to remaining milk mixture, stirring constantly. Cook over medium-low heat, stirring constantly, 2 minutes or until slightly thickened. Pour into a large bowl, and cool.

Line a 15- x 10-inch jellyroll pan with parchment paper; lightly coat paper with cooking spray. Beat egg whites at high speed with an electric mixer until stiff peaks form; fold into batter. Spread evenly in prepared pan.

Bake at 400° for 15 minutes or until a wooden pick inserted in center comes out clean. Cool in pan on a wire rack 5 minutes. Turn out onto a cloth towel; remove paper. Return paper to pan. Top soufflé with vegetable mixture; sprinkle with cheese. Beginning at a long side, roll up, jellyroll fashion; place roll, seam side down, in pan. Bake at 350° for 10 minutes or until heated and cheese melts. Slice with a serrated knife; serve with salsa. Yield: 8 servings.

Country Ham 'n' Scrambled Egg Casserole

prep: 24 min. cook: 1 hr., 29 min.

¼   cup butter or margarine
½   cup all-purpose flour
1   quart milk
¼   teaspoon pepper
2   (2½-ounce) jars sliced mushrooms,
     drained
1   (8-ounce) package thinly sliced
     country ham, cut into 1-inch
     pieces
4   slices bacon, cooked and crumbled
     (optional)
16   large eggs, lightly beaten
1   cup evaporated milk
¼   cup butter or margarine
Garnish: chopped fresh parsley

Melt ¼ cup butter in a heavy saucepan over low heat; add flour, stirring until smooth. Cook, stirring constantly, 1 minute. Gradually add 1 quart milk; cook over medium heat, stirring constantly, until thickened and bubbly. Stir in pepper, mushrooms, country ham, and, if desired, bacon; remove from heat. Set aside.

Combine eggs and evaporated milk, stirring with a wire whisk.

Melt ¼ cup butter in a large nonstick skillet over medium heat; add egg mixture, and cook, without stirring, until egg mixture begins to set on bottom. Draw a spatula across bottom of skillet until eggs form large curds. Continue until eggs are thickened but still moist; do not stir constantly. Remove from heat.

Spoon half of egg mixture into a lightly greased 13- x 9-inch baking dish; cover with half of ham mixture. Repeat procedure. (If desired, cover and chill 8 hours. Let stand at room temperature 30 minutes before baking.)

Bake, covered, at 300° for 30 minutes. Uncover and bake 30 more minutes. Let stand 10 minutes. Garnish, if desired. Yield: 8 to 10 servings.

Cheddar-Egg Casserole

make-ahead

prep: 13 min.   cook: 55 min.
other: 8 hrs., 15 min.

6   cups cubed cooked ham
4   cups (16 ounces) shredded Cheddar
       cheese
8   cups French bread cubes
3   tablespoons butter, melted
½   cup all-purpose flour
1   teaspoon dry mustard
8   large eggs
4   cups milk

Layer ham, cheese, and bread cubes in a lightly greased 13- x 9-inch baking dish; drizzle with butter. Combine flour and mustard; sprinkle over top. Whisk together eggs and milk; pour over casserole. Cover and chill 8 hours.

Remove from refrigerator; let stand at room temperature 15 minutes.

Bake, uncovered, at 350° for 50 to 55 minutes or until set. Yield: 8 to 10 servings.

Hash Brown-Cheese Bake

prep: 5 min.   cook: 45 min.

1   (20-ounce) package refrigerated
       shredded hash browns
1   (10¾-ounce) can cream of celery
       soup, undiluted
1   (8-ounce) container sour cream
1   (2-ounce) jar diced pimiento, drained
½   cup shredded Parmesan cheese
1   cup (4 ounces) shredded sharp
       Cheddar cheese, divided

Combine first 5 ingredients and ½ cup shredded Cheddar cheese; spoon mixture into a lightly greased 13- x 9-inch baking dish.

Bake, uncovered, at 350° for 40 minutes. Sprinkle with remaining Cheddar cheese, and bake 5 more minutes. Yield: 6 to 8 servings.

Hash Brown-Ham-Cheese Bake: Stir in 2 cups chopped cooked ham.

Sugared Bacon

quick & easy

prep: 10 min.   cook: 35 min.

⅓   cup firmly packed brown sugar
3   tablespoons Worcestershire sauce
2   tablespoons spicy honey mustard
1   large egg, beaten
12   slices bacon
1½   cups fine, dry breadcrumbs

Combine first 4 ingredients in a shallow bowl, stirring well. Dip each slice of

bacon into sugar mixture; coat with breadcrumbs. Arrange bacon slices on a rack in a large broiler pan.

Bake at 350° for 35 minutes or until bacon is crisp. Drain well on paper towels. Yield: 12 slices.

Citrus Compote with Caramel Syrup

make-ahead

prep: 30 min.   cook: 35 min.

¾   cup sugar
¾   cup cold water, divided
¼   cup light corn syrup
¼   teaspoon ground cinnamon
⅛   teaspoon ground cloves
5   large navel oranges, peeled and
       sectioned *
4   pink grapefruit, peeled and
       sectioned *

Garnish: cinnamon sticks

Cook sugar, ¼ cup cold water, and corn syrup in a small heavy saucepan over medium heat, stirring constantly, 30 minutes or until mixture is caramel colored. Remove from heat.

Add remaining ½ cup water. (Sugar mixture will clump but will dissolve when heated.) Bring to a boil. Boil, stirring constantly, 5 minutes or until smooth. Stir in ground cinnamon and cloves.

Pour over orange and grapefruit sections. Garnish, if desired, and serve warm. Yield: 6 servings.

* 3⅓ cups jarred orange sections, drained, and 5 cups jarred grapefruit sections, drained, may be substituted for fresh fruit.

Make-Ahead Note: Caramel syrup can be made ahead and chilled. Reheat in a saucepan before serving.

easy holiday cheers

Stir up a festive atmosphere with this mix of tasty drinks. We've included a variety of hot and cold blends, along with several recipes suitable for a crowd.

Spiced Apple Cider

A spicy bundle brimming with cloves, allspice, and orange rind simmers in this apple cider and fruit juice mixture. This seasonal pleasure can be served warm or chilled.

editor's favorite
prep: 7 min.   cook: 20 min.

1   teaspoon whole cloves
½   teaspoon whole allspice
Rind of 1 orange, cut into strips
2   quarts apple cider
3   cups pineapple juice
¾   cup orange juice
2   tablespoons lemon juice

Place first 3 ingredients in a cheesecloth bag; combine spice bag, cider, and remaining ingredients in a Dutch oven.
   Cook, uncovered, over medium heat until thoroughly heated. Remove and discard spice bag. Serve warm or chilled. Yield: about 3 quarts.

Cinnamon Cider

quick & easy
prep: 3 min.   cook: 15 min.

1½   quarts apple cider
1   quart cranberry-apple drink
2   cups pineapple juice
¾   cup red cinnamon candies
2   teaspoons whole cloves
Cinnamon sticks (optional)

Pour first 3 ingredients into an electric percolator. Place cinnamon candies and cloves in percolator basket. Perk through complete cycle of percolator. Serve hot with cinnamon stick stirrers, if desired. Yield: 3 quarts.

Hot Russian Tea

prep: 4 min.   cook: 13 min.

4   quarts water
1   cup sugar
4   (2-inch) cinnamon sticks
2   (12-ounce) cans frozen pineapple-orange-banana juice concentrate, undiluted
1   (12-ounce) can frozen lemonade concentrate, undiluted
⅓   cup unsweetened instant tea powder

Bring 1 quart water, sugar, and cinnamon sticks to a boil in a large Dutch oven over medium-high heat, stirring until sugar dissolves. Stir in remaining 3 quarts water, frozen concentrates, and tea powder. Cook until thoroughly heated; serve immediately. Yield: 5 quarts.

Cranberry-Currant Warmer

prep: 5 min.   cook: 15 min.

1   (12-ounce) jar red currant jelly
1   cup water
1   (32-ounce) bottle cranberry juice drink
2   (12-ounce) cans unsweetened pineapple juice
½   cup lemon juice
Garnish: lemon wedges

Heat jelly and 1 cup water in a large saucepan over medium heat, stirring often, 10 minutes or until jelly melts. Stir in next 3 ingredients, and cook until heated. Garnish, if desired. Yield: 8 servings.

perfect presentation

Use these tips to serve holiday drinks with professional panache.

• Mix and match glassware of similar quality. The variety adds a refreshing look to your buffet and spares you from having to gather large quantities of the same design glasses and mugs.
• Choose clear glassware for colored drinks. Clear glassware showcases the beauty of red wine or vibrant holiday punch. Set out tall and short glasses, and allow your guests to select their preference.
• Break the rules. For example, serve a beverage other than beer in pilsner glasses, pour red wine or eggnog into European bistro glasses, or ladle holiday punch into tall flutes or fountain glasses.

Cranberry-Currant Warmer

White Chocolate
Brandy Alexander

White Chocolate Brandy Alexander

quick & easy
prep: 6 min. cook: 6 min.

3½ cups milk
½ teaspoon vanilla extract
⅛ teaspoon salt
6 ounces white chocolate, finely chopped
⅓ cup brandy
3 tablespoons white crème de cacao
Garnishes: whipped cream, white chocolate shavings

Combine first 3 ingredients in a medium saucepan; cook over medium heat until thoroughly heated (do not boil). Remove from heat; gradually stir about one-fourth of hot mixture into chocolate, stirring with a wire whisk until chocolate melts. Add to remaining hot mixture, stirring constantly. Stir in brandy and crème de cacao. Pour into glasses. Garnish, if desired. Serve immediately. Yield: 4½ cups.

Orange Wassail

Make two batches of this traditional holiday drink—one with bourbon and one without—so that merrymakers, both young and young at heart, can enjoy a toast to good health.

prep: 7 min. cook: 10 min.

1 (64-ounce) carton orange juice
1 (64-ounce) bottle apple juice
4 cups cranberry juice cocktail
1 (12-ounce) can frozen lemonade concentrate, thawed and undiluted
1 (2-inch) cinnamon stick
3 cups bourbon (optional)
1 tablespoon whole cloves
2 oranges, sliced

Combine first 5 ingredients in a large Dutch oven. Stir in bourbon, if desired. Insert cloves into orange slices; add to juice mixture. Cook, uncovered, over medium heat until thoroughly heated. Serve warm. Yield: 6 quarts.

Praline Coffee

quick & easy
prep: 5 min. cook: 5 min.

3 cups hot brewed coffee
¾ cup half-and-half
¾ cup firmly packed light brown sugar
2 tablespoons butter
¾ cup praline liqueur
Sweetened whipped cream

Cook first 4 ingredients in a large saucepan over medium heat, stirring constantly, until thoroughly heated (do not boil). Stir in liqueur; top with sweetened whipped cream. Yield: about 5 cups.

Holiday Hot Chocolate

prep: 9 min. cook: 14 min.

1½ cups sugar
½ cup cocoa
⅛ teaspoon salt
5 cups water
1 (12-ounce) can evaporated milk
2 cups milk
Sweetened whipped cream
Crushed peppermint candy

Combine first 3 ingredients in a large Dutch oven; stir well. Gradually stir in water; bring to a boil.

Add evaporated milk and milk; cook until thoroughly heated, stirring occasionally. Pour into mugs. Top each serving with whipped cream, and sprinkle with crushed candy. Yield: 7 cups.

Spirited Addition: For a spiked version, add ¾ cup peppermint schnapps to this hot chocolate mixture just before serving.

coffee bar

Offer a coffee bar at your next open house or as the ending to a fine meal.

• Prepare your coffee bar with an emphasis on gourmet blends rather than on food. Include treats to complement—not compete with—the beverage.
• Arrange everything on a countertop or sideboard that is easily accessible to a number of people. There should be enough room for cups, saucers, spoons, and flavorings.
• If you don't have an espresso/cappuccino machine, a blend of 30% French and 70% Columbian coffees brewed in a drip pot works nicely. Serve in demitasse or regular cups, and allow two servings for each guest.
• In addition to sugar and cream, include sweetened whipped cream (about 2 tablespoons per person).
• For fun flavorings, include grated chocolate; cinnamon sticks; shakers of ground cinnamon, cocoa and nutmeg; almond slivers; and grated orange rind.
• For spirited versions, offer guests a selection of liqueurs to add to their coffee. You can include almond, orange, hazelnut, praline, and coffee liqueurs. For a similar taste without the alcohol, use flavored syrups. Look for them at your grocery store in the coffee aisle.

Sparkling Citrus Punch

freezer-friendly • make-ahead
prep: 8 min.   other: 4 hrs.

1   (46-ounce) can pineapple juice
1½ cups orange juice
¾   cup lemon juice
¼   cup lime juice
1¼ cups sugar
2   (2-liter) bottles ginger ale, chilled

Stir together first 5 ingredients until sugar dissolves. Pour into ice cube trays. Cover and freeze until firm (approximately 4 hours). To serve, place 4 juice cubes in each tall glass. Pour 1 cup ginger ale into each glass; stir until slushy. Yield: about 17 servings.

Freezing Note: Freeze juice mixture in an airtight container, if desired. Thaw slightly in a punch bowl; add ginger ale, and stir until slushy.

Spiced Coffee-Eggnog Punch

prep: 14 min.   cook: 22 min.   other: 4 hrs.

2   cups strongly brewed coffee
1½ (3-inch) cinnamon sticks
6   whole allspice
6   whole cloves
2   (32-ounce) cans eggnog, chilled
1   tablespoon vanilla extract
1   cup whipping cream, whipped
1   quart vanilla ice cream, softened
Ground nutmeg

Combine first 4 ingredients in a saucepan. Bring to a boil; reduce heat, and simmer, uncovered, 15 minutes. Pour coffee mixture through a wire-mesh strainer into a bowl, discarding spices; chill 3 to 4 hours. Combine coffee

---

■■■■■■■■■■■■■■■■■■■■■■■■■■■■

painted napkins

Dress up paper cocktail napkins with a cheery holiday design. Use a paint pen to write a favorite verse or words to a cherished carol around the edge of each napkin, and then draw a design in the center of the napkin, if desired. For designs, draw stars or trees—anything that's easy and fast.

■■■■■■■■■■■■■■■■■■■■■■■■■■■■

mixture, eggnog, and vanilla in a large bowl; fold in whipped cream.

Spoon softened ice cream into a punch bowl. Pour eggnog mixture over ice cream, and stir gently. Sprinkle punch with ground nutmeg. Yield: 11 cups.

Mocha Eggnog

Eggnog gets a holiday makeover with instant coffee granules, chocolate syrup, and brandy.

prep: 8 min.   other: 2 hrs., 20 min.

1½ tablespoons instant coffee granules
½   cup hot water
1   (32-ounce) carton refrigerated eggnog
¼   to ½ cup brandy (optional)
½   cup chocolate syrup
½   cup whipping cream, whipped
Garnish: grated semisweet chocolate

Dissolve instant coffee granules in hot water; cool. Combine coffee, eggnog, and, if desired, brandy. Add chocolate syrup; cover and chill thoroughly.

Fold in whipped cream just before serving. Garnish, if desired. Yield: about 1½ quarts.

Rich Velvet Punch

quick & easy
prep: 7 min.   cook: 5 min.

6   cups brewed coffee
3   cups half-and-half
1   cup Cookies 'n' Cream liqueur
¾   cup chocolate syrup
1   pint coffee ice cream

Combine first 4 ingredients in a large saucepan; stir well. Cook over medium heat until thoroughly heated. Add ice cream, stirring until ice cream melts. Serve warm. Yield: 3 quarts.

Holiday Cheer

quick & easy
prep: 7 min.

2   (750-milliliter) bottles rosé wine, chilled
2   cups port
1   cup cherry brandy
Juice of 2 oranges (⅔ cup)
Juice of 2 lemons (¼ cup)
½   cup superfine sugar
1   (1-liter) bottle club soda, chilled

Combine first 5 ingredients; add sugar, stirring until sugar dissolves. Stir in club soda just before serving. Serve over crushed ice. Yield: 3 quarts.

■■■■■■■■■■■■■■■■■■■■■■■■■■■■

festive flutes

Decorate holiday glassware using a white opaque paint marker to draw simple snowflake designs. If you want to keep the painted design, you should handwash the glasses. Otherwise, you can easily scratch off the paint with your fingernail after the party.

■■■■■■■■■■■■■■■■■■■■■■■■■■■■

Champagne Punch with Ice Ring

In a hurry? Use one 20-ounce can unsweetened pineapple chunks, drained, instead of fresh pineapple.

prep: 17 min.   other: 6 hrs., 35 min.

6   cups bottled or boiled, cooled water
Fresh strawberries, kiwifruit slices,
        kumquat halves
1   fresh pineapple, cut into bite-size
        pieces
2½ cups sugar, divided
1¾ cups lemon juice
1   (750-milliliter) bottle Champagne,
        chilled
1   (750-milliliter) bottle dry white
        wine, chilled
2   quarts cold water

Pour 4½ cups water into a 6-cup ring mold; freeze. Arrange strawberries, kiwifruit, and kumquats on top of ice, letting fruit extend above top of mold. Pour remaining 1½ cups water over fruit, filling mold to within ½ inch of top; freeze.

Combine pineapple and 1 cup sugar; let stand at room temperature 30 minutes.

Combine lemon juice and remaining sugar, stirring until sugar dissolves.

To serve, combine pineapple mixture, lemon juice mixture, Champagne, wine, and cold water in a punch bowl. Let ice ring stand at room temperature 5 minutes. Carefully remove ice ring from mold, and place in punch bowl, fruit side up. Yield: 4½ quarts.

Sparkling Champagne Punch

Sparkling Champagne Punch

prep: 20 min.   other: 6 hrs.

3¾ cups lemonade
5   lemon slices
5   lime slices
10 maraschino cherries with stems
6   cups water
2   (12-ounce) cans frozen lemonade
        concentrate, thawed and undiluted
2   (12-ounce) cans frozen pineapple
        juice concentrate, thawed and
        undiluted
1   (2-liter) bottle ginger ale, chilled
1   (1-liter) bottle tonic water,
        chilled
1   (750-milliliter) bottle Champagne,
        chilled *

Pour 3 cups lemonade into a lightly greased 4½-cup ring mold; freeze 1 hour or until slushy. Arrange citrus slices and cherries in mold, pressing into slushy mixture, and freeze 1 hour. Pour in remaining ¾ cup lemonade; freeze at least 4 hours or until firm.

Stir together 6 cups water and concentrates in a large container; chill at least 1 hour or until thoroughly chilled.

Add ginger ale, tonic water, and Champagne to chilled juice mixture in container; gently stir. Remove ice ring from mold, and place in a large punch bowl. Add punch; serve immediately. Yield: 28 servings.

* 3 cups sparkling cider may be substituted.

merry party starters

Good friends and good food are a winning combination—especially during the holidays. This selection of yummy appetizers makes any gathering more fun.

Pecan Cheese Ball

make-ahead

prep: 13 min.   other: 2 hrs.

2   (8-ounce) packages cream cheese, softened
1   (8-ounce) can crushed pineapple, drained
¼   cup chopped green bell pepper
2   tablespoons finely chopped onion
2   teaspoons seasoned salt
2   cups chopped pecans, toasted and divided

Combine first 5 ingredients; stir in 1 cup pecans. Cover and chill until firm.

Shape mixture into a ball; roll in remaining 1 cup pecans. Place cheese ball on a serving platter; serve with crackers and strips of green bell pepper and red bell pepper. Yield: 1 (5-inch) cheese ball.

Chicken-Artichoke-Cheese Spread Gift Box

This recipe can make two gifts, if you prefer. Simply cut the loaf into two small "boxes," and garnish each half.

great gift • make-ahead

prep: 18 min.   other: 8 hrs.

3   cups diced cooked chicken
2   (8-ounce) packages cream cheese, softened
2   cups freshly shredded Parmesan cheese
1   (14-ounce) can artichoke hearts, drained and diced
1   cup finely chopped pecans, toasted
4   green onions, minced
1   tablespoon lemon juice
½   teaspoon salt
1   teaspoon seasoned pepper
Garnishes: 7 or 8 green onion stems, 1 red chile pepper, halved

Combine first 9 ingredients in a large bowl; stir until blended. Spoon into a straight-sided 5- x 9-inch loafpan lined with plastic wrap. Cover and chill 8 hours.

Invert chilled mixture onto a serving plate; remove plastic wrap. Cut loaf in half crosswise, place 1 cut half directly on top of remaining cut half, and smooth sides.

Plunge green onion stems into boiling water; plunge stems into ice water to stop the cooking process. Immediately transfer to paper towels; drain stems, and press between paper towels to dry. Press stems into sides of cheese square, beginning with end of 1 stem on each side. Bring stems up and over to center of top; form loops with remaining stems, and secure with wooden picks. Arrange chile pepper halves on top. Cover and chill up to 4 days. Yield: about 24 appetizer servings.

Hearts of Palm Spread

quick & easy

prep: 8 min.   cook: 20 min.

1   (14-ounce) can hearts of palm, drained and chopped
1   cup (4 ounces) shredded mozzarella cheese
¾   cup mayonnaise or salad dressing
½   cup grated Parmesan cheese
¼   cup sour cream
2   tablespoons minced green onions

Combine all ingredients; spoon into a greased 9-inch quiche dish.

Bake, uncovered, at 350° for 20 minutes or until bubbly. Serve hot with crackers. Yield: about 2 cups.

Chicken-Artichoke-Cheese
Spread Gift Box

Crab-and-Muenster Cheesecake

freezer-friendly • make-ahead

prep: 14 min.   cook: 1 hr.   other: 8 hrs.

1¼ cups fine, dry breadcrumbs
      (commercial)
3   tablespoons butter or margarine,
      melted
2   (8-ounce) packages cream cheese,
      softened
3   large eggs
⅔ cup mayonnaise
2   tablespoons all-purpose flour
12 ounces fresh crabmeat, drained and
      flaked
1¼ cups (5 ounces) shredded Muenster
      cheese
¼ cup minced fresh chives
1   (2-ounce) jar diced pimiento, drained

Combine breadcrumbs and butter; stir
well. Firmly press crumb mixture into
bottom of a 9-inch springform pan.

Beat cream cheese at high speed with
an electric mixer until creamy. Add eggs,
1 at a time, beating well after each addition. Add mayonnaise and flour; mix
until blended. Stir in crabmeat and next
3 ingredients. Pour into prepared pan.

Bake, uncovered, at 325° for 1 hour or
until center is set. Cool to room temperature in pan on a wire rack; cover and chill
at least 8 hours. To serve, carefully remove
sides of pan. Yield: 1 (9-inch) cheesecake.

cheesecake appetizers

These savory cheesecakes can be frozen up to
two weeks. To freeze, bake as directed and let
the cheesecakes cool completely on a wire rack.
Remove the sides of the pans, cover the cheesecakes tightly, and freeze. Thaw in the refrigerator.

Chicken Nacho Cheesecake

freezer-friendly • make-ahead

prep: 18 min.   cook: 1 hr., 5 min.   other: 8 hrs.

1⅔ cups finely crushed tortilla chips
¼ cup butter or margarine, melted
3   (8-ounce) packages cream cheese,
      softened
4   large eggs
½ cup mayonnaise
1   (1.25-ounce) package taco
      seasoning mix
2   tablespoons all-purpose flour
1½ cups drained and finely chopped
      canned premium chunk white
      chicken
1½ cups (6 ounces) shredded colby-
      Monterey Jack cheese blend
1   (8-ounce) carton sour cream
Toppings: sliced ripe olives, cooked
      whole kernel corn, chopped green
      onions, chopped fresh tomato
Picante sauce or salsa

Combine tortilla chips and butter; stir
well. Firmly press into bottom of a
10-inch springform pan; set aside.

Beat cream cheese at high speed with
an electric mixer until creamy. Add eggs,
1 at a time, beating well after each addition. Add mayonnaise, taco seasoning
mix, and flour; beat at low speed until
smooth. Stir in chicken and cheese. Pour
batter into prepared pan.

Bake, uncovered, at 325° for 55
minutes. Spread sour cream on top of
cheesecake; bake 10 more minutes. Cool
to room temperature in pan on a wire
rack. Cover and chill at least 8 hours.

To serve, carefully remove sides of
pan. Arrange toppings on cheesecake.
Serve with picante sauce. Yield:
1 (10-inch) cheesecake.

Chicken Nacho Cheesecake

Crab-and-Muenster Cheesecake

Eggnog Dip

make-ahead

prep: 8 min.   cook: 14 min.   other: 8 hrs.

1½ cups refrigerated eggnog
2   tablespoons cornstarch
½   cup whipping cream
1   tablespoon sugar
½   cup sour cream
1   tablespoon light rum (optional)

Combine eggnog and cornstarch in a medium saucepan; cook over medium heat, stirring constantly, until thickened and bubbly. Remove from heat; cover with plastic wrap, gently pressing directly onto mixture. Cool 2 hours in refrigerator.

Beat whipping cream at high speed with an electric mixer until foamy; add sugar, beating until soft peaks form. Fold whipped cream, sour cream, and rum, if desired, into eggnog mixture. Cover and chill 6 hours. Serve with fresh fruit. Yield: 3 cups.

Showstopping Appetizer Torte

make-ahead

prep: 30 min.   cook: 17 min.   other: 2 hrs.

1½ cups chopped pecans
4   (8-ounce) packages cream cheese, softened and divided
3   tablespoons mustard-mayonnaise sauce, divided (we tested with Durkee's)
1   (8-ounce) package shredded sharp Cheddar cheese
1   (7-ounce) can crushed pineapple, drained
½   cup chopped green onions
2   teaspoons dried mint
1¼ cups orange marmalade, divided
2   tablespoons dried orange peel
1   tablespoon mayonnaise
2   to 3 teaspoons orange extract

Bake chopped pecans in a shallow pan at 350°, stirring occasionally, 5 to 10 minutes or until lightly toasted. Remove from pan.

Process 2 packages cream cheese, 2 tablespoons mustard-mayonnaise sauce, and next 4 ingredients in a food processor until blended, stopping to scrape down sides. Press mixture into bottom of a plastic wrap-lined 9-inch springform pan, and sprinkle with chopped pecans.

Process remaining cream cheese, remaining mustard-mayonnaise sauce, ⅔ cup orange marmalade, and next 3 ingredients in food processor until smooth, stopping to scrape down sides.

Spread mixture over pecans, pressing until smooth. Cover and chill 2 hours or up to 3 days. Remove from pan; spread with remaining marmalade. Serve with gingersnaps. Yield: about 30 appetizer servings.

Layered Nacho Dip

This family favorite is so simple to make. Serve it with red and green tortilla chips to carry out the holiday theme.

editor's favorite

prep: 10 min.   cook: 30 min.

2   (16-ounce) cans refried beans
1   (4.5-ounce) can chopped green chiles
1   (1¼-ounce) package taco seasoning mix
1   (8-ounce) package shredded Mexican four-cheese blend
1   (8-ounce) container refrigerated avocado dip
1   (8-ounce) carton sour cream
3   green onions, thinly sliced
2   (2¼-ounce) cans sliced ripe olives, drained
1   large tomato, chopped

Combine first 3 ingredients, stirring well; spread into a lightly greased 7- x 11-inch baking dish or 9-inch deep-dish pieplate.

Bake at 350° for 25 minutes or until thoroughly heated. Sprinkle evenly with cheese; bake 5 more minutes or until cheese melts.

Spread avocado dip over cheese; spread sour cream over avocado dip. Top evenly with green onions, olives, and tomato. Serve warm with tortilla chips or corn chips. Yield: 10 servings.

Microwave Option: If you're in a hurry, heat this dip in your microwave oven. Cook bean mixture at HIGH 3 to 4 minutes or until thoroughly heated. Top with cheese, and cook at HIGH 2 more minutes or until cheese melts. Proceed with recipe as directed.

Layered Nacho Dip

quick dips

Try these shortcut ideas for your next holiday gathering. They go from kitchen to table in a snap.

Pesto Dip: Combine 1 (3.4-ounce) jar pesto sauce; 1 (8-ounce) container sour cream; and ⅓ cup chopped dried tomatoes in oil, drained. Serve with vegetables. Makes 1½ cups.

Fruit Dip: Combine 1 (8-ounce) container sour cream, 1 tablespoon sugar, ½ teaspoon pumpkin pie spice, and 1 teaspoon vanilla extract. Serve with fruit. Makes 1 cup.

Easy Guacamole: Combine 1 ripe avocado, peeled and mashed; 2 tablespoons picante sauce; ¾ teaspoon lime juice; and ¼ teaspoon garlic salt. Serve with tortilla chips. Makes 1 cup.

Sugar-and-Spice Pecans

These pecans taste yummy as a snack or dessert. You can also finely chop them and use them to top Cookies 'n' Cream Dessert (page 19).

prep: 11 min.   cook: 50 min.   other: 15 min.

¾   cup sugar
1   teaspoon ground cinnamon
½   teaspoon salt
¼   teaspoon ground nutmeg
¼   teaspoon ground allspice
¼   teaspoon ground cloves
1   egg white, lightly beaten
2½   tablespoons water
8   cups pecan halves
¾   teaspoon edible gold-leaf powder
    (optional) *

Stir together first 8 ingredients in a bowl. Add pecans; stir until coated. Spread in a lightly greased, aluminum foil-lined 15- x 10-inch jellyroll pan.

Bake at 275° for 50 minutes, stirring occasionally. Remove from pan; cool on wax paper. If desired, place in a zip-top plastic bag, and sprinkle with gold-leaf powder, shaking to coat. Store in an airtight container. Yield: 8 cups.

* You can find edible gold-leaf powder at most cooking specialty stores.

Hot Seafood Dip

prep: 21 min.   cook: 27 min.

1¼   pounds unpeeled, small fresh shrimp
2   tablespoons butter or margarine
2   cups mayonnaise
1   cup freshly grated Parmesan cheese
½   cup chopped green onions
3   jalapeño peppers, seeded and chopped
2   tablespoons lemon juice
2   or 3 drops of hot sauce
1   pound fresh lump crabmeat, drained
2   (14-ounce) cans artichoke hearts, drained and finely chopped
½   teaspoon salt
⅓   cup sliced almonds

Peel shrimp, and devein, if desired. Cook shrimp in butter in a medium skillet over medium-high heat 2 minutes, stirring constantly. Drain and set aside.

Combine mayonnaise and next 5 ingredients in a large bowl. Add shrimp, crabmeat, artichoke hearts, and salt; stir well. Spoon into a greased 13- x 9-inch baking dish. Sprinkle with almonds.

Bake, uncovered, at 375° for 25 minutes or until mixture is thoroughly heated. Serve with melba toast rounds. Yield: 9 cups.

Hot Spinach-Jalapeño Dip

prep: 13 min.   cook: 25 min.

2   (10-ounce) packages frozen chopped spinach
¼   cup butter or margarine
2   tablespoons all-purpose flour
½   cup evaporated milk
1   (6-ounce) roll jalapeño cheese, cubed
2   tablespoons finely chopped onion
1   teaspoon Worcestershire sauce
¾   teaspoon celery salt
¾   teaspoon garlic powder
½   teaspoon ground black pepper
¼   teaspoon lemon juice
Dash of ground red pepper
Dash of hot sauce
½   cup soft, buttered breadcrumbs

Cook spinach according to package directions, omitting salt. Drain, reserving ½ cup liquid. Melt butter in a saucepan over low heat; add flour, stirring until smooth. Cook, stirring constantly, 1 minute.

Add spinach, reserved ½ cup liquid, milk, and remaining ingredients except breadcrumbs; stir until smooth. Spoon into a greased 1-quart casserole; sprinkle with breadcrumbs.

Bake, uncovered, at 350° for 25 minutes. Serve hot with crackers. Yield: 4 cups.

Southern Spiced Nuts

prep: 7 min.   cook: 20 min.   other: 15 min.

1   egg white
1   teaspoon water
1½   cups dry-roasted peanuts
1   cup pecan halves
¾   cup sugar
1   tablespoon pumpkin pie spice
¾   teaspoon salt

Beat egg white and water in a large bowl until foamy. Add dry roasted peanuts and pecan halves; toss gently to coat. Combine sugar, pumpkin pie spice, and salt; add to nuts, and toss until coated.

Spread mixture in a single layer in a lightly greased 15- x 10-inch jellyroll pan. Bake at 300° for 20 minutes or until lightly browned.

Transfer immediately to wax paper. Cool completely, breaking large clusters apart as they cool. Yield: 4 cups.

Holiday Party Mix

great gift
prep: 11 min.   cook: 1 hr.

1   cup butter or margarine, melted
1   tablespoon Worcestershire sauce
1   teaspoon curry powder
½   teaspoon garlic salt
⅛   teaspoon hot sauce
6   cups corn chips
4   cups cheese crackers
3   cups mixed nuts
6   cups popped popcorn
1½   cups walnut pieces

Stir together first 5 ingredients in a bowl. Combine corn chips and remaining 4 ingredients in a large roasting pan; add butter mixture, stirring to coat.

Bake at 250° for 1 hour, stirring every 15 minutes. Spread on paper towels to cool. Store in an airtight container. Yield: 16 cups.

Pear-Pecan Appetizers

prep: 10 min.   cook: 5 min.
other: 30 min.

1   cup finely chopped pecans
2   ripe pears
1   quart water
2   tablespoons lemon juice
½   cup butter or margarine,
        softened
2   tablespoons crumbled blue cheese

Bake pecans in a shallow pan at 350°, stirring often, 5 minutes or until toasted.

Cut each pear into thin slices, leaving stems intact. Combine pear slices, water, and lemon juice in a large bowl.

Beat butter and blue cheese at medium speed with an electric mixer until smooth.

Drain pear slices on paper towels. Spread butter mixture on bottom half of pear slices; coat with pecans, and place on a serving plate. Cover and chill 30 minutes. Yield: 2½ dozen.

This classic pairing of blue cheese and pears is always a favorite.

Pear-Pecan Appetizers

Brie Cheese Wafers

prep: 17 min.   cook: 8 min.   other: 8 hrs.

½ pound Brie, softened
½ cup butter, softened
2 cups all-purpose flour
¼ teaspoon salt
¼ teaspoon ground red pepper
¼ teaspoon Worcestershire sauce

Position knife blade in food processor bowl; add Brie (with rind) and butter. Process until blended, stopping often to scrape down sides. Add flour and remaining ingredients, pulsing until a soft dough forms.

Divide dough in half, and shape each portion into an 8-inch log; wrap in plastic wrap, and chill 8 hours. Cut into ¼-inch slices; or use a cookie press fitted with a star-shaped disk to shape dough into straws, following manufacturer's instructions. Place slices or straws on ungreased baking sheets.

Bake at 375° for 8 minutes or until lightly browned. Transfer to wire racks to cool. Yield: 5 dozen wafers or 7 dozen straws.

Parmesan Cheese Straws

For a twist on the wine-and-cheese theme, pair these elegant appetizers with your favorite vino.

prep: 15 min.   cook: 10 min.

⅔ cup refrigerated shredded Parmesan cheese
½ cup butter or margarine, softened
1 cup all-purpose flour
¼ teaspoon salt
¼ teaspoon ground red pepper
¼ cup milk
Pecan halves (optional)

Position knife blade in food processor bowl; add cheese and butter. Process until blended.

Add flour, salt, and ground red pepper; process about 30 seconds or until mixture forms a ball, stopping often to scrape down sides.

Divide dough in half. Roll each portion into a ⅛-inch-thick rectangle, and cut into 2- x ½-inch strips; or shape dough into ¾-inch balls, and flatten each ball to about ⅛-inch thickness.

Place strips or rounds of dough on ungreased baking sheets; brush with milk. Top with pecan halves, if desired.

Bake at 350° for 7 minutes for strips and 10 minutes for rounds or until lightly browned. Transfer to wire racks to cool. Yield: 5 dozen straws or 3 dozen wafers.

Savory Cheese Puffs

freezer-friendly • make-ahead
prep: 29 min.   cook: 15 min.

2 large eggs
1 (3-ounce) package cream cheese, softened
¼ cup cottage cheese
4 ounces feta cheese
1 (16-ounce) package frozen phyllo pastry, thawed
Unsalted butter, melted

Beat eggs at medium speed with an electric mixer 1 minute; beat in cheeses.

Unfold phyllo, and cover with a slightly damp towel to prevent pastry from drying out.

Place 1 phyllo sheet on a flat surface covered with wax paper; cut lengthwise into 3 (12- x 6-inch) strips. Brush 1 long side of each strip with melted butter; fold strips in half lengthwise, and brush with butter.

Place 1 teaspoon cheese mixture onto base of each strip; fold right bottom corner over to form a triangle. Continue folding back and forth into a triangle, gently pressing corners together.

Place triangles, seam sides down, on ungreased baking sheets, and brush with butter. Repeat procedure with remaining phyllo sheets, cheese mixture, and butter.

Bake at 375° for 15 minutes or until golden. Yield: 5¼ dozen.

Freezer Option: You may freeze unbaked pastries on baking sheets; remove to airtight containers, and freeze up to 2 weeks. Bake as directed without thawing.

Baked Gouda in Pastry

pastry pointers

Be sure to thaw the pastry sheets properly before unfolding them, or they may crumble.

Spinach Pom-Poms

Freeze these unbaked bites on a jellyroll pan up to one week. To serve, let stand at room temperature one hour; bake as directed.

freezer-friendly • make-ahead

prep: 12 min.   cook: 20 min.   other: 8 hrs.

2   (10-ounce) packages frozen chopped
    spinach, thawed and drained
2   cups herb-seasoned stuffing mix,
    crushed
1   cup grated Parmesan cheese
⅓   cup butter or margarine, softened
6   large eggs, lightly beaten
Dash of ground nutmeg
Spicy mustard

Squeeze spinach between paper towels until barely moist. Combine spinach, stuffing mix, and next 4 ingredients; shape into 2-inch balls. Place balls on a lightly greased 15- x 10-inch jellyroll pan; cover and chill 8 hours.

Bake at 350° for 15 to 20 minutes or until hot. Drain on paper towels. Serve with your favorite spicy mustard. Yield: 14 appetizer servings.

Baked Gouda in Pastry

You can assemble this appetizer in advance; just cover and chill it up to 24 hours before baking.

make-ahead

prep: 13 min.   cook: 25 min.

½   (17.3-ounce) package frozen puff
    pastry sheets
1   cup finely chopped pecans, divided
2   (6- or 7-ounce) rounds Gouda cheese,
    rinds removed

Thaw 1 pastry sheet according to package directions; reserve second sheet in freezer for another use. Cut thawed pastry sheet in half, and roll each half on a lightly floured surface to a 9-inch square.

Sprinkle ¼ cup pecans in center of each pastry square. Place cheese rounds over pecans; sprinkle ¼ cup pecans over each cheese round. Bring corners of each pastry square to center of each cheese round. Fold pastry to fit cheese round; twist top to completely enclose cheese. Place pastries on a lightly greased baking sheet.

Bake at 400° for 25 minutes or until puffed and golden. Transfer to serving plates, and serve immediately. Yield: 12 appetizer servings.

Sausage-Date Balls

quick & easy

prep: 19 min.   cook: 20 min.

1   pound ground pork sausage
2   cups biscuit mix
½   cup finely chopped pecans
1   (8-ounce) package pitted dates, chopped

Combine all ingredients; stir well, and shape into 1-inch balls. Place on lightly greased baking sheets.

Bake at 350° for 20 minutes or until browned. Serve warm or at room temperature. Yield: 4½ dozen.

Crispy Prosciutto Pinwheels

prep: 22 min.   cook: 25 min.   other: 30 min.

1   (17.3-ounce) package frozen puff pastry, thawed
1   (4.25-ounce) jar champagne mustard
1   cup grated Parmesan cheese
1½   tablespoons dried oregano
2   teaspoons garlic powder
8   ounces thinly sliced prosciutto
1   large egg, lightly beaten

Place 1 pastry sheet on a work surface; spread half of mustard evenly over pastry. Combine cheese, oregano, and garlic powder; sprinkle half of cheese mixture over mustard. Arrange half of prosciutto slices evenly over cheese mixture. Lightly press prosciutto into cheese.

Roll up pastry from both long sides, jellyroll fashion, until rolls meet in the middle. Repeat procedure with remaining pastry sheet, mustard, cheese mixture, and prosciutto. Cover and chill rolls at least 30 minutes.

Cut rolls crosswise into ½-inch slices. (Slices will resemble a figure 8.) Place slices on lightly greased baking sheets. Brush tops with egg.

Bake at 350° for 25 minutes or until puffed and golden. Serve warm or at room temperature. Yield: about 3½ dozen.

Sweet-and-Sour Meatballs

For a speedy and spicy entrée, serve these meatballs over hot cooked rice or noodles.

quick & easy

prep: 5 min.   cook: 17 min.

½   (38-ounce) package frozen Italian-style meatballs
1   (12-ounce) bottle chili sauce
1   (10-ounce) jar grape jelly
1   (8-ounce) can pineapple chunks, drained (optional)

Cook meatballs in a large nonstick skillet over medium heat 4 minutes or until browned. Drain meatballs, and return to skillet.

Add chili sauce and jelly, and cook until jelly melts, stirring constantly. Add pineapple, if desired. Bring to a boil; reduce heat, and simmer 10 minutes, stirring mixture occasionally. Yield: 12 appetizer servings.

Swedish Meatballs: Cook and drain meatballs as directed. Instead of the ingredients listed above, add 2 (3-ounce) packages cream cheese, cubed; ¾ cup milk; ½ cup water; 2 tablespoons chopped fresh parsley; ⅛ teaspoon salt; and ⅛ teaspoon dried thyme. Cook over medium heat until mixture is smooth and thickened, stirring constantly.

Baked Horseradish Squares

You can freeze these morsels, unbaked, up to one week. To serve, let stand 10 minutes. Remove crusts, quarter slices, and bake as directed.

freezer-friendly • make-ahead

prep: 16 min.   cook: 14 min.   other: 20 min.

½   pound cooked ham, coarsely chopped
1   small onion, quartered
8   ounces extra-sharp Cheddar cheese, coarsely chopped
1½   tablespoons prepared horseradish
½   teaspoon salt
½   teaspoon hot pepper sauce
¼   teaspoon pepper
1   (16-ounce) loaf very thinly sliced sandwich bread
Paprika

Position knife blade in food processor bowl; add ham and onion. Process until finely chopped. Remove from bowl; set aside. Add Cheddar cheese to processor bowl; process until finely chopped. Return ham and onion to processor bowl. Add horseradish and next 3 ingredients; process just until mixture begins to form a ball.

Spread about 1 tablespoon mixture on each bread slice. Place slices on ungreased baking sheets; cover and freeze about 20 minutes or until spread is firm. Remove crusts; cut each slice into 4 squares. Sprinkle with paprika.

Bake at 400° for 12 to 14 minutes. Remove from oven; serve immediately. Yield: 9 dozen.

Pork Tenderloin with Mustard Sauce

It's okay for pork to have a slightly pink color when it's cooked. As long as the temperature reaches 160°, the pork is done.

prep: 10 min. cook: 30 min. other: 8 hrs.

½ cup teriyaki sauce
2 tablespoons brown sugar
¼ cup bourbon
4 (¾-pound) pork tenderloins
Mustard Sauce
Commercial party rolls

Combine first 3 ingredients in a shallow dish or zip-top freezer bag. Add tenderloins; cover or seal, and chill 8 hours, turning meat occasionally.

Remove from marinade, discarding marinade. Place on a rack in a shallow roasting pan.

Bake at 400° for 30 minutes or until a meat thermometer inserted into thickest portion registers 160°. Thinly slice, and serve with Mustard Sauce on party rolls. Yield: 25 appetizer servings.

Mustard Sauce

prep: 4 min.

⅔ cup sour cream
⅔ cup mayonnaise
2 tablespoons dry mustard
3 to 4 green onions, finely chopped

Combine all ingredients; cover and chill. Yield: 1⅓ cups.

Creamed Shrimp in Mini Pastry Shells

Baking the unfilled phyllo shells adds extra crispness, but you can omit the baking if you're short on time.

make-ahead

prep: 19 min. cook: 46 min.

4 (2.1-ounce) packages frozen mini phyllo shells (we tested with Athens Mini Fillo Shells)
1½ pounds unpeeled, medium-size fresh shrimp
⅔ cup dry white wine
½ cup chopped onion
2 tablespoons chopped fresh parsley
½ teaspoon salt
3 tablespoons butter or margarine
3 tablespoons all-purpose flour
1 cup milk
1 cup (4 ounces) shredded Swiss cheese
2 teaspoons lemon juice
½ teaspoon pepper

Bake phyllo shells according to package directions, if desired; cool. Set aside.

Peel and devein shrimp, if desired.

Combine wine and next 3 ingredients in a saucepan; bring to a boil. Add shrimp, and cook 3 to 5 minutes. Drain, reserving ¼ cup liquid. Chop shrimp, and set aside.

Melt butter in a large saucepan over low heat; add flour, stirring until smooth. Cook 1 minute, stirring constantly. Gradually add milk, and cook over medium heat, stirring constantly, until mixture is thickened and bubbly.

Add cheese, stirring until cheese melts. Gradually stir in shrimp, reserved ¼ cup liquid, lemon juice, and pepper.

Spoon mixture into a greased 2-quart shallow baking dish. (Cover baking dish, and chill up to 8 hours at this point if you wish. Before serving, let dish stand at room temperature 30 minutes.)

Bake, covered, at 350° for 20 minutes or until thoroughly heated. Spoon mixture into phyllo shells, and serve immediately. Yield: 5 dozen.

New Orleans-Style Canapés

Olive salad is a component of the New Orleans Muffuletta sandwich. Here, we repackage the colorful chopped salad as a filling for these flaky mouthfuls.

prep: 17 min. cook: 20 min. other: 1 hr.

1 (12-ounce) jar pickled mixed vegetables, drained
¼ cup pimiento-stuffed olive slices, chopped
2 ounces thinly sliced salami, finely chopped
1 tablespoon minced garlic
1 tablespoon olive oil
2 (10.2-ounce) cans refrigerated flaky biscuits
½ cup finely shredded provolone cheese

Chop mixed vegetables. Combine vegetables, olives, and next 3 ingredients. Cover and chill at least 1 hour.

Bake biscuits according to package directions. Cool slightly. Using a melon baller or small spoon, carefully scoop out centers of 16 biscuits. (Reserve remaining biscuits for another use.)

Stir cheese into olive salad mixture. Spoon 1 heaping tablespoon into each hollowed-out biscuit.

Bake at 400° for 8 to 10 minutes or until cheese melts. Serve warm. Yield: 16 appetizers.

wine and cheese pairings

Use this handy reference as a starting point for some favorite combinations of wine and cheese. Feel free to mix-and-match according to your preferences.

reds

Cabernet Sauvignon:
- sharp Cheddar
- Swiss
- Asiago
- Monterey Jack
- Parmesan

Merlot:
- sharp Cheddar
- Monterey Jack
- Gouda

whites

Chardonnay:
- mild Cheddar
- smoked mozzarella

Sauvignon Blanc:
- blue cheeses (Gorgonzola and Roquefort)
- goat
- Gruyère

Champagne or sparkling wine:
- Brie
- Camembert
- fontina

simple accompaniments
- crusty bread and crackers
- fresh fruit
- whole nuts
- assorted olives
- hard breadsticks
- bell pepper strips

entrées for every occasion

Let one of these main-dish recipes be the star attraction of a festive holiday meal. With over 30 recipes, ranging from Apple-Stuffed Tenderloin to Traditional Christmas Goose, you're sure to find just what you're looking for.

Hazelnut-Crusted Rack of Lamb with Cherry-Wine Sauce

Rustic yet refined, this nut-coated rack of lamb is sumptuous. Crisscrossing the racks for baking makes a fabulous presentation.

editor's favorite
prep: 8 min.   cook: 45 min.

¼   cup coarse grained Dijon mustard
2   (8-rib) lamb rib roasts (2¾ to 3 pounds each), trimmed
¼   cup fine, dry breadcrumbs (commercial)
½   cup finely chopped hazelnuts
¼   cup finely chopped fresh parsley
1   tablespoon chopped fresh thyme or 1 teaspoon dried thyme
½   teaspoon freshly ground pepper
¼   teaspoon salt
Cherry-Wine Sauce or mint sauce
Garnish: fresh thyme sprigs

Spread mustard over lamb rib roasts. Stir together breadcrumbs and next 5 ingredients; pat over roasts.

Place roasts, fat side out and ribs crisscrossed, in a lightly greased roasting pan. Insert meat thermometer into thickest portion of lamb, making sure it does not touch bone.

Bake at 400° for 10 minutes. Remove from oven. Cool slightly. Cover exposed bones with strips of aluminum foil to prevent excessive browning. Reduce oven temperature to 375°; bake 35 more minutes or until thermometer registers 150° (medium-rare). Serve with Cherry-Wine Sauce. Garnish, if desired. Yield: 8 servings.

Time-Saving Tip: Ask the butcher to "french" (trim fat from) the chine bones for you.

Cherry-Wine Sauce

prep: 5 min.   cook: 7 min.

⅔   cup dry red wine
⅓   cup beef broth
3   tablespoons honey
1½   teaspoons chopped fresh thyme or ½ teaspoon dried thyme
¼   teaspoon salt
¼   teaspoon dry mustard
2   teaspoons cornstarch
2   tablespoons balsamic vinegar
1   (15-ounce) can pitted dark cherries, drained

Stir together first 6 ingredients in a heavy saucepan; bring to a boil, and boil 5 minutes.

Combine cornstarch and vinegar, stirring well; add to wine mixture, stirring well. Bring to a boil over medium-high heat; boil 1 minute. Stir in cherries. Yield: 1½ cups.

Standing Rib Roast

prep: 5 min.   cook: 2 hrs.   other: 10 min.

1   (5- to 6-pound) rib roast (3 ribs)
Freshly ground black pepper
Steamed new potatoes (optional)
Steamed carrots (optional)
Garnishes: fresh sage sprigs, fresh rosemary sprigs

Place roast, fat side up, on a rack in a shallow roasting pan. Sprinkle roast with pepper. Insert a meat thermometer into roast, making sure it does not touch fat or bone.

Bake at 350° for 2 hours or until meat thermometer registers 145° (medium-rare) or 160° (medium). Let stand 10 minutes before slicing. If desired, serve with new potatoes and carrots, and garnish. Yield: 8 to 10 servings.

Hazelnut-Crusted Rack of Lamb
with Cherry-Wine Sauce

Peppered Rib-Eye Steaks

prep: 6 min.   cook: 20 min.   other: 1 hr.

¾   teaspoon freshly ground black
      pepper
1   teaspoon dried thyme
1½ teaspoons garlic powder
½   teaspoon salt
½   teaspoon ground red pepper
½   teaspoon lemon pepper
½   teaspoon dried parsley flakes
2   (1½-inch-thick) rib-eye steaks
1   tablespoon olive oil

Stir together first 7 ingredients. Brush
steaks with oil; rub with pepper mixture.
Cover and chill 1 hour.

Grill steaks, covered with grill lid, over
medium-high heat (350° to 400°) about
10 minutes on each side or to desired
degree of doneness. Yield: 2 servings.

Royal Beef Tenderloin

prep: 10 min.   cook: 55 min.   other: 8 hrs.

1   cup soy sauce
⅔   cup canola oil
3   tablespoons brown sugar
2   tablespoons Dijon mustard
1   tablespoon white vinegar
1   teaspoon garlic powder
1   green onion, chopped
1   (5- to 6-pound) beef tenderloin,
      trimmed
Royal Butter

Combine first 7 ingredients; stir well.
Place tenderloin in a large zip-top freezer
bag. Pour marinade mixture over tenderloin. Seal bag securely. Marinate in
refrigerator 8 hours, turning occasionally.
Remove tenderloin from marinade,
reserving marinade. Bring marinade to
a boil in a small saucepan; set aside.

Place tenderloin on a rack in a shallow
roasting pan. Bake at 400° for 45 to 55
minutes or until thermometer inserted in
thickest part registers 145° (medium-
rare) or 160° (medium), basting occasionally with marinade. Let stand 10
minutes before slicing. Transfer to a
serving platter. Serve with Royal Butter.
Yield: 10 servings.

Royal Butter

prep: 2 min.

1½ cups butter or margarine, softened
1   (8-ounce) package cream cheese,
      softened
¼   cup mayonnaise
¼   cup prepared horseradish, drained

Combine all ingredients in a medium
mixing bowl; beat at medium speed with
an electric mixer until blended. Serve at
room temperature. Yield: 2 cups.

Herb-Peppered
Veal Chops

prep: 10 min.   cook: 46 min.   other: 1 hr.

4   (1½- to 2-inch-thick) veal chops
      (about 3½ pounds)
2   tablespoons vegetable oil, divided
2   garlic cloves, minced
2   teaspoons paprika
1½ teaspoons dried thyme
1½ teaspoons dried oregano
¾   teaspoon salt
¾   teaspoon ground cumin
¾   teaspoon lemon pepper
1   teaspoon ground black pepper
¾   teaspoon ground red pepper
1   (14-ounce) can beef broth
1   tablespoon cornstarch
2   tablespoons water
¼   teaspoon Worcestershire sauce
Garnish: whole roasted shallots

Brush chops with 1 tablespoon oil, and
rub with garlic.

Stir together paprika and next
7 ingredients in a small bowl. Gently
rub mixture on chops. Cover and chill
1 hour.

Heat remaining 1 tablespoon oil in a
large ovenproof skillet over medium-
high heat. Cook chops in hot oil 3 minutes on each side or until browned.

Bake at 350° for 20 minutes or until
done. Remove chops from skillet, and
keep warm, reserving drippings in
skillet.

Add broth to reserved drippings,
stirring to loosen particles; bring to a
boil. Boil until reduced to 1 cup (about
10 minutes); skim fat from broth
mixture.

Stir together cornstarch, water, and
Worcestershire sauce. Gradually stir
into broth mixture; bring to a boil. Boil,
stirring constantly, 1 minute. Serve
with chops. Garnish, if desired. Yield:
4 servings.

Herb-Peppered Pork Chops:
Substitute 4 (1½-inch-thick) pork chops
for veal chops and 1 (14-ounce) can
chicken broth for beef broth.

Crown Roast of Pork with Stuffing

prep: 35 min.   cook: 3 hrs., 15 min.

1   (16-rib) crown roast of pork
        (about 8 pounds)
3   tablespoons vegetable oil, divided
¾   teaspoon salt
¼   teaspoon pepper
3½ pounds baking potatoes, peeled
        and cubed (about 7 medium)
½   teaspoon salt
1   pound sweet Italian sausage,
        casings removed
3   large onions, chopped (about 4 cups)
5   celery ribs, finely chopped (about
        2 cups)
4   carrots, scraped and finely chopped
        (about 2 cups)
2   garlic cloves, minced
⅓   cup chopped fresh parsley
1   teaspoon fennel seeds, crushed
¾   teaspoon salt
⅛   teaspoon pepper

Brush roast with 1 tablespoon oil; sprinkle with ¾ teaspoon salt and ¼ teaspoon pepper. Place roast, bone ends up, in a lightly greased shallow roasting pan. Insert meat thermometer into roast, making sure it does not touch fat or bone.

Bake at 475° for 15 minutes. Reduce oven temperature to 325°, and bake 1½ hours.

Combine potato, ½ teaspoon salt, and water to cover in a large saucepan. Bring to a boil; cover, reduce heat, and simmer 10 minutes or until tender. Drain.

Brown sausage in a large skillet, stirring until it crumbles. Remove from skillet with a slotted spoon, reserving drippings in skillet. Add remaining 2 tablespoons oil to drippings. Add onion and next 3 ingredients to skillet; cook, stirring constantly, 15 minutes or until tender. Stir in potato, sausage, parsley, and remaining 3 ingredients.

Spoon about 3 cups stuffing mixture into cavity of roast, mounding slightly. Cover stuffing and exposed ends of ribs with aluminum foil. Spoon remaining stuffing mixture into a lightly greased 11- x 7-inch baking dish; cover with foil.

Bake roast and stuffing at 325° for 30 minutes or until meat thermometer registers 160°. Remove roast from oven; let stand, covered. Bake stuffing in baking dish 15 more minutes. Yield: 8 servings.

Tuscan Pork Roast

This Italian-inspired roast is typically served with garlic, pepper, and rosemary.

prep: 25 min.   cook: 1 hr., 27 min.

¼   cup fresh parsley sprigs
¼   cup olive oil
4   garlic cloves
2   tablespoons fresh rosemary leaves
1   tablespoon fresh thyme leaves
1   tablespoon chopped fresh sage
1   teaspoon salt
½   teaspoon freshly ground pepper
1   (4½-pound) boneless pork loin
        roast, trimmed
3   tablespoons all-purpose flour
2½ cups chicken broth
½   cup dry white wine or chicken broth
1   teaspoon sugar
½   teaspoon salt
1   teaspoon chopped fresh parsley
1   teaspoon chopped fresh thyme
Garnishes: fresh sage sprigs, fresh thyme
        sprigs, fresh rosemary leaves,
        roasted garlic

Process parsley sprigs and next 7 ingredients in a food processor or blender 2 minutes until smooth, stopping once to scrape down sides; set herb mixture aside.

Butterfly roast by making a lengthwise cut down center of 1 flat side, cutting to within ½ inch of other side. Unfold roast, forming a rectangle, and place between 2 sheets of heavy-duty plastic wrap; flatten to ½-inch thickness using a mallet or rolling pin.

Spread about two-thirds herb mixture over roast. Roll up roast, jellyroll fashion, starting with long side, and secure at 2-inch intervals using kitchen string.

Place roast in a shallow roasting pan; top with remaining herb mixture.

Bake at 450° for 15 minutes. Reduce heat to 350°; bake 45 minutes to 1 hour or until meat thermometer inserted into thickest portion registers 155°. Remove from pan, reserving drippings in pan; keep roast warm. Temperature will rise to 160°.

Whisk flour into drippings in pan, and cook over medium-high heat 2 minutes, stirring constantly. Add broth and next 3 ingredients; simmer 10 minutes or until thickened. Pour gravy through a wire-mesh strainer into a bowl, discarding solids. Stir in 1 teaspoon each of parsley and thyme. Serve gravy with roast. Garnish, if desired. Yield: 8 servings.

Molasses-Grilled Pork Tenderloin

quick & easy

prep: 5 min.   cook: 20 min.   other: 8 hrs.

¼ cup molasses
2 tablespoons coarse grained Dijon mustard
1 tablespoon apple cider vinegar
4 (¾-pound) pork tenderloins, trimmed

Combine first 3 ingredients, and brush over the tenderloins. Cover and marinate 8 hours in refrigerator.

Grill tenderloins, covered with grill lid, over medium-hot coals (350° to 400°) about 10 minutes on each side or until a meat thermometer inserted into thickest portion registers 160°, turning once. Yield: 8 servings.

Apple-Stuffed Tenderloin with Praline-Mustard Glaze

prep: 20 min.   cook: 50 min.   other: 1 hr.

¼ cup raisins
⅓ cup bourbon or apple juice
2 (¾- to 1-pound) pork tenderloins
1 medium-size cooking apple, thinly sliced
1 medium onion, thinly sliced
2 to 3 garlic cloves, halved
1 tablespoon chopped fresh rosemary
¼ cup maple syrup
2 tablespoons dark brown sugar
2 tablespoons prepared mustard

Combine raisins and bourbon in a bowl; let stand 1 hour.

Cut tenderloins lengthwise down center, cutting to but not through bottom. Alternate apple and onion slices down center of each tenderloin. Top slices evenly with raisins, garlic, and rosemary.

Close tenderloins over filling, and tie at 1-inch intervals. Place on sheets of heavy-duty aluminum foil.

Stir together syrup, sugar, and mustard; brush half of mixture over tenderloins. Close foil, and fold to seal. Place in a 13- x 9-inch pan.

Bake at 325° for 25 minutes. Open foil, and brush with remaining syrup mixture. Close foil, and bake 20 to 25 more minutes or until a meat thermometer inserted into thickest portion reaches 160°. Yield: 6 servings.

Pork Medaillons in Mustard Sauce

prep: 6 min.   cook: 25 min.   other: 8 hrs.

3 tablespoons vegetable oil
1 tablespoon coarse grained mustard
½ teaspoon salt
½ teaspoon pepper
2 (¾-pound) pork tenderloins
¼ cup dry white wine
Mustard Cream Sauce
Garnish: fresh basil sprigs

Stir together first 4 ingredients; rub over pork tenderloins. Place in a large zip-top freezer bag; seal bag, and marinate in refrigerator 8 hours.

Place tenderloins on a lightly greased rack in a shallow roasting pan. Insert a meat thermometer into thickest part of 1 tenderloin. Bake at 400° for 25 minutes or until thermometer registers 160°, basting every 10 minutes with wine.

Slice tenderloins into ¾-inch slices; arrange slices evenly on dinner plates. Spoon Mustard Cream Sauce around slices. Garnish, if desired. Yield: 4 servings.

Mustard Cream Sauce

prep: 4 min.   cook: 16 min.

1¾ cups whipping cream
¼ cup coarse grained mustard
¼ teaspoon salt
⅛ teaspoon ground white pepper

Cook whipping cream in a heavy saucepan over medium heat, stirring often, until reduced to 1¼ cups (about 15 minutes). Do not boil. Stir in mustard, salt, and pepper; cook, stirring constantly, 1 minute. Yield: 1¼ cups.

Ham-and-Turkey Spaghetti

A cheesy white sauce dresses this pasta. It's a pleasant diversion from typical tomato-topped spaghetti.

prep: 15 min.   cook: 55 min.

1 (8-ounce) package thin spaghetti, uncooked
2 tablespoons butter or margarine
6 green onions, sliced
1½ cups sliced fresh mushrooms
1½ cups chopped cooked ham
1½ cups chopped cooked turkey
1 (12-ounce) carton cottage cheese
1 (8-ounce) carton sour cream
2 tablespoons milk
¼ teaspoon salt
¼ teaspoon celery salt
¼ to ½ teaspoon pepper
1 cup (4 ounces) shredded sharp Cheddar cheese

Cook spaghetti according to package directions; drain and set aside.

Melt butter in a skillet over medium-high heat. Add green onions and mushrooms; cook, stirring constantly, until crisp-tender. Add ham and turkey; toss gently.

Combine cottage cheese, sour cream, milk, salt, celery salt, and pepper in a large bowl; add pasta and meat mixture. Toss gently. Spoon mixture into a lightly greased 13- x 9-inch baking dish.

Bake, covered, at 350° for 45 minutes. Uncover; sprinkle with shredded cheese. Bake, uncovered, 5 more minutes. Yield: 8 servings.

Grilled Ham and Apples

quick & easy

prep: 3 min.   cook: 21 min.

½   cup orange marmalade
2   teaspoons butter or margarine
¼   teaspoon ground ginger
2   (½-inch-thick) ham slices (about
      2½ pounds)
4   apples, cut into ½-inch-thick slices

Combine first 3 ingredients in a 1-cup glass measuring cup; microwave at HIGH 1 minute or until melted, stirring once.

Grill ham and apples, covered with grill lid, over medium-hot coals (350° to 400°), turning occasionally and basting with marmalade mixture, 20 minutes or until thoroughly heated. Yield: 4 to 6 servings.

Grilled Ham and Apples

Orange marmalade basting glaze adds zest to this easy-to-prepare dish. Thanks to packaged ham slices, you can satisfy a craving without buying the whole hog.

Pasta with Broccoli and Sausage

Pasta with Broccoli and Sausage

prep: 5 min.   cook: 28 min.

1   pound fresh broccoli, cut into
    florets
1   (9-ounce) package refrigerated
    fettuccine
2   tablespoons butter or margarine
1   cup sliced fresh mushrooms
1   garlic clove, minced
1   pound reduced-fat smoked sausage,
    sliced
3   large eggs
¾   cup whipping cream
¾   teaspoon pepper
1   cup grated Parmesan cheese

Cook broccoli and fettuccine in boiling water to cover in a Dutch oven 4 minutes or until broccoli is crisp-tender; drain. Rinse with cold water; drain. Place in a large bowl.

Melt butter in a large heavy skillet; add mushrooms and garlic, and sauté 3 minutes or until tender. Add to fettuccine mixture.

Cook sausage in skillet over medium-high heat 5 minutes or until done; drain and add to fettuccine mixture. Wipe skillet clean with a paper towel.

Stir together eggs, whipping cream, and pepper in skillet until blended. Add fettuccine mixture; toss well. Cook over low heat, stirring constantly, 3 to 5 minutes or until thickened. Sprinkle with Parmesan cheese, and toss. Serve immediately. Yield: 4 servings.

Wild Rice and Sausage

This hefty casserole actually tastes better with reduced-sodium products. And it freezes nicely, so you can make it well ahead.

freezer-friendly • make-ahead

prep: 17 min.   cook: 1 hr., 42 min.   other: 5 min.

1   (16-ounce) package ground pork
    sausage
1   cup chopped celery
1   large onion, chopped
1   medium-size green pepper, seeded
    and chopped
1   garlic clove, minced
2   (14-ounce) cans ready-to-serve
    chicken broth
1   (10¾-ounce) can reduced-sodium,
    reduced-fat cream of mushroom
    soup, undiluted
1   (10¾-ounce) can reduced-sodium,
    reduced-fat cream of chicken
    soup, undiluted
1   (8-ounce) can sliced water
    chestnuts, drained
2   (4-ounce) cans sliced mushrooms,
    drained
1   (6-ounce) package long-grain and
    wild rice mix
¼   teaspoon dried thyme
1   (2-ounce) package sliced almonds

Combine first 5 ingredients in a large skillet; cook over medium heat until sausage is browned and vegetables are tender, stirring until meat crumbles. Drain.

Stir in chicken broth and next 6 ingredients; spoon into a lightly greased 3-quart baking dish. Sprinkle with almonds.

Bake, uncovered, at 350° for 1½ hours. Let stand 5 minutes before serving. Yield: 8 to 10 servings.

just toss a salad

People gravitate towards casual entertaining during the holidays, and these three recipes offer easy options. Just pick up a loaf of crusty bread at the bakery, and toss a salad—and you're ready to entertain with one of these one-dish meals.

Tipsy Chicken 'n' Dressing

prep: 19 min.   cook: 50 min.

1   (8-ounce) package cornbread
    stuffing mix
3   slices bread, crumbled
2   large eggs, lightly beaten
1   (14-ounce) can chicken broth
1   small onion, finely chopped
1   celery rib, finely chopped
1   (14-ounce) can quartered artichoke
    hearts, drained
8   skinned and boned chicken breasts
8   (1-ounce) slices Swiss cheese
1   (10¾-ounce) can cream of celery
    soup, undiluted
1   cup dry white wine
½   teaspoon dried basil
4   mushrooms, sliced
¼   cup grated Parmesan cheese
2   tablespoons minced fresh parsley

Combine first 6 ingredients; stir well. Divide mixture among 8 greased individual 2-cup baking dishes. Place 3 artichoke quarters in middle of dressing mixture in each dish; place chicken over artichokes. Top with Swiss cheese.

Combine soup, wine, and basil; pour over chicken. Top with mushrooms, Parmesan cheese, and minced parsley.

Bake, covered, at 350° for 40 minutes. Uncover and bake 10 more minutes. Yield: 8 servings.

Oven-Roasted Chicken

prep: 9 min.   cook: 1 hr., 10 min.

1   (3- to 4-pound) whole chicken
6   garlic cloves, peeled
½   teaspoon salt
½   teaspoon pepper
1   (14-ounce) can chicken broth
2   (0.87-ounce) packages brown gravy
      mix

Place chicken in a lightly greased shallow pan. Place garlic in chicken cavity. Sprinkle cavity and outside of chicken evenly with salt and pepper. Pour broth in pan around chicken.

Bake, uncovered, at 400° until meat thermometer inserted in thickest part of thigh registers 180° (about 55 to 60 minutes), basting often with broth. Remove chicken to a serving plate, reserving drippings. Remove garlic from chicken, and mash.

Pour drippings through a wire-mesh strainer into a 2-cup glass measuring cup. Add enough water to measure 2 cups. Pour into a medium saucepan. Whisk in mashed garlic and gravy mix. Bring mixture to a boil over medium-high heat, stirring constantly. Reduce heat, and simmer, stirring constantly, 9 to 10 minutes or until thickened. Serve with chicken. Yield: 4 to 6 servings.

Chicken and Dumplings

prep: 23 min.   cook: 1 hr., 40 min.

1   (3-pound) whole chicken, cut up
7   cups water
3   tablespoons chicken bouillon
      granules
1   teaspoon pepper
2   cups all-purpose flour
1   tablespoon baking powder
½   teaspoon salt
¼   cup shortening
⅔   to ¾ cup milk
4   hard-cooked eggs, chopped

Bring chicken and water to a boil in a large Dutch oven; cover, reduce heat, and simmer 1 hour. Remove chicken; cool. Pour broth through a wire-mesh strainer into a large saucepan, discarding solids. Skim off fat. Return broth to Dutch oven; stir in bouillon granules and pepper.

Skin and bone chicken. Cut chicken into bite-size pieces, and add chicken to broth. Return to a simmer.

Meanwhile, combine flour, baking powder, and salt in a bowl. Cut in shortening with a pastry blender until mixture is crumbly. Add milk, stirring until dry ingredients are moistened.

Turn dough out onto a lightly floured surface. Gather dough into a ball, and knead lightly 4 or 5 times. Roll dough to ⅛-inch thickness; sprinkle lightly with flour, and cut into 2- x 2-inch squares.

Drop strips, 1 at a time, into simmering broth, stirring gently, until all are added. Reduce heat, and simmer, stirring often, 15 minutes. Stir in egg just before serving. Yield: 6 to 8 servings.

Caramelized Chicken with Cranberry Conserve

prep: 15 min.   cook: 22 min.   other: 1 hr.

3   tablespoons frozen orange juice
      concentrate, thawed
2   tablespoons balsamic vinegar
2   tablespoons dry sherry
1   garlic clove, minced
4   skinned and boned chicken breasts
3   tablespoons brown sugar
1   tablespoon dark sesame oil
1   small onion, chopped
½   cup dried cranberries
1   to 2 tablespoons sesame seeds,
      toasted (optional)
1   to 2 tablespoons minced green
      onions (optional)

Combine first 4 ingredients in a large zip-top freezer bag; add chicken. Seal bag and chill at least 1 hour. Remove chicken from marinade, reserving marinade.

Cook sugar and sesame oil in a large nonstick skillet over medium-high heat, stirring constantly, 4 minutes. Add chicken, and cook 3 to 4 minutes on each side. Add reserved marinade, onion, and cranberries; cook, stirring and turning chicken often, 10 minutes or until done. Remove chicken, and let stand 5 minutes. Slice and serve with cranberry mixture. Sprinkle with sesame seeds and green onions, if desired. Yield: 4 servings.

Chicken-Cheddar Tetrazzini

freezer-friendly

prep: 36 min.   cook: 2 hrs.

1   (3- to 4-pound) whole chicken
1   teaspoon salt
1   teaspoon black pepper
1   (8-ounce) package spaghetti
1   large green bell pepper, seeded and
      chopped
1   cup sliced fresh mushrooms
1   small onion, chopped
¼   cup butter or margarine,
      melted
¼   cup all-purpose flour
½   teaspoon salt
½   teaspoon garlic powder
½   teaspoon poultry seasoning
½   teaspoon black pepper
1   cup half-and-half
2   cups (8 ounces) shredded sharp
      Cheddar cheese, divided
1   (10¾-ounce) can cream of
      mushroom soup, undiluted
¾   cup grated Parmesan cheese,
      divided
¼   cup sherry
1   (4-ounce) jar diced pimiento,
      drained
1   teaspoon paprika
¾   cup sliced almonds, toasted

Place chicken in a Dutch oven, and cover with water. Add 1 teaspoon salt and 1 teaspoon black pepper, and bring to a boil. Cover, reduce heat, and simmer 1 hour or until tender. Remove chicken from broth, reserving broth. Cool chicken to touch. Bone and shred chicken.

Add enough water to reserved broth to measure 3 quarts. Bring to a boil. Cook spaghetti in broth according to package directions. Drain and set aside.

Chicken-Cheddar
Tetrazzini

Cook bell pepper, mushrooms, and onion in butter in Dutch oven over medium heat, stirring constantly, until tender. Add flour and next 4 ingredients; stir until smooth. Cook, stirring constantly, 1 minute. Gradually stir in half-and-half, and cook until thickened. Add ¾ cup Cheddar cheese, stirring until cheese melts. Add shredded chicken, mushroom soup, ½ cup Parmesan cheese, sherry, and pimiento; stir well.

Combine chicken mixture and spaghetti, tossing gently. Spread in a greased 13- x 9-inch baking dish.

Bake, uncovered, at 350° for 20 to 25 minutes or until thoroughly heated. Combine remaining Parmesan cheese and paprika. Sprinkle remaining Cheddar cheese in diagonal rows across top of casserole. Repeat procedure with almonds and Parmesan mixture.

Bake 5 more minutes or until Cheddar melts. Yield: 6 to 8 servings.

shredded chicken shortcut

Boil the chicken for Chicken-Cheddar Tetrazzini ahead of time, seasoning it and reserving the broth as directed in the first paragraph. Cool the chicken completely; then bone it, and shred or chop the meat. Cover and store in the refrigerator up to 24 hours, or cover and freeze the meat and broth up to a month. Then you'll be one step ahead when you start to prepare this recipe.

King Ranch Chicken

prep: 35 min.   cook: 40 min.   other: 5 min.

4   skinned and boned chicken breasts
¼   teaspoon salt
¼   teaspoon black pepper
2   tablespoons butter
1   medium-size green bell pepper,
        seeded and chopped
1   medium onion, chopped
2   (10-ounce) cans diced tomatoes
        and green chiles
1   (10¾-ounce) can cream of
        mushroom soup, undiluted
1   (10¾-ounce) can cream of
        chicken soup, undiluted
12   (6-inch) corn tortillas, cut into
        quarters
2   cups (8 ounces) shredded Cheddar
        cheese

Sprinkle chicken with salt and black
pepper; place in a lightly greased
13- x 9-inch baking dish.

Bake at 325° for 25 minutes or until
done; cool. Coarsely chop chicken.

Melt butter in a large skillet over
medium heat; add bell pepper and
onion, and sauté until crisp-tender.
Remove from heat, and stir in chicken,
tomatoes and green chiles, and soups.

Place one-third of tortilla quarters in
bottom of a lightly greased 13- x 9-inch
baking dish; top with one-third chicken
mixture, and sprinkle evenly with ⅔ cup
cheese. Repeat layers twice, reserving
⅔ cup Cheddar cheese.

Bake at 325° for 35 minutes; sprinkle
with reserved ⅔ cup Cheddar cheese,
and bake 5 more minutes. Let stand
5 minutes before serving. Yield: 6 to
8 servings.

Chicken Fettuccine Supreme

prep: 12 min.   cook: 20 min.

1   (12-ounce) package fettuccine
6   skinned and boned chicken breasts
¼   teaspoon salt
¼   teaspoon black pepper
¼   cup butter
1   garlic clove, minced
1   large green bell pepper, chopped
1   large red bell pepper, chopped
1   (16-ounce) jar Alfredo sauce
1   cup chopped pecans, toasted
Freshly grated Parmesan cheese

Cook fettuccine according to package
directions. Drain; set aside, and keep
warm.

Meanwhile, sprinkle chicken with salt
and black pepper. Melt butter in a large
skillet; cook chicken in butter 5 minutes
on each side or until golden, fork-tender,
and no pink remains. Remove chicken
from skillet, reserving drippings in pan.
Slice chicken diagonally into finger-
length strips, and set aside.

Add garlic and bell peppers to skillet;
cook, stirring constantly, until tender.

Combine bell peppers, sauce, pecans,
and pasta; toss gently. To serve, divide
fettuccine mixture evenly among 6 individual plates; top each with chicken, and
sprinkle with Parmesan cheese. Serve
immediately. Yield: 6 servings.

Turkey-Noodle-Poppy Seed Casserole

freezer-friendly • make-ahead
prep: 12 min.   cook: 1 hr., 24 min.

1   (8-ounce) package medium-size egg
        noodles, uncooked
½   cup chopped onion
¼   cup chopped green bell pepper
¼   cup butter or margarine, melted
3   tablespoons all-purpose flour
3   cups milk
¼   cup grated Parmesan cheese
1   tablespoon poppy seeds
1   teaspoon salt
⅛   teaspoon ground red pepper
3   cups diced cooked turkey
1   (4-ounce) jar diced pimiento, drained
2   tablespoons grated Parmesan cheese

Cook noodles according to package
directions. Drain well.

Cook onion and bell pepper in butter
in a Dutch oven over medium-high heat,
stirring constantly, until tender; add
flour, stirring until smooth. Cook, stirring constantly, 1 minute. Gradually add
milk; cook over medium heat, stirring
constantly, until thickened and bubbly.
Stir in noodles, ¼ cup Parmesan cheese,
poppy seeds, and next 4 ingredients.

Spoon into a lightly greased 13- x 9-
inch baking dish. (If desired, cover and
chill 8 hours. Let stand at room temperature 30 minutes before baking.)

Bake, covered, at 350° for 45 minutes.
Uncover; sprinkle with 2 tablespoons
Parmesan. Bake, uncovered, 10 more
minutes or until thoroughly heated.
Yield: 6 to 8 servings.

Make-Ahead Note: You can freeze the
casserole before baking. To bake, thaw
in refrigerator 24 hours. Let stand at
room temperature 30 minutes. Bake as
directed above.

Cornish Hens with
Barley-Mushroom Stuffing

Cornish Hens with Barley-Mushroom Stuffing

prep: 18 min.   cook: 2 hrs., 27 min.   other: 3 hrs.

3   (1½-pound) Cornish hens
⅓   cup soy sauce
1½ tablespoons honey
1½ tablespoons dry sherry
½   teaspoon garlic powder
1   cup uncooked barley
2½ cups chicken broth
1½ cups chopped fresh mushrooms
¾   cup chopped water chestnuts
4   green onions, chopped
Garnish: green onions

Place hens in a large zip-top freezer bag.

Stir together soy sauce and next 3 ingredients; pour into cavities and over hens. Seal bag and chill, turning often, 3 to 4 hours.

Bring barley and broth to a boil in a saucepan; cover, reduce heat, and simmer 45 minutes or until liquid is absorbed. Remove from heat; stir in mushrooms, water chestnuts, and chopped green onions.

Remove hens from marinade, reserving marinade. Bring marinade to a boil in a small saucepan; set aside.

Stuff hen cavities with barley mixture, reserving extra mixture. Place hens, breast sides up, on a rack in a shallow roasting pan.

Bake hens at 375° for 1 hour and 30 minutes or until a meat thermometer inserted into meaty part of thigh registers 180° and center of stuffing registers 165°, basting hens occasionally with reserved marinade. Serve with reserved barley mixture. Garnish, if desired. Yield: 3 servings.

Traditional Christmas Goose with Sweet Bread Dressing

Fruit and spices sweeten this bread dressing for the holidays. This recipe makes a hefty amount, so after you stuff the goose, spoon the rest of the dressing into a greased baking dish and bake at 350° until lightly browned.

prep: 24 min.   cook: 3 hrs.   other: 10 min.

1   (10-pound) dressed goose
8   cups cubed day-old bread
3   cups chopped cooking apple
2   cups raisins
⅓   cup sugar
1   tablespoon ground cinnamon
1   teaspoon salt
¼   teaspoon ground ginger
¼   teaspoon ground mace
¼   teaspoon dried thyme
½   cup water
¼   cup butter, melted

Remove giblets and neck from goose; reserve for another use. Rinse goose thoroughly with cold water; pat dry. Prick skin with a fork at 2-inch intervals. Set goose aside.

Combine bread cubes and next 8 ingredients; stir in water and butter. Spoon bread cube mixture into cavity of goose; close cavity with skewers, and truss. Place goose, breast side up, on a rack in a shallow roasting pan. Bake, uncovered, at 350° for 2½ to 3 hours or until a meat thermometer inserted in turkey thigh registers 180° and inserted into stuffing registers 165°.

Transfer goose to a serving platter; let stand 10 minutes before slicing. Yield: 6 to 8 servings.

■■■■■■■■■■■■■■■■■■■■■■■■■■■■■■

safe stuffing

When stuffing poultry, it's okay to prepare the stuffing mixture ahead, but don't add it to the bird until just before cooking. If stuffed in advance and allowed to stand, even if refrigerated, harmful bacteria may develop that may not be destroyed during cooking. Make sure the stuffing cooks to 165°. If the stuffing isn't done but the bird is, transfer the stuffing to a baking dish and bake until it tests done.

■■■■■■■■■■■■■■■■■■■■■■■■■■■■■■

Rosemary-Orange Turkey Breast

prep: 13 min.   cook: 20 min.   other: 8 hrs.

1   (1½- to 2-pound) skinned and
      boned turkey breast
½   cup fresh orange juice
3   tablespoons olive oil
2   tablespoons balsamic vinegar
1   tablespoon honey
2   teaspoons dried rosemary, crushed
1   teaspoon salt
⅛   teaspoon dried crushed red pepper

Place turkey between 2 sheets of heavy-duty plastic wrap; flatten to 1-inch thickness, using a meat mallet or rolling pin. Place turkey in a large zip-top freezer bag.

Combine orange juice and next 6 ingredients in a jar. Cover tightly, and shake vigorously. Pour marinade mixture over turkey; seal bag securely. Marinate in refrigerator 8 hours, turning occasionally.

Remove turkey from marinade, reserving marinade. Bring marinade to a boil in a small saucepan. Grill turkey, covered, over medium-hot coals (350° to 400°) 15 minutes or until a meat thermometer inserted into thickest portion registers 170°, turning and basting occasionally with marinade. Yield: 6 servings.

Shrimp Lafayette

prep: 22 min.   cook: 39 min.

1¼ pounds unpeeled, medium-size
        fresh shrimp
2   cups water
1   teaspoon salt, divided
½   teaspoon ground black pepper,
        divided
2   tablespoons butter or margarine,
        melted and divided
2   medium-size red bell peppers,
        chopped (2 cups)
1   large onion, chopped (1 cup)
1   tablespoon seeded and chopped
        jalapeño pepper
4   medium tomatoes, peeled, seeded,
        and chopped (4 cups)
¼   teaspoon brown sugar
¼   teaspoon ground red pepper
⅛   teaspoon ground white pepper
2   garlic cloves, chopped
Hot cooked linguine

Peel shrimp, reserving shells. Devein
shrimp, if desired. Set shrimp aside.
Combine shrimp shells, 2 cups water,
½ teaspoon salt, and ¼ teaspoon black
pepper in a medium saucepan; bring to
a boil. Reduce heat, and simmer, uncovered, 15 minutes. Pour mixture through
a wire-mesh strainer into a bowl, discarding shells. Set aside ¼ cup shrimp
stock. Reserve remaining shrimp stock
for other uses, if desired.

Cook shrimp in 1 tablespoon butter
in a large saucepan over medium-high
heat, stirring constantly, 3 minutes or
until shrimp turn pink. Remove shrimp
from pan; set aside, and keep warm.

Cook bell pepper, onion, and jalapeño
pepper in remaining 1 tablespoon butter
in pan over medium-high heat, stirring
constantly, 5 minutes or until vegetables
are tender. Stir in remaining ½ teaspoon

salt and ¼ teaspoon ground black pepper, tomato, and next 4 ingredients; cook
5 minutes, stirring occasionally.

Add reserved ¼ cup shrimp stock;
cook 5 minutes, stirring occasionally.
Add shrimp; cook until mixture is thoroughly heated, stirring occasionally.
Serve over linguine. Yield: 4 servings.

Seafood Casserole

make-ahead
prep: 19 min.   cook: 1 hr., 4 min.   other: 10 min.

1   pound unpeeled, medium-size
        fresh shrimp
1   cup dry white wine
1   tablespoon butter or margarine
1   tablespoon chopped fresh parsley
1   teaspoon salt
1   medium onion, thinly sliced
1   pound fresh bay scallops
3   tablespoons butter or margarine
3   tablespoons all-purpose flour
1   cup half-and-half
½   cup (2 ounces) shredded Swiss
        cheese
2   teaspoons lemon juice
⅛   teaspoon pepper
½   pound crab-flavored seafood
        product
1   (4-ounce) can sliced mushrooms,
        drained
1   cup soft breadcrumbs
¼   cup grated Parmesan cheese
Paprika

Peel and devein shrimp.

Combine wine and next 4 ingredients
in a Dutch oven; bring to a boil. Add
shrimp and scallops, and cook 3 to 5
minutes; drain, reserving ⅔ cup liquid.

Melt 3 tablespoons butter in Dutch
oven over low heat; add flour, stirring
until smooth. Cook 1 minute, stirring

constantly. Gradually add half-and-half;
cook over medium heat, stirring constantly, until mixture is thickened and
bubbly. Stir in Swiss cheese. Gradually
stir in reserved ⅔ cup liquid, lemon
juice, and pepper; add shrimp mixture,
seafood product, and mushrooms. Spoon
mixture into a lightly greased 11- x 7-
inch baking dish. (If desired, cover and
chill 8 hours. Let stand 30 minutes at
room temperature before baking.)

Bake, covered, at 350° for 40
minutes. Combine breadcrumbs and
Parmesan cheese, and sprinkle over
casserole; bake 5 more minutes. Sprinkle
with paprika; let stand 10 minutes before
serving. Yield: 8 servings.

Gumbo Pot Pies

prep: 30 min.   cook: 2 hrs., 12 min.
other: 15 min.

1   (2½-pound) whole chicken
2   quarts water
1   onion, quartered
2   bay leaves
½   cup all-purpose flour
½   cup vegetable oil
1   large green bell pepper, chopped
1   large onion, chopped
3   garlic cloves, chopped
2   pounds fresh or frozen okra, cut
        in ¾-inch slices
2   (10-ounce) cans whole tomatoes
        and green chiles
1   pound andouille sausage, sliced
1   tablespoon dried thyme
1   pound unpeeled, large fresh shrimp
2   (17.3-ounce) packages frozen
        puff pastry, thawed
1   large egg, lightly beaten

Combine chicken, 2 quarts water, quartered onion, and bay leaves in a Dutch

oven. Bring to a boil. Cover, reduce heat, and simmer 1 hour or until chicken is tender.

Remove chicken; reserve 1½ cups broth, and discard onion and bay leaves. Set chicken aside to cool.

Combine flour and oil in Dutch oven. Cook over medium heat, stirring constantly, 15 to 20 minutes or until roux is chocolate colored. Add bell pepper, chopped onion, and garlic; sauté 2 minutes. Add okra, tomatoes and green chiles, sausage, thyme, and reserved 1½ cups broth. Cover and simmer 30 minutes.

Meanwhile, skin, bone, and coarsely chop chicken. Peel and devein shrimp; stir shrimp and chicken into gumbo. Cook just until shrimp turn pink. Remove from heat, and set aside to cool slightly.

Roll each pastry sheet out on a floured surface. Cut 4 circles out of each sheet of pastry, ½ inch larger than rims of individual 2-cup soup crocks. Return pastry to freezer for at least 15 minutes. Cut out decorative leaf shapes from excess pastry strips.

Ladle gumbo into crocks, filling three-fourths full. Brush top edges of pastry circles with beaten egg. Invert and place 1 pastry circle over each bowl, pressing firmly to sides of bowl to seal edges. Cut slits in pastry to allow steam to escape. Apply decorative leaves on top of pastry. Brush top of each pastry circle and leaves with beaten egg. Bake pot pies at 400° for 20 minutes or until pastry is puffed and golden. Yield: 8 servings.

Garden Lasagna

**prep: 24 min.   cook: 2 hrs., 37 min.
other: 10 min.**

½   cup chopped celery
4   medium zucchini, coarsely chopped
3   garlic cloves, minced
1   large onion, chopped
1   medium-size green bell pepper, seeded and chopped
1   medium carrot, scraped and diced
3   tablespoons olive oil
2   (16-ounce) cans stewed tomatoes, undrained
1   (8-ounce) can tomato sauce
1   (6-ounce) can tomato paste
¼   cup chopped fresh parsley
¼   cup dry red wine
1   tablespoon dried Italian seasoning
½   teaspoon salt
¼   teaspoon freshly ground black pepper
9   lasagna noodles, uncooked
1   (15-ounce) carton ricotta cheese
2   cups (8 ounces) shredded mozzarella cheese
1   cup grated Parmesan cheese

Cook first 6 ingredients in hot oil in a large Dutch oven over medium heat, stirring constantly, 15 minutes or until vegetables are tender. Stir in tomato and next 7 ingredients. Bring to a boil; cover, reduce heat, and simmer 30 minutes, stirring occasionally. Uncover and simmer 45 minutes or until sauce is thick, stirring occasionally.

Cook noodles according to package directions; drain. Spread one-fourth of sauce in a lightly greased 13- x 9-inch baking dish. Top with 3 noodles, one-third of ricotta cheese, one-fourth of mozzarella cheese, and one-fourth of Parmesan cheese; repeat layers twice. Top entire mixture with remaining

sauce, mozzarella cheese, and Parmesan cheese.

Bake, uncovered, at 350° for 35 to 40 minutes. Let stand 10 minutes before serving. Yield: 8 servings.

Mediterranean Ravioli

prep: 15 min.   cook: 49 min.

2   cups peeled, cubed eggplant
1   cup chopped onion
2   garlic cloves, minced
2   tablespoons olive oil
1   (15-ounce) container refrigerated chunky tomato sauce, pasta sauce, or spaghetti sauce
¼   cup sliced ripe olives
1   tablespoon balsamic vinegar
1   teaspoon dried thyme
1   (9-ounce) package refrigerated cheese-filled ravioli
⅔   cup freshly grated Parmesan cheese

Sauté first 3 ingredients in hot oil in a large skillet over medium-high heat until tender. Stir in tomato sauce and next 3 ingredients. Remove from heat; set aside.

Cook ravioli according to package directions; drain. Rinse with cold water; drain.

Combine vegetable mixture and ravioli, tossing gently; spoon into a lightly greased shallow 2-quart baking dish. Cover and bake at 350° for 20 minutes. Uncover and sprinkle with cheese; bake, uncovered, 10 more minutes or until thoroughly heated. Yield: 4 servings.

all the trimmings

Dressings, gravies, and sauces take any meal to the next level. This collection of recipes offers lots of choices for the perfect complement to your Christmas menu.

Sausage Cornbread Dressing

Southern sensibilities favor cornbread crumbs when it comes to making dressing. Choose either hot or mild ground pork sausage to create this go-with-everything side dish.

editor's favorite
prep: 26 min.   cook: 56 min.

1   pound mild or hot ground pork sausage
4   celery ribs, diced
2   medium onions, diced
5   cups cornbread crumbs
3½ cups chicken or turkey broth
3   cups white bread cubes, toasted
2   teaspoons rubbed sage
¼   teaspoon pepper
2   large eggs, lightly beaten

Cook first 3 ingredients in a large skillet over medium heat until sausage is browned and vegetables are tender, stirring until sausage crumbles. Drain.

Combine sausage mixture, cornbread crumbs, and remaining ingredients, stirring well. Spoon mixture into a greased 13- x 9-inch baking dish.

Bake, uncovered, at 350° for 35 to 40 minutes or until lightly browned and thoroughly heated. Yield: 8 servings.

Fruited Wild Rice Dressing

Dried fruits add sweetness and color to this dressing that's equally at home with turkey, chicken, or pork.

prep: 29 min.   cook: 1 hr., 55 min.

1   (6-ounce) package long-grain and wild rice mix
6   cups (½-inch cubes) country-style bread (we tested with Italian ciabatta)
1   pound ground pork sausage
2   small onions, chopped
4   celery ribs, chopped
¼   cup butter
1   cup dried apricots, coarsely chopped
¾   cup dried cherries
½   cup chopped fresh Italian parsley
½   teaspoon salt
½   teaspoon pepper
1   cup chicken broth

Prepare rice mix according to package directions. Transfer to a large bowl, and fluff with a fork. Set aside.

Meanwhile, place bread cubes on a large-rimmed pan and toast at 325° for 20 minutes or until dry. Set aside.

Cook sausage in a large skillet over medium heat, stirring until it crumbles and is well browned; drain.

Sauté onion and celery in butter in a large skillet over medium heat until tender.

Combine rice, bread, sausage, sautéed vegetables, dried fruit, parsley, salt, and pepper in a large bowl; toss well. Drizzle broth evenly over dressing. Toss well. Transfer dressing to a lightly greased 3-quart baking dish.

Bake, covered, at 375° for 20 minutes. Uncover and bake 25 to 30 more minutes or until browned. Yield: 8 to 10 servings.

dressing for dinner

• All manner of dressings can be found in Southern cookbooks dating back to the early 1800s. Over time, the dish came to be thought of as an essential part of holiday tables, often the most anticipated item on Thanksgiving and Christmas menus.

• Most Southerners seem to want dressing like their mother used to make, but no one's mother made it the same. Dressing can be crisp and crumbly or thick and moist, depending on personal preference, the amount of broth added, and how long it is cooked.

• The main variation lies in the moistness of the dressing. If you prefer yours moist, add a little more broth or other liquid—add a little less if you prefer it on the dry side.

• You know you've added enough broth to the dressing mixture when you can shake it and it shimmies or jiggles. Adding any more will make it soupy.

Fruited Wild Rice
Dressing

Green Chile-Cheddar-Pecan Dressing

prep: 29 min. cook: 1 hr., 5 min.

1   cup pecan pieces
2   tablespoons butter, melted
½   teaspoon garlic powder
¼   teaspoon salt
1   teaspoon paprika
¼   teaspoon ground red pepper
1   (8-ounce) package shredded sharp
      Cheddar cheese, divided
7   cups cornbread crumbs *
6   cups biscuit crumbs (we tested with
      Pillsbury Frozen Buttermilk
      Biscuits)
1   (15.25-ounce) can sweet whole
      kernel corn, drained
1   (4.5-ounce) can chopped green
      chiles, drained
2   large eggs, lightly beaten
¼   cup chopped fresh cilantro
½   teaspoon salt
½   teaspoon dried oregano
¼   teaspoon black pepper
3½ cups chicken broth
Garnish: fresh cilantro

Combine first 6 ingredients in a small bowl, tossing well. Spread in a single layer on a baking sheet. Bake at 350° for 10 minutes or until toasted; set aside.

Combine 1½ cups cheese and next 9 ingredients in a large bowl. Add broth, stirring just until moistened. Spoon into a greased 13- x 9-inch baking dish. Sprinkle with remaining ½ cup cheese and reserved pecans.

Bake, uncovered, at 350° for 50 to 55 minutes or until set and lightly browned. Garnish, if desired. Yield: 12 servings.

* 1 (28-ounce) package of frozen Sister Schubert's Southern Cornbread is equal to 7 cups cornbread crumbs.

Green Chile-Cheddar-Pecan Dressing

This dressing sports the favorite Southern flavors of pecans and cornbread, and gets a kick from green chiles.

Creole Dressing

prep: 39 min.   cook: 1 hr., 18 min.

1   (16-ounce) container chicken
      livers, drained
1   (10-ounce) container fresh oysters,
      undrained
½   (16-ounce) loaf day-old French
      bread, crumbled
½   cup butter or margarine
5   celery ribs, chopped
4   garlic cloves, minced
2   bunches green onions, chopped
2   large onions, chopped
1   cup chopped fresh parsley
½   pound ground beef, cooked
      and drained
½   pound ground pork, cooked
      and drained
1   teaspoon rubbed sage
1   teaspoon ground thyme
½   teaspoon pepper
2   tablespoons Creole seasoning

Chop chicken livers; cook in boiling
water until tender. Drain; set aside.

Drain oysters, reserving liquid;
coarsely chop oysters. Place bread in a
bowl. Pour reserved liquid over bread.

Melt butter in a large skillet over
medium-high heat; add celery and next
4 ingredients. Cook, stirring constantly,
until vegetables are tender. Add livers,
oysters, bread mixture, beef, and
remaining ingredients. Reduce heat;
simmer, uncovered, about 15 minutes.
Spoon into a lightly greased 13- x 9-inch
baking dish. Bake at 350° for 30 minutes or until lightly browned. Yield: 10
servings.

Vidalia Onion and Giblet Gravy

editor's favorite

prep: 36 min.   cook: 1 hr., 28 min.

Giblets and neck bone from 1 turkey or
      chicken
1   celery rib, chopped
1   carrot, scraped and chopped
4   black peppercorns
1   whole clove
5   cups chicken broth
4   cups diced Vidalia onion (3 pounds)
¼   cup butter, melted
2   tablespoons peanut oil
¼   cup cornstarch
½   cup heavy whipping cream
Pan drippings from 1 roasted turkey or
      chicken
Salt and pepper to taste

Combine first 6 ingredients in a large
saucepan. Bring to a boil; cover, reduce
heat, and simmer 45 minutes. Pour mixture through a wire-mesh strainer into a
bowl; discard celery, carrot, peppercorns,
and clove. Remove meat from neck;
finely chop neck meat and giblets.

Cook onion in butter and oil in a large
Dutch oven over medium-high heat, stirring constantly, until onion is lightly
browned and tender. Sprinkle cornstarch
over onion and cook, stirring constantly,
2 minutes. Add strained broth. Cook
over medium-high heat, stirring constantly with a wire whisk, until thickened and bubbly. Stir in chopped neck
meat and giblets and heavy cream.

Skim fat from reserved pan drippings
of roasted turkey; discard fat. Stir pan
drippings into gravy. Cook over low
heat, stirring constantly, until thoroughly
heated. Sprinkle with salt and pepper as
desired. Yield: 6 cups.

Old-Fashioned Giblet Gravy

prep: 10 min.   cook: 1 hr., 10 min.

Giblets and neck bone from 1 turkey or
      chicken
1   small onion
2   celery ribs, chopped
½   teaspoon salt
Pan drippings from 1 roasted turkey or
      chicken
3   tablespoons all-purpose flour
¼   cup water
1   hard-cooked egg, chopped
¼   teaspoon pepper

Combine giblets (except liver), neck,
onion, celery, and salt in a saucepan.
(Set liver aside.) Cover with water. Bring
to a boil; cover, reduce heat, and simmer
45 minutes or until giblets are fork tender. Add liver, and simmer 10 more
minutes. Drain, reserving broth. Remove
meat from neck; coarsely chop neck
meat and giblets. Discard onion and celery. Set aside.

Skim fat from pan drippings of poultry; discard fat. Add reserved broth to
pan drippings; stir until sediment is
loosened from bottom of roaster.
Measure broth mixture; add water to
equal 1½ cups, if necessary.

Combine flour and ¼ cup water in a
medium saucepan; stir until smooth.
Add broth mixture; cook over medium
heat, stirring constantly, until thickened
and bubbly. Stir in reserved neck meat,
giblets, egg, and pepper. Serve hot with
roasted poultry. Yield: 2 cups.

Raisin Sauce

prep: 5 min.   cook: 15 min.

1   cup firmly packed brown sugar
1½ tablespoons cornstarch
¾   cup raisins
½   cup water
2   tablespoons orange juice
2   tablespoons white vinegar
1   tablespoon butter or margarine
⅛   teaspoon salt

Combine brown sugar and cornstarch
in a small saucepan, stirring well; add
raisins and remaining ingredients. Cook,
uncovered, over low heat 15 minutes,
stirring often. Serve warm. Yield: 1 cup.

Slow-Cooker Apple Butter

make-ahead

prep: 16 min.   cook: 10 hrs.

4   pounds cooking apples, peeled and
      sliced
½   cup apple cider vinegar
3   cups granulated sugar
1   cup firmly packed brown sugar
1   teaspoon ground nutmeg

Place sliced apple and vinegar in a
4-quart slow cooker.
   Cook, covered, at HIGH 6 hours. Stir
in sugars and nutmeg. Reduce setting to
LOW; cook, covered, 4 hours. Cool. Store
in refrigerator up to 1 week. Yield: 6 cups.

Honey-Cinnamon Butter

prep: 4 min.

½   cup unsalted butter, softened
2   tablespoons honey
½   teaspoon ground cinnamon

Combine all ingredients in a small
mixing bowl; beat at low speed with an
electric mixer 1 minute or until creamy.
Cover and chill, if desired. If chilled, let
stand at room temperature 20 minutes
before serving. Yield: ½ cup.

Cranberry Chutney

prep: 5 min.   cook: 25 min.   other: 2 hrs.

½   medium onion, chopped
1   garlic clove, minced
½   jalapeño pepper, seeded and
      chopped
1   (½-inch-thick) slice fresh ginger,
      peeled and chopped
2   tablespoons white wine vinegar
½   teaspoon grated lime rind
1   tablespoon fresh lime juice
2   (16-ounce) cans whole-berry
      cranberry sauce
¼   cup sugar

Cook first 7 ingredients in a large
saucepan over medium-high heat,
stirring constantly, 10 to 15 minutes or
until mixture is tender. Stir in cranberry
sauce and sugar; bring to a boil.
Remove from heat.
   Cover and chill 2 hours. Store chutney
in refrigerator up to 2 weeks. Yield:
3½ cups.

Slow-Cooker
Apple Butter

Citrus-Spiked Cranberry Sauce

This easy recipe makes a great gift. For the gift bag, fold a length of tulle in half and glue the sides together.

prep: 5 min.   cook: 15 min.   other: 5 min.

1   pound fresh or frozen cranberries, thawed (4 cups)
1   to 1½ cups sugar
1   tablespoon grated orange rind
1   cup orange juice
Dash of salt

Combine all ingredients in a 2-quart microwaveable casserole. Cover with heavy-duty plastic wrap; fold back a small corner of wrap to allow steam to escape. Microwave at HIGH 15 minutes, stirring every 5 minutes, until cranberry skins pop. Let stand, covered, 5 minutes. Stir. Serve warm or chilled. Yield: 2¾ cups.

Cranberry-Cherry Relish

quick & easy

prep: 8 min.   cook: 20 min.

1   (16-ounce) can whole-berry cranberry sauce
1   cup fresh or frozen pitted dark cherries
½   cup raisins
¼   cup minced onion
¼   cup firmly packed brown sugar
2   tablespoons balsamic vinegar
1   tablespoon minced fresh ginger

Combine all ingredients in a heavy non-aluminum saucepan. Bring to a boil; reduce heat, and simmer, uncovered, 20 minutes or until thickened. Store in refrigerator. Yield: 2½ cups.

Citrus-Spiked Cranberry Sauce

save room for the sides

Vegetable and fruit side dishes contribute variety and often a colorful component to the meal. This selection of both hot and cold recipes makes it easy to round out a special holiday menu.

Asparagus with Jalapeño Hollandaise Sauce

A sprinkling of diced jalapeño pepper and pimiento caps off these hollandaise-enhanced asparagus spears in colorful holiday fashion. To save time and effort, cook frozen asparagus spears instead of the fresh vegetable.

quick & easy
prep: 12 min.   cook: 6 min.

1½ pounds fresh asparagus or
    2 (10-ounce) packages frozen
    asparagus spears
1 (0.9-ounce) package hollandaise
    sauce mix (we tested with Knorr)
2 tablespoons grated Parmesan cheese
1 tablespoon seeded and diced
    jalapeño pepper
2 teaspoons diced pimiento
Garnishes: fresh cilantro sprigs, lemon
    slices, red jalapeño pepper fan

Snap off tough ends of asparagus. Arrange asparagus in a steamer basket over boiling water. Cover and steam 5 to 6 minutes or until crisp-tender. Arrange asparagus on a serving plate, and keep warm.

Prepare hollandaise sauce mix according to package directions; stir in Parmesan cheese, diced jalapeño pepper, and pimiento. Serve over asparagus. Garnish, if desired. Yield: 6 servings.

Buttery Broccoli Medley

make-ahead
prep: 30 min.   cook: 15 min.

1 pound fresh broccoli
1 head fresh cauliflower, broken into
    florets
⅓ cup butter or margarine
1 red bell pepper, chopped
2 garlic cloves, minced
2 tablespoons Dijon mustard
¼ to ½ teaspoon salt
½ teaspoon freshly ground black pepper
3 green onions, chopped

Cut broccoli into florets, reserving stems for another use.

Arrange broccoli and cauliflower in a steamer basket over boiling water. Cover and steam 10 minutes or until crisp-tender.

Melt butter in a Dutch oven over medium-high heat; add bell pepper and garlic, and sauté 3 to 5 minutes or until tender. Stir in broccoli, cauliflower, mustard, salt, and black pepper; sprinkle with onions. Yield: 6 to 8 servings.

Make-Ahead Note: Spoon cooked broccoli mixture into a greased 11- x 7-inch baking dish (do not sprinkle with onions); cover and chill. Bake, covered, at 350° for 20 minutes or until heated. Sprinkle with onions before serving.

Bacon-Pecan Brussels Sprouts

Shredded Brussels sprouts burst with flavor when paired with crisp bacon and toasted pecans.

prep: 21 min.   cook: 34 min.

1 pound fresh Brussels sprouts
5 slices bacon
¼ cup chopped pecans
2 green onions, sliced
⅛ teaspoon ground nutmeg
⅛ teaspoon salt
⅛ teaspoon pepper

Wash Brussels sprouts thoroughly; remove discolored leaves. Cut off stem ends; cut Brussels sprouts vertically into thin shreds.

Cook bacon in a skillet until crisp. Remove bacon, reserving drippings in skillet. Crumble bacon and set aside. Add pecans to drippings; cook over medium-high heat, stirring constantly, until golden. Add Brussels sprouts, green onions, nutmeg, salt, and pepper. Cook over medium heat 18 minutes or until Brussels sprouts are tender, stirring often. Spoon into a serving dish; sprinkle with bacon. Yield: 4 servings.

Asparagus with Jalapeño
Hollandaise Sauce

Green Beans with Mushrooms and Sage

prep: 12 min.   cook: 20 min.

1   pound fresh green beans, trimmed
      and cut into 2-inch pieces
2   tablespoons butter or margarine
2   tablespoons olive oil
½   cup fresh sage leaves, chopped
½   (8-ounce) package sliced fresh
      mushrooms
3   garlic cloves, minced
½   cup chicken broth
2   tablespoons dry white wine
1   teaspoon Worcestershire sauce
½   teaspoon salt
¼   teaspoon coarsely ground pepper

Cook beans in boiling salted water 10 to 12 minutes or until crisp-tender; drain. Plunge into ice water to stop the cooking process; drain and set aside.

Melt butter with oil in a large skillet over medium-high heat; add sage, and sauté 1 minute or until crisp and dark green. Remove with a slotted spoon.

Add mushrooms and garlic to skillet; sauté 2 minutes or until liquid evaporates. Stir in green beans, broth, and next 4 ingredients; cook 5 minutes or until liquid is reduced by half. Stir in sage just before serving. Yield: 4 servings.

Potato Puff Soufflé

prep: 17 min.   cook: 45 min.

1   tablespoon minced onion
¼   cup butter or margarine, melted
¼   cup all-purpose flour
1   teaspoon salt
¼   teaspoon pepper
2   cups cooked, mashed potato
1   (8-ounce) carton sour cream
4   large eggs, separated

Cook onion in butter in a large skillet over medium-high heat, stirring constantly, until tender. Reduce heat to medium. Add flour, stirring until blended. Cook, stirring constantly, until thickened and bubbly. Stir in salt and pepper; remove from heat. Stir in mashed potato and sour cream.

Beat egg yolks until thick and pale. Gradually stir about one-fourth of hot mixture into yolks, and add to remaining hot mixture, stirring constantly.

Beat egg whites in a large bowl at high speed with an electric mixer until stiff peaks form; gently fold beaten egg white into potato mixture, one-third at a time. Spoon into a buttered 1½-quart soufflé dish. Bake, uncovered, at 350° for 40 minutes or until puffed and set. Serve immediately. Yield: 6 servings.

Sweet Potatoes with Apples

A kiss of honey, a spritz of orange juice, and a golden crown of toasty marshmallows elevate this sweet potato-apple casserole to lofty heights.

editor's favorite
prep: 19 min.   cook: 1 hr., 5 min.
other: 30 min.

6   large sweet potatoes (about
      5 pounds)
3   tablespoons frozen orange juice
      concentrate, thawed and
      undiluted
2   tablespoons water
2   tablespoons honey
1   tablespoon butter or margarine,
      melted
¼   cup sugar
2   Golden Delicious apples, peeled and
      thinly sliced
20   large marshmallows, halved

Cook sweet potatoes in boiling water to cover 35 minutes or until tender. Drain; cool. Peel sweet potatoes, and place in a large mixing bowl.

Combine orange juice concentrate and next 3 ingredients; stir well. Add ⅓ cup orange juice mixture and sugar to sweet potatoes. Reserve remaining orange juice mixture. Beat sweet potato mixture at medium speed with an electric mixer until smooth.

Spoon mixture into a greased shallow 2½-quart baking dish; smooth top. Arrange apple slices over sweet potato mixture; brush apple slices with remaining orange juice mixture. Bake, uncovered, at 350° for 20 minutes. Arrange marshmallow halves over apple slices; bake 20 more minutes or until marshmallows are puffed and lightly browned. Yield: 12 servings.

Sweet Potatoes with Bacon in Tangy Vinaigrette

prep: 8 min.   cook: 35 min.

3   medium-size sweet potatoes
      (about 2 pounds)
      Tangy Vinaigrette
6   slices bacon, cooked and coarsely
      crumbled
1   tablespoon chopped fresh
      parsley

Cook sweet potatoes in boiling water to cover 30 to 35 minutes or just until tender. Drain and cool completely.

Peel potatoes; coarsely chop, and place in a serving bowl.

Pour Tangy Vinaigrette over sweet potatoes, and toss gently. Sprinkle with crumbled bacon and chopped parsley before serving. Yield: 6 servings.

Tangy Vinaigrette

prep: 4 min.

½ cup vegetable oil
¼ cup cider vinegar
3 tablespoons honey
½ teaspoon dry mustard
¼ teaspoon ground cumin
¼ teaspoon pepper

Combine all ingredients in a small jar; cover tightly, and shake vigorously. Serve at room temperature. Yield: about 1 cup.

Sweet Potato-Eggnog Casserole

Crumbled oatmeal cookies form the base for an easy streusel topping.

prep: 10 min.   cook: 1 hr.

5 pounds large sweet potatoes
½ cup golden raisins
¼ cup brandy
⅔ cup refrigerated eggnog
3 tablespoons butter or margarine, melted
2 tablespoons sugar
⅛ teaspoon salt
Oatmeal Cookie Topping

Cook sweet potatoes in water to cover in a large Dutch oven 40 minutes or until tender; drain and cool to touch. Peel and mash.

While potatoes cook, combine raisins and brandy; let stand 30 minutes. Drain.

Combine potato, eggnog, and next 3 ingredients; reserve 2 cups. Stir raisins into remaining potato mixture; spoon into a lightly greased 2-quart baking dish. Sprinkle with Oatmeal Cookie Topping. Pipe or dollop reserved potato mixture around edge of dish. Bake at 350° for 20 minutes or until heated. Yield: 6 to 8 servings.

Oatmeal Cookie Topping

prep: 2 min.

2 (2-inch) oatmeal cookies, crumbled
2 tablespoons dark brown sugar
2 tablespoons chopped pecans, toasted

Combine ingredients in a small bowl. Yield: ½ cup.

Squash Casserole

prep: 21 min.   cook: 56 min.

1 pound yellow squash, sliced
1 medium onion, chopped
⅓ cup water
¼ teaspoon salt
¾ cup (3 ounces) shredded Cheddar cheese, divided
½ cup fine, dry breadcrumbs (commercial) or buttery cracker crumbs, divided
¼ cup butter or margarine
2 large eggs, lightly beaten
1 tablespoon sugar
¼ teaspoon salt
¼ teaspoon soy sauce
⅛ teaspoon pepper
⅛ teaspoon paprika

Combine first 4 ingredients in a large saucepan. Bring to a boil; reduce heat, and simmer, uncovered, 15 minutes or until tender. Drain and mash squash mixture. Add ½ cup Cheddar cheese, ¼ cup breadcrumbs, and next 6 ingredients; stir well. Spoon into a lightly greased 1½-quart baking dish.

Bake, uncovered, at 350° for 20 minutes; top with remaining cheese and remaining breadcrumbs. Sprinkle with paprika, and bake 15 more minutes or until cheese melts and mixture is thoroughly heated. Yield: 4 servings.

Holiday Rice

prep: 13 min.   cook: 50 min.

1¼ cups uncooked long-grain rice
¼ cup butter or margarine, melted
1 cup chopped celery
4 green onions, sliced
1 (14-ounce) can beef broth
1 (4-ounce) can sliced mushrooms, undrained
1 bay leaf
1 tablespoon chopped fresh parsley
1 teaspoon Beau Monde seasoning
¼ to ½ teaspoon dried tarragon

Stir together first 4 ingredients in a 13- x 9-inch baking dish. Stir in broth and remaining ingredients.

Bake, covered, at 350° for 50 minutes, stirring occasionally. Discard bay leaf. Yield: 6 to 8 servings.

Pecan Wild Rice

prep: 10 min.   cook: 45 min.

5½ cups chicken broth
1 cup wild rice, uncooked
4 green onions, thinly sliced
1 cup pecan halves, toasted
1 cup golden raisins
⅓ cup orange juice
¼ cup chopped fresh parsley
¼ cup olive oil
1 tablespoon grated orange rind
1½ teaspoons salt
¼ teaspoon freshly ground pepper

Combine broth and rice in a medium saucepan. Bring to a boil; reduce heat, and simmer, uncovered, 45 minutes or until rice is done. Drain and place in a medium bowl. Add green onions and remaining ingredients; toss gently. Serve immediately. Yield: 6 servings.

congealed salad secrets

Follow these tips for a perfectly shaped congealed salad.

• Lightly spray the inside of the mold with vegetable cooking spray before filling.

• Be sure gelatin is firm before unmolding. Gently press the top with your finger—it should spring back or jiggle.

• Before unmolding, gently run a small knife around the outer edge to break the seal.

• Dip the bottom of the mold in warm water for about 15 seconds before unmolding. Be careful not to get any water in the mold.

• If the salad sticks to the mold, return it to warm water for 5 more seconds and try again.

• You may also wrap the outside of the mold with a warm, damp tea towel. Wet the towel with hot water, and wring it out. Wrap the towel around the bottom and partially up the sides of the mold. Let stand 1 to 2 minutes before unmolding the salad.

• To serve on a bed of crisp lettuce leaves, place the greens facedown on the salad in the mold. Top with the platter, and turn over.

• When serving directly on a platter, moisten the platter with a little water before inverting the mold to help the gelatin adhere to the surface.

• Be sure to include the whipped cream or topping in the center of the ring, or serve on the side.

• To fix a small broken piece of congealed salad, put it back into place; then use a tiny bit of water to seal the edges of the seam.

• If you have a major mishap, cube the entire congealed salad and serve in a large bowl.

Congealed Cherry Salad

make-ahead

prep: 9 min.   other: 3 hrs., 20 min.

1 (15-ounce) can pitted dark sweet cherries, undrained
1 (11-ounce) can mandarin oranges, undrained
1 (8-ounce) can crushed pineapple, undrained
1 (6-ounce) package cherry-flavored gelatin
1 cup cold water
½ cup chopped pecans
Lettuce leaves
Garnish: fresh cherries

Drain all canned fruit into a bowl, reserving juice. Set fruit aside. Stir juice well, and reserve 1½ cups. Bring reserved juice mixture to a boil in a saucepan. Add gelatin and cook, stirring constantly, 2 minutes or until gelatin dissolves. Remove from heat. Stir in cold water. Chill until the consistency of unbeaten egg white.

Fold in drained fruit and pecans. Pour mixture into a lightly oiled 6-cup mold. Cover and chill until firm. Unmold onto a lettuce-lined serving plate. Garnish, if desired. Yield: 8 to 10 servings.

Easy Out: To unmold with ease, run a knife around the edge of the mold to break the suction. Gently pull the salad away from the sides of the mold using your fingers. Wrap the mold in a damp, warm cloth towel. Place a serving platter on top of the mold and invert. Remove the mold.

Double Berry Salad

For a double dose of cranberries, substitute a package of cranberry-flavored gelatin for the raspberry.

make-ahead

prep: 10 min.   other: 3 hrs., 20 min.

1 (3-ounce) package raspberry-flavored gelatin
1 cup boiling water
1 (16-ounce) can whole-berry cranberry sauce
¾ cup finely chopped celery
½ cup chopped pecans
Lettuce leaves
Garnishes: celery leaves, fresh cranberries

Combine gelatin and boiling water, stirring 2 minutes or until gelatin dissolves. Chill until mixture is the consistency of unbeaten egg white. Stir in cranberry sauce, celery, and pecans.

Spoon mixture into lightly oiled individual molds or a 4-cup mold. Cover and chill until firm. Unmold onto lettuce-lined plates. Garnish, if desired. Yield: 8 servings.

Double Berry Salad

Gingered Peach Salad

prep: 21 min.   other: 3 hrs.

2   (15-ounce) cans spiced peaches,
       undrained
1   (8-ounce) can unsweetened crushed
       pineapple, undrained
1   (3-ounce) package orange-flavored
       gelatin
1   (3-ounce) package lemon-flavored
       gelatin
1   cup boiling water
1   tablespoon lemon juice
1   tablespoon orange juice
1   teaspoon ground ginger
½   teaspoon salt
½   cup chopped celery
½   cup chopped pecans
Lettuce leaves
½   cup sour cream
¼   teaspoon ground ginger
Garnish: celery leaves

Drain peaches and crushed pineapple,
reserving 1¾ cups liquid. Chop peaches.

Combine gelatins and boiling water,
stirring 2 minutes or until gelatins dissolve. Stir in reserved 1¾ cups liquid,
lemon juice, and next 3 ingredients. Add
reserved fruit, celery, and pecans, stirring well.

Pour into a lightly oiled 9-inch square
dish. Cover and chill until firm. Cut into
squares. Serve on lettuce leaves.

Combine sour cream and ¼ teaspoon
ginger; spoon sour cream mixture evenly
over each serving. Garnish, if desired.
Yield: 9 servings.

Candied-Brandied Cranberries

*Brandy spikes this sweet and succulent
creation that makes enough to enjoy at
home and to package for gift-giving.*

make-ahead • quick & easy

prep: 6 min.   cook: 1 hr.   other: 30 min.

3   (12-ounce) packages fresh or frozen
       cranberries, thawed
3   cups sugar
½   cup brandy

Arrange cranberries evenly in a single
layer in 2 lightly greased 15- x 10-inch
jellyroll pans. Sprinkle sugar evenly over
cranberries in each pan. Cover tightly
with aluminum foil; bake at 350° for
1 hour, switching pans to opposite oven
racks after 30 minutes.

Spoon cranberry mixture into a large
serving bowl; stir in brandy. Cool. Serve
at room temperature, or cover and chill.
Yield: 5½ cups.

Make-Ahead Note: You can store
Candied-Brandied Cranberries, covered,
in the refrigerator up to 1 week.

Brandied Cranberry Oranges

prep: 20 min.   cook: 5 min.   other: 8 hrs.

6   fresh blood red or navel oranges
2   (12-ounce) packages fresh or frozen
       cranberries, thawed
3   cups sugar
1   cup orange juice
½   cup plus 2 tablespoons brandy
       (optional)

Peel oranges, if desired. Cut oranges into
⅛-inch slices, discarding ends. Cut slices
into quarters.

Layer one-third of orange slices, one-
third of cranberries, and 1 cup sugar in
a large bowl. Repeat layers twice with
remaining fruit and sugar. Cover and let
stand 8 hours.

Spoon mixture into a Dutch oven. Stir
in orange juice; bring to a boil, and boil,
stirring constantly, until sugar dissolves.

Pack hot fruit into hot jars, filling to
½ inch from top. Add 2 tablespoons
brandy to each jar, if desired. Cover fruit
with boiling syrup, filling to ½ inch
from top. Remove air bubbles; wipe jar
rims. Cover at once with metal lids;
screw on bands. Process in a boiling-
water bath 15 minutes. Yield: 5 pints.

Frozen Fruit Salads

*Served in individual cups, this frozen
fruit salad with cherries, bananas, and
pecans is a great make-ahead salad for
any luncheon.*

prep: 15 min.   cook: 9 min.
other: 8 hrs., 30 min.

¾   cup plus 2 tablespoons sugar
½   cup sifted cake flour
¼   teaspoon salt
1   cup pineapple juice
3   tablespoons lemon juice
1   large egg, lightly beaten
1   cup whipping cream
1   (15-ounce) can pitted white sweet
       Royal Anne cherries in heavy
       syrup, drained
1   (15¼-ounce) can peach slices in
       heavy syrup, drained
1   (8-ounce) can pineapple chunks,
       in juice, drained
1   medium banana, sliced
½   cup chopped pecans
¼   cup maraschino cherries,
       chopped
Green leaf lettuce (optional)

Combine first 3 ingredients in a heavy saucepan; stir in pineapple juice and lemon juice. Cook over medium heat, stirring constantly, 6 minutes or until thickened. Gradually stir a small amount of hot mixture into beaten egg; add to remaining hot mixture, stirring constantly. Cook over medium heat, stirring constantly, until candy thermometer registers 160° (about 2 to 3 minutes). Remove from heat; cool slightly. Cover and chill thoroughly.

Beat whipping cream at medium speed with an electric mixer until soft peaks form. Fold whipped cream into chilled mixture. Stir in white cherries and next 5 ingredients. Spoon mixture evenly into paper-lined muffin pans. Cover and freeze at least 8 hours.

To serve, peel paper liner away from each individual salad. Serve salads on lettuce leaves, if desired. Yield: 12 servings.

Spinach-Fruit Salad with Raspberry Vinaigrette

editor's favorite
prep: 36 min.

½   pound fresh spinach, washed, trimmed, and torn
1   head Bibb lettuce, torn
2   oranges, peeled and sectioned
2   Red Delicious apples, thinly sliced
1   kiwifruit, peeled and thinly sliced
½   cup chopped walnuts, toasted
Raspberry Vinaigrette

Combine first 6 ingredients in a large bowl; toss gently. Pour Raspberry Vinaigrette over spinach mixture just before serving; toss gently. Yield: 8 servings.

Raspberry Vinaigrette

prep: 5 min.   other: 30 min.

½   cup vegetable oil
¼   cup raspberry vinegar
1   tablespoon honey
½   teaspoon grated orange rind
¼   teaspoon salt
⅛   teaspoon pepper

Combine all ingredients in a jar; cover tightly, and shake vigorously. Cover and chill thoroughly. Yield: about 1 cup.

Winter Mixed Green Holiday Salad with Cranberry Vinaigrette

prep: 45 min.   cook: 15 min.

¾   cup pecan halves
⅔   cup honey
¼   cup butter or margarine, melted
½   cup sugar
4   heads Belgian endive
2   large watercress bunches
8   kumquats
4   cups finely shredded radicchio
3   seedless tangerines, peeled and sectioned
Cranberry Vinaigrette
1   cup fresh mint leaves, shredded
Garnish: fresh mint sprigs

Stir together first 3 ingredients; spread in a shallow roasting pan.

Bake at 325° for 12 to 15 minutes, stirring often. Remove pecans with a slotted spoon; toss pecans with sugar. Cool.

Separate endive leaves, and cut larger leaves in half. Discard coarse watercress stems. Cut kumquats in half lengthwise.

Toss together endive, watercress, kumquats, and next 4 ingredients. Sprinkle with pecans, and garnish, if desired. Yield: 8 servings.

Cranberry Vinaigrette

prep: 15 min.   cook: 10 min.

½   cup fresh cranberries
⅔   cup tangerine juice or orange juice
⅓   cup tarragon vinegar
2   tablespoons Dijon mustard
2   shallots, minced
½   teaspoon salt
½   teaspoon pepper
½   cup walnut or light olive oil

Bring cranberries and tangerine juice to a boil in a medium saucepan over medium-high heat; boil 5 minutes. Drain cranberries, reserving juice; set aside. Return juice to saucepan, and boil 5 minutes.

Process juice, vinegar, and next 4 ingredients in a blender until blended. With blender running, add oil in a slow, steady stream. Stir in cranberries. Yield: 1½ cups.

Black-Eyed Pea Salad

quick & easy
prep: 12 min.   other: 4 hrs.

4   celery ribs
1   small green or red bell pepper
4   green onions
2   (15.5-ounce) cans black-eyed peas, drained and rinsed
⅓   cup minced fresh cilantro or parsley
⅓   cup Italian dressing
2   tablespoons country-style Dijon mustard

Chop first 3 ingredients. Combine chopped vegetables and next 4 ingredients in a large bowl. Cover and chill at least 4 hours. Yield: 6 servings.

Chicken-and-Black-Eyed Pea Salad: Stir in 2 cups coarsely chopped cooked chicken.

on the rise

Nothing tops the aroma and taste of fresh-baked bread. Feather-light biscuits, gooey coffee cakes, and hot rolls from the oven conjure memories of cozy kitchens brimming with holiday warmth.

Angel Biscuits

This dough keeps in the refrigerator up to one week. (Punch the dough down before rolling and cutting.) You can forgo the 30-minute rise if you're in a hurry, but the biscuits won't be quite as fluffy.

make-ahead

prep: 19 min.   cook: 7 min.   other: 30 min.

2   (¼-ounce) envelopes active dry yeast
2   tablespoons sugar
¼   cup warm water (100° to 110°)
5   cups self-rising flour
1   teaspoon baking soda
1   teaspoon salt
¾   cup shortening
2   cups buttermilk

Combine first 3 ingredients in a 1-cup glass measuring cup; let stand 5 minutes.

Combine flour, soda, and salt in a large mixing bowl; cut in shortening with a pastry blender until mixture is crumbly. Add yeast mixture and buttermilk, stirring until dry ingredients are moistened.

Turn dough out onto a floured surface; knead until smooth and elastic (about 8 minutes). Roll to ¼-inch thickness on a lightly floured surface. Cut with a 2½-inch round cutter; place ½ inch apart on greased baking sheets. Cover and let rise in a warm place (85°), free from drafts, for 30 minutes or until doubled in bulk. Bake at 450° for 6 to 7 minutes or until lightly browned. Yield: 3½ dozen.

Easy Herb Biscuits

Try using any available two herbs in place of chives and parsley.

quick & easy

prep: 8 min.   bake: 8 min.

2   cups biscuit mix
1   tablespoon freeze-dried chives
1   teaspoon dried parsley flakes
¾   cup plain yogurt

Combine all ingredients in a medium bowl, stirring just until dry ingredients are moistened. Turn dough out onto a floured surface, and knead 4 or 5 times.

Roll dough to ½-inch thickness; cut with a 2-inch round cutter. Place on a lightly greased baking sheet.

Bake at 450° for 8 minutes or until lightly browned. Yield: 1 dozen.

Three-Step Biscuits

Commit this simple recipe to memory so you can have homemade biscuits often.

quick & easy

prep: 6 min.   cook: 15 min.

1   (8-ounce) container sour cream
2   cups self-rising flour
3   tablespoons water

Stir together all ingredients. (Dough will be crumbly.) Turn dough out onto a lightly floured surface; knead 3 or 4 times.

Pat or roll dough to ½-inch thickness; cut with a 2½-inch round cutter. Place biscuits on a lightly greased baking sheet.

Bake at 425° for 12 to 15 minutes or until golden. Yield: 8 biscuits.

Hot Raisin Scones

The ingredients in these scones are simple and inexpensive, and the results are impressively tasty.

prep: 5 min.   cook: 10 min.

2   cups all-purpose flour
2   teaspoons baking powder
½   teaspoon baking soda
¼   teaspoon salt
2   tablespoons sugar
1   teaspoon grated lemon zest
½   cup cold butter or margarine
½   cup raisins
¾   cup buttermilk

Combine first 6 ingredients in a bowl. Cut in butter until mixture is crumbly, using a pastry blender. Add raisins, tossing lightly. Add buttermilk, stirring until dry ingredients are moistened.

Turn dough out onto a lightly floured surface, and knead lightly 6 times. Divide dough in half. Shape each portion into a 7-inch circle on an ungreased baking sheet; cut each circle into 6 wedges.

Bake at 425° for 10 minutes. Cool on wire racks. Yield: 1 dozen.

Hot Raisin Scones

Broccoli Cornbread

Broccoli, Cheddar cheese, and spicy seasonings distinguish this cornbread from more traditional versions.

quick & easy

prep: 6 min.   cook: 30 min.   other: 5 min.

1   (10-ounce) package frozen chopped
        broccoli, thawed
1   (8½-ounce) package cornbread mix
1   cup (4 ounces) shredded Cheddar
        cheese
½   cup butter or margarine, melted
½   teaspoon salt
½   teaspoon garlic powder
¼   teaspoon ground red pepper
3   large eggs, lightly beaten
1   medium onion, chopped

Press broccoli between paper towels to remove excess moisture. Combine cornbread mix and next 7 ingredients; stir well. Stir in broccoli (batter will be thick). Pour mixture into a greased 8-inch square pan.

   Bake at 375° for 25 to 30 minutes or until golden. Cool slightly, and cut into squares. Yield: 9 servings.

measuring success

• Measure dry ingredients in metal or plastic measuring cups. Use the cup that holds the exact amount called for in the recipe.
• Measure flour by spooning it lightly into a dry measuring cup and letting it mound slightly; then level the top with a flat edge.
• Measure liquid ingredients on a level surface in a glass or clear plastic measuring cup with a pouring lip. Read liquid measurements at eye level.

Broccoli Cornbread

Bacon-Pecan Cornbread Loaf

prep: 15 min. cook: 58 min. other: 30 min.

4   slices bacon
Vegetable oil
¾   cup chopped pecans
1½ cups yellow cornmeal
1¼ cups all-purpose flour
⅓   cup sugar
1½ teaspoons baking soda
½   teaspoon salt
2   large eggs, lightly beaten
1   cup buttermilk
Yellow cornmeal

Cook bacon in a large skillet until crisp;
crumble bacon, and set aside. Pour
bacon drippings into a measuring cup:
add enough vegetable oil to drippings
to measure ½ cup, and set aside. Add
pecans to skillet; cook over medium heat
until browned, stirring frequently. Set
pecans aside.

Combine 1½ cups cornmeal and next
4 ingredients in a large bowl. Combine
eggs and buttermilk; stir in reserved
drippings. Add to cornmeal mixture, and
stir just until dry ingredients are moistened. Fold in reserved bacon and pecans.

Grease a 9- x 5-inch loafpan; dust with
cornmeal. Pour batter into prepared pan.
Bake at 325° for 50 minutes or until a
wooden pick inserted in center comes
out clean. Cool in pan on a wire rack
30 minutes; remove from pan, and cool
completely. Yield: 1 (9-inch) loaf.

Quick Garlic Bread

quick & easy

prep: 4 min. cook: 5 min.

¼   cup butter or margarine, softened
1   tablespoon grated Parmesan cheese
1½ teaspoons mayonnaise or salad
      dressing
⅛   teaspoon garlic powder
⅛   teaspoon paprika
1   (16-ounce) loaf sliced French bread

Combine first 5 ingredients; spread on
1 side of each bread slice. Place on an
ungreased baking sheet.

Broil 4 inches from heat 4 to 5 minutes
or until golden. Yield: 1 loaf.

Bacon Monkey Bread

*Canned biscuits make this savory pull-
apart bread convenient.*

prep: 19 min. cook: 40 min. other: 10 min.

11 slices bacon, cooked and crumbled
½   cup grated Parmesan cheese
1   small onion, chopped
3   (10.2-ounce) cans refrigerated
      buttermilk biscuits
½   cup butter or margarine, melted

Combine first 3 ingredients, and set
aside.

Cut each biscuit into fourths. Dip one-
third of biscuit pieces into melted butter,
and place in a lightly greased 10-inch
Bundt pan. Sprinkle with half of bacon
mixture. Repeat layers with remaining
biscuit pieces and bacon mixture, ending
with biscuit pieces.

Bake at 350° for 40 minutes or until
golden. Cool in pan 10 minutes; invert
onto a serving platter, and serve bread
immediately. Yield: 1 (10-inch) ring.

Crusty Herbed Popover

Crusty Herbed Popovers

*If you choose fresh herbs for this recipe,
use three times the amount listed for
dried.*

prep: 7 min. cook: 55 min.

2   tablespoons grated Parmesan cheese
1   cup bread flour
1   cup milk
1   tablespoon butter or margarine,
      melted
1   teaspoon dried thyme
1   teaspoon Worcestershire sauce
¾   teaspoon dried oregano
½   teaspoon salt
¼   teaspoon garlic powder
2   large eggs, lightly beaten
2   egg whites

Grease a popover pan with cooking spray
or oil; dust bottom and sides of pan with
Parmesan cheese. Set pan aside.

Combine flour and remaining ingredients; stir with a wire whisk until blended.
Fill prepared pan three-fourths full.
Place in a cold oven. Turn oven on 450°,
and bake 15 minutes. Reduce heat to
350°, and bake 35 to 40 more minutes
or until crusty and browned. Serve
immediately. Yield: 6 popovers.

Fresh Apple Bread

Cinnamon and sugar cozy up to pecans and apples in this comforting quick bread. Buttermilk keeps the loaf moist and adds a subtle tang.

great gift

prep: 14 min.   cook: 1 hr.   other: 10 min.

½   cup shortening
1   cup sugar
2   large eggs
2   cups all-purpose flour
½   teaspoon salt
1   teaspoon baking soda
1½ tablespoons buttermilk
½   teaspoon vanilla extract
1   cup chopped pecans
1   tablespoon all-purpose flour
1   cup peeled, grated cooking apple
1½ tablespoons sugar
½   teaspoon ground cinnamon

Beat shortening at medium speed with an electric mixer until creamy: gradually add 1 cup sugar, beating well. Add eggs, 1 at a time, beating after each addition. Add 2 cups flour and salt, mixing well.

Dissolve soda in buttermilk; add to flour mixture, beating well. Stir in vanilla.

Combine pecans and 1 tablespoon flour: add pecan mixture and apple to batter, stirring well. Pour batter into a greased and floured 9- x 5-inch loafpan. Combine 1½ tablespoons sugar and cinnamon; sprinkle evenly over batter. Bake at 350° for 1 hour or until a wooden pick inserted in center comes out clean. Cool in pan on a wire rack 10 minutes. Remove from pan, and cool completely on wire rack. Yield: 1 (9-inch) loaf.

Holiday Banana Nut Bread

great gift

prep: 10 min.   cook: 1 hr.   other: 10 min.

2   large eggs, lightly beaten
½   cup butter or margarine, melted
1   cup mashed ripe banana
1   teaspoon vanilla extract
1½ cups all-purpose flour
1   teaspoon baking soda
1   cup sugar
½   cup chopped pecans
¼   cup flaked coconut
¼   cup raisins

Combine first 4 ingredients in a large bowl. Combine flour, soda, and sugar; add to butter mixture, stirring just until moistened. Fold in pecans, coconut, and raisins. Pour batter into a greased and floured 8½- x 4½-inch loafpan.

Bake at 350° for 50 to 60 minutes or until a wooden pick inserted in center of loaf comes out clean. Cool in pan 10 minutes; remove from pan, and cool completely on a wire rack. Yield: 1 (8½-inch) loaf.

Cranberry Bread

great gift

prep: 12 min.   cook: 1 hr.   other: 10 min.

1½ cups fresh cranberries
2   cups all-purpose flour
1½ teaspoons baking powder
½   teaspoon baking soda
1   teaspoon salt
1   cup sugar
¼   cup butter or margarine
1   large egg, beaten
1   teaspoon grated orange rind
¾   cup orange juice
1½ cups golden raisins

Position knife blade in food processor bowl; add cranberries. Process until coarsely chopped, stopping once to scrape down sides: set aside.

Combine flour and next 4 ingredients in a large bowl; cut in butter with pastry blender until mixture is crumbly. Add egg, orange rind, and orange juice, stirring just until dry ingredients are moistened. Stir in cranberries and raisins.

Spoon batter into a greased and floured 9- x 5-inch loafpan. Bake at 350° for 55 to 60 minutes or until a wooden pick inserted in center comes out clean. Cool in pan on a wire rack 10 minutes. Remove from pan, and cool completely on wire rack. Yield: 1 (9-inch) loaf.

Pecan Spice Loaf

great gift

prep: 15 min.   cook: 55 min.   other: 5 min.

½   cup butter, softened
¾   cup firmly packed brown sugar
1   large egg
½   cup molasses
1   tablespoon grated orange rind
2   cups all-purpose flour
2   teaspoons baking powder
½   teaspoon baking soda
1½ teaspoons ground ginger
½   teaspoon ground nutmeg
¼   teaspoon ground cloves
1   cup chopped pecans
¾   cup orange juice

Beat butter in a large bowl at medium speed with an electric mixer until creamy; gradually add brown sugar, beating well. Add egg, and beat well. Stir in molasses and orange rind.

Combine flour and next 6 ingredients; add to creamed mixture alternately with orange juice, beginning and ending with flour mixture. Mix after each addition. Pour batter into a greased and floured 9- x 5-inch loafpan.

Bake at 350° for 55 minutes or until a wooden pick inserted in center comes out clean. Cool in pan 5 minutes; remove from pan, and cool completely on a wire rack. Yield: 1 (9-inch) loaf.

Pumpkin Bread with Cream Cheese-and-Peach Preserves

editor's favorite

prep: 13 min. cook: 1 hr., 20 min.
other: 10 min.

2 cups sugar
¾ cup vegetable oil
4 large eggs
1 (16-ounce) can pumpkin
3⅓ cups all-purpose flour
2 teaspoons baking soda
½ teaspoon baking powder
1 teaspoon salt
1 tablespoon pumpkin pie spice
⅔ cup water
2 teaspoons vanilla extract
1 cup chopped pecans
Cream Cheese-and-Peach Preserves

Combine sugar and oil in a large bowl, stirring well. Add eggs, 1 at a time, mixing well after each addition. Stir in pumpkin.

Combine flour and next 4 ingredients; add to pumpkin mixture alternately with water, beginning and ending with flour mixture. Stir in vanilla and pecans. Spoon into 2 lightly greased 9- x 5-inch loafpans.

Bake at 325° for 1 hour and 10 to 20 minutes or until a wooden pick inserted in center comes out clean. Cool in pans 10 minutes. Remove from pans; cool on wire

racks. Serve with Cream Cheese-and-Peach Preserves. Yield: 2 (9-inch) loaves.

Cream Cheese-and-Peach Preserves

prep: 3 min.

¼ cup peach preserves
¼ teaspoon ground ginger
1 (8-ounce) package cream cheese, softened
Combine preserves and ginger; spoon over block of cream cheese. Yield: 1 cup.

Blueberry Crunch Loaf

prep: 17 min. cook: 1 hr. other: 15 min.

¼ cup butter, softened
1 (3-ounce) package cream cheese, softened
1 cup granulated sugar
2 large eggs
2 cups all-purpose flour
2 teaspoons baking powder
¼ teaspoon baking soda
¼ teaspoon salt
⅓ cup milk
1 cup fresh or frozen blueberries *
3 tablespoons brown sugar
2 tablespoons regular oats, uncooked
2 tablespoons chopped pecans
1 tablespoon all-purpose flour
1 tablespoon butter, melted

Beat ¼ cup butter and cream cheese at medium speed with an electric mixer 2 minutes or until creamy. Gradually add 1 cup sugar, beating 5 minutes. Add eggs, 1 at a time, beating after each addition.

Combine 2 cups flour, baking powder, soda, and salt. Add to butter mixture alternately with milk, beginning and ending with flour mixture. Gently fold in blueberries. Spoon batter into a greased and floured 9- x 5-inch loafpan.

Stir together brown sugar and remaining ingredients in a small bowl. Sprinkle over batter. Bake at 350° for 1 hour or until a wooden pick inserted in center comes out clean. Cool in pan on a wire rack 15 minutes. Remove from pan; cool completely on wire rack. Yield: 1 (9-inch) loaf.

* If using frozen blueberries, pat dry on paper towels; toss with 2 tablespoons all-purpose flour before stirring into batter.

Upside-Down Cranberry-Apple Coffee Cake

prep: 14 min. cook: 55 min. other: 5 min.

1 cup fresh or frozen cranberries, thawed
1 cup finely chopped, unpeeled cooking apple
½ cup sugar
½ cup chopped walnuts
½ teaspoon ground cinnamon
⅛ teaspoon ground cloves
1 cup all-purpose flour
1 cup sugar
2 large eggs
¼ cup butter or margarine, melted
¼ cup vegetable oil
1 teaspoon vanilla extract

Combine first 6 ingredients in a bowl; stir well. Spoon mixture into a greased 8-inch round cakepan; set aside.

Combine flour and remaining 5 ingredients in a mixing bowl; beat at medium speed with an electric mixer 2 minutes. Spoon batter over cranberry mixture.

Bake at 350° for 55 minutes or until a wooden pick inserted in center comes out clean. Cool in pan on a wire rack 5 minutes; invert onto a serving plate. Serve warm. Yield: 1 (8-inch) coffee cake.

Raspberry Coffee Cake

This coffee cake complements any breakfast menu. You can vary the flavor and color of the fillings with preserves.

prep: 17 min.   cook: 45 min.   other: 15 min.

2¼ cups all-purpose flour
¾ cup sugar
¾ cup butter or margarine
½ teaspoon baking powder
½ teaspoon baking soda
¼ teaspoon salt
¾ cup sour cream
1 teaspoon almond extract
1 large egg, lightly beaten
1 (8-ounce) package cream cheese, softened
¼ cup sugar
1 large egg
½ cup raspberry preserves
½ cup sliced almonds

Combine flour and ¾ cup sugar in a large bowl. Cut in butter with a pastry blender until mixture is crumbly; set aside 1 cup crumb mixture.

Add baking powder and next 5 ingredients to remaining crumb mixture; stir well. Spread dough in bottom and 2 inches up sides of a greased and floured 9-inch springform pan (dough should be about ¼-inch thick on sides).

Combine cream cheese, ¼ cup sugar, and 1 egg; beat at medium speed with an electric mixer until smooth. Pour batter into prepared pan. Spoon preserves evenly over cream cheese mixture.

Combine reserved 1 cup crumb mixture and sliced almonds; sprinkle over preserves.

Bake at 350° for 45 minutes or until filling is set and crust is lightly browned. Cool 15 minutes in pan; remove sides of pan. Serve warm or at room temperature, if desired. Yield: 8 servings.

Pecan Coffee Cake

prep: 13 min.   cook: 40 min.   other: 15 min.

3 cups biscuit mix
¼ cup sugar
½ cup milk
¼ cup butter or margarine, melted
1 (8-ounce) package cream cheese, softened
½ cup sugar
½ teaspoon vanilla extract
¼ teaspoon butter flavoring
2 large eggs
Brown Sugar Glaze
Pecan halves, toasted

Combine first 4 ingredients in a mixing bowl; stir vigorously until blended. Turn dough out onto a lightly floured surface, and knead 4 or 5 times. Press into bottom and up sides of an ungreased 9-inch round cakepan.

Combine cream cheese and next 4 ingredients in a mixing bowl; beat at medium speed with an electric mixer until smooth. Pour mixture over dough.

Bake at 350° for 35 to 40 minutes or until center is set. Cool in pan 15 minutes. Spoon Brown Sugar Glaze over top, and arrange pecan halves over edge of glaze. Serve warm or at room temperature. Yield: 8 servings.

Brown Sugar Glaze

prep: 5 min.   cook: 2 min.

2 tablespoons brown sugar
2 tablespoons butter or margarine
1 tablespoon milk

Combine all ingredients in a small saucepan. Bring to a boil over medium heat; cook, stirring constantly, 2 minutes. Remove from heat; cool to lukewarm. Yield: about ¼ cup.

Macaroon Coffee Cake

Coconut and almonds give this moist cake the flavor of macaroon cookies.

prep: 22 min.   cook: 45 min.

¾ cup butter, softened
1¼ cups sugar, divided
2 large eggs
2⅓ cups all-purpose flour, divided
2½ teaspoons baking powder
½ teaspoon baking soda
½ teaspoon salt, divided
1 cup sour cream
¼ teaspoon coconut extract
¾ teaspoon almond extract, divided
2 cups sweetened flaked coconut
⅔ cup sweetened condensed milk
½ cup slivered almonds, chopped
¼ cup butter, cut into pieces

Beat ¾ cup butter at medium speed with an electric mixer until creamy. Gradually beat in 1 cup sugar. Add eggs, 1 at a time, beating after each addition.

Combine 2 cups flour, baking powder, soda, and ¼ teaspoon salt; add to butter mixture alternately with sour cream, beginning and ending with flour mixture. Beat at low speed until blended after each addition. Stir in coconut extract and ½ teaspoon almond extract.

Spoon half of batter into a greased 9-inch square pan. Combine coconut, condensed milk, remaining ¼ teaspoon salt, and remaining ¼ teaspoon almond extract; stir well. Spread over batter in pan. Spread remaining batter on top.

Combine almonds, remaining ¼ cup sugar, and remaining ⅓ cup flour. Cut ¼ cup butter into mixture with a pastry blender until crumbly. Spread over batter.

Bake at 350° for 45 minutes or until a wooden pick inserted in center comes out clean. Cool in pan on a wire rack. Cut into squares. Yield: 9 servings.

Macaroon Coffee Cake

Onion-and-Sesame Rolls

These bite-size rolls will hook you with their buttery goodness. Roll them in Italian seasoning or poppy seeds for a quick variation.

prep: 11 min. cook: 15 min.

1½ tablespoons freshly grated
     Parmesan cheese
1   tablespoon instant minced onion
½   teaspoon garlic powder
1   (8-ounce) can refrigerated crescent
     rolls
2   tablespoons Italian dressing
1   tablespoon sesame seeds *

Stir together cheese, minced onion, and garlic powder in a small bowl.

Unroll crescent rolls, and separate into 2 rectangles; press perforations to seal. Sprinkle cheese mixture over rectangles, leaving a ½-inch border.

Roll up each rectangle, jellyroll fashion, starting with a short side, and pinch seams to seal. Cut each roll into 5 (1-inch-thick) slices, and place on an ungreased baking sheet. Brush rolls with Italian dressing, and sprinkle with sesame seeds.

Bake at 375° for 10 to 15 minutes or until rolls are lightly browned. Serve immediately. Yield: 10 rolls.

* 1 tablespoon Italian seasoning or poppy seeds may be substituted for sesame seeds.

Onion-and-Sesame Rolls

Refrigerator Yeast Rolls

These rolls received such a high taste-testing score that we developed two variations from the basic recipe.

editor's favorite • make-ahead
prep: 15 min. cook: 12 min.
other: 5 hrs., 15 min.

1   cup shortening
1   cup sugar
2   teaspoons salt
1   cup boiling water
2   large eggs, lightly beaten
2   (¼-ounce) envelopes active dry yeast
1   cup warm water (100° to 110°)
6   cups all-purpose flour
¼   cup butter or margarine, melted

Combine first 3 ingredients in a large bowl; stir in 1 cup boiling water. Cool. Stir in eggs.

Combine yeast and 1 cup warm water in a 1-cup glass measuring cup; let stand 5 minutes. Stir into egg mixture. Gradually add flour, stirring until blended. Cover and chill at least 4 hours.

Divide dough into 3 portions. Cover and chill 2 portions up to 5 days, if desired.

Roll 1 portion of dough to ¼-inch thickness on a floured surface. Cut with a 2-inch round cutter.

Place 2 inches apart on lightly greased baking sheets. Brush with melted butter. Let rise at room temperature 1 hour or until doubled in bulk.

Bake at 375° for 10 to 12 minutes or until golden. Yield: 1½ dozen per portion.

Cinnamon Rolls: Roll 1 portion of dough into a 14- x 10-inch rectangle. Brush with ¼ cup melted butter; sprinkle with ⅓ cup sugar and 2 teaspoons ground cinnamon. Roll up, jellyroll fashion, starting with long side; cut crosswise into ¾-inch-thick slices. Place in 2 lightly greased 9-inch round cakepans. Let rise, and bake as directed. Stir together ½ cup powdered sugar and 2 teaspoons milk; drizzle glaze over warm rolls. Yield: about 1½ dozen.

Herb Rolls: Follow procedure for Cinnamon Rolls, substituting 1 tablespoon each chopped fresh chives, chopped fresh basil, and chopped fresh rosemary for sugar and cinnamon. Omit powdered sugar glaze. Yield: about 1½ dozen.

Sour Cream Yeast Rolls

make-ahead

prep: 19 min. cook: 12 min.
other: 8 hrs., 45 min.

1   (¼-ounce) envelope active dry yeast
¼   cup warm water (100° to 110°)
¼   cup butter or margarine, cut into
        ½-inch pieces
½   cup sour cream
¼   cup sugar
½   teaspoon salt
1   large egg, lightly beaten
2   cups all-purpose flour
¼   cup butter or margarine, melted

Combine yeast and warm water in a 1-cup glass measuring cup; let stand 5 minutes.

Combine ¼ cup butter and next 3 ingredients in a medium saucepan over low heat; heat until butter melts, stirring occasionally. Cool to 100° to 110°. Transfer to a large bowl; stir in yeast mixture and egg. Gradually add flour, mixing well. (Dough will be wet.) Cover and chill at least 8 hours.

Punch dough down; turn out onto a floured surface, and knead 3 or 4 times.

Roll dough to ¼-inch thickness, and cut with a 2½-inch round cutter.

Make a crease with the dull edge of a knife just off the center on each round. Brush dough lightly with melted butter. Fold larger side over smaller side so edges will meet; press gently to seal. Repeat procedure with remaining dough. Place 12 rolls each in 2 lightly greased 8-inch round cakepans.

Cover and let rise in a warm place (85°), free from drafts, 40 minutes or until doubled in bulk. Bake at 375° for 10 to 12 minutes or until golden brown. Yield: 2 dozen.

Cloverleaf Rolls: Lightly grease 2 muffin pans. Shape dough into 1-inch balls; place 3 dough balls in each muffin cup. Cover and let rise in a warm place (85°), free from drafts, 40 minutes or until doubled in bulk. Bake as directed. Brush with melted butter. Yield: 2 dozen.

Super Dinner Rolls

prep: 27 min. cook: 20 min.
other: 1 hr., 25 min.

7¼ cups bread flour, divided
¾   cup sugar
1   teaspoon salt
2   (¼-ounce) envelopes active dry yeast
2   cups milk
½   cup butter, cut into ½-inch pieces
3   large eggs, lightly beaten

Combine 2 cups flour, sugar, salt, and yeast in a large mixing bowl; stir well. Combine milk and butter in a heavy saucepan; cook over low heat just until butter melts, stirring occasionally. Cool to 120° to 130°.

Gradually add liquid mixture to flour mixture, beating well at low speed with

an electric mixer. Beat 2 more minutes at medium speed. Add eggs and ¾ cup flour, beating 2 minutes at medium speed. Gradually stir in enough of the remaining 4½ cups flour to make a soft dough.

Turn dough out onto a lightly floured surface, and knead until smooth and elastic (about 8 to 10 minutes). Place dough in a large well-greased bowl, turning to grease top. Cover and let rise in a warm place (85°), free from drafts, 45 minutes or until doubled in bulk.

Punch dough down; divide in half. Divide each half into 11 equal portions; shape each portion into a ball. Place at least 1 inch apart on large greased baking sheets.

Cover and let rise in a warm place, free from drafts, 30 minutes or until doubled in bulk. Bake at 325° for 18 to 20 minutes or until lightly browned. Remove rolls from baking sheets; cool on wire racks. Yield: 22 rolls.

Overnight Potato Rolls

These rolls are a Test Kitchens favorite because they're unusually light and can be made ahead. To make ahead, bake them for 3 to 5 minutes; then wrap in aluminum foil, and freeze. To serve, let the rolls thaw and bake at 425° for 5 minutes or until lightly browned.

editor's favorite • make-ahead

prep: 20 min.   cook: 10 min.

other: 10 hrs., 20 min.

1   (¼-ounce) envelope active dry yeast
½   cup warm water (100° to 110°)
1   cup milk
½   cup sugar
1   cup instant mashed potatoes
1½   teaspoons salt
⅔   cup butter-flavored shortening
2   large eggs
5¾ to 6¼ cups all-purpose flour
Melted butter or margarine

Combine yeast and warm water in a 1-cup glass measuring cup; let stand 5 minutes.

Combine milk and next 3 ingredients in a medium saucepan; cook, stirring constantly, until mixture begins to simmer. Pour over shortening in a bowl, and stir until shortening melts. Cool to 100° to 110°.

Combine yeast mixture, milk mixture, and eggs in a large mixing bowl. Gradually add 3 cups flour, beating at medium speed with an electric mixer until smooth. Stir in enough remaining flour to make a soft dough.

Place in a well-greased bowl, turning to grease top; cover and chill 8 hours.

Punch dough down; turn out onto a floured surface, and knead 4 or 5 times. Roll dough to ½-inch thickness; cut with a 2½-inch round cutter.

Dip rolls in butter, and place 1 inch apart on lightly greased baking sheets. Cover and let rise in a warm place (85°), free from drafts, 2 hours.

Bake at 425° for 8 to 10 minutes or until lightly browned. Yield: 2½ dozen.

Cloverleaf Rolls: Shape dough into ¾-inch balls; place 3 balls in each well-greased muffin cup. Let rise, and bake as directed.

Sweet Potato Rolls

prep: 19 min.   cook: 34 min.

other: 1 hr., 36 min.

1   quart water
1   (¾-pound) sweet potato, peeled and chopped
3   tablespoons sugar, divided
1   (¼-ounce) envelope active dry yeast
6¼   cups all purpose flour, divided
1½   teaspoons salt
1   cup milk
1   tablespoon vegetable oil
2   large eggs, lightly beaten

Bring water to a boil; add potato. Cook 10 to 15 minutes or until tender. Drain, reserving 1 cup liquid; cool liquid to 110°. Mash potato; stir in 2 tablespoons sugar. Set aside. Stir remaining 1 tablespoon sugar and yeast into reserved liquid; let stand 10 minutes.

Stir together 5½ cups flour and salt in a large bowl; make a well in center of mixture. Stir together potato mixture, milk, oil, and eggs; add yeast mixture, stirring until blended. Add to flour mixture, stirring to make a soft dough.

Turn dough out onto a floured surface; knead lightly, adding ½ cup flour, as needed, to prevent sticking. Place dough in a well-greased bowl, turning to grease top. Cover and let rise in a warm place

(85°), free from drafts, 1 hour or until doubled in bulk. Punch dough down; turn out onto floured surface, and divide in half. Shape each portion into an 18- x 2½-inch log.

Cut each log diagonally into 1-inch-thick slices; sprinkle slices with remaining ¼ cup flour. Place 1 to 2 inches apart on lightly greased baking sheets.

Cover and let rise in a warm place, free from drafts, 20 minutes. Bake at 400° for 15 to 20 minutes or until golden. Cool on wire racks. Yield: 2½ dozen.

Spoon Rolls

Homemade rolls have never been so simple; just spoon the dough into muffin cups. The rolls don't even need to rise. They bake up with slightly pebbly tops that resemble muffins.

make-ahead

prep: 9 min.   cook: 25 min.   other: 4 hrs., 5 min.

1   (¼-ounce) envelope active dry yeast
2   tablespoons warm water (100° to 110°)
½   cup vegetable oil
¼   cup sugar
1   egg, lightly beaten
4   cups self-rising flour
2   cups warm milk or water (100° to 110°)

Combine yeast and 2 tablespoons warm water in a bowl; let stand 5 minutes.

Combine yeast mixture, oil, and remaining ingredients in a large bowl; stir until smooth.

Cover tightly, and refrigerate at least 4 hours or up to 4 days.

Stir batter; spoon into greased muffin pans, filling three-fourths full. Bake at 350° for 25 minutes or until golden. Yield: 20 rolls.

Spoon Rolls

Rosemary Focaccia

Deliver this popular Italian flatbread on a cutting board for a gift that lasts after the holidays. A great "ripping" bread meant to be torn into serving-size pieces, it can be enjoyed alone or made into gourmet sandwiches.

great gift

prep: 32 min.   cook: 30 min.   other: 1 hr., 35 min.

2   (¼-ounce) envelopes active dry yeast
2   cups warm water (100° to 110°)
6   cups all-purpose flour, divided
½   cup unsalted butter, softened
½   cup finely chopped fresh rosemary, divided
1   teaspoon salt
¼   cup olive oil, divided
8   garlic cloves, minced
1   tablespoon diced pimiento
2½ teaspoons kosher salt
½   teaspoon freshly ground pepper

Rosemary Focaccia

Combine yeast and warm water in a 4-cup glass measuring cup; let stand 5 minutes.

Place 5 cups flour in a large bowl; make a well in center. Add yeast mixture; stir until a soft dough forms.

Cover and let rise in a warm place (85°), free from drafts, 45 minutes or until doubled in bulk. (Dough will be spongy.)

Sprinkle remaining 1 cup flour on a flat surface. Turn dough out onto floured surface; knead until flour is incorporated to make a firm dough. Gradually knead in butter, ¼ cup rosemary, and 1 teaspoon salt.

Knead until dough is smooth and elastic (about 9 minutes), adding additional flour, if necessary.

Brush 2 (15- x 10-inch) jellyroll pans with 1 tablespoon oil each. Divide dough in half. Press each portion into a jellyroll pan. Cover and let rise in a warm place, free from drafts, 30 to 45 minutes or until dough is almost doubled in bulk.

Using fingertips, dimple the dough all over in both pans; sprinkle with minced garlic, diced pimiento, and remaining ¼ cup rosemary. Drizzle with remaining 2 tablespoons olive oil, and sprinkle with kosher salt and pepper.

Bake at 375° for 25 to 30 minutes or until golden. Cut or tear into squares. Yield: 2 flatbreads (8 servings each).

dimpling focaccia dough

Using your fingertips, make indentations all over the surface of the dough in the pan.

Onion-Poppy Seed Twist

Slender onion-filled strips of dough are intertwined to create this savory loaf. Pair it with your favorite soup for a simple, satisfying cold-weather supper.

prep: 27 min.   cook: 35 min.   other: 40 min.

2½ cups all-purpose flour, divided
3   tablespoons sugar
1   (¼-ounce) envelope active dry yeast
1   teaspoon salt
½   cup milk
¼   cup water
1   large egg, lightly beaten
3   tablespoons butter, melted
1   cup diced onion
2   tablespoons butter, melted
2   tablespoons poppy seeds
⅛   teaspoon salt
1   large egg, lightly beaten
1   tablespoon water
Poppy seeds

Combine 1 cup flour, sugar, yeast, and salt in a large bowl.

Cook milk and ¼ cup water over low heat in a saucepan until very warm (120° to 130°); gradually stir into flour mixture. Stir in 1 egg, 3 tablespoons melted butter, and remaining 1½ cups flour until blended.

Turn dough out onto a floured surface, and knead until smooth and elastic (4 to 6 minutes). Place in a well-greased bowl, turning to grease top. Cover and let stand 10 minutes.

Combine onion and next 3 ingredients in a small bowl.

Roll dough into a 14- x 10-inch rectangle on a lightly floured surface; cut in half lengthwise. Spoon half of onion mixture down center of each rectangle. Bring long sides over filling, pinching seams to seal. Place, seam sides down and side by side, on a lightly greased baking sheet. Pinch portions together at 1 end to seal; braid portions, and pinch ends to seal.

Cover and let rise in a warm place (85°), free from drafts, 20 to 30 minutes or until doubled in bulk.

Stir together remaining egg and 1 tablespoon water until blended; brush over dough. Sprinkle with poppy seeds. Bake at 350° for 35 minutes, shielding with aluminum foil after 25 minutes; cool on a wire rack. **Yield: 1 loaf.**

Almond Twists

prep: 35 min.   cook: 15 min.
other: 11 hrs., 5 min.

1   (¼-ounce) envelope active dry yeast
½   cup warm water (100° to 110°)
4½   cups all-purpose flour
¼   cup granulated sugar
1   teaspoon salt
1   teaspoon grated orange rind
1   cup butter or margarine, softened
6   large eggs
1   (8-ounce) can almond paste
¾   cup firmly packed brown sugar
½   cup butter or margarine, softened
¼   cup chopped almonds, toasted
2   cups sifted powdered sugar
3   tablespoons milk

Combine yeast and warm water in a 1-cup glass measuring cup; let stand 5 minutes.

Combine yeast mixture, 3 cups flour, ¼ cup granulated sugar, and next 4 ingredients in a large mixing bowl; beat at low speed with an electric mixer until blended. Beat 4 more minutes at medium speed. Add remaining 1½ cups flour; beat at low speed until blended. Cover and let rise in a warm place (85°),

Almond Twists

free from drafts, 1½ hours or until doubled in bulk. Cover and chill at least 8 hours.

Combine almond paste, brown sugar, ½ cup butter, and almonds; stir well, and set aside.

Punch dough down, and divide in half. Cover and chill 1 portion of dough. Roll remaining portion into a 16- x 10-inch rectangle on a floured surface. Spread half of almond paste mixture over dough. Fold dough lengthwise into thirds, forming a long rectangle. Cut into 16 (1-inch) strips. Twist each strip, and place on a lightly greased baking sheet. Repeat procedure with remaining dough and almond paste mixture.

Cover and let rise in a warm place, free from drafts, 1½ hours or until doubled in bulk.

Bake at 350° for 15 minutes or until lightly browned. Remove to wire racks.

Combine powdered sugar and milk; drizzle over warm rolls. **Yield: 32 twists.**

Herb-Buttered Crescents

Change the flavor of these tender, flaky crescents with a made-to-order herb butter. Experiment by using such herbs as oregano and basil in place of chives and parsley.

make-ahead
prep: 19 min.   cook: 15 min.
other: 9 hrs., 13 min.

2   (¼-ounce) envelopes active dry yeast
½   cup warm water (100° to 110°)
1   cup milk
½   cup sugar
½   cup sour cream
½   cup butter or margarine, cut into
      ½-inch pieces
2   large eggs, beaten
2   teaspoons salt
5½ to 6 cups all-purpose flour
Herb Butter

Combine yeast and warm water in a 1-cup glass measuring cup; let stand 5 minutes.

Combine milk and next 3 ingredients in a medium saucepan; cook over low heat just until butter melts, stirring occasionally. Cool to 100° to 110°.

Combine yeast mixture, milk mixture, eggs, salt, and 2 cups flour; beat at medium speed with an electric mixer 2 minutes. Stir in enough remaining flour to make a medium-stiff dough.

Place in a well-greased bowl, turning to grease top. Cover and chill 8 to 48 hours.

Turn out onto a floured surface; knead until smooth and elastic. Divide into 4 portions. Roll each into a 12-inch circle on a floured surface; spread with 2 tablespoons Herb Butter. Cut each circle into 12 wedges; roll each wedge, jellyroll fashion, starting at wide end.

Place rolls, point sides down, 2 inches apart on greased baking sheets; curve into crescent shapes. Cover and let rise in a warm place (85°), free from drafts, 40 to 45 minutes or until doubled in bulk.

Bake at 375° for 10 to 15 minutes or until lightly browned. Yield: 4 dozen.

Herb Butter

prep: 5 min.

½   cup butter or margarine, softened
2   tablespoons chopped fresh chives
1½ tablespoons minced fresh parsley
2   teaspoons lemon juice
⅛   teaspoon ground red pepper

Combine all ingredients. Yield: ½ cup.

---

better butters

Stir together one of these delicious bread spreads in about 5 minutes. Before chilling, shape into logs or spoon into plastic wrap-lined bowls. Garnish with fresh cranberries and herbs, such as thyme or rosemary, for an attractive presentation.

Honey Butter: Stir together ½ cup softened butter and 2 to 4 tablespoons honey. Cover and chill 1 hour. Makes about ½ cup. Prep: 5 min.

Honey-Pecan Butter: Stir together ½ cup softened butter; ¼ cup honey; and ⅓ cup toasted, finely chopped pecans. Cover and chill 1 hour. Makes ¾ cup. Prep: 5 min.

Cinnamon-Caramel Butter: Stir together ½ cup softened butter, 6 tablespoons bottled caramel sauce (we tested with Smucker's Caramel Sauce), and ¾ teaspoon ground cinnamon. Cover and chill 1 hour. Makes 1 cup. Prep: 5 min.

Tavern Bread

Peel labels from four 16-ounce cans, and sterilize the cans in your dishwasher for use in this recipe.

prep: 11 min.   cook: 30 min.
other: 1 hr., 20 min.

1   teaspoon instant coffee granules
½   cup water
3   tablespoons molasses
1   tablespoon honey
1   (¼-ounce) envelope active dry yeast
1   (12-ounce) can evaporated milk
2   tablespoons regular oats, uncooked
2   tablespoons vegetable oil
2   teaspoons salt
¼   teaspoon ground ginger
1½ cups whole wheat flour
3   cups all-purpose flour, divided

Combine first 4 ingredients in a heavy saucepan; cook over low heat until granules dissolve. Cool to 100° to 110°; transfer to a large mixing bowl. Stir in yeast; let stand 5 minutes. Add milk and next 4 ingredients. Stir in whole wheat flour and 1 cup all-purpose flour.

Beat at medium speed with an electric mixer 1 minute. Gradually add remaining 2 cups all-purpose flour, stirring with a wooden spoon.

Divide dough into 4 well-greased 16-ounce cans. Let rise, uncovered, in a warm place (85°), free from drafts, 1 hour or until doubled in bulk.

Bake at 350° for 30 minutes. Remove from cans immediately, and cool on wire racks. Yield: 4 loaves.

Tavern Bread

Norwegian Christmas Bread

Whole cardamom is much more fragrant than ground cardamom. If the whole form isn't available, you can use 1 to 2 teaspoons ground cardamom.

prep: 46 min.   cook: 50 min.   other: 1 hr., 45 min.

Whole cardamom pods
1   (¼-ounce) envelope active dry yeast
¼   cup warm water (100° to 110°)
9   to 9¼ cups all-purpose flour, divided
1   cup sugar
2   cups milk
1   cup butter or margarine, melted
1   teaspoon salt
3   large eggs, beaten
1½   cups golden raisins
½   cup chopped red or green candied cherries
½   cup chopped red or green candied pineapple
½   cup coarsely chopped pecans

Place whole cardamom pods in a mortar; use a pestle to crack pods open. Discard pod fragments from the brown or black seeds, and crush enough seeds with pestle to equal 2 teaspoons. Set aside.

Combine yeast and warm water in a 1-cup glass measuring cup; let stand 5 minutes.

Combine yeast mixture, 2 cups flour, and next 4 ingredients in a large mixing bowl; beat at medium speed with an electric mixer 2 minutes. Beat in cardamom and eggs. Stir in fruit and pecans. Gradually stir in enough of remaining 7¼ cups flour to make a soft dough.

Turn dough out onto a well-floured surface, and knead until smooth and elastic (about 10 minutes). Place in a well-greased bowl, turning to grease top. Cover and let rise in a warm place (85°), free from drafts, 1 hour and 15 minutes or until doubled in bulk.

Punch dough down, and divide in half; roll 1 portion of dough into a 14- x 7-inch rectangle. Roll up dough, starting at short end, pressing firmly to eliminate air pockets; pinch ends to seal. Place dough, seam side down, in a well-greased 9- x 5-inch loafpan. Repeat procedure with remaining portion of dough.

Cover and let rise in a warm place, free from drafts, 25 minutes or until doubled in bulk.

Bake at 350° for 30 minutes. Shield loaves with aluminum foil to prevent excessive browning. Bake for 20 more minutes or until loaves sound hollow when tapped. Remove bread from pans immediately; cool on wire racks. Yield: 2 loaves.

Norwegian Christmas Bread

The predominant flavor of this traditional holiday bread comes from cardamom—a pungent, aromatic spice with an exotically sweet flavor.

Raisin Bread

make-ahead

prep: 21 min.   cook: 45 min.

other: 10 hrs., 35 min.

1   (¼-ounce) envelope active dry
    yeast
½   cup warm water (100° to 110°)
¼   cup granulated sugar
1   cup butter or margarine, softened
6   large eggs
1   teaspoon salt
1   teaspoon grated orange rind
4½ cups all-purpose flour
1   cup golden raisins
1½ cups sifted powdered sugar
½   teaspoon rum flavoring
1   to 2 tablespoons water

Combine yeast and warm water in a
1-cup glass measuring cup; let stand
5 minutes.

Combine yeast mixture, ¼ cup granulated sugar, and next 4 ingredients in a
large mixing bowl; add 2 cups flour, and
beat at low speed with an electric mixer
until blended. Beat 4 more minutes. Stir
in remaining 2½ cups flour and raisins.

Cover and let rise in a warm place
(85°), free from drafts, 1½ hours or until
doubled in bulk. Punch down; cover and
chill at least 8 hours.

Turn out onto a floured surface; shape
into an 18-inch rope. Shape into a ring;
pinch ends together to seal. Place in a
greased and floured 12-cup Bundt pan.
Cover and let rise in a warm place, free
from drafts, 1 hour or until doubled
in bulk.

Bake at 350° for 45 minutes or until
loaf sounds hollow when tapped. Remove
from pan, and cool on a wire rack.

Combine powdered sugar, rum
flavoring, and 1 to 2 tablespoons water;
drizzle over loaf. Yield: 1 loaf.

Easy Stollen

Easy Stollen

*Frozen bread dough speeds up the
preparation of this classic German
Christmas bread laden with fruit and
nuts. The dough will be very elastic, so
make sure to press the fruit mixture into
the dough until it's incorporated.*

prep: 16 min.   cook: 30 min.   other: 50 min.

½   cup raisins
½   cup chopped walnuts
¼   cup chopped red and green candied
     cherries
1½ teaspoons orange juice
½   (32-ounce) package frozen bread
     dough loaves, thawed
1   tablespoon butter, melted
1½ cups sifted powdered sugar
2   to 3 tablespoons orange juice

Combine the first 4 ingredients in a
medium bowl.

Place dough on a lightly floured surface; press to 1-inch thickness. Spoon
fruit mixture in center of dough. (Fruit
mixture will be heaping.) Press fruit
mixture into dough until fruit mixture
is evenly distributed.

Press dough into a ½-inch thick oval.
Fold in half lengthwise. Pinch seams
together. Place on a well-greased baking
sheet; brush with butter. Cover and let
rise in a warm place (85°), free from
drafts, 40 minutes or until doubled
in bulk.

Bake at 350° for 25 to 30 minutes or
until loaf sounds hollow when tapped.
Cool 10 minutes on a wire rack.

Meanwhile, combine powdered sugar
and 2 to 3 tablespoons orange juice;
stir well. Drizzle loaf with glaze. Yield:
1 loaf.

Candy Cane Bread

Candy Cane Bread

This recipe yields three luscious loaves. Keep one, and give the others as gifts.

great gift
prep: 32 min.   cook: 15 min.
other: 2 hrs., 20 min.

1½ cups chopped dried apricots
2   cups boiling water
1   (16-ounce) carton sour cream
⅓   cup granulated sugar
¼   cup butter or margarine, cut into
       ½-inch pieces
1½ teaspoons salt
2   (¼-ounce) envelopes active dry yeast
½   cup warm water (100° to 110°)
2   large eggs, lightly beaten
6   to 6½ cups all-purpose flour, divided
1½ cups chopped maraschino cherries
¼   cup butter or margarine, melted
1   cup sifted powdered sugar
1   tablespoon plus 1 to 2 teaspoons
       milk
Garnish: candied cherry halves

Combine apricots and boiling water; cover and let stand 1 hour. Drain apricots, and set aside.

Combine sour cream and next 3 ingredients in a heavy saucepan; stir over low heat just until butter melts. Cool to 100° to 110°.

Dissolve yeast in warm water in a large mixing bowl; let stand 5 minutes. Add sour cream mixture, eggs, and 2 cups flour; beat at low speed with an electric mixer until smooth. Stir in enough remaining flour to make a soft dough.

Turn dough out onto a floured surface, and knead until smooth and elastic (8 to 10 minutes). Place in a greased bowl, turning to grease top. Cover and let rise in a warm place (85°), free from drafts, 1 hour or until doubled in bulk.

Punch dough down; divide into thirds. Roll each portion into a 15- x 6-inch rectangle on a lightly floured surface; transfer to greased baking sheets. Make 2-inch cuts at ½-inch intervals on long sides of rectangles, leaving a 2-inch uncut strip down the center of each.

Combine apricots and maraschino cherries; spread down center of each dough rectangle. Fold and overlap strips diagonally over fruit filling in a braided fashion; gently stretch each dough rectangle to measure 22 inches. Curve 1 end of each to resemble a cane.

Bake at 375° for 15 minutes or until golden. Brush each cane with melted butter; cool. Combine powdered sugar and milk; stir until smooth, and drizzle over bread. Garnish, if desired. Yield: 3 loaves.

Cream Cheese Braids

freezer-friendly
prep: 45 min.   cook: 20 min.
other: 9 hrs., 20 min.

1   (8-ounce) container sour cream
½   cup sugar
½   cup butter or margarine, cut into
       ½-inch pieces
1   teaspoon salt
2   (¼-ounce) envelopes active dry
       yeast
½   cup warm water (100° to 110°)
2   large eggs, lightly beaten
4   cups all-purpose flour
Cream Cheese Filling
Powdered Sugar Glaze

Heat first 4 ingredients over low heat in a medium saucepan, stirring occasionally, just until butter melts. Cool to 100° to 110°.

Combine yeast and warm water in a large mixing bowl; let stand 5 minutes. Stir in sour cream mixture and eggs; gradually stir in flour (dough will be soft). Cover and chill at least 8 hours.

Divide dough into fourths. Turn out each portion onto a heavily floured surface, and knead 4 or 5 times.

Roll each portion into a 12- x 8-inch rectangle, and spread each rectangle with one-fourth of Cream Cheese Filling, leaving a 1-inch border around edges. Carefully roll up, starting at a long side; press seam, and fold ends under to seal. Place, seam side down, on lightly greased baking sheets. Cut 6 equally spaced Xs across top of each loaf; cover and let rise in a warm place (85°), free from drafts, about 1 hour or until doubled in bulk.

Bake at 375° for 15 to 20 minutes or until browned. Drizzle warm loaves with Powdered Sugar Glaze. Yield: 4 loaves.

Cream Cheese Filling

prep: 5 min.

2   (8-ounce) packages cream cheese,
       softened
¾   cup sugar
1   large egg
2   teaspoons vanilla extract

Beat all ingredients at medium speed with an electric mixer until smooth. Yield: about 2½ cups.

Powdered Sugar Glaze

prep: 5 min.

2½ cups sifted powdered sugar
¼   cup milk
2   teaspoons vanilla extract

Stir together all ingredients. Yield: about 1 cup.

Freezing Note: Braids may be frozen after baking. Thaw in refrigerator, and glaze before serving.

Cranberry Coffee Cake

prep: 30 min.   cook: 20 min.
other: 9 hrs., 5 min.

2   (¼-ounce) envelopes active dry yeast
½   cup warm water (100° to 110°)
1   cup milk
½   cup granulated sugar
½   cup sour cream
½   cup butter or margarine, cut into
        ½-inch pieces
2   large eggs, beaten
2   teaspoons salt
2   teaspoons grated orange rind
5½ to 6 cups all-purpose flour
1   (12-ounce) jar cranberry-orange
        relish
2   tablespoons chopped pecans
1   cup sifted powdered sugar
1   tablespoon orange juice

Combine yeast and warm water in a
1-cup glass measuring cup; let stand
5 minutes.

Combine milk and next 3 ingredients
in a medium saucepan over low heat just
until butter melts, stirring occasionally.
Cool to 100° to 110°.

Combine yeast mixture, milk mixture,
eggs, salt, rind, and 2 cups flour; beat
at medium speed with an electric mixer
2 minutes. Gradually stir in enough
remaining flour to make a stiff dough.
Place in a well-greased bowl, turning
to grease top; cover and chill at least
8 hours.

Turn dough out onto a floured surface,
and knead until smooth and elastic
(about 1 minute). Roll into a 15- x 10-
inch rectangle on a floured surface.
Spread relish over dough, leaving a
1-inch border; sprinkle with pecans.

Roll up, jellyroll fashion, starting at
long side; pinch seam to seal. Place roll,
seam side down, on a large greased

baking sheet; shape into a ring, and
pinch ends together to seal.

Cut dough at 1-inch intervals around
ring, using a sharp knife or kitchen
shears, cutting two-thirds of the way
through. Gently turn each piece of dough
on its side, slightly overlapping slices.
Cover and let rise in a warm place (85°),
free from drafts, 45 minutes or until
doubled in bulk.

Bake at 375° for 20 minutes or until
lightly browned. Remove to a wire rack.
Combine powdered sugar and orange
juice, stirring well; drizzle over coffee
cake. Yield: 1 coffee cake.

Cinnamon Loaves

*Just about anyone on your gift list will
appreciate a loaf of homemade bread
swirled with cinnamon and raisins and
drizzled with a sugar glaze. Wrap the
bread loosely with cellophane, and tie
with ribbon.*

great gift
prep: 27 min.   cook: 35 min.
other: 1 hr., 45 min.

1   (¼-ounce) envelope active dry yeast
1   cup warm water (100° to 110°)
3   tablespoons granulated sugar
2   tablespoons shortening
1   large egg
½   teaspoon salt
3   to 3½ cups all-purpose flour
¼   cup butter or margarine, melted
2   tablespoons granulated sugar
2   teaspoons ground cinnamon
⅔   cup raisins
2   cups sifted powdered sugar
2   to 3 tablespoons milk
½   cup chopped pecans

Combine yeast and warm water in a
1-cup glass measuring cup; let stand

5 minutes. Combine yeast mixture,
3 tablespoons granulated sugar, shortening, egg, salt, and half of flour in a large
bowl; beat at low speed with an electric
mixer until smooth. Gradually stir in
enough remaining flour to make a soft
dough.

Place dough in a well-greased bowl,
turning to grease top. Cover and let rise
in a warm place (85°), free from drafts,
1 hour or until doubled in bulk, or cover
and store in refrigerator up to 4 days.
(If chilled, let dough return to room temperature before proceeding.)

Punch dough down; turn out onto a
lightly floured surface, and knead 8 to
10 times.

Divide dough in half, keeping 1 portion covered. Roll 1 portion dough into
a 15- x 7-inch rectangle on a lightly
floured surface; brush with half of melted
butter to within ½ inch of edges.

Combine 2 tablespoons granulated
sugar and cinnamon; sprinkle half of
mixture over butter. Sprinkle ⅓ cup
raisins over top. Roll up, jellyroll fashion,
starting at narrow edge. Pinch seams
and ends together. Place loaf, seam side
down, in a greased 8½- x 4½-inch loafpan. Repeat procedure with other portion of dough.

Cover and let rise in a warm place,
free from drafts, 40 minutes or until
doubled in bulk.

Bake at 350° for 30 to 35 minutes or
until loaves sound hollow when tapped.
Remove loaves from pans, and cool on a
wire rack.

Combine powdered sugar and milk,
stirring until smooth. Drizzle evenly over
loaves, and sprinkle with pecans. Yield:
2 loaves.

Cinnamon Loaves

visions of sugarplums

Cookies and candies delight the child in everyone—never more so than at Christmastime. This array of tasty treats definitely adds new favorites to your list.

Ambrosia Cookies

Savor this cookie's wonderful blend of ambrosia flavors: citrus, nuts, and coconut. The ingredient list is long, but the results are worth it.

big batch • editor's favorite
prep: 15 min.   cook: 16 min. per batch

1   cup butter or margarine, softened
1   cup granulated sugar
1   cup firmly packed dark brown sugar
2   large eggs
2   cups all-purpose flour
2   teaspoons baking powder
½   teaspoon baking soda
½   teaspoon salt
1½ cups regular oats, uncooked
1   cup chopped dates
1   cup golden raisins
1   cup flaked coconut
1   cup chopped pecans
1   teaspoon grated orange rind
1   teaspoon grated lemon rind
1   teaspoon vanilla extract
½   teaspoon almond extract
½   teaspoon orange extract
4   dozen candied cherries, halved

Beat butter at medium speed with an electric mixer until fluffy; gradually add sugars, beating well. Add eggs, 1 at a time, beating well after each addition.

Combine flour and next 4 ingredients; stir well. Add flour mixture and remaining ingredients except candied cherries to creamed mixture; stir well.

Drop by rounded teaspoonfuls 2 inches apart onto lightly greased baking sheets; lightly press a cherry half into each cookie.

Bake at 350° for 14 to 16 minutes; cool cookies on baking sheets 10 minutes. Remove to wire racks to cool. (Cookies become firm as they cool.) Yield: about 8 dozen.

Toasted Almond-and-Cranberry Cookies

big batch
prep: 14 min.   cook: 10 min. per batch

½   cup butter or margarine, softened
½   cup shortening
1   cup firmly packed brown sugar
⅔   cup granulated sugar
2   large eggs
2   cups all-purpose flour
1   teaspoon baking powder
½   teaspoon baking soda
⅛   teaspoon salt
2   (4-ounce) packages white chocolate baking bars, chopped
2   cups cornflakes cereal
1   cup sliced almonds, lightly toasted
1   (6-ounce) package dried cranberries
¾   teaspoon almond extract

Beat butter and shortening at medium speed with an electric mixer until fluffy. Gradually add sugars, beating well. Add

eggs, mixing well. Add flour, baking powder, soda, and salt. Stir in chocolate, cereal, almonds, cranberries, and almond extract.

Drop dough by tablespoonfuls 2 inches apart onto ungreased baking sheets. Bake at 350° for 10 minutes. Remove to wire racks to cool. Yield: 6 dozen.

cookie scoop

• To prevent stiff cookie dough from straining a handheld portable mixer, stir in the last few additions of flour mixture by hand.

• If cookie dough is dry and crumbly, stir in 1 to 2 tablespoons milk.

• A tiny ice cream scoop is a handy gadget that makes dropping dough onto baking sheets a breeze. And you're guaranteed that all the cookies will be the same size.

• If cookies spread too much during baking, the dough may be too soft. Put the dough in the refrigerator until well chilled. Also let hot baking sheets cool completely before reusing them.

• If you don't have wire cooling racks for cooling cookies, place wax paper on the counter and sprinkle it with sugar; then place the cookies on the sugared wax paper to cool.

• Sturdy bar cookies, drop cookies, and fruit cookies are the best candidates for mailing. Tender, fragile cookies are prone to crumbling when mailed. Use a heavy cardboard box as a mailing container, and pack and cushion it tightly so that cookies don't shift around.

Chunky Chip Cookies

You can freeze these cookies in airtight containers up to three months.

big batch • freezer-friendly

prep: 17 min.   cook: 10 min. per batch

1   cup shortening
1   cup butter or margarine, softened
2   cups granulated sugar
2   cups firmly packed brown sugar
4   large eggs
2   teaspoons vanilla extract
4   cups all-purpose flour
2   teaspoons baking powder
2   teaspoons baking soda
2   cups regular oats, uncooked
2   cups cornflakes cereal
2   cups (12 ounces) semisweet
    chocolate morsels
1   cup chopped pecans
1   cup flaked coconut

Beat shortening and butter in a large bowl at medium speed with an electric mixer until creamy; gradually add sugars, beating well. Add eggs, 1 at a time, beating after each addition. Add vanilla, mixing well.

Combine flour, baking powder, and soda; gradually add to creamed mixture, mixing well. Gradually stir in oats and remaining ingredients.

Drop dough by tablespoonfuls, 2 inches apart, onto ungreased baking sheets.

Bake at 350° for 10 minutes or until lightly browned. Remove to wire racks to cool. Yield: 9½ dozen.

Chocolate-Filled Meringue Cookies

prep: 26 min.   cook: 8 hrs., 4 min.   other: 30 min.

2   egg whites
¼   teaspoon cream of tartar
½   cup granulated sugar
1   teaspoon vanilla extract, divided
1   cup finely chopped pecans
1   tablespoon sifted powdered sugar
½   cup butter
2   tablespoons cocoa
3   tablespoons half-and-half
2¼ cups sifted powdered sugar

Preheat oven to 350°. Beat egg whites and cream of tartar at high speed with

Chocolate-Filled Meringue Cookies

an electric mixer until foamy. Gradually add ½ cup granulated sugar, 1 tablespoon at a time, beating until stiff peaks form and sugar dissolves (2 to 4 minutes). Stir in ½ teaspoon vanilla and chopped pecans.

Drop mixture by teaspoonfuls onto aluminum foil-lined baking sheets. Dip finger in 1 tablespoon powdered sugar, and make an indentation in center of each cookie.

Place in oven, and immediately turn oven off. Do not open door for at least 8 hours. Remove from oven, and carefully peel cookies from foil.

Combine butter, cocoa, and half-and-half in a small saucepan; bring to a boil over medium heat. Remove from heat, and cool to room temperature. Add 2¼ cups powdered sugar, and beat well with an electric mixer. Stir in remaining ½ teaspoon vanilla.

Just before serving, pipe cocoa mixture into the indentation of each cookie, using a pastry bag fitted with a star tip. Yield: 4 dozen.

---

cookie storage tips

• Cool cookies completely on a wire rack before storing.

• Store soft, chewy cookies in an airtight container to keep them from drying out.

• After three days, chewy cookies may harden, but can be softened by placing an apple wedge on wax paper in the container.

• Store crisp cookies in a container with a loose-fitting lid.

• Bar cookies can be stored in their baking pan; seal the top of the pan with aluminum foil. Unfrosted bar cookies can be stacked and stored in airtight containers with wax paper between the layers.

• Unfrosted cookies freeze well for eight months if packed in zip-top freezer bags, metal tins, or plastic freezer containers. To serve, thaw in the container for about 15 minutes.

• Cookie dough can be frozen up to six months. Thaw the dough in the refrigerator or at room temperature until it's the right consistency for shaping into cookies as the recipe directs. Some refrigerator cookies can be sliced straight from the freezer without thawing.

Oatmeal-Nut-Chocolate Chip Cookies

Dipping these cookies in chocolate makes them a chocolate-lover's dream.

big batch
prep: 24 min.   cook: 12 min. per batch

1½ cups uncooked regular oats
1   cup butter or margarine, softened
1   cup granulated sugar
1   cup firmly packed brown sugar
2   large eggs
1   tablespoon vanilla extract
2   cups all-purpose flour
1   teaspoon baking soda
½   teaspoon baking powder
½   teaspoon salt
2   cups (12 ounces) semisweet
     chocolate morsels
3   (1.55-ounce) bars milk chocolate,
     grated
1½ cups chopped pecans
12 ounces chocolate bark coating,
     melted (optional)

Place oats in container of an electric blender; cover and process until finely ground. Set aside.

Beat butter in a large bowl at medium speed with an electric mixer until creamy; gradually add sugars, beating well. Add eggs and vanilla, mixing well.

Combine ground oats, flour, and next 3 ingredients; gradually add flour mixture to creamed mixture, mixing well. Stir in chocolate morsels, grated chocolate, and pecans.

Drop dough by heaping teaspoonfuls onto greased baking sheets. Bake at 375° for 10 to 12 minutes or until lightly browned. Cool slightly on pans; remove to wire racks to cool completely.

Dip half of each cookie in melted bark coating, if desired; place on parchment paper to dry. Yield: about 9 dozen.

Oatmeal-Molasses Cookies

Just like Grandma used to make: soft and chewy with just the right amount of sweetness and a little bit of coconut.

big batch
prep: 15 min.   cook: 10 min. per batch

2   cups sugar
1   cup vegetable oil
⅓   cup molasses
2   large eggs
2   cups all-purpose flour
1   teaspoon baking powder
1   teaspoon baking soda
1   teaspoon salt
1   teaspoon ground cinnamon
2   cups quick-cooking oats,
     uncooked
1   cup raisins
1   cup flaked coconut (optional)

Combine first 4 ingredients in a large mixing bowl. Beat at medium speed with an electric mixer until smooth.

Combine flour and next 4 ingredients; stir well. Add to sugar mixture, mixing well. Stir in oats, raisins, and, if desired, coconut.

Drop dough by heaping teaspoonfuls onto lightly greased baking sheets. Bake at 350° for 10 minutes. Cool slightly on pans; remove to wire racks to cool completely. Yield: about 6 dozen.

Fruitcake Cookies

Even those who don't care for traditional fruitcake will beg for seconds of these chunky, chewy gems.

prep: 17 min.   cook: 10 min. per batch
other: 1 hr.

½   cup shortening
1   cup firmly packed light brown
     sugar
1   large egg
¼   cup buttermilk
2   cups all-purpose flour
½   teaspoon baking soda
½   teaspoon baking powder
½   teaspoon salt
1   cup chopped dates
1   cup chopped pecans
1   cup chopped candied cherries
5   dozen pecan halves (optional)

Combine first 3 ingredients in a large bowl; stir in buttermilk.

Combine flour and next 3 ingredients; stir into brown sugar mixture. Stir in dates, pecans, and cherries; cover and chill 1 hour.

Drop dough by rounded teaspoonfuls, 2 inches apart, onto lightly greased baking sheets. Top each cookie with a pecan half, if desired.

Bake at 375° for 10 minutes or until lightly browned. Remove to wire racks to cool. Yield: 5 dozen.

Orange Slice Cookies

big batch

prep: 20 min.   cook: 10 min. per batch

1½ cups finely chopped candy orange
      slices
¼   cup all-purpose flour
1   cup butter or margarine, softened
1   cup firmly packed brown sugar
¾   cup granulated sugar
2   large eggs
2   tablespoons milk
2   tablespoons vanilla extract
2   cups all-purpose flour
1   teaspoon baking soda
½   teaspoon salt
½   teaspoon ground cinnamon
½   teaspoon ground nutmeg
2½ cups quick-cooking oats, uncooked
1   cup flaked coconut

Combine chopped orange slices and
¼ cup flour in a medium bowl; toss to
coat candy. Set aside.

Beat butter at medium speed with an
electric mixer until creamy; gradually
add sugars, beating well. Add eggs, milk,
and vanilla; beat well.

Combine 2 cups flour and next 4
ingredients; gradually add to creamed
mixture, beating well. Stir in reserved
candy mixture, oats, and coconut.

Drop dough by rounded teaspoonfuls
2 inches apart onto greased baking
sheets.

Bake at 375° for 10 minutes. Cool
slightly on pans; remove to wire racks
to cool completely. Yield: 9 dozen.

Salted Peanut Cookies

big batch

prep: 12 min.   cook: 12 min. per batch

1   cup shortening
2   cups firmly packed brown sugar
2   large eggs
2   cups all-purpose flour
1   teaspoon baking powder
1   teaspoon baking soda
½   teaspoon salt
2   cups quick-cooking oats, uncooked
1   cup crispy rice cereal
1   cup salted peanuts

Beat shortening at medium speed with an
electric mixer until fluffy; gradually add
sugar, beating well. Add eggs; beat well.

Combine flour and next 3 ingredients;
add to creamed mixture, mixing well.
Stir in oats, cereal, and peanuts. (Dough
will be stiff.)

Drop dough by rounded teaspoonfuls
onto lightly greased baking sheets.

Bake at 375° for 10 to 12 minutes.
Remove to wire racks to cool. Yield:
7 dozen.

Praline Wafers

prep: 7 min.   cook: 8 min. per batch

⅔   cup butter
1   cup firmly packed brown sugar
1   egg yolk
1   tablespoon vanilla extract
1⅓ cups unbleached all-purpose flour
¼   teaspoon salt
⅓   cup toasted, finely chopped pecans
Pecan halves (optional)

Melt butter in a skillet. Add sugar, and
cook over medium heat, stirring constantly, 3 minutes. Remove from heat,
and cool. Add egg yolk and vanilla,

stirring well. Stir in flour and salt. Add
chopped pecans; stir just until blended.

Drop dough by level tablespoonfuls,
2 inches apart, onto ungreased baking
sheets. Press a pecan half lightly into
each cookie, if desired.

Bake at 375° for 8 minutes or until
edges are golden. Cool on pans 1 minute;
remove to wire racks to cool completely.
Yield: 3 dozen.

Kentucky Sugar Cookies

big batch • freezer-friendly • make-ahead

prep: 13 min.   cook: 10 min. per batch

1   cup butter, softened
1   cup vegetable oil
1   cup granulated sugar
1   cup sifted powdered sugar
2   large eggs
1   teaspoon vanilla extract
4   cups all-purpose flour
1   teaspoon salt
1   teaspoon baking soda
1   teaspoon cream of tartar
Additional sugar (optional)

Beat butter and oil at medium speed with
an electric mixer until blended. Gradually
add 1 cup granulated sugar and powdered sugar, beating well. Add eggs and
vanilla, beating until blended.

Combine flour and next 3 ingredients;
add to butter mixture, mixing well.

Drop dough by rounded teaspoonfuls
onto ungreased baking sheets.

Bake at 350° for 9 to 10 minutes or
until lightly browned. Remove to wire
racks; sprinkle with additional sugar
while warm, if desired. Cool. Yield:
9 dozen.

Freezing Note: Freeze cookies in airtight
containers up to 1 month, if desired.

"Doe-a-Deer" Sugar Cookies

prep: 17 min.   cook: 12 min. per batch

1   cup butter, softened
1½ cups sugar
1   large egg
3⅓ cups all-purpose flour
½   teaspoon baking soda
½   teaspoon salt
1   teaspoon cream of tartar
2   teaspoons vanilla extract
Red decorator sugar crystals
Red cinnamon candies

Beat butter at medium speed with an electric mixer 2 minutes or until soft and creamy. Gradually add sugar, beating well. Add egg, and beat well. Combine flour, soda, salt, and cream of tartar; add to butter mixture, beating at low speed just until blended. Stir in vanilla. Shape dough into a ball. (Dough may be slightly crumbly.)

Roll dough to ¼-inch thickness on parchment paper. Cut with a 3½-inch reindeer-shaped cookie cutter, and place 2 inches apart on ungreased baking sheets. Sprinkle dough with sugar crystals. Place 1 cinnamon candy on each reindeer for an eye.

Bake at 350° for 12 minutes or until edges are golden. Remove to wire racks to cool. Yield: 32 cookies.

Rolled Sugar Cookies

You'll find this to be an easy sugar cookie dough to roll and cut.

prep: 21 min.   cook: 8 min. per batch
other: 1 hr.

½   cup butter or margarine, softened
1   cup sugar
1   large egg
1   teaspoon vanilla extract
2½ cups all-purpose flour
2   teaspoons baking powder
¼   teaspoon salt
Decorator sugar crystals

Beat butter at medium speed with an electric mixer until creamy; gradually add 1 cup sugar, beating well. Add egg and vanilla; beat well.

Combine flour, baking powder, and salt; gradually add to butter mixture, beating just until blended. Shape dough into a ball; cover and chill 1 hour.

Divide dough into thirds. Work with 1 portion of dough at a time, storing remaining dough in refrigerator. Roll each portion to ⅛-inch thickness on a lightly floured surface. Cut with a 3-inch cookie cutter, and place on lightly greased baking sheets. Sprinkle with sugar crystals.

Bake at 375° for 8 minutes or until edges are lightly browned. Cool slightly on pans; remove to wire racks to cool completely. Yield: 20 cookies.

Rolled Sugar Cookies

Peanut Butter Cup Cookies

Peanut Butter Cup Cookies

prep: 21 min.   cook: 15 min. per batch

½   cup sugar
⅓   cup creamy peanut butter
¼   cup butter or margarine, softened
1   large egg
2   tablespoons whipping cream
1   teaspoon vanilla extract
1   cup all-purpose flour
1   teaspoon baking soda
⅛   teaspoon salt
½   cup chopped unsalted peanuts
1   (13-ounce) package miniature
    peanut butter cup candies
    (we tested with Reese's)

Beat first 3 ingredients at medium speed with an electric mixer 2 minutes. Add egg, whipping cream, and vanilla; beat well. Combine flour, soda, and salt. Add to peanut butter mixture; stir well. Stir in peanuts.

Roll dough into 1-inch balls. Press dough into miniature (1¾-inch) muffin pans lined with paper muffin cups.

Bake at 350° for 12 minutes. Remove from oven; press down centers with thumb, and press a peanut butter cup into center of each cookie. Bake for 3 more minutes. Remove from oven. Cool completely in pans on wire racks. Yield: 3 dozen.

Braided Candy Canes

You can also shape this cookie dough into festive wreaths.

prep: 31 min.   cook: 15 min. per batch

¾   cup butter or margarine, softened
1   cup sugar
3   large eggs
1   tablespoon vanilla extract
4   cups all-purpose flour
1   tablespoon baking powder
½   teaspoon baking soda
1   egg white, lightly beaten
Red decorator sugar crystals

Beat butter at medium speed with an electric mixer until creamy; gradually add 1 cup sugar, beating well. Add eggs and vanilla, mixing well.

Combine flour, baking powder, and soda; gradually add flour mixture to butter mixture, beating at low speed just until blended after each addition.

Divide dough into fourths. Divide each portion into 14 pieces; roll each piece into a 9-inch rope. Fold ropes in half, and twist. Shape twists into candy canes; brush with egg white, and sprinkle with sugar crystals.

Place cookies 2 inches apart on ungreased baking sheets. Bake at 350° for 15 minutes or until edges begin to brown. Remove to wire racks to cool. Yield: 4½ dozen.

Vanilla-Almond Crescents

prep: 36 min.   cook: 18 min. per batch

1   cup sifted powdered sugar
1   vanilla bean, split lengthwise
2½ cups all-purpose flour
1⅔ cups finely ground, toasted
    almonds
½   cup sifted powdered sugar
⅛   teaspoon salt
1   cup unsalted butter, cut into small
    pieces
2   egg yolks
2   teaspoons vanilla extract
½   teaspoon almond extract

Place 1 cup powdered sugar in a bowl. Scrape vanilla bean seeds into sugar, and stir well. Cover and set aside.

Combine flour and next 3 ingredients in a large bowl. Cut in butter with a pastry blender until mixture is crumbly. Knead in egg yolks and flavorings. Shape dough into 2-inch crescents.

Place on lightly greased baking sheets. Bake at 325° for 15 to 18 minutes or until golden. Cool on pans 3 minutes; dredge in reserved vanilla sugar. Remove to wire racks to cool completely. Dredge again in vanilla sugar; store in an airtight container. Yield: about 5 dozen.

Cookie Wreaths

prep: 43 min.   cook: 10 min. per batch
other: 2 hrs.

2½ cups all-purpose flour
¼ teaspoon salt
¾ cup sugar
1 tablespoon grated orange rind,
    divided
1 cup butter or margarine
¼ cup orange juice
1 egg white, lightly beaten
1 teaspoon water
¼ cup sugar
⅓ cup ground almonds
Tube of green decorator frosting
Red cinnamon candies

Combine flour, salt, ¾ cup sugar, and
2 teaspoons orange rind; cut in butter
with a pastry blender until mixture is
crumbly.

Sprinkle orange juice evenly over surface; stir mixture with a fork until dry
ingredients are moistened. Shape dough
into a ball; cover and chill.

Divide dough in half. Store 1 portion in
refrigerator. Divide remaining portion into
48 balls. Roll 2 balls into 5-inch ropes.

Place ropes on a lightly greased baking
sheet; pinch ends together at 1 end to
seal. Twist ropes together; shape strip
into a circle, pinching ends to seal.

Repeat procedure with remaining
46 balls and remaining portion of
dough. Combine egg white and water;
brush over cookies.

Combine ¼ cup sugar, ground almonds,
and remaining 1 teaspoon orange rind;
sprinkle mixture on cookies. Bake at 400°
for 8 to 10 minutes or until browned.
Remove to wire racks to cool.

Pipe holly leaves with green frosting,
and top with red cinnamon candies.
Yield: 4 dozen.

Shortbread Cookies

big batch

prep: 19 min.   cook: 16 min. per batch

¾ cup butter, softened
½ cup sugar
1 egg yolk
½ teaspoon vanilla extract
1½ cups all-purpose flour
Pecan halves (optional)

Beat butter at medium speed with an
electric mixer until creamy; gradually
add sugar, beating well. Add egg yolk
and vanilla, beating well. Add flour,
mixing well.

Shape dough into 1-inch balls, and
place on ungreased baking sheets.

Gently press a pecan half in center
of each cookie, if desired.

Bake at 300° for 14 to 16 minutes
or until lightly browned. Cool on pans
5 minutes; remove to wire racks to cool
completely. Yield: 6 dozen.

Swedish Heirloom Cookies

editor's favorite

prep: 30 min.   cook: 15 min. per batch

½ cup shortening
½ cup butter or margarine, softened
1 cup sifted powdered sugar
½ teaspoon salt
2 cups all-purpose flour
1 tablespoon water
1 tablespoon vanilla extract
1¼ cups ground almonds
Additional powdered sugar

Beat shortening and butter at medium
speed with an electric mixer until fluffy.
Add 1 cup powdered sugar and salt,
beating at low speed. Stir in flour. Add
water, vanilla, and almonds, stirring well.

Shape dough into 1-inch balls. Place
on ungreased baking sheets, and flatten.

Bake at 325° for 12 to 15 minutes
or until firm and lightly browned. Roll
warm cookies in additional powdered
sugar. Yield: 4 dozen.

Cinnamon Crisps

prep: 25 min.   cook: 10 min. per batch
other: 5 hrs.

½ cup butter or margarine, softened
1 cup firmly packed brown sugar
1 large egg
1 teaspoon vanilla extract
1½ cups all-purpose flour
2 teaspoons baking powder
¼ teaspoon salt
¼ teaspoon ground cinnamon
1 cup ground pecans, toasted
1 egg white, lightly beaten
1 tablespoon granulated sugar
¼ teaspoon ground cinnamon
Pecan halves (optional)

Beat butter at medium speed with an
electric mixer until creamy; gradually
add brown sugar, beating well. Add egg
and vanilla; mix well. Combine flour and
next 3 ingredients; stir into butter mixture. Cover and chill 2 hours.

Shape dough into 2 (7½-inch) logs.
Roll logs in ground pecans. Wrap in
parchment paper, and freeze until firm.

Slice logs into ¼-inch-thick slices, and
place on lightly greased baking sheets.
Brush each cookie with egg white.
Combine granulated sugar and ¼ teaspoon cinnamon; sprinkle lightly over
cookies. Press a pecan half in center of
each, if desired.

Bake at 350° for 8 to 10 minutes or
until lightly browned. Remove to wire
racks to cool. Yield: 5 dozen.

Eggnog Logs

Enjoy the mellow flavor of eggnog in this shortbread-textured cookie dipped in Vanilla Frosting.

prep: 33 min.   cook: 12 min. per batch

1   cup butter or margarine, softened
¾   cup sugar
1   large egg
2   teaspoons vanilla extract
1   teaspoon rum flavoring
3   cups all-purpose flour
1   teaspoon ground nutmeg
Vanilla Frosting
¾   cup chopped pecans, toasted

Beat butter at medium speed with an electric mixer until creamy; gradually add sugar, beating well. Add egg and flavorings, mixing well.

Combine flour and nutmeg; gradually add to butter mixture, mixing well.

Divide dough into 10 portions. Roll each portion into a 15-inch-long rope; cut each rope into 5 (3-inch) logs. Place 2 inches apart on ungreased baking sheets.

Bake at 350° for 10 to 12 minutes. Remove to wire racks to cool.

Dip log ends into Vanilla Frosting; roll logs in pecans. Yield: 50 cookies.

Vanilla Frosting

prep: 8 min.

¼   cup butter or margarine, softened
2   cups sifted powdered sugar
2   tablespoons milk
1   teaspoon vanilla extract

Beat butter at medium speed with an electric mixer until creamy. Add sugar and milk alternately, beating after each addition. Add vanilla; beat until smooth and mixture is spreading consistency. Yield: about 1 cup.

Cherry Crowns

prep: 20 min.   cook: 15 min. per batch
other: 1 hr.

1   cup butter or margarine, softened
1   (3-ounce) package cream cheese, softened
1   cup sugar
1   large egg, separated
1   teaspoon almond extract
2½   cups all-purpose flour
1   cup finely ground blanched almonds
30   red candied cherries, halved

Beat butter and cream cheese at medium speed with an electric mixer until creamy; gradually add sugar, beating well. Add egg yolk and almond extract, mixing well; gradually stir in flour. Cover and chill 1 hour.

Shape dough into 1-inch balls; dip tops of balls into lightly beaten egg white and then into almonds. Place 2 inches apart on lightly greased baking sheets. Press a cherry half in center of each ball.

Bake at 350° for 15 minutes. Remove to wire racks to cool. Yield: 5 dozen.

Peppermint Pats

prep: 11 min.   cook: 10 min. per batch
other: 2 hrs.

¾   cup butter or margarine, softened
¼   cup sugar
1   large egg
1   teaspoon vanilla extract
1   teaspoon peppermint extract
2   cups all-purpose flour
½   cup finely crushed hard peppermint candy
Red decorator sugar crystals

pretty presentation

• Package soft, chewy cookies in breathable containers, such as cardboard bakery boxes. For a personal touch, collect Chinese take-out boxes, and decorate them with rubber stamps.

• Other creative containers for soft, chewy cookies include hatboxes, shoe boxes, Shaker boxes, or produce crates. Place wax paper between each layer of cookies. If packaging cookies in crates, first wrap them in plastic wrap.

Beat butter at high speed with an electric mixer until soft and creamy. Gradually add ¼ cup sugar, beating well. Add egg, beating well. Stir in flavorings. Gradually add flour; mix well. Stir in crushed candy.

Shape dough into 2 (12-inch) logs, and roll in sugar crystals; wrap logs in parchment paper, and freeze until firm.

Slice logs into ½-inch-thick slices, and place on ungreased baking sheets.

Bake at 350° for 8 to 10 minutes. Remove immediately to wire racks to cool. Yield: 4 dozen.

Sugar-Coated Chocolate Cookies

big batch

prep: 35 min.   cook: 10 min. per batch

other: 2 hrs.

½ cup butter or margarine
3   (1-ounce) unsweetened chocolate
     baking squares
2   cups granulated sugar
2   cups all-purpose flour
2   teaspoons baking powder
3   large eggs, lightly beaten
2   teaspoons vanilla extract
¾ cup sifted powdered sugar

Melt butter and chocolate in a heavy saucepan over low heat.

Combine granulated sugar, flour, and baking powder in a large mixing bowl. Add chocolate mixture, eggs, and vanilla; beat at medium speed with an electric mixer until blended. (Mixture will be very thin.) Cover and chill at least 2 hours.

Shape dough into 1-inch balls, and roll balls in powdered sugar. Place 2 inches apart on lightly greased baking sheets.

Bake at 375° for 10 minutes. Remove to wire racks to cool. Yield: 6½ dozen.

Easy Chocolate Chewies

This is the easiest chocolate cookie recipe around. The cookie tops take on a cracked appearance during baking.

prep: 22 min.   cook: 10 min. per batch

1   (18.25-ounce) package devil's food
     cake mix
½ cup shortening
2   large eggs, lightly beaten
1   tablespoon water
½ cup sifted powdered sugar

Combine first 4 ingredients in a large bowl. Beat at medium speed with an electric mixer just until smooth.

Shape dough into 1-inch balls; roll in powdered sugar. Place balls 2 inches apart on lightly greased baking sheets.

Bake at 375° for 10 minutes. Cool on pans about 10 minutes. Remove to wire racks to cool completely. Yield: 4 dozen.

Chocolate Crunch Cookies

quick & easy

prep: 14 min.   cook: 12 min. per batch

1   large egg, lightly beaten
1   (18.25-ounce) package German
     chocolate cake mix
½ cup butter or margarine, melted
1   cup crisp rice cereal

Combine first 3 ingredients, stirring well. Stir in cereal.

Shape mixture into 1-inch balls; place on lightly greased baking sheets. Dip a fork in flour, and flatten cookies in a crisscross pattern.

Bake at 350° for 10 to 12 minutes. Cool slightly on pans; remove to wire racks to cool completely. Yield: 4 dozen.

Chocolate-Mint Pillows

prep: 25 min.   cook: 25 min.

other: 2 hrs., 15 min.

1   (8-ounce) package cream cheese,
     softened
⅔ cup butter or margarine, softened
2½ cups all-purpose flour
½ cup sifted powdered sugar
2   (4.67-ounce) packages chocolate
     mints (we tested with Andes)
1   tablespoon plus 1 teaspoon
     whipping cream

Beat cream cheese and butter at medium speed with an electric mixer until creamy. Gradually add flour and sugar, beating until blended. Divide dough in half; wrap in parchment paper, and chill thoroughly.

Working with 1 portion of dough at a time, roll dough between 2 sheets of parchment paper into an 18- x 8-inch rectangle. Remove top sheet of parchment paper. Cut dough into 18 (4- x 2-inch) rectangles. Place a mint close to 1 end of each rectangle of dough. Fold dough over to enclose mint and form a small pillow.

Seal edges of dough securely with a fork. Repeat procedure with remaining dough. Place on ungreased baking sheets.

Bake at 375° for 12 to 14 minutes. Remove to wire racks to cool.

Combine remaining 20 mints and whipping cream in top of a double boiler; bring water to a boil. Reduce heat to low; cook until candy melts and mixture is smooth, stirring frequently.

Spoon mint mixture into a zip-top plastic bag or a decorating bag fitted with a No. 2 round tip; seal bag. If using a zip-top bag, snip a tiny hole in 1 corner, using scissors. Drizzle melted chocolate mixture over cookies. Yield: 3 dozen.

Chocolate-Caramel Thumbprints

prep: 23 min. cook: 14 min. other: 1 hr., 2 min.

½   cup butter or margarine, softened
½   cup sugar
2   (1-ounce) semisweet chocolate
      baking squares, melted
1   egg yolk
2   teaspoons vanilla extract
1¼ cups all-purpose flour
¼   teaspoon baking soda
¼   teaspoon salt
¾   cup very finely chopped pecans
16   caramels (we tested with Brach's)
2½ tablespoons whipping cream
⅔   cup semisweet chocolate morsels
2   teaspoons shortening

Beat butter at medium speed with an electric mixer until creamy; gradually add sugar, beating well. Add melted chocolate, egg yolk, and vanilla, beating until blended. Stir together flour, soda, and salt; add to butter mixture, beating well. Cover and chill 1 hour.

Shape dough into 1-inch balls; roll balls in pecans. Place balls 1 inch apart on greased baking sheets. Press thumb gently into center of each ball, leaving an indentation.

Bake at 350° for 12 minutes or until set. Combine caramels and cream in top of a double boiler over simmering water. Cook over medium-low heat, stirring constantly, until caramels melt and mixture is smooth.

Remove cookies from oven; cool slightly, and press center of each cookie again. Quickly spoon ¾ teaspoon caramel mixture into center of each cookie. Remove to wire racks to cool.

Place morsels and shortening in a zip-top freezer bag; seal. Microwave at HIGH 1 to 1½ minutes; squeeze bag until chocolate melts. Snip a tiny hole in 1 corner of bag; drizzle over cooled cookies. Yield: about 2½ dozen.

Gooey caramel centers guarantee these treats will disappear quickly from the platter.

Chocolate-Caramel
Thumbprints

Rum Balls

Rum Balls

prep: 28 min.

1   (12-ounce) package vanilla wafers
1   (16-ounce) package pecan pieces
½   cup honey
⅓   cup bourbon
⅓   cup dark rum
¼   cup vanilla wafer crumbs or ⅓ cup
     powdered sugar

Process vanilla wafers in food processor until crumbs are fine. Transfer to a large bowl. Process pecans in food processor until finely chopped. Stir into vanilla wafer crumbs. Stir in honey, bourbon, and rum.

Shape dough into 1-inch balls, and roll in ¼ cup vanilla wafer crumbs. Place in an airtight container; store in refrigerator up to 1 week. Yield: 6 dozen.

Snowballs

quick & easy
prep: 18 min.

2¼ cups cream-filled chocolate
     sandwich cookie crumbs
1   cup toasted, finely chopped pecans
1½ cups sifted powdered sugar,
     divided
⅓   cup flaked coconut
¼   cup light corn syrup
¼   cup strawberry preserves

Stir together cookie crumbs, pecans, ¾ cup powdered sugar, and coconut in a bowl. Stir in corn syrup and preserves.

Shape mixture into balls, using 1 level tablespoon of mixture for each. Roll balls in remaining ¾ cup powdered sugar; roll again to coat well. Store in an airtight container up to 4 days. Yield: 28 cookies.

Brown Sugar Shortbread

Brown Sugar Shortbread

editor's favorite
prep: 10 min.   cook: 12 min. per batch
other: 35 min.

1   cup butter, softened
½   cup firmly packed dark brown
     sugar
2   cups all-purpose flour
2   to 3 tablespoons white sparkling
     sugar

Beat butter at medium speed with an electric mixer until creamy; gradually add brown sugar, beating until light and fluffy. Gradually add flour, beating at low speed until smooth. Cover and chill 30 minutes.

Roll dough to ¼-inch thickness on a lightly floured surface. Cut with a 2-inch tree-shaped cutter; place 1 inch apart on lightly greased baking sheets. Sprinkle evenly with sparkling sugar.

Bake at 375° for 10 to 12 minutes or until edges are golden; cool on pans on wire racks 5 minutes. Remove to wire racks to cool completely. Yield: 1½ dozen.

Cinnamon-Pecan Icebox Cookies

You can freeze this dough up to a month. Bake a little or a lot at a time when you need it.

freezer-friendly • make-ahead
prep: 23 min.   cook: 12 min. per batch
other: 2 hrs.

1   cup butter or margarine, softened
¾   cup granulated sugar
¼   cup firmly packed brown sugar
1   large egg
1   teaspoon vanilla extract
2¼ cups all-purpose flour
1½ teaspoons baking powder
½   teaspoon salt
1   cup finely chopped pecans
¼   cup granulated sugar
1½ teaspoons ground cinnamon

Beat butter at medium speed with an electric mixer until creamy; gradually add ¾ cup granulated sugar and ¼ cup brown sugar, beating well. Add egg and vanilla, beating well.

Combine flour, baking powder, and salt; add to creamed mixture, beating well. Stir in pecans. Cover and chill dough 2 hours. Shape into 2 (6- x 2½-inch) rolls. Wrap rolls in parchment paper, and freeze until firm.

Combine ¼ cup granulated sugar and cinnamon; stir well. Unwrap dough, and roll in sugar mixture. Slice frozen dough into ¼-inch-thick slices; place on ungreased baking sheets.

Bake at 350° for 12 minutes or until golden. Remove to wire racks to cool. Yield: 4 dozen.

Brown Sugar-Pecan Cookies

prep: 30 min.   cook: 12 min. per batch
other: 30 min.

1   cup butter or margarine, softened
½   cup granulated sugar
½   cup firmly packed brown sugar
1   large egg
1   teaspoon vanilla extract
2   cups all-purpose flour
½   teaspoon baking soda
¼   teaspoon salt
½   cup finely chopped pecans
Brown Sugar Frosting
60   pecan halves (about ⅔ cup)

Beat butter at medium speed with an electric mixer until creamy; gradually add sugars, beating well. Add egg and vanilla; beat well.

Combine flour, soda, and salt; gradually add to butter mixture, beating well. Stir in chopped pecans. Cover and chill at least 30 minutes.

Shape dough into 1-inch balls. Place 2 inches apart on ungreased baking sheets.

Bake at 350° for 10 to 12 minutes. Remove to wire racks to cool. Spread about 1 teaspoon Brown Sugar Frosting on each cookie, and top with a pecan half. Yield: 5 dozen.

Brown Sugar Frosting

prep: 8 min.   cook: 10 min.

1   cup firmly packed brown sugar
½   cup half-and-half
1   tablespoon butter or margarine
1½ to 1⅔ cups sifted powdered sugar

Combine brown sugar and half-and-half in a saucepan. Cook over medium heat, stirring constantly, until mixture comes to a boil; boil 4 minutes. Remove from heat. Stir in butter.

Brown Sugar-
Pecan Cookies

Add 1½ cups powdered sugar; beat at medium speed with an electric mixer until smooth. Gradually add enough remaining powdered sugar to make desired spreading consistency. Yield: 1⅓ cups.

Caramel-Pecan Logs

freezer-friendly

prep: 31 min.   cook: 10 min.   other: 1 hr.

1   (13-ounce) jar marshmallow cream
1   teaspoon vanilla extract
1   to 2 (16-ounce) packages powdered
     sugar, sifted
1   tablespoon milk
2   (14-ounce) packages caramels
     (we tested with Farley)
4   cups chopped pecans, toasted

Stir together marshmallow creme and vanilla in a large bowl. Grease hands with shortening, and gradually knead enough powdered sugar into marshmallow cream mixture until consistency is stiff.

Divide mixture into 4 portions. Shape each portion into a 6-inch log. Wrap in plastic wrap, and freeze 1 hour. (Logs should be hard.)

Combine milk and caramels in a large heavy skillet; cook over medium-low heat until caramels melt and mixture is smooth, stirring often.

Dip each log into caramel mixture; working quickly, roll in pecans, and wrap in plastic wrap. Store in refrigerator or freeze up to 1 month. To serve, cut into ¼-inch slices. Yield: 4 (6-inch) logs.

Pecan Crescent Cookies

prep: 16 min.   cook: 30 min. per batch
other: 2 hrs.

1   cup butter or margarine, cut up
2   cups all-purpose flour
1   cup cottage cheese
¼   cup butter or margarine, melted
1½   cups firmly packed brown sugar
1   cup chopped pecans

Cut 1 cup butter into flour with a pastry blender until crumbly. Stir in cheese. Divide dough into thirds; wrap portions separately in plastic wrap. Chill 2 hours. Roll each portion into a 10-inch circle on a well-floured surface. Brush with butter; sprinkle with brown sugar. Top with pecans. Lightly press sugar and pecans into dough with a rolling pin.

Cut each circle into quarters. Cut each quarter into 4 wedges, and roll up, starting with long end; place, point sides down, on ungreased baking sheets.

Bake at 350° for 25 to 30 minutes or until lightly browned. Remove immediately to wire racks to cool. Yield: 4 dozen.

Swedish Gingersnaps

big batch

prep: 26 min.   cook: 10 min. per batch
other: 2 hrs.

1½   cups butter or margarine, softened
1½   cups sugar
1¼   cups molasses
2   large eggs
2   teaspoons grated orange rind
7   cups all-purpose flour
2   teaspoons baking soda
1   tablespoon ground ginger
1   tablespoon ground cinnamon
2   teaspoons ground cloves
½   teaspoon ground cardamom

Beat butter at medium speed with an electric mixer until creamy; gradually add sugar, beating well. Add molasses, eggs, and orange rind; mix well.

Combine flour and next 5 ingredients; mix well. Gradually add to creamed mixture, mixing until smooth after each addition. Divide dough into 4 equal portions; wrap each portion in plastic wrap, and chill at least 2 hours.

Roll 1 portion of dough (dough will be soft) to ⅛-inch thickness on a well-floured surface; keep remaining dough chilled. Cut with 2- to 3-inch Christmas cookie cutters; place on lightly greased baking sheets.

Bake at 350° for 8 to 10 minutes. Remove to wire racks to cool. Repeat procedure with remaining dough. Yield: about 13½ dozen.

Cranberry-Caramel Bars

prep: 20 min.   cook: 43 min.

1   cup fresh cranberries
2   tablespoons granulated sugar
2⅓   cups all-purpose flour, divided
½   teaspoon baking soda
2   cups regular oats, uncooked
½   cup granulated sugar
½   cup firmly packed light brown
     sugar
1   cup butter or margarine, melted
1   (10-ounce) package dried chopped
     dates
¾   cup chopped pecans
1   (12.25-ounce) jar caramel topping

Stir together cranberries and 2 tablespoons granulated sugar in a small bowl; set aside.

Combine 2 cups flour and next 4 ingredients; stir in melted butter until crumbly. Reserve 1 cup flour mixture.

Press remaining mixture into bottom of a lightly greased 13- x 9-inch baking dish.

Bake at 350° for 18 minutes. Sprinkle with dates, pecans, and cranberry mixture. Stir together caramel sauce and remaining ⅓ cup flour; spoon over cranberries. Sprinkle with reserved 1 cup flour mixture. Bake 25 more minutes or until lightly browned. Cool completely in dish on a wire rack. Cut into bars. Yield: 2 dozen.

Peanut Butter Bars

prep: 9 min.   cook: 40 min.

1   (18.25-ounce) package yellow cake
     mix
1   cup chunky peanut butter
½   cup butter, melted
2   large eggs
1   cup (6 ounces) semisweet chocolate
     morsels
1   (14-ounce) can sweetened
     condensed milk

Combine first 4 ingredients in a large bowl. Beat at medium speed with an electric mixer 1 to 2 minutes.

Press half of mixture into bottom of an ungreased 13- x 9-inch pan.

Bake at 350° for 10 minutes. Remove from oven; sprinkle with chocolate morsels, and drizzle with condensed milk. Sprinkle with remaining cake mix mixture.

Bake at 350° for 30 more minutes. Cool completely in pan on a wire rack. Cut into bars. Yield: 2 dozen.

Mississippi Mud Brownies

prep: 12 min.   cook: 35 min.

4   (1-ounce) unsweetened chocolate
       baking squares
1   cup butter or margarine
2   cups granulated sugar
1   cup all-purpose flour
⅛   teaspoon salt
4   large eggs, lightly beaten
1   cup chopped pecans
2   (1-ounce) unsweetened chocolate
       baking squares
½   cup evaporated milk
½   cup butter or margarine
½   teaspoon vanilla extract
4½ to 5 cups sifted powdered sugar
3   cups miniature marshmallows

Combine 4 chocolate squares and 1 cup
butter in a large saucepan; cook over low
heat, stirring until chocolate and butter
melt. Remove from heat.

Combine 2 cups granulated sugar,
flour, and salt; add to melted chocolate
mixture. Add eggs and pecans; stir until
blended.

Spoon batter into a lightly greased and
floured 13- x 9-inch pan. Bake at 350°
for 20 to 25 minutes or until a wooden
pick inserted in center comes out clean.

Meanwhile, combine 2 chocolate
squares, milk, and ½ cup butter in a
heavy saucepan. Cook over low heat,
stirring often, until chocolate and butter
melt. Remove from heat. Transfer to a
medium bowl. Stir in vanilla. Gradually
add powdered sugar, beating at low
speed with an electric mixer until frosting is smooth.

Sprinkle marshmallows evenly over
warm brownies. Quickly pour frosting
over marshmallows, spreading evenly.
Cool completely in pan on a wire rack.
Cut into bars. Yield: 2 dozen.

Mississippi Mud Brownies

the foil fix

Here's the secret to precision-cut brownies.

• Grease the pan; then line it with a long piece of aluminum foil, allowing the foil to extend
2 inches beyond both ends of the pan. Grease the foil.

• Add the batter; bake and cool according to the recipe.

• Once the brownies are cool, lift the foil with the uncut brownies out of the pan. Invert and peel
off the foil; then turn the brownies right side up.

• Place on a large cutting board; cut into bars or squares using a sharp knife.

Peppermint Brownies

prep: 9 min.   cook: 23 min.

other: 2 hrs., 15 min.

4   large eggs
2   cups sugar
1   cup all-purpose flour
1   cup cocoa
1   cup butter or margarine,
      melted
1   teaspoon vanilla extract
½   teaspoon peppermint extract
Mint Cream Frosting
3   (1-ounce) unsweetened chocolate
      baking squares
3   tablespoons butter or margarine

Beat eggs with a wire whisk in a large bowl. Add sugar, and stir well. Combine flour and cocoa; gradually stir into egg mixture. Stir in 1 cup melted butter and flavorings.

Pour batter into a lightly greased 15- x 10-inch jellyroll pan; bake at 350° for 15 to 18 minutes or until a wooden pick inserted in center comes out clean. Cool in pan on a wire rack.

Spread Mint Cream Frosting over brownie layer; freeze 15 minutes. Melt 3 chocolate squares and 3 tablespoons butter in a heavy saucepan over low heat, stirring constantly, until melted. Spread over frosting with a pastry brush. Chill until firm; cut into squares. Store in refrigerator. Yield: 2 dozen.

Mint Cream Frosting

prep: 6 min.

¼   cup butter or margarine,
      softened
2¾   cups sifted powdered sugar
2   to 3 tablespoons milk
½   teaspoon peppermint extract
3   or 4 drops of green liquid food
      coloring

Beat butter at medium speed with an electric mixer; gradually add powdered sugar, beating after each addition. Add milk, and beat until mixture is spreading consistency. Stir in peppermint extract and food coloring. Yield: about 2 cups.

Cream Cheese-Swirl Brownies

editor's favorite

prep: 24 min.   cook: 40 min.

1   (4-ounce) package sweet baking
      chocolate squares
5   tablespoons butter or margarine,
      divided
½   (8-ounce) package cream cheese,
      softened
¼   cup sifted powdered sugar
3   large eggs, divided
1   tablespoon all-purpose flour
½   teaspoon vanilla extract
½   cup granulated sugar
¼   cup firmly packed brown sugar
½   cup all-purpose flour
½   teaspoon baking powder
¼   teaspoon salt
1   tablespoon Kahlúa or brewed
      coffee

Melt chocolate and 3 tablespoons butter over low heat, stirring constantly. Cool.

Beat remaining 2 tablespoons butter and cream cheese in a medium bowl at medium speed with an electric mixer until creamy. Gradually add powdered sugar, beating until light and fluffy. Stir in 1 egg, 1 tablespoon flour, and vanilla. Set aside.

Beat remaining 2 eggs at medium speed until thick and pale. Gradually add granulated sugar and brown sugar, beating until thickened. Combine ½ cup flour, baking powder, and salt; add to egg mixture, mixing well. Stir in cooled chocolate mixture and liqueur.

Spread half of chocolate batter into a greased 8-inch square pan. Spread with cream cheese mixture; top with remaining chocolate batter. Swirl batter with a knife to create a marbled effect.

Bake at 350° for 35 to 40 minutes. Cool completely in pan on a wire rack; cut brownies into 2-inch squares. Yield: 16 brownies.

Chess Brownies

A box of cake mix makes quick work of these blond brownies studded with pecans and topped with a soft cream cheese layer.

quick & easy

prep: 13 min.   cook: 40 min.

1   cup chopped pecans
½   cup butter, melted
3   large eggs, divided
1   (18.25-ounce) package yellow cake
      mix
1   (8-ounce) package cream cheese,
      softened
1   (16-ounce) package powdered
      sugar

Stir together pecans, butter, 1 egg, and cake mix until blended; press in bottom of a lightly greased 13- x 9-inch pan.

Combine remaining 2 eggs, cream cheese, and powdered sugar in a large mixing bowl; beat at medium speed with an electric mixer until smooth. Pour cream cheese mixture over cake mix layer.

Bake at 325° for 40 minutes or until cheese mixture is set. Cool completely in pan on a wire rack. Cut into squares. Yield: 15 brownies.

Nutty Brownies

Nutty Brownies

prep: 29 min.   cook: 45 min.   other: 1 hr., 10 min.

1   cup quick-cooking oats, uncooked
1¼   cups all-purpose flour, divided
½   cup firmly packed brown sugar
½   cup butter or margarine, melted
¼   teaspoon salt
⅓   cup butter or margarine
2   (1-ounce) unsweetened chocolate
      baking squares
2   large eggs
1   cup granulated sugar
1   teaspoon vanilla extract
¾   cup chopped macadamia nuts
Creamy Frosting
Chocolate-Coated Macadamias

Stir together oats, ½ cup flour, brown sugar, ½ cup butter, and salt. Spread in a greased 9-inch square pan. Bake at 350° for 10 minutes.

Combine ⅓ cup butter and chocolate in a small saucepan; cook over medium-low heat until melted, stirring frequently.

Beat eggs at medium speed with an electric mixer until thick and pale. Add granulated sugar and vanilla; stir well. Stir in melted chocolate mixture, remaining ¾ cup flour, and ¾ cup macadamia nuts. Spread over crust.

Bake at 350° for 25 minutes. Cool completely on a wire rack. Spread Creamy Frosting over brownies. Cut into 16 squares. Top each with a Chocolate-Coated Macadamia. Yield: 16 brownies.

Creamy Frosting

prep: 6 min.

2   cups sifted powdered sugar
¼   cup butter or margarine, softened
1½   tablespoons milk

Beat all ingredients at high speed with an electric mixer until smooth. Yield: 1 cup.

Chocolate-Coated Macadamias

prep: 12 min.   cook: 5 min.

¼   cup semisweet chocolate morsels
16   macadamia nuts

Melt morsels over low heat in a small heavy saucepan, stirring frequently. Remove from heat; cool slightly. Dip each macadamia nut halfway into melted chocolate. Place on parchment paper to dry. Yield: 16 coated nuts.

Frosted Fruitcake Bars

prep: 28 min.   cook: 35 min.   other: 1 hr., 30 min.

¾   cup butter or margarine, softened
⅔   cup firmly packed brown sugar
⅓   cup molasses
3   large eggs
1½   cups all-purpose flour
½   pound candied pineapple, finely
      chopped (about 1¼ cups)
½   pound red and green candied
      cherries, finely chopped (1¼ cups)
1   cup coarsely chopped walnuts
¾   cup golden raisins
¼   cup all-purpose flour
1   teaspoon ground allspice
Caramel Frosting

Beat butter at medium speed with an electric mixer until creamy; gradually add brown sugar, beating well. Beat in molasses and eggs. Stir in 1½ cups flour.

Toss together candied pineapple and next 5 ingredients; stir into batter. (Batter will be thick.) Grease and flour a 13- x 9-inch pan; line with parchment paper, and grease paper. Spread batter in pan.

Bake at 325° for 30 to 35 minutes. Cool completely in pan on a wire rack. Spread warm Caramel Frosting over fruitcake. Let stand 30 minutes. Cut into bars. Yield: 2½ dozen.

Caramel Frosting

prep: 8 min.   cook: 34 min.

6   tablespoons butter or margarine
1½   cups firmly packed brown sugar
¼   cup dark corn syrup
½   cup whipping cream
2½   cups coarsely chopped walnuts

Combine first 3 ingredients in large saucepan. Bring to boil over medium heat, stirring frequently, until sugar dissolves. Cook, without stirring, until reaches hard ball stage (260°). Remove from heat.

Stir in cream and walnuts. Return to heat, and cook just until mixture reaches soft ball stage (240°). Remove from heat, and cool 1 minute before spreading over bars. Yield: 3 cups.

Hermits

prep: 12 min.   cook: 25 min.

1½   cups sugar
½   cup vegetable oil
½   cup molasses
2   large eggs
2½   cups all-purpose flour
1   teaspoon baking soda
½   teaspoon ground cinnamon
½   teaspoon ground nutmeg
½   teaspoon ground cloves
½   teaspoon ground ginger
1   cup raisins

Beat first 3 ingredients in a large mixing bowl at medium speed with an electric mixer until blended. Add eggs, 1 at a time, beating well after each addition.

Combine flour and next 5 ingredients; gradually add to sugar mixture, beating well. Stir in raisins. Spread into a greased 15- x 10-inch jellyroll pan. Bake at 350° for 25 minutes. Cool slightly in pan on a wire rack. Cut into bars. Yield: 32 bars.

Peanutty Clusters

prep: 7 min.   cook: 10 min.

2   cups sugar
1   cup evaporated milk
¼   cup butter or margarine
18   large marshmallows
½   cup (3 ounces) semisweet chocolate
       morsels
½   cup (3 ounces) milk chocolate
       morsels
½   (16-ounce) jar dry-roasted peanuts

Combine first 4 ingredients in a heavy
3-quart saucepan; cook over medium
heat, stirring constantly, about 10 minutes or until a candy thermometer
registers 234°.

Remove from heat; add morsels, and
beat at medium speed with an electric
mixer until morsels melt. Stir in peanuts.

Drop by rounded teaspoonfuls onto
buttered parchment paper; cool. Store in
an airtight container. Yield: 3½ dozen.

fudge factors

Making fudge and some other candies requires cooking the mixture to specific end-point temperatures. A candy thermometer helps you achieve exact temperatures. If you don't have a candy thermometer, these simple tests described below of dropping the candy mixture into cold water will
help you determine doneness.

Stage	Temperature	Test
Thread Stage	223° to 234°	Syrup spins a 2-inch thread when dropped from a metal spoon.
Soft Ball Stage	234° to 240°	In cold water, syrup forms a soft ball that flattens when removed from water.
Firm Ball Stage	242° to 248°	In cold water, syrup forms a firm ball that doesn't flatten when removed from water.
Hard Ball Stage	250° to 268°	Syrup forms a hard, yet pliable, ball when removed from cold water.
Soft Crack Stage	270° to 290°	When dropped into cold water, syrup separates into threads that are hard but not brittle.
Hard Crack Stage	300° to 310°	When dropped into cold water, syrup separates into threads that are hard and brittle.
Caramel Stage	310° to 340°	Syrup will be honey-colored when spooned onto a white plate. The longer it cooks, the darker it becomes.

Chocolate Fudge

prep: 20 min.   cook: 25 min.

1   tablespoon butter or margarine
4½ cups sugar
1   (12-ounce) can evaporated milk
2   tablespoons butter or margarine
¼   teaspoon salt
2   cups (12 ounces) milk chocolate
       morsels
2   cups (12 ounces) semisweet
       chocolate morsels
1   (13-ounce) jar marshmallow cream
1   teaspoon vanilla extract
2   cups chopped pecans, toasted

Butter a large heavy saucepan with
1 tablespoon butter. Stir together sugar
and next 3 ingredients in pan.

Cook over medium heat, stirring constantly, until sugar dissolves and mixture
comes to a boil.

Cook, covered, 2 to 3 minutes to wash
down sugar crystals from sides of pan.
Uncover and cook, without stirring, until
mixture reaches soft ball stage or a
candy thermometer registers 236°.
Remove from heat.

Stir together milk mixture, milk chocolate morsels, semisweet chocolate morsels,
and marshmallow cream in a large mixing bowl; beat at medium speed with an
electric mixer until smooth. Add vanilla;
beat until mixture thickens and begins to
lose its gloss (about 10 minutes). Stir in
pecans. Quickly pour into a buttered 13-
x 9-inch dish. Cool completely on a wire
rack. Cut into squares. Yield: 5 pounds.

Buttermilk Fudge

editor's favorite • quick & easy
prep: 10 min.   cook: 18 min.

2   cups sugar
1   cup buttermilk
½   cup butter
2   tablespoons light corn syrup
1   teaspoon baking soda
¾   cup chopped pecans, toasted
       (optional)
1   teaspoon vanilla extract

Butter sides of a heavy 4-quart saucepan;
add sugar and next 4 ingredients.

Cook over medium heat, stirring constantly, 18 minutes or until candy
thermometer registers 236°. Remove
from heat, and cool, undisturbed, until

temperature drops to 180° (about 15 minutes).

Add pecans, if desired, and vanilla; beat with a wooden spoon until mixture thickens and begins to lose its gloss (about 5 minutes). Quickly pour into a buttered 9- x 5-inch loafpan. Cool completely in pan on wire rack. Cut into squares. Yield: 3 dozen squares (1¼ pounds).

Stained-Glass Divinity

prep: 18 min. cook: 25 min.

2½ cups sugar
½ cup light corn syrup
½ cup water
2 egg whites
1 teaspoon vanilla extract
½ cup toasted, chopped pecans
2 (0.9-ounce) rolls multicolored hard candies, broken into pieces

Combine first 3 ingredients in a large saucepan or Dutch oven; cook over low heat, stirring constantly, until sugar dissolves. Cover and cook over medium heat 2 minutes to wash down sugar crystals from sides of pan.

Uncover and cook over medium heat, without stirring, until mixture reaches hard ball stage or a candy thermometer registers 260°.

Beat egg whites in a large bowl at high speed with a heavy-duty electric mixer until stiff peaks form.

Pour hot syrup mixture in a very thin stream over beaten egg whites, beating constantly at high speed. Add syrup more rapidly toward the end. Add vanilla, and continue beating until mixture loses its gloss and holds its shape (about 5 minutes). Quickly stir in pecans.

Spread mixture into a greased 8-inch square pan. Sprinkle immediately with crushed candy. Let stand at room temperature until firm enough to cut. Cut divinity into 1-inch squares. Yield: 1¾ pounds.

Raspberry Divinity

Raspberry-flavored gelatin and almonds make these rosy candies flush with flavor.

prep: 20 min. cook: 25 min.

3 cups sugar
¾ cup water
¾ cup light corn syrup
¼ teaspoon salt
2 egg whites
1 (3-ounce) package raspberry-flavored gelatin
1 cup chopped slivered almonds, toasted

Combine first 4 ingredients in a heavy 3-quart saucepan; cook over low heat, stirring constantly, until sugar dissolves. Cover and cook over medium heat 2 to 3 minutes to wash down sugar crystals from sides of saucepan. Uncover and cook over medium heat, without stirring, until mixture reaches hard ball stage or candy thermometer registers 258°. Remove saucepan from heat.

Beat egg whites in a large mixing bowl at high speed with an electric mixer until foamy. Add raspberry-flavored gelatin, and beat until stiff peaks form. Gradually pour hot syrup mixture in a thin stream over egg whites, beating constantly at high speed until mixture holds its shape (3 to 4 minutes). Quickly stir in almonds.

Drop mixture by rounded teaspoonfuls onto parchment paper. Cool completely. Store in an airtight container. Yield: 3 dozen.

Chocolate-Almond Pralines

prep: 18 min. cook: 31 min.

1½ cups slivered almonds, toasted
1½ cups granulated sugar
¾ cup firmly packed brown sugar
½ cup milk
⅓ cup butter
½ cup (3 ounces) semisweet chocolate morsels
1 tablespoon Kahlúa (optional)

Combine first 5 ingredients in a heavy saucepan. Cook over low heat, stirring constantly, until sugars dissolve and butter melts. Cover and cook over medium heat 2 to 3 minutes to wash down sugar crystals from sides of pan. Uncover and cook, stirring constantly, until mixture reaches soft ball stage or candy thermometer registers 238°.

Remove saucepan from heat; stir in chocolate morsels and, if desired, Kahlúa. Beat with a wooden spoon until mixture begins to thicken. Working rapidly, drop by tablespoonfuls onto lightly buttered parchment paper. Let pralines stand until firm. Yield: 2½ dozen.

candy tips

• Make candy on a dry, sunny day. If you must make it on a humid or rainy day, cook the candy until the thermometer registers 1 to 2 degrees higher than the recipe specifies.

• To help control the formation of sugar crystals, butter the sides of the saucepan. Also, stir the candy gently until it comes to a boil and the sugar dissolves.

• When ready to pour, do so quickly and don't scrape the sides of the pan since this may add sugar crystals to the candy. Cool completely before cutting or storing.

Chocolate-Praline Truffles

This truffle mixture is wonderful when shaped into balls and rolled in pecans. It also adds richness to Chocolate Truffle Cake (page 189), spread on the cake layers as a ganache.

prep: 20 min.   cook: 24 min.   other: 4 hrs., 50 min.

1½ cups chopped pecans
¼ cup firmly packed light brown sugar
2 tablespoons whipping cream
3 (4-ounce) semisweet chocolate baking bars, broken into pieces
¼ cup whipping cream
3 tablespoons butter, cut up
2 tablespoons almond liqueur

Stir together first 3 ingredients; spread in a lightly buttered 9-inch round cakepan.

Bake at 350° for 20 minutes or until coating appears slightly crystallized, stirring once. Remove from oven; stir and cool. Set aside.

Microwave chocolate and ¼ cup whipping cream in a microwave-safe bowl at HIGH 1½ minutes, stirring halfway through.

Whisk until chocolate melts and mixture is smooth. (If chocolate doesn't melt completely, microwave and whisk at 15-second intervals until melted.) Whisk in butter and liqueur; let stand 20 minutes.

Beat at medium speed with an electric mixer 3 minutes or until soft peaks form. (Do not overbeat.) Cover and chill at least 4 hours.

Shape mixture into 1-inch balls; roll in pecan mixture. Cover and chill up to 1 week, or freeze up to 1 month. Yield: about 2 dozen.

White Chocolate-Praline Truffles: Substitute 3 (4-ounce) white chocolate baking bars for semisweet chocolate baking bars and almonds for pecans.

Chocolate-Marble Truffles: Prepare 1 recipe each of mixture for Chocolate-Praline Truffles and mixture for White Chocolate-Praline Truffles. Spoon both mixtures into a 13- x 9-inch pan; swirl with a knife. Chill and shape as directed; roll in cream-filled chocolate sandwich cookie crumbs, omitting pecan mixture.

White Chocolate Salties

Stir up a big batch of these sweet yet salty goodies, and you'll be set for a party or gift-giving.

great gift
prep: 5 min.   cook: 13 min.   other: 20 min.

3 (6-ounce) packages white chocolate baking squares
2 tablespoons shortening
4 cups pretzel sticks (about 10 ounces)
1½ cups salted Spanish peanuts

Combine baking squares and shortening in top of a double boiler; bring water to a boil. Reduce heat to low; cook, stirring constantly, until baking squares and shortening melt.

Pour into a large bowl. Add pretzels and peanuts, stirring gently to coat.

Spread into a buttered 15- x 10-inch jellyroll pan. Chill 20 minutes; break into pieces. Store in an airtight container. Yield: 2 pounds.

Easy Roasted Nut Clusters

prep: 16 min.   cook: 24 min.   other: 2 min.

3 cups hazelnuts
3 tablespoons butter or margarine
6 (2-ounce) vanilla bark coating squares
¼ cup semisweet chocolate morsels

Place hazelnuts in an ungreased jellyroll pan. Bake at 350° for 15 minutes.

Rub hazelnuts briskly with a towel to remove skins; discard skins. Coarsely chop hazelnuts. Melt butter in a large skillet over medium heat. Add hazelnuts, and toss to coat. Remove from heat.

Place bark coating in top of a double boiler; bring water to a boil. Reduce heat to low; cook until coating melts. Remove from heat. Cool 2 minutes.

Add hazelnuts, and stir until coated. Gently stir in chocolate morsels, creating a marbled effect.

Drop mixture by heaping tablespoonfuls onto parchment paper. Cool completely. Yield: 3½ dozen.

Millionaires

prep: 22 min.   cook: 11 min.   other: 30 min.

1 (14-ounce) package caramels (we tested with Farley)
2 tablespoons milk
2 cups chopped pecans
2 cups (12 ounces) semisweet chocolate morsels

Combine caramels and milk in a heavy saucepan; cook mixture over medium-low heat, stirring often, until smooth. Stir in pecans, and drop by teaspoonfuls onto buttered baking sheets. Let stand until firm.

Microwave chocolate in a 1-quart microwave-safe bowl at HIGH 1 minute or until melted, stirring once.

Dip caramel candies into melted chocolate, allowing excess to drip; place on buttered baking sheets. Let candy stand until firm. Yield: 34 candies.

Benne Seed Brittle

Benne Seed Brittle

prep: 10 min. cook: 31 min.

2   cups sugar
½   cup light corn syrup
½   cup boiling water
1¼ cups cashews, toasted and coarsely
       chopped
1   (2.5-ounce) jar sesame seeds
       (about ½ cup), toasted
3   tablespoons butter or margarine
1   teaspoon baking soda
1   teaspoon vanilla extract

Combine first 3 ingredients in a heavy saucepan. Cook over medium heat, stirring constantly, until sugar dissolves. Cover and cook over medium heat 3 minutes to wash down sugar crystals from sides of pan. Uncover and cook, stirring occasionally, until mixture reaches hard crack stage or a candy thermometer registers 300°. Remove from heat, and stir in cashews and remaining ingredients.

Working rapidly, pour mixture onto a lightly buttered 15- x 10-inch jellyroll

Toast sesame seeds— often referred to as benne seeds—in a skillet or the oven; watch them closely because they brown quickly.

pan; spread in a thin layer. Cool completely in pan on a wire rack; break into large pieces. Store in airtight container. Yield: 1½ pounds.

best home baking

The tempting aromas of holiday cakes and pies wafting from the kitchen are the source of many fond Christmas memories. The recipes gathered here will fill your senses with delightful scents and tastes of the season.

Lane Cake

prep: 33 min.   cook: 18 min.   other: 30 min.

1   cup butter or margarine, softened
2   cups sugar
3   cups sifted cake flour
1   tablespoon plus 1 teaspoon baking
      powder
¾   cup milk
½   teaspoon vanilla extract
¼   teaspoon almond extract
8   egg whites
Lane Cake Filling
Seven-Minute Frosting

Beat butter at medium speed with an electric mixer until creamy; gradually add sugar, beating well.

Combine flour and baking powder; add to creamed mixture alternately with milk, beginning and ending with flour mixture. Beat at low speed after each addition. Stir in flavorings.

Beat egg whites at high speed until stiff peaks form; fold into batter. Pour into 3 greased and floured 9-inch round cakepans.

Bake at 325° for 18 minutes or until a wooden pick inserted in center comes out clean. Cool in pans on wire racks 10 minutes; remove from pans, and cool completely on wire racks.

Spread Lane Cake Filling between layers and on top of cake. Spread Seven-Minute Frosting on sides of cake. Yield: 1 (3-layer) cake.

Lane Cake Filling

prep: 8 min.   cook: 23 min.   other: 30 min.

½   cup butter or margarine
8   egg yolks
1½   cups sugar
1   cup chopped pecans
1   cup chopped raisins
1   cup flaked coconut
½   cup chopped maraschino cherries
⅓   cup bourbon or sherry

Melt butter in a heavy saucepan over low heat. Add egg yolks and sugar; cook, stirring vigorously, until sugar dissolves and mixture thickens (18 to 20 minutes). Remove from heat; stir in pecans and remaining ingredients. Cool completely. Yield: 3½ cups.

Seven-Minute Frosting

prep: 7 min.   cook: 9 min.

1½   cups sugar
⅓   cup warm water
2   egg whites
1   tablespoon light corn syrup
1   teaspoon vanilla extract

Combine first 4 ingredients in top of a large double boiler; beat at low speed with an electric mixer 30 seconds or until blended.

cake wisdom

• Use shortening to grease cakepans when possible. Oil, butter, or margarine may cause cakes to stick or burn.

• Dust a greased cakepan with flour, tilting to coat the bottom and the sides. Then shake out excess flour. This helps a baked cake come easily out of the pan.

• Use the correct pan size. Recipes suitable for a 10-inch tube pan, which holds 16 cups, won't always fit in a 12- or 13-cup Bundt pan.

• Beat butter and sugar 5 minutes with a heavy-duty stand mixer, 6 minutes with a standard mixer, or 7 minutes with a portable, handheld mixer.

• Eggs should be room temperature when you add them to cake batter. To warm refrigerated eggs safely, run them, still in their shells, under warm water about 30 seconds.

• Preheat your oven 10 minutes before baking, unless otherwise specified.

• Stagger cakepans in the oven for even baking, and don't let pans touch.

• Bake cake layers on the center rack of oven unless the recipe says otherwise.

Place over boiling water; beat constantly at high speed 7 to 9 minutes or until stiff peaks form and temperature reaches 160°. Remove from heat. Add vanilla; beat 2 minutes or until frosting is spreading consistency. Yield: 4½ cups.

Lane Cake

Italian Cream Cake

Italian Cream Cake

This cake is sure to win raves from your family—it did in our Test Kitchens.

editor's favorite

prep: 28 min.   cook: 25 min.   other: 30 min.

½   cup butter or margarine, softened
½   cup shortening
2   cups sugar
5   large eggs, separated
1   tablespoon vanilla extract
2   cups all-purpose flour
1   teaspoon baking soda
1   cup buttermilk
1   cup flaked coconut
Nutty Cream Cheese Frosting
Garnishes: toasted pecan halves, chopped pecans

Beat butter and shortening in a large mixing bowl at medium speed with an electric mixer until creamy; gradually add sugar, beating well. Add egg yolks, 1 at a time, beating until blended after each addition. Add vanilla; beat until blended.

Combine flour and soda; add to butter mixture alternately with buttermilk, beginning and ending with flour mixture. Beat at low speed until blended after each addition. Stir in coconut.

Beat egg whites until stiff peaks form; fold into batter. Pour into 3 greased and floured 9-inch round cakepans.

Bake at 350° for 23 to 25 minutes or until a wooden pick inserted in center comes out clean. Cool layers in pans on wire racks 10 minutes; remove from pans, and cool layers completely on wire racks.

Spread Nutty Cream Cheese Frosting between layers and on top and sides of cake. Garnish, if desired. Yield: 1 (3-layer) cake.

Nutty Cream Cheese Frosting

prep: 8 min.   cook: 10 min.

1   cup chopped pecans
1   (8-ounce) package cream cheese, softened
½   cup butter or margarine, softened
1   tablespoon vanilla extract
1   (16-ounce) package powdered sugar, sifted

Bake pecans in a shallow pan at 350°, stirring occasionally, 5 to 10 minutes or until toasted. Cool.

Beat cream cheese, butter, and vanilla at medium speed with an electric mixer until creamy. Add sugar, beating at low speed until blended. Beat at high speed until smooth; stir in pecans. Yield: 4 cups.

Fresh Coconut Cream Cake

make-ahead
prep: 30 min. cook: 36 min. other: 30 min.

1   cup butter, softened
2   cups sugar
3   large eggs
3   cups all-purpose flour
2   teaspoons baking powder
1   cup milk
1   teaspoon vanilla extract
½   teaspoon butter flavoring
½   cup water
1   tablespoon sugar
Coconut Frosting
3   cups flaked coconut

Beat butter at medium speed with an electric mixer until creamy; gradually add 2 cups sugar, beating well. Add eggs, 1 at a time, beating after each addition.

Combine flour and baking powder; add to butter mixture alternately with milk, beginning and ending with flour mixture. Mix at low speed after each addition until blended. Stir in flavorings. Pour batter into 3 greased and floured 9-inch round cakepans.

Bake at 350° for 25 to 28 minutes or until a wooden pick inserted in center comes out clean. Cool in pans on wire racks 10 minutes; remove from pans, and cool completely on wire racks.

Combine water and 1 tablespoon sugar in a small saucepan; bring to a boil. Reduce heat, and simmer 3 minutes. Spoon sugar mixture over cake layers.

Stack layers, spreading about 1 cup Coconut Frosting between layers, and sprinkling ½ cup coconut on frosting between layers. Spread remaining Coconut Frosting on top and sides of cake, and sprinkle with remaining coconut. Store in refrigerator. Yield: 1 (3-layer) cake.

Coconut Frosting

prep: 6 min.

2   cups whipping cream
½   cup sifted powdered sugar
1   teaspoon vanilla extract
1   teaspoon coconut extract
2   drops of butter flavoring

Combine all ingredients in a medium bowl; beat at medium speed with an electric mixer until soft peaks form. Yield: 4 cups.

Best Carrot Cake

Buttermilk Glaze adds moisture to this carrot cake, while swirls of Cream Cheese Frosting provide a classic finishing touch.

prep: 26 min. cook: 30 min. other: 35 min.

2   cups all-purpose flour
2   teaspoons baking soda
½   teaspoon salt
2   teaspoons ground cinnamon
3   large eggs
2   cups sugar
¾   cup vegetable oil
¾   cup buttermilk
2   teaspoons vanilla extract
2   cups grated carrot
1   (8-ounce) can crushed pineapple, drained
1   (3.5-ounce) can sweetened flaked coconut
1   cup chopped pecans or walnuts
Buttermilk Glaze
Cream Cheese Frosting

Line 3 (9-inch) round cakepans with wax paper; lightly grease and flour wax paper. Set pans aside.

Stir together first 4 ingredients. Beat eggs and next 4 ingredients at medium speed with an electric mixer until smooth. Add flour mixture, beating at low speed until blended. Fold in carrot and next 3 ingredients. Pour batter into prepared cakepans.

Bake at 350° for 25 to 30 minutes or until a wooden pick inserted in center comes out clean.

Drizzle Buttermilk Glaze evenly over layers; cool layers in pans on wire racks 15 minutes. Remove from pans; cool completely on wire racks. Spread Cream Cheese Frosting between layers and on top and sides of cake. Yield: 1 (3-layer) cake.

Buttermilk Glaze

prep: 9 min. cook: 4 min.

1   cup sugar
1½ teaspoons baking soda
½   cup buttermilk
½   cup butter or margarine
1   tablespoon light corn syrup
1   teaspoon vanilla extract

Bring first 5 ingredients to a boil in a large Dutch oven over medium-high heat. Boil, stirring often, 4 minutes. Remove from heat, and stir in vanilla. Yield: 1½ cups.

Cream Cheese Frosting

prep: 6 min.

1   (8-ounce) package cream cheese, softened
1   (3-ounce) package cream cheese, softened
¾   cup butter or margarine, softened
1   (16-ounce) package powdered sugar, sifted
1½ teaspoons vanilla extract

Beat first 3 ingredients at medium speed with an electric mixer until creamy. Add powdered sugar and vanilla; beat until smooth. Yield: 4 cups.

Peppermint Candy Cake

prep: 45 min.　cook: 25 min.　other: 20 min.

⅔　cup shortening

1¾　cups sugar

3　cups sifted cake flour

3½　teaspoons baking powder

½　teaspoon salt

1⅓　cups milk

1　teaspoon vanilla extract

4　egg whites

Peppermint Glaze

1　cup crushed hard peppermint
　　candy (about 36 candies)

Fluffy Frosting

Peppermint sticks (optional)

Round peppermint candies (optional)

Beat shortening at medium speed with an electric mixer until fluffy; gradually add sugar, beating at medium speed 5 to 7 minutes.

Combine flour, baking powder, and salt; add to shortening mixture alternately with milk, beginning and ending with flour mixture. Mix at low speed after each addition until blended. Stir in vanilla.

Beat egg whites at high speed until stiff peaks form. Gently fold into batter. Pour into 3 greased and floured 8-inch round cakepans. Bake at 350° for 25 minutes or until a wooden pick inserted in center comes out clean. Cool in pans on wire racks 10 minutes; remove from pans, and cool 10 minutes on wire racks. Prick warm layers at 1-inch intervals with a fork.

Place 1 layer on a cake plate; pour one-third of Peppermint Glaze over layer, and sprinkle with ¼ cup peppermint candy. Repeat with remaining layers, but don't sprinkle top layer with candy. Frost top and sides with Fluffy Frosting; sprinkle top with remaining peppermint candy. Garnish with additional candies, if desired. Yield: 1 (3-layer) cake.

Peppermint
Candy Cake

Peppermint Christmas candy gives this cake its whimsical charm. Seal candy in a zip-top plastic bag; gently crush with a rolling pin.

Peppermint Glaze

prep: 3 min.　cook: 6 min.

⅓　cup butter or margarine, melted

1　cup sugar

⅓　cup milk

½　teaspoon peppermint extract

Combine all ingredients in a small saucepan. Bring to a boil, stirring constantly, and cook, stirring constantly, 1 minute. Yield: 1 cup.

Fluffy Frosting

prep: 5 min.　cook: 18 min.

1½　cups sugar

½　teaspoon cream of tartar

½　cup water

3　egg whites

1　teaspoon vanilla extract

Combine first 3 ingredients in a saucepan. Cook, stirring constantly, over medium heat until sugar dissolves. Cook, without stirring, to soft ball stage or until candy thermometer registers 240°.

Beat egg whites at high speed with an electric mixer until soft peaks form; continue beating, adding syrup mixture in a heavy stream. Add vanilla; beat until spreading consistency. Yield: 5 cups.

Black Forest Cake

editor's favorite • make-ahead

prep: 25 min.   cook: 35 min.   other: 8½ hrs.

2   cups sifted cake flour
1¼   teaspoons baking powder
¼   teaspoon baking soda
¾   teaspoon salt
2   cups granulated sugar
¾   cup cocoa
½   cup shortening
½   cup sour cream
½   cup milk
⅓   cup Kirsch or other cherry-flavored
        brandy
2   large eggs
2   egg yolks
4   cups whipping cream
⅓   cup sifted powdered sugar
2   tablespoons Kirsch or other cherry-
        flavored brandy
2   (21-ounce) cans cherry pie filling

Grease 2 (9-inch) round cakepans; line bottoms with wax paper. Grease and flour wax paper and sides of pans. Set aside.

Combine first 6 ingredients in a large mixing bowl; stir well. Add shortening and ¼ cup sour cream. Beat at low speed with an electric mixer 30 seconds or until blended. Add remaining ¼ cup sour cream, milk, and ⅓ cup Kirsch. Beat at medium speed 1½ minutes. Add eggs and egg yolks, 1 at a time, beating 20 seconds after each addition. Pour batter into prepared pans.

Bake at 350° for 30 to 35 minutes or until a wooden pick inserted in center comes out clean. Cool in pans on wire racks 10 minutes; remove from pans. Peel off wax paper, and cool layers on wire racks.

Split cake layers in half horizontally to make 4 layers. Position knife blade in food processor bowl. Break 1 cake layer into pieces, and place in processor bowl. Pulse 5 or 6 times or until cake resembles fine crumbs. Set crumbs aside.

Beat whipping cream until foamy; gradually add powdered sugar, beating until soft peaks form. Add 2 tablespoons Kirsch, beating until stiff peaks form. Reserve 1½ cups whipped cream mixture for garnish.

Place 1 cake layer on a cake plate, cut side up; spread with 1 cup whipped cream mixture, and top with 1 cup pie filling. Repeat procedure once, and top with remaining cake layer.

Frost sides and top of cake with whipped cream mixture. Carefully pat cake crumbs generously around sides of frosted cake.

Pipe or spoon reserved 1½ cups whipped cream mixture around top edges of cake; spoon 1 cup pie filling in center. (Reserve any remaining pie filling for another use.) Cover and chill cake 8 hours before serving. Store in refrigerator. Yield: 1 (3-layer) cake.

Black Forest Cake

Chocolate Truffle Cake

Chocolate Truffle Cake

You can freeze the cake layers several weeks ahead; then assemble the cake one or two days before your party.

prep: 34 min.   cook: 20 min.
other: 2 hrs., 30 min.

1   cup butter, softened
1¼ cups sugar
3   large eggs
2   cups sifted cake flour
1   teaspoon baking soda
¼   teaspoon salt
⅓   cup cocoa
1   (8-ounce) container sour cream
2   teaspoons vanilla extract
1   recipe Chocolate-Praline Truffles
      (page 180; omit pecan mixture
      and rolling procedure)
Milk Chocolate-Buttercream Frosting

Beat butter at medium speed with an electric mixer until creamy; gradually add sugar, beating well. Add eggs, 1 at a time, beating until blended after each addition. Combine flour and next 3 ingredients; add to butter mixture alternately with sour cream, beginning and ending with flour mixture. Beat at low speed until blended after each addition. Stir in vanilla. Spread into 3 greased and floured 8-inch round cakepans.

Bake at 350° for 18 to 20 minutes or until a wooden pick inserted in center comes out clean. Cool in pans on wire racks 10 minutes. Remove from pans, and cool completely on wire racks.

Prepare mixture for Chocolate-Praline Truffles; spread a thin layer between cake layers and on top and sides of cake. Cover and chill cake at least 1 hour.

Spread Milk Chocolate-Buttercream Frosting on top and sides of cake. Chill at least 1 hour and up to 2 days. Yield: 1 (3-layer) cake.

Milk Chocolate-Buttercream Frosting

prep: 7 min.   cook: 45 sec.

2   (1.55-ounce) milk chocolate candy
      bars, broken into pieces
¼   cup whipping cream, divided
¾   cup butter, softened
4½ cups sifted powdered sugar
1½ teaspoons vanilla extract

Microwave chocolate and 2 tablespoons whipping cream in a 1-quart microwave-safe bowl at MEDIUM (50% power) 45 seconds. Whisk until chocolate melts and mixture is smooth. (Do not overheat.)

Beat butter and ¾ cup sugar at low speed with an electric mixer until blended. Add remaining sugar alternately with remaining whipping cream; beat at low speed until blended after each addition.

Add chocolate mixture and vanilla. Beat at medium speed until spreading consistency. Yield: about 3 cups.

Black Walnut-Spice Cake

For a milder flavor, substitute English walnuts or pecans for black walnuts.

prep: 35 min.   cook: 25 min.   other: 35 min.

1½ cups boiling water
1   cup chopped black walnuts
½   cup shortening
½   cup butter or margarine, softened
2   cups firmly packed light brown sugar
3   large eggs
3   cups all-purpose flour
1   tablespoon baking powder
Dash of salt
½   teaspoon ground cinnamon
½   teaspoon ground nutmeg
½   teaspoon ground cloves
1   cup milk
Buttery Cinnamon Frosting

Combine boiling water and 1 cup walnuts; let stand 5 minutes. Drain well; set aside.

Beat shortening and butter at medium speed with an electric mixer in a large mixing bowl until creamy; gradually add brown sugar, beating well. Add eggs, 1 at a time, beating until blended after each addition.

Combine flour and next 5 ingredients; add to creamed mixture alternately with milk, beginning and ending with flour mixture. Mix at low speed after each addition just until blended.

Fold in prepared walnuts. Pour batter into 3 greased and floured 9-inch round cakepans.

Bake at 350° for 20 to 25 minutes or until a wooden pick inserted in center comes out clean. Cool in pans on wire racks 10 minutes. Remove from pans, and cool completely on wire racks.

Spread Buttery Cinnamon Frosting between layers and on top and sides of cake. Yield: 1 (3-layer) cake.

Buttery Cinnamon Frosting

prep: 14 min.

1   cup butter or margarine,
      softened
7½ cups sifted powdered sugar,
      divided
1¼ teaspoons ground cinnamon
¼   cup plus 1 tablespoon milk
2½ teaspoons vanilla extract

Beat butter at high speed with an electric mixer until creamy. Combine 2 cups powdered sugar and cinnamon; add to butter, and beat at medium speed until smooth.

Add remaining 5½ cups sugar to creamed mixture alternately with milk, beating well after each addition. Add vanilla; beat until blended. Yield: enough for 1 (3-layer) cake.

Pound Cake with Easy Caramel Frosting

Spread Easy Caramel Frosting on the cake immediately after the frosting has reached the desired spreading consistency, or it will become too stiff.

prep: 32 min.   cook: 1 hr., 20 min.   other: 45 min.

2   cups butter, softened
2⅔   cups sugar
8   large eggs
3½   cups all-purpose flour
½   cup half-and-half
1   teaspoon vanilla extract
Easy Caramel Frosting

Beat butter at medium speed with an electric mixer until creamy. Gradually add sugar, beating at medium speed 5 to 7 minutes. Add eggs, 1 at a time, beating just until yellow disappears.

Add flour to creamed mixture alternately with half-and-half, beginning and ending with flour. Mix at low speed just until blended after each addition. Stir in vanilla. Pour batter into a greased and floured 10-inch tube pan.

Bake at 325° for 1 hour and 15 to 20 minutes. Cool in pan on a wire rack 10 to 15 minutes. Remove from pan, and cool completely on wire rack.

Spread Easy Caramel Frosting on top and sides of cake. Yield: 1 (10-inch) cake.

Easy Caramel Frosting

prep: 7 min.   cook: 5 min.

½   cup butter
1   cup firmly packed brown sugar
¼   cup whipping cream
2½   cups sifted powdered sugar
1   teaspoon vanilla extract

Melt butter in a heavy saucepan. Add brown sugar; cook over low heat, stirring constantly, 1½ to 2 minutes or until sugar dissolves. (Do not boil.) Remove from heat.

Stir in whipping cream. Add powdered sugar and vanilla. Beat at high speed with an electric mixer until frosting is spreading consistency. Yield: enough for 1 (10-inch) cake.

Triple Chocolate Cake

prep: 16 min.   cook: 1 hr.   other: 45 min.

1   (18.25 ounce) package chocolate cake mix (we tested with Duncan Hines)
1   (3.9-ounce) package chocolate instant pudding mix
1   (8-ounce) container sour cream
4   large eggs
½   cup water
½   cup vegetable oil
2   cups (12 ounces) semisweet chocolate morsels
½   cup chopped pecans
Cocoa
Chocolate Glaze

Combine first 6 ingredients in a large bowl; beat for 1 minute until blended. Stir in chocolate morsels and pecans. Spoon batter into a well-greased 12-cup Bundt pan dusted lightly with cocoa.

Bake at 350° for 1 hour or until cake begins to pull away from sides of pan. Cool in pan on a wire rack 15 minutes; remove cake from pan, and cool completely on wire rack. Spoon glaze over top of cake. Yield: 1 (10-inch) cake.

Chocolate Glaze

prep: 5 min.   cook: 4 min.

3   (1-ounce) unsweetened chocolate baking squares, melted
1½   cups sifted powdered sugar
¼   cup hot water
½   cup egg substitute
¼   cup butter or margarine, softened

Combine melted chocolate, sugar, and water; beat at medium speed with an electric mixer until blended. Gradually add egg substitute, and beat until mixture cools. Add butter, 1 tablespoon at a time, beating until blended. Yield: 1¼ cups.

---

high-altitude adjustments

Cakes, more than any other type of baked goods, are affected by the lower air pressure at high altitudes. When baked above 3,000 feet, cakes will not rise properly and may be dry and tough. Use this chart as a guide when baking cakes at high altitudes. In addition, when baking a cake above 3,000 feet in altitude, increase the baking temperature by 25°.

Ingredients	3,000 ft.	5,000 ft.	7,000 ft.	10,000 ft.
Sugar: for each cup, decrease ...	1 to 3 teaspoons	1 to 2 tablespoons	1½ to 3 tablespoons	2 to 3½ tablespoons
Liquid: for each cup, add ...	1 to 2 tablespoons	2 to 3 tablespoons	3 to 4 tablespoons	3 to 4 tablespoons
Baking Powder: for each teaspoon, decrease ...	⅛ teaspoon	⅛ to ¼ teaspoon	¼ teaspoon	¼ to ½ teaspoon

Triple Chocolate Cake

Old South Fruitcake

Old South Fruitcake

prep: 49 min.   cook: 4 hrs.
other: 1 hr., 10 min.

1½ cups butter, softened
1¼ cups firmly packed brown sugar
⅓   cup molasses
7   large eggs, separated
3   cups all-purpose flour
1½ pounds yellow, green, and red
         candied pineapple, chopped
         (about 3¾ cups)
1   pound red and green candied
         cherries, halved (about 2½ cups)
3   cups pecan halves, lightly toasted
1   cup walnuts, coarsely chopped
¾   cup golden raisins
¾   cup raisins
½   cup all-purpose flour
1   teaspoon ground allspice
¼   cup brandy
1   tablespoon powdered sugar
Additional brandy (optional)

Draw a 10-inch circle on a piece of non-recycled brown paper, using a 2-piece tube pan as a guide. Cut out circle; set tube pan insert in center, and draw around inside tube. Cut out smaller circle. Grease paper; set aside. Heavily grease and flour 10-inch tube pan; set aside.

Beat butter at medium speed with an electric mixer until creamy; gradually add brown sugar, beating well. Stir in molasses. Beat egg yolks; alternately add beaten yolks and 3 cups flour to creamed mixture. (Batter will be very thick.)

Combine candied pineapple and next 5 ingredients in a large bowl; sprinkle with ½ cup flour and allspice, stirring to coat well. Stir mixture into batter.

Beat egg whites until stiff peaks form; gradually fold into batter. Spoon batter into prepared pan. Cover pan with 10-inch paper circle, greased side down.

Store this cake in an airtight container for three weeks. Soak it each week with brandy to keep it moist. Then chill so it will slice neatly and easily.

Bake at 250° for 4 hours or until cake tests done. Remove from oven. Discard paper cover. Cool in pan 10 minutes. Loosen cake from sides of tube pan, using a narrow metal spatula; invert pan, and remove cake. Invert cake again onto a wire rack.

Combine ¼ cup brandy and powdered sugar; slowly pour evenly over cake. Cool completely on wire rack.

Wrap cake in brandy-soaked cheesecloth. Store in an airtight container in a cool place 3 weeks. Pour a small amount of brandy over cake each week, if desired. Yield: 1 (10-inch) cake.

Fruitcake Loaves: Spoon batter into 3 greased and floured 8½- x 4½-inch loafpans or 6 greased and floured 6- x 3½-inch miniature loafpans. Bake at 250° for 2½ hours or until cake tests done.

Chocolate Fruitcakes

Reduce the butter to ½ cup and the chocolate to 4 (1-ounce) baking squares to make this rich chocolate fruitcake a little lighter.

prep: 15 min.   cook: 35 min.
other: 8 hrs., 30 min.

1   cup butter or margarine
6   (1-ounce) semisweet chocolate
       baking squares
1¼ cups sugar
3   large eggs
1   cup all-purpose flour
¼   teaspoon salt
1   cup red candied cherries, cut in
       half
1   cup green candied pineapple, cut
       into ½-inch wedges
¾   cup walnut halves
¾   cup pecan halves
Garnish: red candied cherries

Melt butter and chocolate in a heavy saucepan over low heat, stirring often. Remove from heat; cool 15 minutes.

Stir in sugar. Add eggs, 1 at a time, stirring well after each addition. Add flour and salt, stirring until blended. Stir in cherries and next 3 ingredients. Spoon mixture into 4 greased and floured 5- x 3-inch loafpans.

Bake at 350° for 35 minutes or until a wooden pick inserted in center comes out clean. Cool in pans on wire racks 10 minutes. Remove from pans, and cool on wire racks.

Wrap in heavy-duty plastic wrap; chill 8 hours before cutting. Garnish, if desired. Yield: 4 loaves.

Chocolate-Marbled Pound Cake

Gently swirl vanilla and chocolate batters together to create a pretty swirl in each slice.

prep: 27 min.   cook: 1 hr., 12 min.
other: 45 min.

½   cup shortening
½   cup butter, softened
3   cups sugar
5   large eggs
3   cups all-purpose flour
½   teaspoon baking powder
¼   teaspoon salt
1   cup milk
1   teaspoon vanilla extract
1   (1-ounce) unsweetened
       chocolate baking square
1   tablespoon shortening
½   cup chopped pecans

Beat ½ cup shortening and butter at medium speed with an electric mixer about 2 minutes or until creamy. Gradually add sugar, beating mixture at

medium speed 5 to 7 minutes. Add eggs, 1 at a time, beating just until yellow disappears.

Combine flour, baking powder, and salt; add to creamed mixture alternately with milk, beginning and ending with flour mixture. Mix at low speed just until blended after each addition. Stir in vanilla. Reserve 2 cups batter.

Combine chocolate and 1 tablespoon shortening in a small, heavy saucepan; cook over low heat, stirring constantly, until chocolate melts. Add chocolate mixture to reserved 2 cups batter, stirring until blended.

Pour one-third of plain batter into a greased and floured 10-inch tube pan; top with half of chocolate batter. Repeat batter layers, ending with plain batter. Swirl batter with a knife to create a marbled effect; sprinkle with pecans.

Bake at 350° for 1 hour and 10 minutes or until a wooden pick inserted in center comes out clean. Cool in pan on a wire rack 15 minutes. Remove from pan, and cool completely on wire rack. Yield: 1 (10-inch) cake.

Chocolate-Cranberry Roulage

freezer-friendly

prep: 26 min. cook: 14 min. other: 1 hr., 20 min.

4   large eggs
½   cup water
1   (18.25- or 18.5-ounce) package
     Swiss chocolate, devil's food, or
     fudge cake mix
2   to 4 tablespoons cocoa
1   (12-ounce) carton cranberry-orange
     crushed fruit
¾   cup cranberry juice cocktail
2   tablespoons powdered sugar
1½   tablespoons cornstarch
4   to 5 tablespoons crème de cassis
     or other black currant-flavored
     liqueur, divided *
2   cups whipping cream
Cocoa
Garnish: fresh cranberries

Coat 2 (15- x 10-inch) jellyroll pans with cooking spray; line with wax paper, and coat with cooking spray. Set aside.

Beat eggs 5 minutes in a large mixing bowl at medium-high speed with an electric mixer. Add water, beating at low speed until blended. Gradually add cake mix, beating at low speed until moistened. Beat at medium-high speed 2 minutes. Divide batter in half, and spread batter evenly into prepared pans. (Layers will be thin.)

Bake each cake at 350° on the middle rack in separate ovens for 13 minutes or until cake springs back when lightly touched in the center. (If you don't have a double oven, set 1 pan aside and bake after the first one is done.) Sift 1 to 2 tablespoons cocoa in a 15- x 10-inch rectangle on a cloth towel; repeat with second towel. When cakes are done, immediately loosen from sides of pans,

and turn each out onto a prepared towel. Peel off wax paper. Starting at narrow end, roll up each cake and towel together; cool completely on wire racks, seam sides down.

Combine crushed fruit and next 3 ingredients in container of an electric blender or food processor; process until smooth, stopping several times to scrape down sides.

Pour cranberry mixture into a small saucepan; bring to a boil over medium heat, stirring constantly. Boil 1 minute, stirring constantly. Stir in 2 tablespoons crème de cassis. Cool.

Beat whipping cream at medium-high speed with an electric mixer until soft peaks form. Fold in ⅔ cup cranberry mixture; cover and chill the remaining cranberry mixture for garnish.

Unroll cake rolls; brush lightly with remaining 2 to 3 tablespoons crème de cassis. Spread each cake with half of whipped cream mixture. Reroll cakes without towels; place, seam sides down, on a baking sheet. Cover and freeze cakes at least 1 hour or up to 3 months.

Dust cakes with cocoa, and cut into 1- to 2-inch slices. Spoon remaining cranberry mixture evenly onto dessert plates. Top each with a cake slice. Garnish, if desired. Yield: 2 filled cake rolls (8 servings each).

* 4 to 5 tablespoons cranberry juice cocktail may be substituted for crème de cassis.

Chocolate-Cranberry Roulage

Bûche de Noël

To save a little time, you can use 1 (16-ounce) can chocolate fudge frosting in place of the Mocha Buttercream Frosting. Just stir in 1 to 2 tablespoons strongly brewed coffee to add the touch of mocha.

prep: 54 min.   cook: 10 min.   other: 20 min.

Vegetable oil
4   large eggs, separated
¼   cup granulated sugar
1   tablespoon vegetable oil
1   teaspoon almond extract
½   cup granulated sugar
⅔   cup sifted cake flour
1   teaspoon baking powder
¼   teaspoon salt
2   tablespoons powdered sugar
Amaretto Filling
Mocha Buttercream Frosting
Garnishes: chocolate leaves,
       cranberries

Grease bottom and sides of a 15- x 10-inch jellyroll pan with vegetable oil; line with wax paper, and grease and flour wax paper. Set aside.

Beat egg yolks in a large mixing bowl at high speed with an electric mixer until thick and pale. Gradually add ¼ cup granulated sugar, beating constantly. Stir in 1 tablespoon vegetable oil and almond extract.

Beat egg whites at high speed until foamy. Gradually add ½ cup granulated sugar, 1 tablespoon at a time, beating until stiff peaks form. Fold egg white mixture into yolk mixture.

Combine flour, baking powder, and salt; fold into egg mixture, and spread batter evenly into prepared pan.

Bake at 350° for 8 to 10 minutes. Sift powdered sugar in a 15- x 10-inch rectangle on a cloth towel. When cake is done, immediately loosen from sides of pan; turn out onto sugar-coated towel. Peel off wax paper. Starting at narrow end, roll up cake and towel together; cool completely on a wire rack, seam side down.

Unroll cake; spread with Amaretto Filling, and reroll without towel. Place on a serving plate, seam side down.

Cut a 1-inch piece diagonally from 1 end of cake. Position short piece against top center of longer piece, cut side up, to resemble the knot of a tree (see photo above). Spread Mocha Buttercream Frosting over cake roll. Score frosting with fork tines to resemble bark. Garnish, if desired. Yield: 8 servings.

Amaretto Filling

prep: 13 min.   cook: 2 min.

½   teaspoon unflavored gelatin
1   tablespoon cold water
1   tablespoon powdered sugar
1   tablespoon cocoa
½   cup whipping cream
1½   teaspoons almond liqueur

Sprinkle gelatin over cold water in a small saucepan; let stand 1 minute.

Cook over low heat, stirring until gelatin dissolves, about 2 minutes. Set aside.

Combine powdered sugar and cocoa.

Beat whipping cream at low speed with an electric mixer, gradually adding dissolved gelatin. Beat at medium speed until mixture begins to thicken. Add powdered sugar mixture, and beat at high speed until soft peaks form. Stir in almond liqueur. Yield: 1 cup.

Mocha Buttercream Frosting

prep: 5 min.

¼   cup butter or margarine, softened
2½   cups sifted powdered sugar
2½   tablespoons cocoa
2   to 3 tablespoons strongly brewed
       coffee
1   teaspoon vanilla extract

Beat butter at medium speed with an electric mixer until creamy; add powdered sugar, cocoa, 2 tablespoons coffee (at room temperature), and vanilla, beating until blended. Add enough remaining coffee, if necessary, for spreading consistency. Yield: 1¼ cups.

dessert with a French twist

Southerners have a fondness for rolled cakes. They look pretty on a plate, they store easily, and you can garnish them in a number of ways. This traditional French Christmas cake, shaped and decorated to look like a tree log, is filled with a delectable amaretto filling and frosted with silky chocolate buttercream. Be sure to roll the cake as soon as you remove it from the oven and turn it out of the pan. If you let it cool before rolling, it's likely to crack.

Chocolate-Pecan Torte

Chocolate-Pecan Torte

prep: 45 min.　cook: 18 min.　other: 30 min.

4　large eggs, separated
½　cup sugar
⅔　cup all-purpose flour
½　teaspoon baking soda
¼　teaspoon salt
¾　cup ground pecans
⅓　cup cocoa
¼　cup water
1　teaspoon vanilla extract
¼　cup sugar
Chocolate Frosting
¾　cup chopped pecans,
　　　toasted
Rich Chocolate Glaze

Grease bottoms of 2 (9-inch) round cakepans. Line bottoms of pans with wax paper; grease wax paper. Set pans aside.

Beat egg yolks at high speed with an electric mixer; gradually add ½ cup sugar, beating until mixture is thick and pale. Combine flour and next 4 ingredients; add to yolk mixture alternately with water, beginning and ending with flour mixture. Stir in vanilla.

Beat egg whites at high speed with an electric mixer until foamy; gradually add

¼ cup sugar, beating until stiff peaks form. Fold into batter. Pour batter into prepared pans.

Bake at 375° for 16 to 18 minutes or until a wooden pick inserted in center comes out clean. Cool in pans on wire racks 10 minutes; remove from pans, and cool completely on wire racks.

Split layers in half horizontally to make 4 layers. Place 1 layer on a serving plate; spread 1 cup Chocolate Frosting on top of layer. Repeat procedure with second and third layers and 2 additional cups frosting. Top stack with fourth layer. Spread remaining frosting on sides of cake; press chopped pecans into frosting. Spread Rich Chocolate Glaze over top. Yield: 1 (4-layer) cake.

Chocolate Frosting

prep: 7 min.

⅔　cup sifted powdered sugar
⅓　cup cocoa
2　cups whipping cream
1½　teaspoons vanilla extract

Combine sugar and cocoa; gradually stir in cream and vanilla. Beat at low speed with an electric mixer until mixture is blended; then beat at high speed until stiff peaks form. Yield: 3½ cups.

Rich Chocolate Glaze

prep: 3 min.　cook: 5 min.

2　tablespoons cocoa
2　tablespoons water
1　tablespoon butter or margarine
1　cup sifted powdered sugar
¼　teaspoon vanilla extract

Combine first 3 ingredients in a small saucepan; cook over medium heat, stirring constantly, until mixture thickens. Remove from heat; stir in sugar and vanilla. Yield: ⅓ cup.

Coconut-Chocolate-Almond Cheesecake

prep: 38 min.　cook: 1 hr.　other: 8 hrs.

1½　cups chocolate wafer cookie
　　　crumbs (28 to 30 cookies; we
　　　tested with Nabisco)
3　tablespoons sugar
¼　cup butter or margarine,
　　　melted
4　(8-ounce) packages cream cheese,
　　　softened
3　large eggs
1　cup sugar
1　(14-ounce) package sweetened
　　　flaked coconut
1　(11.5-ounce) package milk
　　　chocolate morsels
½　cup slivered almonds, toasted
1　teaspoon vanilla extract
½　cup (3 ounces) semisweet
　　　chocolate morsels
Garnish: toasted chopped almonds

Stir together first 3 ingredients; press mixture into bottom of a 10-inch springform pan. Bake at 350° for 8 minutes. Cool.

Beat cream cheese, eggs, and 1 cup sugar at medium speed with an electric mixer until fluffy.

Stir in coconut and next 3 ingredients. Pour batter into prepared crust.

Bake at 350° for 1 hour. Cool on a wire rack.

Place semisweet chocolate morsels in a zip-top plastic bag; seal. Submerge bag in warm water until morsels melt. Snip a tiny hole in 1 corner of bag; drizzle chocolate over cheesecake.

Cover cheesecake, and chill at least 8 hours. Store in refrigerator up to 5 days, if desired. Remove sides of springform pan when ready to serve. Garnish, if desired. Yield: 1 (10-inch) cheesecake.

Coconut-Chocolate-Almond
Cheesecake

This rich, decadent dessert is the perfect finale to an elegant Christmas dinner.
Sprinkle chopped almonds around the outer edge for a simple yet showy garnish.

Chocolate Crunch Cheesecake

prep: 24 min.   cook: 43 min.
other: 10 hrs., 15 min.

½   cup butter or margarine
1   (1-ounce) semisweet chocolate
     baking square
1½ cups crushed unsalted pretzels
½   cup finely chopped pecans
3   tablespoons sugar
1   (8-ounce) package cream cheese,
     softened
1   (3-ounce) package cream cheese,
     softened
⅔   cup sugar
5   large eggs
8   (1-ounce) semisweet chocolate
     baking squares, melted and
     cooled
⅓   cup whipping cream
2   cups frozen whipped topping,
     thawed
3   (1.55-ounce) milk chocolate
     with crisped rice bars, finely
     chopped
Garnishes: additional milk chocolate
     with crisped rice bars, chocolate
     shavings

Combine butter and 1 ounce chocolate
in a medium saucepan. Cook over
medium-low heat, stirring frequently,
until melted. Remove from heat, and stir
in crushed pretzels, pecans, and 3 tablespoons sugar. Press mixture firmly in
bottom and 2 inches up sides of a
9-inch springform pan. Bake at 350°
for 5 minutes. Cool on a wire rack.

Beat cream cheese at medium speed
with an electric mixer 2 minutes.
Gradually add ⅔ cup sugar, beating
well. Add eggs, 1 at a time, beating just
until blended after each addition. Add
melted chocolate and whipping cream;
beat at low speed until blended. Pour
batter into prepared crust. Bake at 375°
for 35 minutes or until center is almost
set. Cool to room temperature on a wire
rack. Cover and chill 8 hours.

Combine whipped topping and
chopped candy bars, stirring gently.
Spread over cheesecake. Cover and
chill until ready to serve. Remove
sides of pan. Garnish, if desired. Yield:
1 (9-inch) cheesecake.

Caramel-Brownie Cheesecake

prep: 13 min.   cook: 1 hr., 20 min.
other: 6 hrs., 15 min.

1¾ cups vanilla wafer crumbs
⅓   cup butter or margarine, melted
1   (14-ounce) package caramels
1   (5-ounce) can evaporated milk
2   cups coarsely crumbled unfrosted
     brownies *
3   (8-ounce) packages cream cheese,
     softened
1   cup firmly packed light brown sugar
3   large eggs
1   (8-ounce) container sour cream
2   teaspoons vanilla extract
Garnishes: whipped cream, chocolate-
     lined wafer roll cookies

Combine vanilla wafer crumbs and butter, stirring well. Press mixture firmly in
bottom and 2 inches up sides of a 9-inch
springform pan. Bake at 350° for 5 minutes. Cool completely on a wire rack.

Combine caramels and milk in a small
heavy saucepan; cook over low heat, stirring often, until caramels melt. Pour
caramel mixture over crust. Sprinkle
crumbled brownies over caramel.

Beat cream cheese at medium speed
with an electric mixer 2 minutes or until
light and fluffy. Gradually add brown
sugar, mixing well. Add eggs, 1 at a time,
beating just until blended. Stir in sour
cream and vanilla.

Pour batter into prepared crust. Bake
at 350° for 50 to 60 minutes or until
cheesecake is almost set. Remove from
oven, and cool to room temperature on a
wire rack. Cover and chill at least 4 hours.

Remove sides of pan; garnish, if
desired. Yield: 1 (9-inch) cheesecake.

* Buy prepackaged unfrosted brownies
from a bakery, or prepare your favorite
mix; cool and crumble enough to yield
2 cups.

New Orleans Triple Chocolate-Espresso Pecan-Praline Christmas Volcano Cakes

*Insert a chunky praline into each warm-
from-the-oven volcano cake to initiate
the "flow" of molten chocolate.*

prep: 13 min.   cook: 16 min.   other: 3 min.

1½ tablespoons butter, melted
1½ tablespoons unsweetened cocoa
4   (3-ounce) dark chocolate candy
     bars, coarsely chopped (we tested
     with Ghirardelli candy bars [not
     baking bars])
1   cup butter
2   teaspoons vanilla extract
⅔   cup all-purpose flour
¼   cup espresso powder
¾   cup egg substitute
½   cup sugar
12 dark chocolate candies (we tested
     with Dove)
Cocoa
Pecan Pralines or 12 ready-made
     pralines

New Orleans Triple Chocolate-Espresso Pecan-Praline Christmas Volcano Cake

Pecan Pralines

The secret to making these pralines extra yummy is the use of molasses instead of corn syrup. An extra set of hands is helpful when you start dropping the pralines and sprinkling them with toppings because the pralines start to harden quickly.

prep: 8 min.   cook: 13 min.   other: 19 min.

1½ cups firmly packed light brown
     sugar
½   cup heavy whipping cream
1   tablespoon light molasses
⅛   teaspoon salt
2   tablespoons butter or margarine
1   cup pecan pieces
½   teaspoon vanilla extract
Assorted holiday sprinkles

Bring first 4 ingredients to a boil in a 2-quart heavy saucepan over medium heat, stirring constantly. Wash sugar crystals from sides of pan with a small brush dipped in hot water. Insert a candy thermometer into mixture. Cook, stirring occasionally, until thermometer registers 236° (soft ball stage).

Remove from heat; add butter (do not stir). Let candy stand until thermometer reaches 150°. Stir in pecans and vanilla. Using a wooden spoon, stir candy constantly until it begins to thicken and lose its gloss.

Quickly drop by heaping teaspoonfuls onto wax paper; quickly sprinkle with holiday sprinkles. Let stand until firm. Yield: 1½ dozen (1 pound).

Brush 12 (½-cup-capacity) muffin cups with 1½ tablespoons melted butter. Sprinkle evenly with 1½ tablespoons cocoa, shaking out excess; set aside.

Place chocolate and 1 cup butter in a medium-size heavy saucepan. Cook over low heat, stirring often, until chocolate and butter melt. Remove from heat; stir in vanilla. Combine flour and espresso powder; stir into chocolate mixture.

Beat egg substitute and sugar in a small bowl at medium speed with an electric mixer 5 minutes or until slightly thickened. Gradually whisk one-fourth of chocolate mixture into egg mixture; add to remaining chocolate mixture in pan, whisking constantly.

Place 1 chocolate candy in center of each muffin cup. Pour batter into muffin cups, filling three-fourths full. Bake at 400° for 11 minutes or just until edges of cakes spring back when lightly touched but centers are still very soft. Let stand 3 minutes; quickly loosen with a small sharp knife, and invert cakes onto a baking sheet. Carefully transfer cakes to dessert plates using a spatula. Lightly sift cocoa over cakes, and insert 1 Pecan Praline into the top of each cake. Yield: 12 servings.

Reheating Note: Leftover volcano cakes reheat nicely on HIGH in the microwave; it takes only 20 to 30 seconds per cake.

Apple-Bourbon Pie

prep: 33 min.   cook: 1 hr.   other: 2 hrs.

½   cup raisins
½   cup bourbon
3   pounds cooking apples
¾   cup sugar
2   tablespoons all-purpose flour
1   teaspoon ground cinnamon
¼   teaspoon salt
⅛   teaspoon ground nutmeg
½   cup chopped pecans or walnuts,
       toasted
1   (15-ounce) package refrigerated
       piecrusts, divided
2   teaspoons apricot preserves, melted
1   tablespoon buttermilk
1   tablespoon sugar

Combine raisins and bourbon, and let soak at least 2 hours.

Peel apples, and cut into ½-inch slices; arrange apple slices in a steamer basket over boiling water. Cover and steam 10 minutes or until apple slices are tender.

Combine ¾ cup sugar and next 4 ingredients in a large bowl; stir in apple slices, soaked raisins, and pecans.

Fit 1 piecrust into a 9-inch pieplate according to package directions; brush preserves over bottom. Spoon apple mixture into piecrust.

Unroll remaining piecrust; cut with a 3-inch leaf-shaped cutter. Mark veins on leaves with a pastry wheel or sharp knife. Arrange pastry leaves over apple mixture; brush leaves with buttermilk, and sprinkle pie with 1 tablespoon sugar.

Bake at 450° on lower rack of oven 15 minutes. Shield edges of pie with strips of aluminum foil to prevent excessive browning. Bake at 350° for 30 to 35 more minutes. Cool on a wire rack. Yield: 1 (9-inch) pie.

Festive Cranberry Pie

A twist of the wrist while weaving the pastry strips into a lattice atop this pie creates a stunning visual treat.

**prep: 20 min.   cook: 58 min.
other: 2 hrs., 45 min.**

¾   cup sugar
¾   cup light corn syrup
½   cup water
2   tablespoons grated orange rind
1   tablespoon cornstarch
3   cups fresh cranberries
½   cup raisins
½   cup coarsely chopped pecans
2   tablespoons butter or margarine
Pastry for double-crust 9-inch pie
2   teaspoons sugar

Combine first 5 ingredients in a large saucepan; bring to a boil, stirring constantly. Stir in cranberries, raisins, and pecans. Cover, reduce heat, and cook 7 to 10 minutes or until cranberry skins pop. Remove from heat, and stir in butter; cool completely without stirring.

Roll half of pastry to ⅛-inch thickness on a lightly floured surface; place in a 9-inch pieplate. Spoon filling into pastry shell.

Roll remaining pastry to ¼-inch thickness; cut into 1-inch strips. Weave strips over filling in a lattice fashion, twisting each strip while weaving. Press ends of strips into rim of crust; flute edge. Sprinkle pie with 2 teaspoons sugar. Bake at 400° for 40 minutes. Cool on a wire rack. Yield: 1 (9-inch) pie.

Cranberry Surprise Pie

The surprise? You won't have to worry about rolling pastry for this pie. The "crust" is spooned over the top and bakes until golden, like a cobbler. Spoon it into bowls for serving.

prep: 13 min.   cook: 1 hr.

3   cups fresh or frozen coarsely
       chopped cranberries
½   cup fresh or frozen blueberries
½   cup chopped pecans or sliced
       almonds
⅓   cup flaked coconut
1½ cups sugar, divided
1   large egg
½   cup all-purpose flour
6   tablespoons butter or margarine,
       melted

Combine cranberries and blueberries. Spoon cranberry mixture into a lightly greased 9-inch pieplate.

Combine pecans and coconut, and sprinkle over cranberry mixture. Top with 1 cup sugar.

Beat egg and remaining ½ cup sugar at medium speed with an electric mixer until blended. Add flour and butter; beat at low speed until blended.

Spread batter evenly over pie filling. Bake at 325° for 1 hour or until golden. Cool completely on a wire rack. Store in refrigerator. Yield: 8 servings.

foil facts

If the crust browns too fast, your oven may be too hot or may not be heating evenly. Shield the crust edges with strips of aluminum foil after the crust turns golden, earlier if your recipe specifies.

Cranberry Surprise Pie

pastry pointers

- Cut shortening or cold butter pieces into flour mixture using a pastry blender. The mixture should form small clumps, which give your piecrust its flakiness.
- Roll pastry on a lightly floured surface, but remember that too much flour toughens the crust. A stockinette rolling pin cover minimizes the amount of flour needed during rolling.
- Always roll pastry from the center to the edge to form a circle. Avoid stretching the dough when transferring it; this prevents shrinking during baking.
- One way to transfer pastry to a pieplate is to slide a baking sheet under the pastry; then slip the pastry into the plate. This prevents the pastry from tearing.
- Here's another way to get your pastry into the pieplate in one piece: Roll the pastry circle carefully onto a rolling pin; then lay the pin across the top of the pieplate, and unroll the pastry into the pieplate.
- Here's a final way to transfer pastry: Fold the pastry circle in half on a floured surface; then fold it in half again. Lift the pastry, place the point in the center of the pieplate, and gently unfold it.

favorite flutes

- Fluting refers to crimping edges between your fingers for a decorative finish. Leave about ½ inch of pastry beyond the rim of the pieplate for a pretty design.
- Give the scalloped edge a different look by gently pressing a fork imprint into each scallop. If the fork sticks to the pastry, dip it in flour.
- Create a spiral fluted crust by pressing the handle of a wooden spoon diagonally into the edge of the chilled pastry at ½-inch intervals.

Cranberry-Cherry Pie

Two tangy fruits mingle under a flaky pastry of star cutouts. Tapioca is the old-fashioned thickener.

prep: 27 min.   cook: 40 min.   other: 15 min.

1   (21-ounce) can cherry pie filling
1   (16-ounce) can whole-berry cranberry sauce
¼   cup quick-cooking tapioca
2   tablespoons sugar
1   tablespoon butter, melted
1   teaspoon lemon juice
¼   teaspoon ground cinnamon
Pastry for double-crust 9-inch pie
Milk

Combine first 7 ingredients; stir well. Let stand 15 minutes.

Roll half of pastry to ⅛-inch thickness on a lightly floured surface. Place in a 9-inch pieplate. Spoon cherry mixture into pastry shell.

Roll remaining pastry to ⅛-inch thickness. Using 2½- and 1½-inch star cookie cutters, cut out 5 stars. Moisten edges of filled pastry shell with water. Transfer remaining pastry to top of pie. Trim off excess pastry along edges. Fold edges under, and crimp.

Arrange pastry cutouts on top of pie. Gently brush pastry top and cutouts with milk.

Bake at 400° for 20 minutes. Shield edges of pie with aluminum foil to prevent excessive browning, and bake 20 more minutes. Yield: 1 (9-inch) pie.

Mincemeat Pie with Orange Hard Sauce

prep: 19 min.   cook: 30 min.

1   (15-ounce) package refrigerated piecrusts, divided
1   teaspoon all-purpose flour
1   (28-ounce) jar prepared mincemeat
1   cup chopped pecans, toasted
2   tablespoons Grand Marnier or orange juice
Orange Hard Sauce

Unroll 1 piecrust; sprinkle with flour, spreading over surface. Place crust, floured side down, in a 9-inch pieplate; set aside.

Combine mincemeat, pecans, and Grand Marnier; spoon into pastry shell.

Unroll remaining piecrust. Cut into ½-inch strips, using a knife or pastry wheel, and arrange in a lattice design over filling. Trim off any excess pastry along the edges. Fold edges under, and crimp.

Bake at 425° for 30 minutes or until golden. Serve warm or cold with Orange Hard Sauce. Yield: 1 (9-inch) pie.

Orange Hard Sauce

prep: 5 min.

2   cups sifted powdered sugar
⅔   cup butter or margarine, softened
2   tablespoons Grand Marnier or orange juice

Combine all ingredients; beat at medium speed with an electric mixer until smooth. Yield: 1 cup.

Pear-Mincemeat Pie

editor's favorite

prep: 40 min.   cook: 1 hr., 45 min.

3   pounds pears, peeled and diced
1   (15-ounce) package raisins
3½ cups sugar
⅓   cup cider vinegar
½   teaspoon salt
1½ teaspoons ground nutmeg
1½ teaspoons ground cinnamon
1½ teaspoons ground allspice
1½ teaspoons ground cloves
1   (15-ounce) package refrigerated
     piecrusts, divided
⅓   cup chopped pecans, toasted
1   large egg, lightly beaten

Bring first 9 ingredients to a boil in a large heavy saucepan, stirring often; reduce heat to medium-high, and cook, stirring often, 25 to 30 minutes or until thickened. Cool.

Unroll 1 piecrust, and fit into a 9-inch deep-dish pieplate according to package directions.

Stir pecans into pear mixture; spoon into piecrust.

Unroll remaining piecrust. Cut out and remove leaf shapes from center of piecrust using a leaf-shaped cookie cutter, leaving a 3-inch border around edges. Brush piecrust and leaves with beaten egg. Carefully place piecrust over filling; fold edges under. Make diagonal cuts into edge at ¼-inch intervals; fold every other piece inward. Arrange leaves on pie.

Bake pie on lowest oven rack at 350° for 1 hour or until golden brown, shielding with aluminum foil to prevent excessive browning, if necessary. Yield: 1 (9-inch) pie.

Pear-Mincemeat Pie

Pear-Macadamia Pie

Ripe pears make a big difference in this dessert. Plan ahead so that the fruit will be ripe when you're ready to bake.

prep: 16 min.   cook: 1 hr., 15 min.
other: 15 min.

½   (15-ounce) package refrigerated
     piecrusts
½   cup pear preserves
2   tablespoons Frangelico or other
     hazelnut liqueur
⅔   cup macadamia nuts
½   cup sugar
1½ tablespoons all-purpose flour
¼   cup butter or margarine, softened
1   large egg
2½ pounds ripe cooking pears, peeled,
     cored, and thinly sliced

Unroll piecrust, and lightly roll to fit a 10-inch pieplate. Fit piecrust into pieplate according to package directions. Bake as directed.

Combine preserves and Frangelico in a small heavy saucepan; cook over medium heat, stirring constantly, until warm. Pour mixture through a wire-mesh strainer, discarding solids. Gently brush a thin layer of glaze over warm pastry, reserving remaining glaze.

Position knife blade in food processor bowl; add nuts, sugar, and flour. Process until finely ground. Add butter and egg; process until smooth. Spread mixture evenly over pastry; freeze 15 minutes.

Arrange pear slices over nut mixture; bake at 350° for 30 minutes. Cover loosely with aluminum foil, and bake 40 more minutes or until pears are tender and golden. Remove from oven; immediately brush pears with reserved glaze. Cool on a wire rack. Yield: 1 (10-inch) pie.

fancy finish

Cut a scalloped edge for a piecrust by rolling the tip of a teaspoon around the edge of the pastry after you transfer the pastry to the pieplate.

Pumpkin Pie with Spiced Cream Sauce

This holiday favorite boasts pumpkin pie spice in the filling and in the accompanying cream sauce.

prep: 12 min.   cook: 1 hr., 3 min.

½   (15-ounce) package refrigerated
        piecrusts
1   (16-ounce) can pumpkin
1   (14-ounce) can sweetened
        condensed milk
2   large eggs, beaten
¼   cup firmly packed brown sugar
1   teaspoon pumpkin pie spice
¼   teaspoon vanilla extract
Spiced Cream Sauce (optional)

Fit piecrust into a 9-inch pieplate according to package directions; fold edges under, and crimp. Prick bottom and sides of piecrust generously with a fork. Bake at 450° for 8 minutes; cool.

Combine pumpkin and next 5 ingredients, stirring well; pour into prepared piecrust. Bake at 350° for 50 to 55 minutes or until a knife inserted in center comes out clean. Cool on a wire rack. Serve with Spiced Cream Sauce, if desired. Yield: 1 (9-inch) pie.

Spiced Cream Sauce

prep: 4 min.   other: 3 min.

½   cup sour cream
2   tablespoons brown sugar
¼   teaspoon pumpkin pie
        spice
¼   cup whipping cream

Combine first 3 ingredients in a small bowl, stirring well. Let stand at room temperature 3 minutes. Gradually add whipping cream, stirring until blended. Cover and chill. Yield: ¾ cup.

Bourbon-Pecan-Pumpkin Pie

Mashed sweet potato instead of pumpkin would also be a delight in this dessert laced with bourbon.

prep: 12 min.   cook: 56 min.

3   large eggs, lightly beaten
1   (15-ounce) can pumpkin
1   cup half-and-half
¾   cup firmly packed dark brown
        sugar
3   tablespoons bourbon
1   teaspoon ground cinnamon
½   teaspoon ground ginger
¼   teaspoon salt
1   unbaked 9-inch pastry shell
2   tablespoons butter or margarine
¼   cup firmly packed dark brown
        sugar
1   cup chopped pecans, toasted
2   tablespoons bourbon

Combine first 8 ingredients, stirring until blended. Pour into pastry shell.

Bake at 425° for 10 minutes. Reduce heat to 350°; bake 40 more minutes or until set. Cool on a wire rack.

Combine butter and ¼ cup brown sugar in a saucepan; cook over medium heat, stirring until sugar dissolves. Add pecans and 2 tablespoons bourbon, stirring to coat pecans. Spoon mixture over pie. Yield: 1 (9-inch) pie.

Rum-Laced Pecan Pie

**prep: 16 min.   cook: 1 hr., 16 min.
other: 2 hrs., 15 min.**

1   cup sugar
1   cup light corn syrup
⅓   cup butter or margarine
4   large eggs, lightly beaten
3   tablespoons dark rum
1   teaspoon vanilla extract
¼   teaspoon salt
1   (15-ounce) package refrigerated
        piecrusts
1¼ cups pecan halves

Combine sugar, corn syrup, and butter in a medium saucepan; cook over low heat, stirring constantly, until sugar dissolves and butter melts. Remove from heat; cool slightly. Stir in eggs and next 3 ingredients.

Unroll 1 piecrust, and fit into a 9-inch pieplate according to package directions. Cut leaf shapes or other desired shapes from remaining piecrust, using cookie cutters. Arrange cutouts around edge of pieplate, pressing gently.

Pour filling into prepared piecrust; top with pecan halves. Bake at 325° for 1 hour and 10 minutes or until pie is set. Cool on a wire rack. Yield: 1 (9-inch) pie.

Buttermilk Chess Pie

This easy recipe takes only minutes to prepare and is a Test Kitchens favorite.

editor's favorite
prep: 8 min.   cook: 45 min.

5   large eggs, lightly beaten
2   cups sugar
⅔   cup buttermilk
½   cup butter or margarine, melted
2   tablespoons all-purpose flour
1   teaspoon vanilla extract
1   unbaked 9-inch pastry shell

Combine first 6 ingredients; stir well. Pour filling into pastry shell.

Bake at 350° for 45 minutes or until set. Cool on a wire rack. Yield: 1 (9-inch) pie.

Hot Cranberry Bake

prep: 22 min.   cook: 1 hr.

4   cups peeled, chopped cooking apples
2   cups fresh cranberries
1½ teaspoons lemon juice
1   cup granulated sugar
1⅓ cups quick-cooking oats, uncooked
1   cup chopped walnuts
⅓   cup firmly packed brown sugar
½   cup butter or margarine, melted
Vanilla ice cream

Layer apples and cranberries in a lightly greased 2-quart baking dish. Sprinkle with lemon juice; spoon granulated sugar over fruit.

Combine oats and next 3 ingredients; stir just until dry ingredients are moistened and mixture is crumbly; sprinkle over fruit. Bake, uncovered, at 325° for 1 hour. Serve dessert warm with vanilla ice cream. Yield: 8 servings.

Lemon Pie

This is one of the easiest all-occasion dessert recipes you'll find.

quick & easy
prep: 12 min.   cook: 45 min.

2   medium lemons
6   large eggs, lightly beaten
2½   cups sugar
¼   cup fresh lemon juice
½   cup butter or margarine, melted
1   unbaked 9-inch pastry shell
Garnishes: frozen whipped topping (thawed), lemon wedges

Grate rind from lemons; set aside grated rind. Remove and discard pith from lemons. Quarter and seed lemons.

Combine lemon quarters, grated rind, eggs, sugar, and lemon juice in container of an electric blender; cover and process 1 minute or until smooth, stopping once to scrape down sides. Add butter; cover and process 30 seconds. Pour into pastry shell.

Bake at 350° for 40 to 45 minutes or until slightly firm in center. Cool on a wire rack. Garnish, if desired. Yield: 1 (9-inch) pie.

Lemon Pie

- Tarts are shallow pastry crusts filled with sweet or savory fillings; they range from bite-size tartlets to individual to full size.
- Trace a small dessert plate or saucer to make a circle of dough for an individual tart or pie.
- The best way to be sure all tartlet shells are the same size is to divide the dough in half; then pinch off equal-size mounds of dough to fill each little tartlet pan.

Cranberry-Walnut Tart

prep: 21 min.   cook: 30 min.
other: 4 hrs., 10 min.

1½ cups all-purpose flour
1   cup chopped walnuts
¼   cup sugar
½   cup butter or margarine
1   large egg. lightly beaten
1   teaspoon vanilla extract
1   envelope unflavored gelatin
¼   cup cold water
3   cups fresh cranberries
1   cup sugar
½   cup red currant jelly
½   cup whipping cream. whipped

Combine first 3 ingredients in a medium mixing bowl; cut in butter with a pastry blender until mixture is crumbly. Add egg and vanilla; stir with a fork until dry ingredients are moistened. Press mixture on bottom and 1¼ inches up sides of a lightly greased 9-inch springform pan.

Bake at 350° for 15 to 20 minutes or until golden. Cool completely.

Sprinkle gelatin over cold water in a small bowl. Combine cranberries. 1 cup sugar. and jelly in a saucepan; cook over low heat 10 minutes or until cranberry

skins pop. Remove from heat; cool cranberry mixture 5 minutes.

Add softened gelatin; stir until dissolved. Cool completely.

Pour cranberry mixture into tart shell. Chill. Place tart on a platter; remove sides of pan before serving. Pipe whipped cream on top of tart. Yield: 1 (9-inch) tart.

Southern Pecan Tartlets

prep: 25 min.   cook: 1 hr., 1 min.
other: 45 min.

1   tablespoon butter or margarine
1   cup chopped pecans
⅛   teaspoon salt
1   (15-ounce) package refrigerated
        piecrusts
½   cup butter or margarine
1   cup light corn syrup
1   cup sugar
1   teaspoon vanilla extract
½   teaspoon lemon juice
¼   teaspoon ground cinnamon
3   large eggs. lightly beaten

Place 1 tablespoon butter in a large shallow pan; bake at 350° until melted. Add pecans, stirring to coat; bake 8 to 10 minutes or until toasted. stirring once. Remove from oven, and sprinkle with salt; cool.

Unroll 1 piecrust. Cut into rounds with a 2½-inch round cutter. Fit pastry rounds into miniature (1¾-inch) muffin pans. (Do not trim edges.) Repeat procedure with remaining piecrust. Sprinkle toasted pecans evenly into tart shells; set aside.

Place ½ cup butter in a small heavy saucepan; cook over medium heat, stirring constantly. until lightly browned. (Do not burn.) Remove from heat; cool 10 minutes.

Add corn syrup and remaining 5 ingredients to butter. stirring well; spoon mixture evenly over pecans in tart shells.

Bake at 350° for 35 to 40 minutes or until set. Cool in pans 5 minutes. Remove from pans; cool completely on wire racks. Yield: 4½ dozen.

Hazelnut-Pumpkin Tart

prep: 28 min.   cook: 40 min.
other: 3 hrs., 25 min.

1   (15-ounce) package refrigerated
        piecrusts. divided
1   cup hazelnuts. toasted. skinned.
        and finely chopped
3   large eggs
1   (16-ounce) can pumpkin
½   cup firmly packed brown sugar
⅓   cup granulated sugar
1   cup half-and-half
¾   teaspoon ground ginger
¾   teaspoon ground cinnamon
⅛   teaspoon salt
Dash of ground nutmeg
Dash of ground allspice
Dash of ground cloves
1   cup whipping cream
½   cup sifted powdered sugar
1   tablespoon minced crystallized ginger
30   whole hazelnuts, toasted and skinned

Roll 1 piecrust into a 12-inch circle on a floured surface. Fit into an 11-inch tart pan with removable bottom. Prick bottom and sides of pastry shell. Bake at 375° for 5 minutes. Cool in pan on a wire rack. Sprinkle with chopped hazelnuts.

Beat eggs at high speed with an electric mixer. Add pumpkin and next 9 ingredients; beat well. Pour into pastry. Bake at 375° for 35 minutes. Cool in pan on wire rack. Cover and chill at least 2 hours.

Hazelnut-Pumpkin Tart

Cut 30 shapes from remaining piecrust using a small leaf cookie cutter. Place on an ungreased baking sheet. Bake at 450° for 6 minutes. Remove to a wire rack to cool.

Beat whipping cream until foamy; gradually add powdered sugar, beating until soft peaks form. Fold in crystallized ginger. Cover and chill 1 hour.

Arrange whole hazelnuts and pastry leaves on tart. Serve with whipped cream mixture. Yield: 1 (11-inch) tart.

Whole hazelnuts and dainty leaves cut from piecrust combine to make a charming seasonal garnish.

toasting hazelnuts

• The most common way to buy hazelnuts is whole, with their cinnamon brown skins intact.

• The easiest way to toast hazelnuts and to remove their skins is to spread whole nuts in an ungreased jellyroll pan. Bake at 350° for 12 to 15 minutes. The skins will begin to split. Using a hot pad, scoop the hot nuts into a colander. Cover them with a kitchen towel, and let sit 1 minute. Rub the nuts briskly in the towel to remove the skins.

Cinnamon-Sugar Fig Tarts

Cinnamon-Sugar Fig Tarts

prep: 32 min. cook: 15 min.
other: 1 hr., 5 min.

¾ cup unsalted butter, softened
1 cup granulated sugar
1 large egg
1 teaspoon vanilla extract
3 cups all-purpose flour
2 teaspoons baking powder
½ teaspoon baking soda
½ teaspoon ground cinnamon
¼ teaspoon salt
1 (10.5- or 11-ounce) jar fig
     preserves (we tested with
     Braswell's)
½ cup chopped pitted dates
½ cup chopped walnuts or pecans,
     toasted
2 tablespoons brown sugar
¼ teaspoon ground allspice

Beat butter at medium speed with an
electric mixer until fluffy; gradually add
granulated sugar, beating well. Add egg
and vanilla, beating well. Combine flour
and next 4 ingredients; gradually add to
butter mixture, beating until blended.
Shape dough into a ball. Cover and chill
30 minutes.

Roll dough to ¼-inch thickness on a
lightly floured surface. Cut and fit dough
into 9 lightly greased 3-inch tart pans,
reserving dough scraps.

Combine preserves and remaining
4 ingredients; stir well. Spoon filling
mixture into tart pans.

Roll dough scraps to ⅛-inch thickness;
cut into ¼-inch strips. Arrange strips
of dough, lattice fashion, across tops
of tarts.

Place tarts on a baking sheet. Bake at
375° for 15 minutes or until golden.
Cool on a wire rack. Gently remove from
pans. Yield: 9 tarts.

Apple Dumplings with
Maple-Cider Sauce

Apple Dumplings with Maple-Cider Sauce

prep: 47 min. cook: 55 min.
other: 30 min.

3 cups all-purpose flour
1 teaspoon salt
¾ cup butter or margarine, chilled
     and cut into pieces
¼ cup plus 1 tablespoon shortening
½ cup apple cider, chilled
8 large Granny Smith apples
½ cup firmly packed brown sugar
½ cup currants
½ cup chopped walnuts
⅓ cup butter or margarine, softened
1 large egg
1 tablespoon water
4 (3-inch) cinnamon sticks, broken
     in half
Maple-Cider Sauce

Combine flour and salt; cut in chilled
butter and shortening with pastry
blender until crumbly. Sprinkle cider, 1
tablespoon at a time, over top; stir with
fork until moistened. Shape into 2 (½-
inch-thick) squares; cover and chill.

Core each apple, leaving ½ inch intact
on bottom. Peel top two-thirds of each.

Combine sugar, currants, and walnuts;
stir in softened butter, blending well.
Spoon evenly into each apple.

Roll pastry squares to ⅛-inch thickness on a floured surface; cut each
square into 4 (7-inch) squares.

Press 1 pastry square around each
apple; remove excess pastry from bottom
so that apple will sit level. Reroll pastry
scraps, if desired; cut into leaf shapes.

Combine egg and water, beating lightly
with a fork. Brush over apples, and
attach leaf shapes, if desired.

Place a cinnamon stick half in top
of each apple to resemble a stem. Place
apples in a lightly greased 15- x 10-inch
jellyroll pan.

Bake at 375° for 40 minutes. Pour
Maple-Cider Sauce over apples; bake
15 more minutes or until apples are
tender. Place apples on a serving plate,
and spoon sauce around apples. Yield:
8 servings.

Maple Whipped Cream: Serve maple
whipped cream with the apples, if
desired. To make it, combine 1 cup
whipping cream and 3 tablespoons
maple syrup in a medium bowl. Beat at
high speed with an electric mixer until
soft peaks form.

Maple-Cider Sauce

prep: 3 min. cook: 9 min.

2 teaspoons cornstarch
1½ cups apple cider
⅔ cup maple syrup
¼ cup firmly packed brown sugar
¼ cup fresh lemon juice

Combine cornstarch and cider in a
saucepan, stirring until smooth; add
maple syrup and remaining ingredients.
Bring to a boil over medium-high heat;
boil 1 minute. Yield: 2 cups.

souper suppers

For a quick meal after a day of shopping or for a casual gathering of friends, this assortment of hearty soups and stews makes menu planning easy.

Potato-Sausage Soup

prep: 8 min.   cook: 46 min.

½   pound ground pork sausage
16   ounces frozen hash browns (4 cups)
1   large onion, chopped
1   (14-ounce) can chicken broth
2   cups water
1   (10¾-ounce) can cream of celery soup, undiluted
1   (10¾-ounce) can cream of chicken soup, undiluted
2   cups milk
Garnish: shredded Cheddar cheese

Brown sausage in a large Dutch oven over medium heat, stirring until it crumbles and is no longer pink. Drain; return to Dutch oven.

Add hash brown potatoes and next 3 ingredients; bring to a boil. Cover, reduce heat, and simmer 30 minutes. Stir in soups and milk; cook, stirring often, until thoroughly heated. Garnish, if desired. Yield: 10 cups.

Chicken-and-Wild Rice Soup

To save time, bone and chop a deli roasted chicken. One deli-roasted chicken will yield about 3 cups chopped cooked chicken; freeze 1 cup for another use.

editor's favorite
prep: 20 min.   cook: 15 min.

1   small onion, chopped
1   cup shredded carrots
2   teaspoons vegetable oil
5   cups water
1   (6.2-ounce) package fast cooking long-grain and wild rice mix (we tested with Uncle Ben's Long Grain & Wild Rice Fast Cook Recipe)
1   (10-ounce) package frozen chopped broccoli
2   cups chopped cooked chicken
1   (8-ounce) loaf pasteurized prepared cheese product, cubed
1   (10¾-ounce) can cream of chicken soup, undiluted

Sauté onion and carrots in hot oil in a Dutch oven over medium heat 5 minutes. Add 5 cups water, seasoning packet from rice, broccoli, and chicken.

Bring to a boil, and stir in rice; reduce heat, cover, and cook 5 minutes. Add cheese and soup; cook, stirring constantly, 5 minutes or until cheese melts. Serve immediately. Yield: about 10 cups.

Oyster-Artichoke Soup

Tender curly morsels of oysters mingle with chunks of artichoke hearts in this velvety cream soup.

prep: 18 min.   cook: 35 min.

2   (12-ounce) containers fresh Standard oysters
½   cup butter or margarine
2   bunches green onions, chopped
6   bay leaves
⅛   teaspoon dried thyme
⅛   teaspoon ground red pepper
¼   cup all-purpose flour
2   (14-ounce) cans chicken broth
1   (14-ounce) can artichoke hearts, drained and cut into eighths
2   teaspoons chopped fresh parsley
1   cup whipping cream

Drain oysters, reserving 1 cup liquid. Cut each oyster into fourths.

Melt butter in a Dutch oven over medium heat. Add green onions and next 3 ingredients; cook, stirring constantly, until green onions are tender. Add flour, stirring until blended. Cook 1 minute, stirring constantly. Gradually stir in reserved 1 cup oyster liquid and chicken broth. Bring to a boil; reduce heat, and simmer, uncovered, 15 minutes. Remove and discard bay leaves. Add oysters, artichoke hearts, and parsley; simmer, uncovered, 10 minutes. Stir in cream, and cook just until thoroughly heated. Serve immediately. Yield: 8 cups.

Oyster-Artichoke Soup

Oyster Stew

Using small oysters in a stew allows them to be more evenly distributed than with larger ones. Oyster liquor is simply the juice that is in the oyster shell in which they are packed. Be sure to use shucked oysters before the sell-by date on the container.

prep: 15 min.   cook: 30 min.

1   (12-ounce) container fresh oysters, undrained
2   tablespoons butter
1   tablespoon canola oil
1   small onion, chopped
1   medium carrot, diced
2   celery ribs, chopped
½   cup dry white wine
4   cups whipping cream
2   medium Yukon gold potatoes, cut into 1-inch cubes
1½ teaspoons salt
½   teaspoon freshly ground pepper
2   plum tomatoes, chopped
8   bacon strips, cooked and crumbled
Chopped fresh chives

Drain oysters, reserving liquor (liquid from oyster container); set aside.

Melt butter in canola oil in a Dutch oven over medium heat; add onion, carrot, and celery, and sauté 5 minutes or until tender.

Add white wine and reserved oyster liquor; simmer 5 minutes, or until reduced by half. Stir in whipping cream, cubed potatoes, salt, and pepper; simmer 15 minutes or until cream is slightly thickened and potatoes are tender. Add oysters, and cook 3 minutes or just until edges begin to curl; stir in tomatoes.

Remove from heat, and serve; sprinkle each serving evenly with crumbled bacon and chives. Yield: 4 servings.

Easy Vegetable Chowder

editor's favorite

prep: 10 min.   cook: 45 min.

11 new potatoes
2   large carrots
1   large onion
3   tablespoons olive oil
2   (10¾-ounce) cans Cheddar cheese soup, undiluted
4   cups water
1   (1.0-ounce) envelope dry onion soup mix
1   teaspoon pepper
½   cup sliced green onions
Garnishes: sliced green onions, shredded Cheddar cheese

Cut potatoes into ½-inch cubes and carrots into ½-inch slices; coarsely chop onion.

Sauté potato, carrot, and chopped onion in hot oil in a Dutch oven until vegetables are tender.

Stir together Cheddar cheese soup, water, onion soup mix, and pepper; add to vegetable mixture. Bring to a boil; reduce heat, and simmer 30 minutes. Stir in ½ cup green onions just before serving. Garnish, if desired. Yield: 6 cups.

Tempting Turkey Soup

Keep leftover cooked turkey in the refrigerator up to two days. Leftover turkey also can be frozen.

prep: 22 min.   cook: 45 min.

3   cups water
1   (10¾-ounce) can cream of chicken soup, undiluted
1   (14½-ounce) can stewed tomatoes
2   to 3 cups chopped cooked turkey
5   small potatoes, peeled and cut into ½-inch cubes
3   carrots, scraped and chopped
1   medium onion, chopped
1   garlic clove, minced
2   chicken bouillon cubes
1   teaspoon salt
1   teaspoon dried basil
½   teaspoon dried thyme
¼   teaspoon pepper
½   teaspoon poultry seasoning (optional)
1½ cups milk
2   tablespoons chopped fresh cilantro

Bring first 13 ingredients, and, if desired, poultry seasoning, to a boil in a Dutch oven. Reduce heat, and simmer, stirring occasionally, 30 minutes or until vegetables are tender. Stir in milk and cilantro; cook, stirring often, just until thoroughly heated. Yield: 10 cups.

Turkey Stew in a Bread Bowl

Use your leftover turkey in this thick, rich stew. Hollow out small bread loaves to make delicious edible bowls.

prep: 27 min.   cook: 50 min.

6   (7½-inch) sourdough sub rolls or
     (8-ounce) round loaves sour-
     dough bread
2   cups chopped carrot
2   tablespoons butter or margarine,
     melted
2   large baking potatoes, peeled and
     chopped
1   large onion, chopped
2   cups water
2   (10¾-ounce) cans cream of
     mushroom soup
1   (12-ounce) can evaporated milk
2   bay leaves
2   teaspoons dried thyme
3   cups chopped cooked turkey
1   (10-ounce) package frozen sweet
     green peas
1   cup (4 ounces) shredded mozzarella
     cheese

Using a serrated knife, hollow out the center of each loaf to form a ¾-inch-thick shell. Place hollow loaves on a baking sheet. Bake at 350° for 15 minutes.

Cook carrot in butter in a Dutch oven over medium-high heat, stirring constantly, 4 to 5 minutes. Add potatoes and next 6 ingredients.

Bring mixture to a boil; cover, reduce heat, and simmer 30 minutes or until vegetables are tender, stirring often. Stir in turkey, peas, and cheese. Simmer, uncovered, 5 more minutes. Remove and discard bay leaves.

To serve, ladle stew into individual bread bowls. Yield: 6 servings.

Turkey Stew in a Bread Bowl

Tear off pieces of the bread bowl to dip in the stew as you eat.

Duck-and-Sausage Gumbo

prep: 41 min.   cook: 3 hrs.

1   (5- to 6-pound) duck, dressed
      and skinned
2   celery ribs with leaves, cut into pieces
1   large carrot, cut into pieces
1   large onion, quartered
1½ cups all-purpose flour
1   teaspoon ground red pepper
1   teaspoon paprika
¾   teaspoon dry mustard
¾   teaspoon ground white pepper
¾   teaspoon black pepper
½   teaspoon salt
1   cup vegetable oil
2   cups chopped green bell pepper
2   cups chopped onion
2   cups chopped celery
2   tablespoons minced fresh garlic
4   cups chopped smoked sausage
      (about 1¼ pounds)
1   (16-ounce) package frozen sliced
      okra
1   bay leaf
Hot cooked rice

Place duck in a Dutch oven; add water to cover. Bring water to a boil. Skim off foam. Add celery pieces, carrot, and quartered onion. Cover, reduce heat, and simmer 1 hour. Remove duck from broth, reserving 8 cups broth. Discard vegetables. Set meat and broth aside to cool. Remove meat from bones, and chop into bite-size pieces.

Combine flour and next 6 ingredients; stir well. Heat oil in Dutch oven or large cast-iron skillet. Add flour mixture, and cook over medium heat, stirring constantly, until roux is chocolate colored (about 30 to 45 minutes). Reduce heat to medium-low; add bell pepper, chopped onion, chopped celery, and garlic. Cook, stirring constantly, until vegetables are tender.

Gradually add reserved 8 cups broth to roux, stirring well. Add chopped duck meat, sausage, okra, and bay leaf. Bring to a boil; reduce heat, and simmer, uncovered, 50 minutes. Remove and discard bay leaf. Serve gumbo with hot cooked rice. Yield: 3½ quarts.

Big-Batch Chili

freezer-friendly • slow cooker
prep: 20 min.   cook: 6 hrs.

4   pounds ground chuck
2   medium onions, chopped
1   green bell pepper, chopped
2   garlic cloves, minced
3   (14½-ounce) cans diced tomatoes,
      undrained
4   (8-ounce) cans tomato sauce
1   (6-ounce) can tomato paste
¼   cup chili powder
1   tablespoon sugar
1   teaspoon salt
1   teaspoon black pepper
½   teaspoon paprika
½   teaspoon ground red pepper
1   bay leaf
2   (16-ounce) cans light red kidney
      beans, rinsed and drained
      (optional)
Toppings: sour cream, shredded
      Cheddar cheese, chopped green
      onions, sliced ripe black olives

Cook ground chuck, in batches, in a large skillet over medium-high heat about 5 minutes, stirring until meat crumbles and is no longer pink; drain. Place meat in a 6-quart slow cooker; stir in onion, next 12 ingredients, and, if desired, beans. Cook, covered, at HIGH 5 to 6 hours or at LOW 8 to 9 hours. Remove and discard bay leaf. Serve with desired toppings. Yield: 15 to 18 cups.

Cooktop Preparation: Cook ground chuck, in batches, in a large Dutch oven. Drain beef; return to Dutch oven. Add onion, next 12 ingredients, and, if desired, beans. Bring to a boil over medium-high heat; reduce heat, cover, and simmer 4 to 6 hours. Remove and discard bay leaf.

Duck-and-Sausage Gumbo

Freezing Note: Let chili stand 30 minutes. Evenly divide the chili mixture into 3 (1-gallon) zip-top freezer bags; seal and lay each bag flat. Stack bags of chili in freezer. Freeze up to 1 month. Thaw frozen chili overnight in refrigerator, or defrost in microwave. Pour thawed chili into a 9-inch square baking dish. Cover tightly with heavy-duty plastic wrap, and fold back a corner to allow steam to escape. Microwave at HIGH 6 to 7 minutes or until bubbly, stirring after 3½ minutes.

Venison Chili

prep: 22 min.   cook: 1 hr.

½   pound mild Italian sausage links
8   slices bacon
1½ pounds coarsely ground venison
2   large onions, chopped
2   large green bell peppers, seeded and chopped
3   garlic cloves, minced
2   jalapeño peppers, seeded and chopped
2   dried red chile peppers, crumbled
1½ tablespoons chili powder
1   teaspoon ground cumin
1   teaspoon dried oregano
½   teaspoon salt
1   (14½-ounce) can diced tomatoes, undrained
1   (12-ounce) can tomato paste
1   (12-ounce) can beer
1   (16-ounce) can pinto beans, drained
Garnishes: sour cream, sliced green onions, shredded Monterey Jack cheese, sliced ripe olives

Brown sausage in a large Dutch oven over medium heat. Drain on paper towels, and slice.

Venison Chili

Cook bacon in Dutch oven until crisp; remove bacon, reserving half the drippings. Crumble bacon.

Heat reserved drippings over medium heat until hot. Add venison, onion, bell peppers, and garlic. Cook until meat is browned and vegetables are tender,

stirring often. Add reserved sausage, bacon, jalapeño peppers, and next 8 ingredients; stir well. Bring to a boil; cover, reduce heat, and simmer 45 minutes, stirring often. Add beans during last 15 minutes of cooking. Garnish, if desired. Yield: 11 cups.

Thanksgiving specialties

Welcome the season with happy gatherings of family and friends, made even more special with these time-honored favorites.

Crabmeat-and-Oyster Dressing

Offer this seafood- and rice-based dressing for a tasty change of pace.

prep: 15 min.   cook: 40 min.

1   (6-ounce) package long-grain and wild rice mix
2⅓ cups water
5   tablespoons butter or margarine, divided
1   medium onion, chopped
½   medium-size green bell pepper, chopped
1   cup chopped fresh mushrooms
1   pound fresh crabmeat, drained and flaked
1   (12-ounce) container fresh oysters, drained
1   (10¾-ounce) can cream of celery soup
1   cup chopped pecans, toasted
½   cup Italian-seasoned breadcrumbs
1   green onion, chopped
¼   teaspoon salt
¼   teaspoon ground black pepper
⅛   teaspoon ground red pepper

Bring rice mix, 2⅓ cups water, and 1 tablespoon butter to a boil in a saucepan. Reduce heat to low, cover, and simmer 25 minutes or until rice is tender.

Melt remaining 4 tablespoons butter in a large nonstick skillet over medium heat; add onion, bell pepper, and mushrooms, and sauté 8 minutes or until tender.

Stir in crabmeat and oysters, and cook 4 minutes. Stir in rice, soup, and remaining ingredients; cook, stirring occasionally, 5 to 10 minutes or until thoroughly heated. Yield: 8 servings.

Sugar-and-Spice Cured Turkey

editor's favorite
prep: 10 min.   cook: 3 hrs., 5 min.
other: 8 hrs., 15 min.

1   (12-pound) whole turkey
¼   cup firmly packed light brown sugar
2   tablespoons kosher or coarse sea salt
1   teaspoon onion powder
½   teaspoon garlic powder
½   teaspoon ground allspice
½   teaspoon ground cloves
½   teaspoon ground mace
1   large onion, quartered
2   (14-ounce) cans low-sodium chicken broth
Additional chicken broth
2   tablespoons all-purpose flour
Garnishes: apple slices, nuts

Remove giblets and neck from turkey; rinse turkey with cold water. Pat dry. Tie legs together with string; tuck wingtips under. Combine brown sugar and next 6 ingredients. Rub over turkey. Cover with plastic wrap; chill 8 hours.

Place turkey on a rack in a roasting pan, breast side up. Arrange onion quarters around turkey. Pour 2 cans broth in bottom of pan.

Bake, loosely covered with foil, at 325° for 1½ hours. Uncover and bake 1½ more hours or until meat thermometer registers 180°. (Cover with foil to prevent excessive browning, if necessary.) Remove onion; discard, reserving pan drippings. Let turkey stand 15 minutes before carving.

Combine pan drippings and enough chicken broth to equal 2 cups in a saucepan over medium heat. Whisk in flour, and cook, whisking constantly, 5 minutes or until thickened. Serve with turkey. Garnish, if desired. Yield: 8 to 10 servings.

Sugar-and-Spice Cured Turkey

Marinating the bird in a brown sugar rub keeps the meat flavorful and succulent.

Maple-Plum Glazed Turkey Breast

To enjoy the turkey breast the day you make it, let it stand 30 minutes before carving. Serve with reserved maple-plum sauce.

editor's favorite

prep: 15 min.   cook: 2 hrs., 30 min.

other: 8 hrs.

2   cups red plum jam
1   cup maple syrup
¼   cup cider vinegar
1   tablespoon grated lemon rind
2   tablespoons fresh lemon juice
1   teaspoon dry mustard
1   (5- to 5½-pound) bone-in turkey
       breast
½   teaspoon salt
8   fresh sage sprigs

Bring jam, maple syrup, vinegar, rind, juice, and mustard to a boil in a large saucepan over medium-high heat; reduce heat to medium-low, and cook, stirring often, 25 minutes or until thickened and bubbly. Remove from heat, and cool completely. Reserve 1½ cups sauce; cover and chill. Set aside remaining sauce for basting.

Loosen skin from turkey without totally detaching skin; sprinkle salt evenly under skin, and carefully place 4 sage sprigs on each side of breast. Replace skin, and place turkey in a lightly greased 11- x 7-inch baking dish. Spread ¾ cup maple-plum sauce evenly over turkey; cover loosely with aluminum foil.

Bake at 325° for 1 hour; uncover and bake 1 more hour or until a meat thermometer registers 170°, basting with remaining ¾ cup maple-plum sauce every 15 minutes.

Remove turkey from baking dish; cool. Wrap in plastic wrap and then in aluminum foil, and chill 8 hours. Serve turkey at room temperature.

Cook reserved 1½ cups maple-plum sauce until thoroughly heated; serve with turkey. Yield: 10 servings.

Maple-Plum Glazed Turkey Tenderloins: Substitute 2 (16-ounce) packages turkey tenderloins for breast. Place tenderloins on a rack in a broiler pan coated with cooking spray; sprinkle evenly with salt, omitting sage. Baste with ¾ cup maple-plum sauce. Bake at 425° for 25 to 30 minutes or until done, basting often with remaining ¾ cup maple-plum sauce. Yield: 6 servings.

Slow-Cooker Turkey and Dressing

Turkey and dressing have never been so simple—just see our series of photos. You may never go back to roasting the bird after you try this easy version.

prep: 10 min.   cook: 7 hrs.

1   (8-ounce) package herb-seasoned
       stuffing mix (we tested with
       Pepperidge Farm)
1   onion, chopped
2   celery ribs, chopped
1   cup dried cranberries
¾   cup chicken broth
3   tablespoons butter or margarine,
       melted
1   (3-pound) frozen boneless turkey
       breast, thawed
¼   teaspoon salt
½   teaspoon pepper
¼   teaspoon dried thyme
1   (0.88-ounce) package turkey gravy
       mix *

Coat inside of a 4-quart electric slow cooker with cooking spray. Add stuffing mix, onion, celery, and cranberries. Combine broth and melted butter. Pour over stuffing, and stir gently.

Remove string from turkey breast. Rinse turkey breast. Place turkey in slow cooker on top of stuffing. Combine salt, pepper, and thyme; sprinkle over turkey. Cover and cook at HIGH 1 hour. Reduce to LOW, and cook 5 to 6 hours or until a meat thermometer inserted in turkey registers 170°.

Remove turkey to a serving platter. Stir stuffing gently in slow cooker; cover and let stand 3 to 4 minutes. Prepare gravy. Spoon stuffing around turkey on platter. Yield: 5 to 6 servings.

* Some turkey breasts come with a gravy packet; some don't. We liked the flavor and color of gravy using a 0.88-ounce package of turkey gravy mix (we tested with French's).

◀ Add stuffing mix to greased slow cooker.

◀ Pour broth and melted butter over stuffing ingredients, and stir gently.

◀ Place turkey over stuffing. Sprinkle with seasonings; cover and cook.

Slow-Cooker Turkey
and Dressing

Cornbread Dressing

We voted unanimously to award this classic Southern side dish our highest rating.

freezer-friendly • make-ahead
prep: 30 min.   cook: 1 hr., 30 min.

2 cups cornmeal
½ cup all-purpose flour
2 teaspoons baking powder
1 teaspoon baking soda
1 teaspoon salt
1 teaspoon sugar (optional)
6 large eggs, divided
2 cups buttermilk
2 tablespoons bacon drippings or
    melted butter
½ cup butter or margarine
3 bunches green onions, chopped
4 celery ribs, chopped
1 (16-ounce) package herb-seasoned
    stuffing mix
5 (14-ounce) cans chicken broth

Combine first 5 ingredients, and, if desired, sugar in a large bowl. Stir together 2 eggs and buttermilk; add to dry ingredients, stirring just until moistened.

Heat bacon drippings in a 10-inch cast-iron skillet or 9-inch round cakepan in a 425° oven 5 minutes. Stir hot drippings into batter. Pour batter into hot skillet.

Bake at 425° for 25 minutes or until golden; cool and crumble. Freeze in a large zip-top freezer bag up to 1 month, if desired. Thaw in refrigerator.

Melt butter in a large skillet over medium heat; add green onions and celery, and sauté until tender.

Stir together remaining 4 eggs in a large bowl; stir in cornbread, onion mixture, stuffing mix, and broth until blended.

Spoon dressing into 1 lightly greased 13- x 9-inch baking dish and 1 lightly greased 9-inch square baking dish. (Cover and freeze up to 3 months, if desired; thaw in refrigerator 8 hours.)

Bake 13- x 9-inch dish, uncovered, at 350° for 1 hour or until lightly browned. Bake 9-inch square baking dish, uncovered, 50 minutes or until lightly browned. Yield: 12 to 15 servings.

Andouille Dressing

An andouille-laced dressing highlights the Cajun trinity of celery, onion, and green pepper.

prep: 12 min.   cook: 1 hr., 5 min.

½ cup butter
1 (1-pound) package Cajun-style
    cooked andouille sausage, diced
3 cups diced onion
2 cups diced celery
2 cups diced green bell pepper
2 garlic cloves, minced
2 teaspoons rubbed sage
1 teaspoon dried thyme
½ teaspoon salt
½ teaspoon pepper
1 (16-ounce) package cornbread
    stuffing mix
4 cups chicken broth

Melt butter in a large nonstick skillet over medium-high heat. Add sausage; cook 4 minutes or until browned. Transfer sausage to a large bowl, reserving drippings in skillet.

Add onion and next 7 ingredients to skillet; cook 8 minutes or until tender, stirring occasionally. Add vegetables and stuffing mix to sausage. Add broth, stirring just until moistened.

Spoon dressing into a greased 15- x 10-inch roasting pan.

Bake, covered, at 350° for 30 minutes. Uncover and bake 20 more minutes. Yield: 12 servings.

Cranberry Relish

Fresh citrus adds a lively twist to this traditional condiment.

quick & easy
prep: 15 min.   other: 30 min.

1 medium-size orange
½ lemon
1 pound fresh cranberries (4 cups)
1 cup sugar

Cut orange and lemon into quarters, removing white membrane down center of pulp. Process the orange and lemon in a food processor until finely chopped.

Add cranberries and sugar; process until coarsely chopped and well combined.

Pour cranberry mixture into a bowl; cover and chill at least 30 minutes. Yield: 3 cups.

Spiced Cranberry Sauce

prep: 7 min.   cook: 21 min.   other: 45 min.

1   cup water
1   cup sugar
1   (3-inch) piece fresh ginger, peeled
1   firm, ripe pear, diced
1   teaspoon grated lemon rind
1   (12-ounce) package fresh or frozen cranberries
2   tablespoons fresh lemon juice

Bring first 3 ingredients to a boil in a heavy saucepan, stirring constantly; boil 5 minutes. Add pear and lemon rind; return mixture to a boil, and cook, stirring occasionally, 3 minutes. Stir in cranberries. Reduce heat, and simmer, without stirring, 3 to 5 minutes or until cranberries pop. Remove from heat; cool. Cover and chill.

Remove ginger; chill sauce up to 2 days. Stir in lemon juice just before serving. Yield: 2½ cups.

Glazed Carrots with Bacon and Onion

quick & easy

prep: 5 min.   cook: 30 min.

1   (1-pound) package baby carrots
3   bacon slices
1   small onion, chopped
3   tablespoons brown sugar
¼   teaspoon pepper

Cook carrots in boiling water to cover in a large saucepan 15 minutes or until carrots are tender; drain.

Cook bacon in a skillet until crisp; remove bacon, and drain on paper towels, reserving 1 tablespoon drippings in skillet. Crumble bacon; set aside.

Sauté onion in reserved drippings over medium-high heat 3 minutes or until tender. Stir in brown sugar, pepper, and carrots. Cook, stirring often, 5 minutes or until carrots are glazed and thoroughly heated.

Transfer carrots to a serving dish, and sprinkle with crumbled bacon. Yield: 4 servings.

Spicy Green Beans with Red Onion

prep: 20 min.   cook: 5 min.   other: 8 hrs.

2   pounds green beans, trimmed *
¼   cup olive oil
1   tablespoon lemon juice
1   teaspoon sugar
1   teaspoon Dijon mustard
½   teaspoon salt
¼   teaspoon black pepper
2   tablespoons chopped red bell pepper
2   tablespoons sliced water chestnuts
½   cup diced red onion

Cook green beans in boiling salted water to cover 5 minutes or until crisp-tender; drain. Plunge into ice water to stop the cooking process; drain.

Whisk together oil and next 5 ingredients in a large bowl. Add green beans, bell pepper, water chestnuts, and onion; toss well to coat. Cover and chill 8 hours. Yield: 6 servings.

* 2 (9-ounce) packages frozen whole green beans (cooked according to package directions) may be substituted for fresh green beans.

Spinach-Artichoke Casserole

prep: 20 min.   cook: 35 min.

2   (10-ounce) packages frozen chopped spinach, thawed
1   (14-ounce) can artichoke hearts, drained and chopped
1   (10¾-ounce) can fat-free cream of mushroom soup, undiluted
1   (8-ounce) container light sour cream
3   green onions, chopped
2   tablespoons all-purpose flour
1   tablespoon minced fresh parsley
¼   teaspoon Worcestershire sauce
1   tablespoon butter or margarine
1   cup sliced fresh mushrooms
2   garlic cloves, pressed
1   tablespoon lemon juice
½   teaspoon black pepper
2   cups (8 ounces) shredded Monterey Jack cheese with peppers

Drain spinach well, pressing between layers of paper towels. Stir together spinach and next 7 ingredients.

Melt butter in a skillet over medium-high heat. Add mushrooms and next 3 ingredients, and sauté 5 minutes or until mushrooms are tender.

Stir mushroom mixture and 1 cup cheese into spinach mixture; spoon into a lightly greased 11- x 7-inch baking dish. Sprinkle with remaining cheese.

Bake at 400° for 30 minutes. Yield: 8 to 10 servings.

Mashed Sweet Potatoes

make-ahead

prep: 25 min.   cook: 1 hr., 15 min.

4   pounds sweet potatoes
½   teaspoon salt
½   cup butter or margarine,
    melted
½   cup half-and-half
1   teaspoon ground cinnamon
1   teaspoon ground nutmeg
40 large marshmallows

Cook potatoes with ½ teaspoon salt in boiling water to cover in a large Dutch oven 30 minutes or until tender; drain. Cool potatoes slightly; peel and cut into chunks.

Beat potato, butter, and next 3 ingredients, in batches, at medium speed with an electric mixer until smooth.

Spoon into a lightly greased 13- x 9-inch baking dish. (If desired, cover and refrigerate up to 3 days, or freeze up to 1 month. Thaw at least 12 hours in refrigerator.)

Bake at 350° for 30 minutes; top with marshmallows, and bake 15 more minutes or until marshmallows are golden. Yield: 12 servings.

Cranberry Congealed Salad

Find pickled peaches on the aisle with canned fruits in your grocery store.

editor's favorite

prep: 30 min.   other: 8 hrs., 30 min.

1   (12-ounce) package fresh
    cranberries
½   cup sugar
3   (3-ounce) packages raspberry-
    flavored gelatin
2   cups boiling water
2   cups cranberry juice, chilled
1   (8-ounce) can crushed pineapple,
    undrained
2   celery ribs, diced (1 cup)
⅔   cup chopped pecans, toasted
Lettuce leaves
Pickled peaches
Fresh mint sprigs
Garnish: chopped pecans, toasted

Process cranberries in a food processor 30 seconds or until coarsely chopped, stopping to scrape down sides. Stir together cranberries and sugar in a bowl; let stand 10 minutes.

Stir together gelatin and boiling water in a large bowl 2 minutes or until gelatin dissolves. Add juice, and chill 30 minutes or until consistency of unbeaten egg whites. Stir in cranberry mixture, pineapple, celery, and ⅔ cup chopped pecans. Spoon mixture into a lightly greased 10-cup Bundt pan; cover and chill 8 hours or until firm.

Unmold onto a lettuce-lined platter. Fill center of ring with pickled peaches and fresh mint sprigs. Garnish, if desired. Yield: 12 servings.

Frosted Cranberry Congealed Salad Parfaits: Beat 8 ounces softened cream cheese at medium speed with an electric mixer until fluffy. Fold in 8 ounces frozen whipped topping, thawed. Layer parfait glasses evenly with leftover salad and cream cheese mixture.

Cranberry Congealed Salad

Butter Rolls

editor's favorite • freezer-friendly

prep: 15 min. cook: 20 min. other: 2 hrs.

1   (¼-ounce) envelope active dry
      yeast
¼   cup warm water (100° to 110°)
2½ to 3 cups all-purpose flour, divided
¼   cup sugar
1¼ teaspoons salt
2   large eggs, divided
¼   cup milk
¼   cup butter or margarine, softened
1   tablespoon water
Sesame or poppy seeds

Stir together yeast and ¼ cup water
in a 1-cup glass measuring cup; let stand
5 minutes.

Pulse 1 cup flour, sugar, and salt in a
food processor until blended. Add yeast
mixture, 1 egg, and milk; pulse until
blended. (Pulsing prevents mixture from
overheating, which would kill yeast.)
Add butter, 1 tablespoon at a time,
pulsing until combined. Gradually add
enough of remaining flour until dough
is no longer sticky. (Dough should be
smooth.)

Place dough in a well-greased bowl,
turning to grease top.

Cover and let rise in a warm place
(85°), free from drafts, 1 hour or until
doubled in bulk. Punch dough down,
and divide into fourths; shape each
portion into 6 (1-inch) balls. Place on
a lightly greased 13- x 9-inch pan.

Cover and let rise in a warm place
(85°), free from drafts, 1 hour. Stir
together remaining egg and 1 tablespoon
water; brush over rolls, and sprinkle
with sesame seeds.

Bake at 375° for 15 to 20 minutes
or until golden brown. Freeze up to
3 months, if desired. Yield: 2 dozen.

Butter Rolls

Buttery Herb-Cheese Muffins

*The secret to these delectable muffins is
a garlic-and-herb cheese spread from
the grocery store.*

prep: 10 min. cook: 25 min.

2   cups self-rising flour
1   cup butter, melted
1   (6.5-ounce) package buttery garlic-
      and-herb spreadable cheese,
      softened (we tested with Alouette
      Garlic and Herbes Gourmet
      Spreadable Cheese)
½   cup sour cream

Stir together all ingredients just until
blended.

Spoon muffin batter into lightly
greased miniature muffin pans, filling
to the top.

Bake at 350° for 25 minutes or until
lightly browned. Yield: 2½ dozen.

Chestnut Soup

editor's favorite

prep: 30 min.   cook: 1 hr., 25 min.

1   leek
3   tablespoons butter or margarine,
        divided
2   Macintosh apples, peeled and
        chopped
2   celery ribs, chopped
1   small onion, thinly sliced
1   bay leaf
1   thyme sprig
1   teaspoon salt
⅛   teaspoon ground nutmeg
2   (32-ounce) containers chicken
        broth
¾   pound whole chestnuts, shelled
        (about 2 cups nut meat)
1   cup whipping cream or half-and-
        half
2   tablespoons all-purpose flour
Toppings: sour cream, grated fresh
        nutmeg (optional)

Remove root, tough outer leaves, and
tops from leek, leaving 2 inches of dark
leaves. Cut into quarters lengthwise.
Thinly slice leek; rinse well, and drain.

   Melt 1 tablespoon butter in a medium
saucepan over medium heat. Add leek,
apples, celery, and onion; sauté 5 minutes.

Add bay leaf and next 3 ingredients;
sauté 8 to 12 minutes or until apples and
vegetables are tender.

   Stir in chicken broth and chestnuts.
Bring to a boil; reduce heat, and simmer
1 hour or until chestnuts are tender. Stir
in cream. Discard bay leaf.

   Process leek mixture, in batches,
in a food processor or blender until
smooth. Return mixture to saucepan.

   Melt remaining 2 tablespoons butter in
a small skillet. Stir in flour until smooth;
cook, stirring constantly, 2 to 3 minutes.

   Add flour mixture to pureed mixture.
Bring to a boil; reduce heat, and simmer
3 to 5 minutes or until thickened. Serve
warm. Top with sour cream and grated
fresh nutmeg, if desired. Yield: 10 cups.

Black Walnut Pie

prep: 9 min.   cook: 35 min.   other: 2 hrs.

3   large eggs
⅓   cup firmly packed brown sugar
1   cup maple syrup
1   teaspoon grated lemon rind
1   teaspoon fresh lemon juice
½   teaspoon vanilla extract
⅛   teaspoon salt
3   tablespoons butter, softened
1   cup black walnut pieces
1   (9-inch) unbaked pastry shell
Sweetened whipped cream

Beat eggs and sugar at medium speed
with an electric mixer until smooth. Add
syrup and next 5 ingredients, beating
until smooth.

   Place walnuts in pastry shell; pour filling over nuts.

   Bake at 375° for 35 minutes (center of
pie will not be set). Cool completely, and
serve with sweetened whipped cream.
Yield: 1 (9-inch) pie.

Cranberry-Apple-Raisin Pie

editor's favorite

prep: 40 min.   cook: 1 hr.

1½   (15-ounce) packages refrigerated
        piecrusts, divided
1   cup sugar, divided
2   tablespoons cornstarch
1   teaspoon ground cinnamon
3   large Golden Delicious apples,
        peeled and sliced
1   cup fresh cranberries
½   cup golden raisins
½   cup pecan pieces, toasted and
        chopped
3   tablespoons butter, cut into pieces
1   large egg
1   tablespoon water
Vanilla ice cream (optional)

Fit 1 piecrust into a 9-inch pieplate
according to package directions; chill.

   Stir together ¾ cup sugar, cornstarch,
and cinnamon in a large bowl; add
apple and next 3 ingredients, tossing
well. Spoon into prepared piecrust; dot
with butter.

   Unroll another piecrust; transfer to top
of pie. Fold edges under, and seal by
pressing with tines of a fork. Cut slits in
top for steam to escape.

   Unroll remaining piecrust. Cut with a
tree-shaped cutter; arrange trees on top
of pie.

   Whisk together egg and 1 tablespoon
water; brush evenly over top of pie.
Sprinkle with remaining ¼ cup sugar.

   Bake at 400° for 20 minutes; reduce
temperature to 350°, and bake 40 minutes. Serve warm, or cool on a wire rack.
(To reheat, cover loosely with aluminum
foil, and bake at 350° for 20 to 25 minutes.) Serve with vanilla ice cream, if
desired. Yield: 1 (9-inch) pie.

Cranberry-Apple-Raisin Pie

Elegant Pumpkin-Walnut
Layered Pie

Elegant Pumpkin-Walnut Layered Pie

A pecan pie-like filling nestles beneath the creamy pumpkin topping.

editor's favorite

prep: 20 min.   cook: 57 min.

1   (15-ounce) package refrigerated piecrusts, divided
1   large egg, lightly beaten
1¼ cups firmly packed light brown sugar, divided
1   cup walnuts, finely chopped and toasted
3   tablespoons butter, melted
¼   teaspoon vanilla extract
1   (16-ounce) can pumpkin
1   (8-ounce) package cream cheese, softened
2   large eggs
2   tablespoons all-purpose flour
1   teaspoon ground cinnamon
½   teaspoon ground ginger
½   teaspoon ground allspice
½   teaspoon ground nutmeg
Whipped cream (optional)

Unroll 1 piecrust; cut out leaves with a leaf-shaped cutter. Brush leaves with lightly beaten egg, and place on a baking sheet; set aside.

Fit remaining piecrust into a 9-inch pieplate according to package directions; fold edges under, and crimp.

Bake leaves at 350° for 10 to 12 minutes or until golden. Bake piecrust for 6 minutes or until lightly browned. Remove leaves and piecrust from oven; cool. Increase oven temperature to 425°.

Combine ½ cup brown sugar, chopped walnuts, butter, and vanilla; spread on the bottom of baked piecrust.

Beat pumpkin, cream cheese, eggs, and remaining ¾ cup brown sugar at medium speed with an electric mixer.

Add flour, cinnamon, ginger, allspice, and nutmeg, beating until blended. Spoon pumpkin mixture over walnut mixture.

Bake at 425° for 15 minutes. Reduce temperature to 350°, and bake 30 minutes or until pie is set. Remove pie to a wire rack; cool.

Arrange leaves on top of pie. Serve warm or chilled with whipped cream, if desired. Yield: 1 (9-inch) pie.

Nutty Yam Tartlets

This recipe makes a generous number. The tartlets freeze beautifully, allowing you to keep some on hand.

freezer-friendly • make-ahead

prep: 15 min.   cook: 1 hr., 45 min.

2   pounds sweet potatoes
¼   cup butter or margarine
3   large eggs, lightly beaten
1   cup chopped pecans, toasted
½   cup granulated sugar
½   cup firmly packed dark brown sugar
⅓   cup coconut milk
¼   cup sweetened flaked coconut
¼   cup honey
1   teaspoon light or dark rum
¼   teaspoon ground nutmeg
¼   teaspoon ground allspice
¼   teaspoon ground cinnamon
¼   teaspoon vanilla extract
4   (10-ounce) packages frozen tart shells *
Whipped cream

Cook potatoes in boiling water to cover in a Dutch oven 1 hour or until tender; drain. Peel potatoes, and discard skins.

Mash potatoes with a potato masher. Stir in butter until melted. Stir in eggs and next 11 ingredients, blending well.

Spoon about 2 tablespoons mixture into each tart shell.

Bake at 350° for 45 minutes or until set. Store in an airtight container in refrigerator; freeze, if desired. Serve tartlets with whipped cream. Yield: about 4 dozen.

* 2 unbaked 9-inch pastry shells may be substituted. Spoon mixture evenly into pastry shells; bake as directed.

nut knowledge

• If you buy nuts already shelled, store them in airtight containers in the freezer.
• Unsalted nuts have a longer storage life than salted nuts. Be sure to refrigerate or freeze after opening.
• The flavor of most nuts is enhanced when you toast them before use. You can toast a small amount of nuts in a dry skillet over medium heat for just a few minutes, stirring often. Use your sense of smell to judge when they're toasted.
• To remove the skins from hazelnuts, peanuts, and pistachios, spread them on a rimmed baking sheet and roast at 350° for 10 to 15 minutes; then rub off the skins.

New Year's sampler

Ring in the New Year with a festive array of goodies, ranging from savory appetizers to top-rated entrées.

Spicy Jack Cheese Crisps

great gift • make-ahead

prep: 30 min.   cook: 10 min.   other: 8 hrs.

½   cup butter, softened
2   (8-ounce) blocks Monterey Jack
      cheese with peppers, shredded
2   cups all-purpose flour
96 pecan halves

Beat softened butter and Monterey Jack cheese at medium speed with an electric mixer until blended; add flour, beating until blended.

Divide dough into 3 equal portions; shape each portion into a 6-inch log. Cover and chill at least 8 hours.

Cut each log into 32 (⅛-inch) slices, and place on ungreased baking sheets. Gently press 1 pecan half into center of each wafer.

Bake, in batches, at 350° for 8 to 10 minutes. Remove crisps to wire racks to cool. Store in an airtight container. Yield: 8 dozen.

Spiced Holiday Pecans

Hot sauce and red pepper dictate how spicy these snacking nuts are. Bake them ahead, and cool; they'll stay fresh up to five days in a cookie tin.

great gift • make-ahead

prep: 4 min.   cook: 28 min.

3   tablespoons butter or margarine,
      melted
½   teaspoon ground red pepper
½   teaspoon ground cinnamon
1   teaspoon salt
3   tablespoons Worcestershire sauce
Dash of hot sauce
4   cups pecan halves

Stir together first 6 ingredients. Add pecans; toss gently until coated. Place in an ungreased 15- x 10-inch jelly-roll pan.

Bake at 300° for 25 to 28 minutes, stirring twice. Cool completely. Store pecans in an airtight container. Yield: 4 cups.

Chutney-Glazed Cheese Pâté

Shred your own Cheddar rather than buying preshredded; it's stickier and blends better with the cream cheese.

prep: 10 min.   other: 8 hrs.

1   (8-ounce) block sharp Cheddar
      cheese, shredded
1   (8-ounce) package cream cheese,
      softened
3   tablespoons dry sherry
½   teaspoon curry powder
¼   teaspoon salt
1   (9-ounce) jar mango chutney
3   green onions, sliced
Garnishes: cucumber peel, fresh
      cranberries

Stir together first 5 ingredients in a large bowl until blended. Spread mixture evenly into a 4-cup shallow serving dish. Cover and chill 8 hours.

Spread chutney evenly over top of pâté; sprinkle with green onions. Garnish, if desired. Yield: about 8 to 10 appetizer servings.

Chutney-and-Blue Cheese Pâté:
Substitute 1 (3-ounce) package cream cheese and 1 (4-ounce) package blue cheese for sharp Cheddar cheese. Proceed with recipe as directed, substituting cranberry chutney for mango chutney, if desired. Leftovers are great on roast beef sandwiches or burgers.

Chutney-Glazed
Cheese Pâté

Pear-and-Gorgonzola Crostini

quick & easy

prep: 15 min.   cook: 2 min.

1   pear, cut lengthwise into 12 wedges
1   teaspoon lemon juice
12   (½-inch-thick) French bread slices
1   cup crumbled Gorgonzola cheese
4   teaspoons milk
¼   cup chopped walnuts, toasted
4   bacon slices, cooked and crumbled

Toss together pear slices and lemon juice; set aside.

Broil bread slices 5 inches from heat 1 minute on each side or until lightly toasted.

Stir together cheese and milk until smooth; spread evenly on 1 side of each bread slice. Sprinkle each slice with 1 teaspoon walnuts; top with 1 pear. Sprinkle with bacon. Yield: 6 servings.

Hot Cider Punch

prep: 5 min.   cook: 1 hr.

1   (64-ounce) bottle apple cider
2   cups orange juice
¾   cup fresh lemon juice
¼   cup honey
10   whole allspice
5   whole cloves
1   (2½-inch) cinnamon stick
1   lemon, sliced

Bring first 7 ingredients to a boil in a Dutch oven; reduce heat, and simmer 1 hour. Pour mixture through a wire-mesh strainer into a container; discard spices. Add lemon slices to punch just before serving. Serve warm. Yield: 8 servings.

Mulled Wine

quick & easy

prep: 5 min.   cook: 15 min.

2   cups water
2   cups sugar
1   orange, sliced
1   lemon, sliced
2   (2½-inch) cinnamon sticks
12   whole cloves
12   allspice berries
2   (750-milliliter) bottles or
      1 (1.5-liter) bottle dry red wine
Garnishes: cinnamon sticks, orange
      rind curls

Combine first 7 ingredients in a Dutch oven over medium heat; bring to a boil, reduce heat, and simmer 5 minutes. Add wine; simmer 10 minutes. Pour mixture through a wire-mesh strainer into a container; discard solids. Garnish, if desired. Yield: 10 servings.

Happy New Year Punch

quick & easy

prep: 6 min.

4   cups grape juice
2   cups white grape juice
3   cups lemon juice
3   cups pineapple juice
4   cups cranberry juice
4   cups orange juice
1   cup sugar
1   (2-liter) bottle ginger ale, chilled
1   (1-liter) bottle club soda, chilled

Stir together first 7 ingredients in a large punch bowl until sugar dissolves. Stir in ginger ale and club soda, and serve over ice. Yield: 2 gallons.

Bourbon-Barrel Coffee

For a gentler brew, omit the ¾ cup bourbon.

prep: 10 min.

¾   cup bourbon
Bourbon Syrup
3   cups hot brewed coffee
Whipped cream

Place 3 tablespoons bourbon and 2 tablespoons Bourbon Syrup in each of 4 coffee cups. Stir ¾ cup hot brewed coffee into each mug. Top with whipped cream. Yield: 4 servings.

Bourbon Syrup

Use leftover syrup on waffles, pancakes, roasted bananas, or ice cream. Or add to iced tea along with fresh mint for a refreshing tea julep. You can purchase superfine sugar at the supermarket, or make your own by processing granulated sugar in a food processor until powdery.

prep: 5 min.   cook: 10 min.

1   cup superfine sugar
1   cup firmly packed light brown
      sugar
1   cup water
1   cup bourbon (we tested with
      Maker's Mark Bourbon)

Bring superfine sugar, brown sugar, and water to a boil in a small saucepan over medium-high heat; cook 10 minutes until reduced by half. Remove from heat, and stir in bourbon. Yield: 2 cups.

1-2-3 Jambalaya

prep: 16 min.   cook: 45 min.

1   large onion, diced
1   large green bell pepper, diced
1   pound smoked sausage, cut into
      ¼-inch slices
1   tablespoon olive oil
4   cups chopped cooked chicken
3   cups uncooked long-grain rice
2   (10½-ounce) cans French onion
      soup, undiluted
1   (14-ounce) can chicken broth
1   (14-ounce) can beef broth
2   to 3 teaspoons Creole seasoning
2   to 3 teaspoons hot sauce
Garnish: fresh cilantro sprigs

Sauté first 3 ingredients in hot oil in
a Dutch oven 4 to 5 minutes or until
sausage is browned. Stir in chicken and
next 6 ingredients.

Bake, covered, at 350° for 40 minutes,
stirring after 30 minutes. Garnish, if
desired. Yield: 8 to 10 servings.

Ham 'n' Pot Liquor Soup

prep: 30 min.   cook: 1 hr., 15 min.

2   pounds fresh collard greens
1   (2-pound) ham steak, chopped
2   tablespoons hot sauce
3   tablespoons olive oil
3   medium onions, chopped
1   garlic clove, minced
6   red potatoes, diced
3   (14-ounce) cans chicken broth
2   (16-ounce) cans field peas, drained
2   (16-ounce) cans crowder peas,
      drained
2   cups water
½   cup vermouth
1   tablespoon white vinegar
1   teaspoon salt

Ham 'n' Pot Liquor Soup

Remove and discard stems and discolored spots from collards; rinse with cold
water. Drain and tear into 1-inch pieces.

Bring collards and water to cover to a
boil in a large Dutch oven. Remove from
heat; drain. Repeat procedure once.

Toss together ham and hot sauce.
Cook ham in hot oil in a Dutch oven
over medium-high heat 8 to 10 minutes
or until browned. Add onion and garlic,
and sauté until tender.

Stir in collards, potato, and remaining
ingredients; bring to a boil. Reduce heat,
and simmer, stirring occasionally, 45
minutes. Yield: 10 cups.

New Year's Day Soup

prep: 20 min.   cook: 1 hr., 30 min.

1   cup diced smoked lean ham
2   celery ribs, chopped
1   medium onion, chopped
2   carrots, chopped
2   garlic cloves, minced
2   (15-ounce) cans black-eyed peas, undrained
2   (14-ounce) cans low-sodium, fat-free chicken broth
2   (14½-ounce) cans no-salt-added stewed tomatoes, undrained
1   (14½-ounce) can no-salt-added diced tomatoes, undrained
1   (8-ounce) can tomato sauce
1½ cups chopped fresh spinach
½   cup chopped fresh parsley
½   teaspoon pepper

Sauté first 5 ingredients over medium heat in a Dutch oven until vegetables are tender.

Stir in peas and next 4 ingredients; bring to a boil. Cover, reduce heat, and simmer 1 hour and 30 minutes. Stir in 1½ cups spinach, parsley, and pepper. Yield: 10 cups.

Corn Sticks

prep: 10 min.   cook: 28 min.

2   jalapeño peppers, seeded and chopped
2   garlic cloves, minced
⅓   cup vegetable oil
½   cup yellow cornmeal
½   cup all-purpose flour
2   teaspoons baking powder
¾   teaspoon salt
1   tablespoon sugar
1   large egg, lightly beaten
½   cup milk

Cook jalapeño peppers and garlic in oil in a saucepan over medium heat, stirring constantly, until tender.

Combine cornmeal and next 4 ingredients; add jalapeño pepper mixture, egg, and milk, stirring until smooth.

Coat a cast-iron breadstick or corn stick pan with cooking spray; heat in a 425° oven 3 minutes or until hot. Remove pan from oven; spoon batter into pan. Bake at 425° for 15 to 20 minutes or until lightly browned. Yield: 8 breadsticks or 6 corn sticks.

Pork Roast with Hopping John Stuffing

editor's favorite

prep: 30 min.   cook: 1 hr.

1   small onion, chopped
½   green bell pepper, chopped
2   tablespoons vegetable oil
1½ cups cooked long-grain rice
1½ cups frozen chopped collard greens, thawed
1   (15-ounce) can black-eyed peas, rinsed and drained
½   cup diced cooked country ham
½   teaspoon sugar
½   teaspoon salt
1   large egg, lightly beaten
1   (2½-pound) boneless pork loin roast

Sauté onion and bell pepper in hot oil in a large skillet over medium-high heat 5 to 7 minutes or until tender. Remove from heat. Add rice and next 5 ingredients; stir in egg. Set stuffing aside.

Butterfly roast by making a lengthwise cut down center of 1 flat side, cutting to within ½ inch of bottom. From bottom of cut, slice horizontally to ½ inch from left side; repeat on right side. Open roast; place between 2 sheets of heavy-duty plastic wrap. Flatten to ½-inch thickness using a meat mallet or rolling pin.

Spoon 1½ cups stuffing evenly over roast, leaving a ½-inch border. Roll up roast, and tie with string at 1-inch intervals. Place roast, seam side down, in a lightly greased 11- x 7-inch baking dish.

Bake at 375° for 1 hour or until a meat thermometer inserted in center registers 160°. Reheat remaining hopping John; serve with roast. Yield: 6 to 8 servings.

New Year's Turkey

The stuffing for this turkey is a rich mixture of veal, ham, raisins, apples, and walnuts. Cajun seasoning spices things up for the holiday!

prep: 43 min.   cook: 3 hrs., 46 min. other: 6 hrs.

1   (10- to 12-pound) turkey
2   tablespoons salt
1   tablespoon pepper
⅓   cup balsamic vinegar
1   tablespoon minced garlic
2   tablespoons olive oil
⅔   cup butter or margarine
1½ cups chopped onion, divided
1   pound ground veal
½   pound ground boiled ham
6   white bread slices
1   cup milk
1   large egg, lightly beaten
1   cup chopped apple
1   tablespoon Cajun seasoning
1   teaspoon salt
1   teaspoon pepper
1   cup raisins
½   cup chopped walnuts
½   cup minced fresh parsley
1½ cups sweet vermouth
½   cup honey
Garnishes: fresh parsley sprigs, kumquat leaves, kumquats

New Year's Turkey

Remove giblets and neck from turkey, and reserve for another use. Rinse turkey with cold water, and pat dry.

Place turkey in a shallow dish. Stir together 2 tablespoons salt and next 4 ingredients; pour over turkey. Cover and chill at least 6 hours.

Melt butter in a large skillet; add ½ cup onion, and sauté until tender. Add veal and ham; cook over medium heat, stirring often, 5 minutes. Remove from heat.

Remove crusts from bread, and discard; crumble bread. Combine breadcrumbs, milk, and egg in a large bowl; stir in apple and next 6 ingredients. Stir in veal mixture.

Remove turkey from refrigerator, and brush cavity with oil mixture. Spoon stuffing into cavity; truss turkey using string. Lift wingtips up and over back, and tuck them under bird. Place turkey, breast side up, into a large roasting pan.

Cover turkey with aluminum foil, and

bake at 400° for 30 minutes. Reduce heat to 350°, and bake 2 hours, basting occasionally with pan drippings.

Process remaining 1 cup onion, vermouth, and honey in a blender until smooth. Pour mixture over turkey, and bake 1 more hour or until meat thermometer inserted into turkey thigh registers 180° and stuffing registers 165°.

Broil turkey 5 inches from heat until golden. Garnish, if desired. Yield: 10 to 12 servings.

Hearty Black-Eyed Peas

Many Southerners believe that eating black-eyed peas on New Year's Day will bring good luck all year long. Any kind of cooked greens ensures financial success.

Hearty Black-Eyed Peas

prep: 20 min.   cook: 1 hr.

1   (16-ounce) package dried black-
      eyed peas
4   cups water
1   medium onion, chopped
½   teaspoon pepper
¾   teaspoon salt
1   (1-pound) ham steak, cut into
      ½ inch cubes, or 1 ham hock
4   whole jalapeño peppers (optional)

Bring first 6 ingredients and, if desired, jalapeños to a boil in a Dutch oven; cover, reduce heat, and simmer 1 hour or until the peas are tender. Yield: 8 servings.

Nana's Collard Greens.

prep: 20 min.   cook: 1 hr., 15 min.

4   bacon slices
1   large carrot, chopped
1   large onion, chopped
2   garlic cloves, minced
2   to 3 tablespoons balsamic vinegar
4   (1-pound) packages fresh collard
      greens, washed, trimmed, and
      chopped
1½ cups low-sodium, fat-free chicken
      broth
½   teaspoon red bell pepper flakes
½   teaspoon salt
¼   teaspoon black pepper

Cook bacon in a Dutch oven until crisp. Remove bacon; drain on paper towels,

reserving 2 tablespoons drippings. Crumble bacon.

Cook carrot in hot bacon drippings in Dutch oven over medium-high heat, stirring occasionally, 5 minutes. Add onion, and cook, stirring occasionally, 5 minutes or until carrot and onion begin to caramelize. Add garlic; cook, stirring constantly, 30 seconds. Add balsamic vinegar, and cook 30 seconds. Add collards, crumbled bacon, broth, and remaining ingredients. Bring to a boil; cover, reduce heat, and simmer 1 hour or until collards are tender. Yield: 6 to 8 servings.

Champagne Sabayon

prep: 8 min.   cook: 10 min.

8   egg yolks
⅔   cup sugar
1½ cups Champagne
1   pint fresh raspberries, blueberries,
      and strawberries

Whisk together egg yolks and sugar in a heavy saucepan over low heat until blended. Whisk in Champagne; cook, whisking constantly, 10 minutes or until mixture reaches 160° and is thickened. Chill, if desired.

Spoon Champagne mixture over fresh berries. Yield: 2¾ cups.

Chocolate Mousse with Orange Liqueur

prep: 18 min.   cook: 8 min.   other: 30 min.

1   (4-ounce) package sweet chocolate
      baking bars, chopped
4   (1-ounce) semisweet chocolate
      baking squares, chopped
¼   cup orange liqueur
2   cups whipping cream
½   cup powdered sugar
Orange Whipped Cream

Place chocolate and orange liqueur in top of a double boiler. Bring water to a boil in bottom of double boiler; remove from heat. Place chocolate over simmering water, and cook, stirring occasionally, until chocolate melts. Cool to lukewarm.

Beat whipping cream at medium speed with an electric mixer until foamy; gradually add powdered sugar, beating until soft peaks form.

Fold about one-fourth of whipped cream into melted chocolate, working quickly; fold chocolate mixture into remaining whipped cream.

Spoon evenly into individual small serving cups. Chill until ready to serve. Dollop with Orange Whipped Cream. Yield: 4 cups.

Orange Whipped Cream

prep: 5 min.

½   cup whipping cream
3   tablespoons powdered sugar
1   tablespoon orange liqueur

Beat all ingredients at medium speed with an electric mixer until soft peaks form. Cover and chill until ready to serve. Yield: 1¼ cups.

Serve warm over Ice Cream

made from a mix

Get a head start on holiday desserts with these recipes that begin with mixes.
(Your secret's safe with us!)

Easy Cookies

quick & easy
prep: 10 min.   cook: 10 min. per batch

1 (18.25-ounce) package chocolate
   or yellow cake mix
½ cup vegetable oil
2 large eggs
1 cup (6 ounces) semisweet
   chocolate morsels
½ cup chopped pecans

Beat first 3 ingredients at medium speed
with an electric mixer until smooth.

Stir in chocolate morsels and pecans.
Drop by heaping teaspoonfuls onto
ungreased baking sheets.

Bake at 350° for 8 to 10 minutes.
Remove to wire racks to cool. Yield:
4½ dozen.

Walnut-Date Bars

*Wrap these treats in plastic wrap, and
place them in a zip-top freezer bag;
freeze up to three months, if desired.*

freezer-friendly • make-ahead
prep: 20 min.   cook: 35 min.   other: 30 min.

1 (18.25-ounce) package yellow
   cake mix
⅔ cup firmly packed brown sugar
2 large eggs
¾ cup butter or margarine, melted
2 cups chopped dates, divided
2 cups chopped walnuts or pecans

Combine cake mix and brown sugar in
a mixing bowl. Add eggs and melted
butter, beating at medium speed with
an electric mixer until blended (batter
will be stiff). Spoon half of batter into
a lightly greased 13- x 9-inch pan; sprinkle with 1 cup each of dates and walnuts.

Stir remaining dates and remaining
walnuts into remaining batter; spread
over mixture in pan.

Bake at 350° for 30 to 35 minutes
or until golden. Run a knife around edge
of pan to loosen sides. Let stand 30 minutes before cutting. Cut into bars, and
store bars in an airtight container. Yield:
16 squares.

Chewy Almond-Fudge Bars

*Coconut candy bars and almonds give
these moist brownies personality. If you
like firm bars, chill them. If you prefer
even firmer brownies, bake them at the
longer end of the time range.*

editor's favorite
prep: 17 min.   cook: 38 min.

1 (19.8-ounce) package chewy fudge
   brownie mix (we tested with
   Duncan Hines)
3 tablespoons vegetable oil
1 cup sweetened condensed milk
14 miniature dark chocolate coconut
   candy bars, chopped (1¼ cups)
   (we tested with Mounds)
¾ cup chopped natural almonds,
   toasted

Prepare brownie mix according to
package directions, reducing vegetable
oil to 3 tablespoons; pour into a lightly
greased 13- x 9-inch pan. Pour sweetened condensed milk over batter;
sprinkle with chopped candy bars
and almonds.

Bake at 350° for 36 to 38 minutes.
Cool completely in pan on a wire rack.
Cut into bars. Yield: 2 dozen.

Chewy Almond-Fudge Bars

Santa Claus Cupcakes

Butter Toffee Loaf Cakes

You can wrap one or both loaf cakes tightly in plastic wrap and heavy-duty aluminum foil, and freeze up to three months.

freezer-friendly • great gift
prep: 13 min.　cook: 1 hr.　other: 10 min.

1　cup chopped pecans, toasted
1　(18.25-ounce) package yellow cake mix
1　(3.4-ounce) package vanilla instant pudding mix
4　large eggs
¾　cup water
½　cup vegetable oil
½　teaspoon butter flavoring
1　cup almond toffee bits

Bake pecans on a baking sheet at 350° for 5 minutes or until toasted, stirring once. Set aside.

Beat cake mix and next 5 ingredients at medium speed with an electric mixer 5 minutes. Stir in toffee bits just until blended.

Sprinkle pecans evenly over bottoms of 2 lightly greased 9- x 5-inch loafpans. Pour cake batter evenly over pecans.

Bake at 350° for 55 minutes or until a wooden pick inserted in center comes out clean. Cool in pans on wire rack 10 minutes. Remove from pans, and cool completely. Yield: 2 loaf cakes.

Chocolate Chip Loaf Cakes: Substitute 1 cup (6 ounces) semisweet chocolate morsels for toffee bits.

Santa Claus Cupcakes

A fluffy white coconut beard, jolly red cinnamon nose, and twinkling candy eyes make Santa Claus come to life—cupcake fashion.

prep: 45 min.　cook: 27 min.　other: 20 min.

1　(18.25-ounce) package white cake mix with pudding
18　flat-bottomed jumbo "cake cup" ice cream cones
1　(16-ounce) container ready-to-spread cream cheese frosting
Flaked coconut
Miniature marshmallows
Red cinnamon candies
Miniature candy-coated chocolate pieces

Prepare cake mix according to package directions. Spoon 5 tablespoons batter into each cone; place cones in muffin pans.

Bake at 350° for 25 to 27 minutes or until a wooden pick inserted in center of cupcakes comes out clean. Remove cones from pans, and cool completely on wire racks.

Spread tops of cupcakes with cream cheese frosting, and decorate with flaked coconut and remaining ingredients. (Do not store cupcakes in an airtight container, or the cones will become soft.) Yield: 1½ dozen.

Brownie Trifle

make-ahead
prep: 18 min.   cook: 28 min.   other: 8 hrs.

1   (19.8-ounce) package fudge
      brownie mix (we tested with
      Betty Crocker)
¼   cup Kahlúa or other coffee-flavored
      liqueur (optional)
2   (3.9-ounce) packages chocolate
      instant pudding mix
1   (12-ounce) container frozen
      whipped topping, thawed
6   (1.4-ounce) chocolate-covered
      toffee candy bars, crushed (we
      tested with Heath bars)

Prepare and bake brownie mix according to package directions in a 13- x 9-inch pan. Prick top of warm brownies at 1-inch intervals with a wooden pick, and, if desired, brush with Kahlúa. Cool brownies, and crumble into small pieces.

Prepare pudding mix according to package directions, omitting chilling procedure.

Place one-third of crumbled brownies in a 3-quart trifle bowl; top with one-third each of pudding, whipped topping, and crushed candy bars.

Repeat layers twice using remaining ingredients, ending with crushed candy bars. Cover and chill trifle at least 8 hours. Yield: 16 servings.

Mint Chocolate Mousse Pie

This smooth and silky pie cuts best if you chill it overnight.

prep: 13 min.   other: 1 hr.

1   (11.1-ounce) package no-bake
      cheesecake mix (we tested with
      Jell-O brand)
⅓   cup butter or margarine, melted
2   tablespoons sugar
1   cup milk
½   cup chocolate-mint flavored syrup
      (we tested with Hershey's)
2   (1.55-ounce) minty milk chocolate
      bars with crunchy cookie bits,
      finely chopped
Garnishes: sweetened whipped cream,
      additional chopped chocolate bars

Combine graham cracker crumbs from cheesecake mix, butter, and sugar. Firmly press mixture in bottom and up sides of a 9-inch pieplate.

Combine milk and chocolate syrup in a medium bowl, stirring well. Add cheesecake filling mix; beat at low speed with an electric mixer until blended. Beat at medium speed 3 minutes. Fold in finely chopped chocolate.

Spoon chocolate mixture into prepared crust. Cover and chill at least 1 hour. Garnish, if desired. Before serving, dip bottom of pieplate in hot water for 30 seconds. Yield: 1 (9-inch) pie.

Mint Chocolate
Mousse Pie

Satiny Mocha Torte

with second and third layers and remaining mousse. Top stack with fourth layer. Chill 30 minutes.

Combine whipping cream and coffee powder in a saucepan; bring to a simmer over medium heat. Remove from heat; add chocolate. Let stand 1 minute. Stir until chocolate melts. Cool 30 minutes.

Pour chocolate glaze over torte, letting excess drip down sides onto wax paper. Using a small spatula, smooth excess glaze onto sides of torte. Gently press hazelnuts onto sides of glazed torte. Carefully pull wax paper strips from beneath torte. Store in refrigerator. Yield: 1 (9-inch) torte.

White Chocolate Charlotte Russe with Cranberry Sauce

It seems fitting to tie such a delicate molded dessert with a sheer ribbon for a beautiful presentation. Tie on the ribbon just before you put it on display for serving.

prep: 20 min.   other: 4 hrs.

2 (3.3-ounce) packages fat-free white chocolate instant pudding mix (we tested with Jell-O brand)
2 cups milk
2 teaspoons grated orange rind
2 tablespoons Grand Marnier or other orange liqueur or orange juice, divided
1 teaspoon vanilla extract
1 cup whipping cream, whipped
22 ladyfingers, split
1 (12-ounce) tub cranberry-orange crushed fruit (we tested with Ocean Spray) *

Prepare both packages of pudding mix according to package directions, using

Satiny Mocha Torte

Convenience products do most of the work in this stunning four-layer cake.

editor's favorite
prep: 37 min.   cook: 46 min.
other: 3 hrs.

¾ cup whole hazelnuts in the skins
1 (18.25-ounce) package devil's food cake mix without pudding (we tested with Duncan Hines devil's food cake mix)
2 (2.8-ounce) packages mocha mousse mix (we tested with Nestlé mocha mousse mix)
1⅓ cups milk
¾ cup whipping cream
1½ tablespoons Swiss-style flavored instant coffee powder (we tested with General Foods International Coffees Suisse Mocha)
6 (1-ounce) semisweet chocolate baking squares, chopped

Place hazelnuts in an ungreased 15- x 10-inch jellyroll pan. Toast at 350° for 12 minutes or until skins begin to split. Transfer hot nuts to a colander; cover with a kitchen towel. Rub nuts briskly with towel to remove skins. Cool nuts, and chop.

Grease and flour 2 (9-inch) cakepans. Prepare cake mix according to package directions; pour into prepared pans. Bake at 350° for 30 minutes or until a wooden pick inserted in center comes out clean. Cool in pans on wire racks 15 minutes; remove from pans, and cool completely on wire racks.

Prepare mousse mix according to package directions, using 1⅓ cups milk; cover and chill.

Split cake layers in half horizontally to make 4 layers. Place 1 layer on a serving plate; place 4 strips of wax paper under and around cake layer. Spread one-third of mousse over layer. Repeat procedure

White Chocolate Charlotte Russe with Cranberry Sauce

White Chocolate Charlotte Russe

2 cups milk. Stir in orange rind, 1 table-spoon Grand Marnier, and vanilla. Gently fold in whipped cream.

Line bottom and sides of a 9-inch springform pan with ladyfingers (see note at right). Spoon pudding mixture into pan. Cover and chill at least 4 hours or until dessert is set.

Combine crushed fruit and remaining Grand Marnier, stirring well. Place dessert on a serving platter; carefully remove sides of pan. Serve with cran-berry sauce. Yield: 12 servings.

* Find the crushed fruit on the same supermarket aisle as canned fruit.

Ladyfinger Note: Here's an easy way to arrange ladyfingers in the springform pan. Simply remove rows of connected ladyfingers intact from their package, and unfold them into the bottom of the pan and then again around the sides of the pan.

Carrot Cake Roulage

Carrot Cake Roulage

Carrot cake claims a new shape in this jellyroll. Look for the lavish cream cheese frosting rolled up inside.

great gift • make-ahead
prep: 35 min. cook: 13 min.
other: 1 hr., 30 min.

4   large eggs
½   cup water
1   (18.25-ounce) package spice cake
       mix (we tested with Duncan
       Hines spice cake mix)
1   cup grated carrot
3   tablespoons powdered sugar, divided
1   (15¼-ounce) can crushed
       pineapple in heavy syrup
2   (16-ounce) containers ready-to-
       spread cream cheese frosting
½   cup chopped pecans, toasted
Additional powdered sugar
Garnish: toasted chopped pecans

Coat 2 (15- x 10-inch) jellyroll pans with cooking spray; line with wax paper, and coat wax paper with cooking spray. Set aside.

Beat eggs in a large bowl at medium-high speed with an electric mixer 5 minutes. Add water, beating at low speed until blended. Gradually add cake mix, beating at low speed until moistened. Beat mixture at medium-high speed 2 minutes. Fold in grated carrot.

Spread batter evenly in prepared pans (layers will be thin). Bake, 1 at a time or in separate ovens, at 350° on the middle rack 13 minutes or until each cake springs back when lightly touched in center.

Sift 1½ tablespoons powdered sugar in a 15- x 10-inch rectangle on a cloth towel; repeat with 1½ tablespoons sugar and a second towel. When cakes are done, immediately loosen from sides of pan, and turn each out onto a sugared towel. Peel off wax paper. Starting at narrow end, tightly roll up each cake and towel together; place each, seam side down, on wire racks to cool completely.

Drain pineapple, reserving ¼ cup syrup. Press pineapple between paper towels to remove excess moisture. Combine pineapple, cream cheese frosting, and ½ cup pecans; stir well.

Unroll cakes; brush each lightly with 2 tablespoons reserved pineapple syrup. Spread each cake with half of frosting mixture. Reroll cakes without towels; place, seam side down, on serving plates.

Cover and chill at least 1 hour. Dust cakes with additional powdered sugar before serving. Garnish, if desired. Yield: 2 cake rolls (8 servings each).

Twice the Goodness: This recipe makes 2 cake rolls, so it's ideal for a make-ahead dessert for a crowd. Or give the second roll as a gift.

Apple-Oat Snack Squares

To give this old-fashioned spice cake as a gift, deliver it in a disposable baking pan or cut it into squares and transfer them to a plate. Either way, your friends will relish a taste with a glass of milk right away!

prep: 16 min. cook: 40 min.

3   cups all-purpose baking mix
2   cups quick-cooking oats,
       uncooked
⅔   cup firmly packed light brown sugar
1   teaspoon ground cinnamon
½   cup butter or margarine, cut into
       pieces
1   cup milk
1   (21-ounce) can apple fruit filling
2   tablespoons light brown sugar

Stir together first 4 ingredients in a medium bowl; cut in butter with a pastry blender until crumbly. Add milk, stirring just until dry ingredients are moistened. Fold in fruit filling, and spoon into a lightly greased 13- x 9-inch pan. Sprinkle with 2 tablespoons brown sugar.

Bake at 350° for 40 minutes or until golden. Cool on a wire rack, and cut into squares. Yield: 16 squares.

Holiday Brownie Cupcakes

Here's a gift kids love that's easy enough for them to help make, too. So be sure to share the recipe.

prep: 16 min. cook: 20 min.

1   (12-ounce) package brownie mix
½   cup vegetable oil
¼   cup cranberry juice
2   large eggs
Toppings: semisweet chocolate morsels,
       candy-coated chocolate pieces,
       chopped pecans, holiday candy
       sprinkles
Powdered sugar (optional)

Stir together first 4 ingredients until smooth. Spoon batter into 12 lightly greased muffin cups. Sprinkle with desired toppings.

Bake at 350° for 20 minutes or until a wooden pick inserted in center of cupcakes comes out clean. Remove from pan, and cool on a wire rack. Sprinkle with powdered sugar, if desired. Yield: 1 dozen.

merry Christmas treats

Delight everyone on your gift list with tasty gifts from your kitchen.
We've even included creative packaging ideas.

Minted Coffee Mix

Give this coffee mix along with a bag of cinnamon sticks that can be used to stir up the tasty treat.

quick & easy

prep: 6 min.

¼   cup instant coffee granules
¼   cup powdered non-dairy coffee creamer
⅓   cup sugar
2   tablespoons cocoa
1½ tablespoons crushed hard peppermint candies

Process all ingredients in a blender until blended. Store in an airtight container. Yield: 1 cup.

Directions for Gift Card: Combine 2 tablespoons Minted Coffee Mix and ¾ cup boiling water, stirring well. Yield: ¾ cup.

Hot Cocoa Mix

Give a friend the delightful gift of hot cocoa—enough for a warming mugful every day of the week. Our minted interpretation tastes like chocolate mint candies. Place this custom-made cocoa mix in a plastic bag, and tuck the bag inside a holiday mug.

editor's favorite • quick & easy

prep: 6 min.

1   cup powdered non-dairy coffee creamer
1   cup sifted powdered sugar
½   cup miniature marshmallows
¼   cup cocoa
¼   cup mint chocolate morsels

Combine all ingredients; store in an airtight container. Yield: 2⅓ cups.

Directions for Gift Card: Combine ⅓ cup Hot Cocoa Mix and ⅔ cup boiling water, stirring well. Yield: about 1 cup.

Spiced Tea Punch Mix

The flavors of citrus and cinnamon combine to create a refreshing holiday drink. Pour the mix into a decorative jar tied up with ribbon; include a recipe card.

prep: 5 min.

1   (21.1-ounce) jar instant orange breakfast drink mix
¾   cup instant tea with lemon
1½ cups sugar
1½ teaspoons ground cloves
1½ teaspoons ground cinnamon

Combine all ingredients in a large bowl; store in an airtight container. Yield: 5 cups.

Directions for Gift Card: Bring ¾ cup Spiced Tea Punch Mix, 1 (46-ounce) can unsweetened pineapple juice, 1 (46-ounce) can apple juice, and 2 cups water to a boil in a Dutch oven. Reduce heat, and simmer, stirring occasionally, 15 minutes. Serve hot or cold. Yield: 15 cups.

bejeweled jars

Put a drop of clear silicone on the flat side of a glass gem. Press it firmly against a glass jar in the desired position (see photo at right). Hold it in place for a few seconds to let the glue set. Let dry for 24 hours.

Spiced Tea Punch Mix

Russian Tea Mix

Russian Tea Mix

Pop a bag of this fragrant spiced tea mix in a pretty teacup or mug as a thoughtful holiday gift.

prep: 5 min.

2   cups sugar
2   cups orange breakfast drink mix
⅔   cup presweetened lemonade mix
½   cup instant tea mix
1   tablespoon ground cinnamon
1   tablespoon ground cloves

Combine all ingredients. Package in an airtight container. Yield: 4½ cups.

Directions for Gift Card: To prepare, spoon 2 heaping tablespoons mix into a cup or mug; stir in ¾ cup boiling water.

Homemade Coconut Granola

prep: 10 min. cook: 1 hr., 4 min.

3½ cups uncooked regular oats
½   cup grated coconut
½   cup sliced almonds
½   cup coarsely chopped pecans
½   cup wheat germ
¼   cup sesame seeds
¼   cup sunflower kernels
½   cup honey
¼   cup firmly packed brown sugar
¼   cup vegetable oil
½   cup crunchy peanut butter
1   teaspoon vanilla extract
¾   cup raisins (optional)

Combine first 7 ingredients in a large bowl. Stir well.

   Combine honey, brown sugar, and oil in a small saucepan. Cook over medium heat, stirring until sugar melts and mixture is thoroughly heated. Remove from heat; add peanut butter and vanilla, stirring until blended. Drizzle over oat mixture; toss to coat. Spread mixture in a greased 15- x 10-inch jellyroll pan.

Bake at 250° for 50 to 60 minutes or until toasted and dry, stirring gently every 20 minutes; add raisins after 40 minutes, if desired. Cool completely. Store in an airtight container. Yield: 8 cups.

Granola Bars: Press unbaked granola mixture (without raisins) into a greased 15- x 10-inch jellyroll pan, using greased fingertips. Press mixture flat with the back of a wide metal spatula. Bake at 250° for 1 hour and 20 minutes to 1½ hours or until toasted. Cut granola into bars while warm. Cool completely in pan. Remove bars from pan, and store in an airtight container. Yield: 2½ dozen.

Elf Gorp

prep: 14 min.   cook: 1 hr.

8   cups popped corn
2   cups toasted oat O-shaped cereal
2   cups goldfish cracker pretzels
2   cups bite-size crispy rice cereal
1   cup peanuts
½   cup butter or margarine, melted
½   teaspoon seasoned salt
½   teaspoon garlic powder
1   tablespoon Worcestershire sauce

Combine first 5 ingredients in a large bowl. Combine butter, salt, garlic powder, and Worcestershire sauce in a small bowl; stir well. Pour over popcorn mixture; toss gently to coat, and pour into a large roasting pan.

Bake at 250° for 1 hour, stirring mixture at 15-minute intervals. Cool completely; store in an airtight container. Yield: 2½ quarts.

stocking stuffers

Fill a Christmas stocking with a favorite snack mix or nut mix. Just package the mix in large zip-top plastic bags. Tuck holiday napkins into the stocking.

Parmesan Nuts and Bolts

quick & easy

prep: 5 min.   cook: 15 min.

3   cups corn-and-rice cereal
1   cup honey graham cereal or bear-shaped graham cereal
⅓   cup grated Parmesan cheese
¼   teaspoon garlic powder
1   (12-ounce) jar unsalted, dry-roasted peanuts
¼   cup butter or margarine, melted

Combine first 5 ingredients in a 15- x 10-inch jellyroll pan. Pour butter evenly over mixture; stir gently to coat.

Bake at 300° for 15 minutes, stirring every 5 minutes. Remove from oven; cool completely. Store in an airtight container. Yield: 6¼ cups.

Honey-and-Spice Crunch

prep: 13 min.   cook: 40 min.

3   quarts popped corn
3   tablespoons butter or margarine
¼   cup honey
¼   cup light corn syrup
3   tablespoons sugar
⅛   teaspoon salt
½   teaspoon ground cinnamon
¼   teaspoon baking soda
½   teaspoon vanilla extract
2   (0.9-ounce) packages dried fruit bits (about ½ cup)

Pour popcorn into a bowl coated with cooking spray; set aside.

Melt butter in a saucepan over low heat; stir in honey and next 3 ingredients. Bring to a boil over medium heat, stirring constantly. Boil, without stirring, 7 minutes or until a candy thermometer registers 250°.

Remove from heat. Stir in cinnamon, soda, and vanilla; pour over popcorn, stirring to coat. Spoon mixture into a lightly greased 15- x 10-inch jellyroll pan.

Bake at 250° for 25 minutes or until golden, stirring every 5 minutes. Stir in dried fruit; cool. Store in airtight containers. Yield: 3 quarts.

Peanut-Pretzel Mix

quick & easy

prep: 8 min.   cook: 12 min.

¾   cup butter or margarine, melted
2   to 3 tablespoons Worcestershire sauce
2   teaspoons garlic powder
1½   teaspoons curry powder
½   teaspoon ground red pepper
½   teaspoon chili powder
4   cups bite-size twisted pretzels
3   cups crispy corn cereal squares
2   cups mini shredded whole wheat cereal biscuits
1½   cups roasted peanuts

Combine first 6 ingredients in a small bowl; stir well. Combine pretzels and remaining 3 ingredients in a large bowl. Drizzle butter mixture over cereal mixture, stirring gently.

Spread mixture in 2 (15- x 10-inch) jellyroll pans. Bake at 350° for 10 to 12 minutes, stirring every 5 minutes. Remove from oven, and cool completely. Store in an airtight container. Yield: 9 cups.

Pepper Pecans

*The light-colored Worcestershire sauce
gives a more attractive coating to the
pecans than the darker sauce.*

quick & easy

prep: 4 min.   cook: 35 min.   other: 30 min.

¼   cup white wine Worcestershire sauce
2   tablespoons butter or margarine,
     melted
¼   teaspoon hot sauce
⅛   teaspoon pepper
2   cups pecan halves

Combine first 4 ingredients in a medium
bowl; stir in pecans. Let mixture stand
30 minutes.

   Drain pecans, and spread in a single
layer in a 13- x 9-inch pan.

   Bake at 250° for 35 minutes, stirring
every 10 minutes. Remove from oven,
and cool completely. Store in an airtight
container up to 2 weeks. Yield: 2 cups.

Chili Nuts

quick & easy

prep: 6 min.   cook: 35 min.

1   pound shelled raw peanuts
¼   cup peanut oil
1   tablespoon chili powder
1   teaspoon salt
¾   teaspoon paprika
½   teaspoon ground red pepper

Place peanuts in a shallow roasting pan;
pour oil over nuts, stirring well. Roast
peanuts at 350° for 35 minutes or until
browned. Drain on paper towels.

   Combine chili powder and remaining
3 ingredients; sprinkle over peanuts, and
stir until coated. Yield: about 2½ cups.

Raspberry Vinegar

*Choose clear decorative bottles to let
the crimson color shine through.*

prep: 8 min.   cook: 10 min.
other: 8 hrs., 30 min.

2   cups fresh raspberries *
2   (17-ounce) bottles white wine
     vinegar
2   (3-inch) cinnamon sticks
½   cup honey

Combine raspberries and vinegar in a
nonmetal bowl; cover and let stand at
room temperature 8 hours.

   Transfer to a large nonaluminum
saucepan, and add cinnamon; bring to a
boil. Reduce heat, and simmer, uncovered, 3 minutes. Remove from heat; stir
in honey, and cool.

   Pour mixture through a large wire-mesh
strainer into bottles or jars, discarding
solids. Seal with a cork or an airtight lid.
Store vinegar in refrigerator 1 week
before using. Yield: 4 cups.

* You can substitute 1 (16-ounce)
package frozen whole raspberries,
thawed and drained, for the fresh
raspberries. Yield: 3½ cups.

❋ **Directions for Gift Card:** Store in
refrigerator. Use in vinaigrettes or
marinades.

Herb-Cheese Croutons

*Package these croutons in a basket with
a gift card that suggests serving them
atop salads and soups. You might also
include directions for storing the croutons.*

prep: 9 min.   cook: 10 min.

1   (13-ounce) package small soft
     breadsticks
¼   cup olive oil
¼   cup butter or margarine, melted
2   cloves garlic, minced
¼   cup grated Parmesan cheese
2   teaspoons dried Italian seasoning
¼   teaspoon ground red pepper

Slice bread into ⅜-inch-thick rounds
with a serrated knife. Combine oil,
butter, and garlic. Drizzle over bread
rounds, tossing to coat. Combine
Parmesan cheese, Italian seasoning, and
pepper; sprinkle over bread rounds, tossing to coat.

   Place on baking sheet; bake at 400° for
5 minutes. Turn rounds over, and bake
2 to 5 more minutes or until crisp and
brown. Cool and store in an airtight container up to 2 weeks. Yield: 10 cups.

Stir-Fry Sauce

prep: 5 min.   other: 8 hrs.

1   (15-ounce) bottle soy sauce
1½ cups dry white wine
½   cup dry sherry
⅓   cup firmly packed brown sugar
2   cloves garlic, halved
2   tablespoons chicken bouillon
      granules
2   tablespoons grated fresh ginger
2   teaspoons black peppercorns
1½ teaspoons sesame oil

Combine all ingredients; cover and chill
8 hours. Pour through a large wire-mesh
strainer into bottles, discarding solids.
Store in refrigerator up to 2 weeks.
Yield: 4½ cups.

Directions for Gift Card: Store Stir-Fry
Sauce in refrigerator up to 2 weeks.

To use with vegetables and chicken or
pork, marinate 1 pound chicken or pork
strips in ½ cup Stir-Fry Sauce 30 minutes. Drain, reserving sauce. Bring sauce
to a boil; set aside. Cook meat in 1
tablespoon vegetable oil in a large skillet,
stirring constantly, until done; remove
from skillet, and drain on paper towels.
Add 4 cups mixed vegetables to skillet;
stir-fry 2 minutes or until crisp-tender.
Combine 1 tablespoon cornstarch, ½
cup water, and reserved sauce; add to
vegetable mixture. Cook 1 minute. Add
meat, and cook until thoroughly heated.
Serve over rice. Yield: 4 servings.

Stir-Fry Sauce,
Raspberry Vinegar

Hot Pineapple Sauce

prep: 9 min.   cook: 11 min.   other: 1 hr.

1   (12-ounce) jar apricot preserves
1   (8-ounce) can unsweetened crushed
       pineapple, drained
½   cup finely chopped red bell pepper
¼   cup finely chopped green onions
2   tablespoons finely chopped jalapeño
       peppers
2   tablespoons balsamic vinegar

Combine all ingredients in a small saucepan; bring to a boil, stirring often. Reduce heat, and simmer 5 minutes. Spoon sauce into a gift container; cover and chill. Yield: 1⅓ cups.

Directions for Gift Card: Store in refrigerator. Heat Hot Pineapple Sauce in a small saucepan; serve with pork, ham, and turkey.

Southwestern Black Bean-Corn Salsa

prep: 30 min.   cook: 3 min.

2   teaspoons cumin seeds
4   (15-ounce) cans black beans, rinsed
       and drained
2   (15.25-ounce) cans sweet whole
       kernel corn, drained
2   red bell peppers, minced
1   red onion, minced
1   cup minced fresh cilantro
1   cup minced fresh parsley
⅔   cup lime juice
½   cup olive oil
6   garlic cloves, pressed
2   teaspoons dried crushed red pepper
1   teaspoon ground black pepper

Cook cumin seeds in a small cast-iron skillet over medium heat 2 to 3 minutes

or until browned, stirring often. Stir together cumin seeds, black beans, and remaining ingredients; toss well. Cover and store in refrigerator up to 1 week. Yield: 10 cups.

Directions for Gift Card: Serve with tortilla chips, fajitas, fish, or steak.

Walnut-Basil Cheese Spread

prep: 7 min.   other: 2 hrs.

1   (11-ounce) log goat cheese
1   (8-ounce) container sour cream
⅔   cup toasted, chopped walnuts
½   cup finely chopped dried tomatoes
       in oil
½   cup minced fresh basil

Combine goat cheese and sour cream in a bowl; stir well. Stir in walnuts and remaining ingredients. Cover and chill at least 2 hours. Serve at room temperature with French bread. Yield: 3 cups.

Roasted Shallot-Garlic Confit

This aromatic dish takes its name, confit (kohn-FEE), from an old method of preserving. It's like a thick relish.

prep: 11 min.   cook: 35 min.

¼   cup butter, cut into pieces
2   tablespoons coarse sea salt
8   shallots, unpeeled
8   large garlic cloves,
       unpeeled
4   sprigs fresh thyme

Combine all ingredients in a small ovenproof skillet or pan; cover with aluminum foil.

Bake at 350° for 35 minutes or until shallots and garlic are tender. Remove shallots and garlic, reserving melted butter and discarding thyme and salt.

Peel and finely chop shallots and garlic. Stir melted butter into shallot mixture. Spoon into a small decorative jar. Store in refrigerator. Yield: about ½ cup.

Directions for Gift Card: Store in refrigerator. Serve on French bread, crackers, toast, or croutons.

Jambalaya Mix

prep: 7 min.

1   cup uncooked long-grain rice
1   tablespoon dried minced onion
1   tablespoon green bell pepper flakes
1   tablespoon dried parsley flakes
2   teaspoons beef bouillon granules
½   teaspoon garlic powder
½   teaspoon ground black pepper
¼   teaspoon dried thyme
⅛   to ¼ teaspoon dried crushed red
       pepper
1   bay leaf

Combine all ingredients; store in an airtight container. Yield: 1½ cups.

Directions for Gift Card: Bring Jambalaya Mix, 3 cups water, and 1 (8-ounce) can tomato sauce to a boil in a Dutch oven. Stir in 1 cup chopped cooked chicken and 1 cup chopped cooked ham or smoked sausage. Cover, reduce heat, and simmer 20 to 25 minutes or until rice is tender. Discard bay leaf. Yield: about 8 cups.

New Year's Day Chili Mix

prep: 8 min.

1   (16-ounce) package dried kidney beans
1   tablespoon dried minced onion
2   teaspoons beef bouillon granules
1   teaspoon salt
½   teaspoon garlic powder
2½ tablespoons chili powder
1   teaspoon dried oregano
¼   teaspoon ground red pepper
1   small bay leaf

Place beans in a zip-top plastic bag; set aside.

Combine minced onion and next 3 ingredients; place in a small zip-top plastic bag and, if desired, in a decorative paper bag, and label "Flavoring Packet."

Combine chili powder and remaining 3 ingredients; place in a small airtight plastic bag and, if desired, in a decorative paper bag, and label "Seasoning Packet."

Place 1 bag beans, 1 Flavoring Packet, and 1 Seasoning Packet in each gift container. Yield: 1 (3-bag) gift.

Directions for Gift Card: Sort and wash beans; place in a large Dutch oven. Cover with water 2 inches above beans; let soak 8 hours. Drain.

Combine beans, Flavoring Packet, and 7 cups water in a large Dutch oven. Bring to a boil; cover, reduce heat, and simmer 1 hour, stirring occasionally.

Stir in 1 pound ground beef, cooked and drained; 1 (8-ounce) can tomato sauce; 1 (6-ounce) can tomato paste; and Seasoning Packet. Bring to a boil; reduce heat, and simmer, uncovered, 30 minutes, stirring occasionally. Remove and discard bay leaf. Yield: 11 cups.

Quick-Soak Method: Place beans in a Dutch oven; cover with water 2 inches above beans. Bring to a boil; boil 1 minute. Cover, remove from heat, and let stand 1 hour. Drain.

New Year's Day Chili Mix

Nine-Bean Soup Mix

Nine-Bean Soup Mix

If you want to make a big batch of gifts, try this soup mix. It makes enough to give to 10 people. Package it by the 2-cupfuls in plastic bags, and then place inside sheer fabric bags. Be sure to attach the Nine Bean-Chicken Soup Recipe.

prep: 5 min.

1   (16-ounce) package barley
1   (16-ounce) package dried red beans
1   (16-ounce) package dried pinto beans
1   (16-ounce) package uncooked lentils
1   (16-ounce) package dried black-eyed peas
1   (16-ounce) package dried black beans
1   (16-ounce) package dried navy beans
1   (16-ounce) package dried great Northern beans
1   (16-ounce) package dried split peas

Combine all ingredients in a large bowl. Store in airtight containers. Yield: 21 cups.

Directions for Gift Card: Write the recipe below on a card.

Nine Bean-Chicken Soup

prep: 9 min.   cook: 2 hrs., 14 min.   other: 30 min.

2   cups Nine-Bean Soup Mix
2   quarts water
2   cups chopped cooked chicken
1   large onion, chopped
1   garlic clove, minced
1   chicken bouillon cube
1   teaspoon salt
½   teaspoon pepper
1   (14½-ounce) can diced tomatoes
1   (10-ounce) can diced tomatoes and green chiles

Place Nine-Bean Soup Mix in a Dutch oven; add water to cover, and let stand 30 minutes. Drain.

Bring soup mix, 2 quarts water, and next 6 ingredients to a boil in Dutch oven. Cover, reduce heat, and simmer 1 to 1½ hours.

Stir in diced tomatoes and tomatoes with chiles; return to a boil. Cover and simmer 30 minutes or until beans are tender, adding more water, if necessary. Yield: 9 cups.

Bean-Pasta Soup Mix

If your thoughts drift to Christmas in July, get a head start on your gift list and make a batch of this soup mix. It will keep for several months.

prep: 23 min.

¾   cup dried onion flakes
½   cup dried parsley flakes
2   (½-ounce) jars dried celery flakes
3   tablespoons dried basil
3   tablespoons dried oregano
2   teaspoons garlic powder
2   teaspoons coarsely ground pepper
2   (2¼-ounce) jars beef bouillon granules
1   (16-ounce) package dried black-eyed peas
1   (16-ounce) package dried black beans
1   (16-ounce) package dried kidney beans
1   (16-ounce) package dried navy beans
1   (16-ounce) package small shell pasta

Combine first 7 ingredients; divide evenly into 6 portions, and place in 6 zip-top plastic bags. Add 2 tablespoons plus ¼ teaspoon bouillon granules to each bag. Label "Herb Mix," and seal.

Combine black-eyed peas and next 3 ingredients. Divide evenly into 6 portions; place in 6 zip-top plastic bags. Label "Bean Mix," and seal.

Place ⅓ cup pasta in 6 zip-top plastic bags. Label "Pasta," and seal.

Place 1 bag each of Herb Mix, Bean Mix, and Pasta in each gift container. Yield: 6 (3-bag) gifts.

Directions for Gift Card: Sort and wash Bean Mix; place in a Dutch oven. Cover with water 2 inches above beans; let soak 8 hours. Drain.

Combine beans, 3 quarts water, Herb Mix, 1 carrot (scraped and chopped), and ⅔ cup chopped cooked ham in Dutch oven. Bring to a boil; reduce heat, and simmer 2½ hours, stirring occasionally.

Add 1 (14½ ounce) can Mexican-style stewed tomatoes, undrained, and pasta; cook 20 minutes. Yield: 9 cups.

Quick-Soak Method: Place beans in a Dutch oven; cover with water 2 inches above beans. Bring to a boil; boil 1 minute. Cover, remove from heat, and let stand 1 hour. Drain.

Bean-Pasta
Soup Mix

Chocolate Chip Gift-Tub Cookies

prep: 13 min.

1	cup butter or margarine, softened
¾	cup firmly packed brown sugar
½	cup granulated sugar
1	large egg
¼	cup sour cream
1	teaspoon vanilla extract
2	cups all-purpose flour
1	teaspoon baking soda
¾	teaspoon salt
1½	cups (9 ounces) semisweet chocolate morsels
1	cup coarsely chopped pecans

Beat butter in a large mixing bowl at medium speed with an electric mixer. Gradually add sugars; beat until blended. Add egg, sour cream, and vanilla; mix well.

Combine flour, soda, and salt; add to butter mixture, mixing well. Stir in chocolate morsels and pecans. Divide dough into 2 airtight gift containers. Keep refrigerated. Yield: 2 gifts.

Directions for Gift Card: Store in refrigerator up to 5 days. To bake, drop by tablespoonfuls onto lightly greased baking sheets. Bake at 375° for 10 to 12 minutes. Cool on wire racks. Yield: 2 dozen.

terrific topper

For a quick packaging idea, cap a jar with a colorful topper. Simply cut a small square from a fabric remnant, place the square on the jar lid, and tie on with ribbon.

Oatmeal-Raisin-Nut Cookie Mix in a Jar

Bakers on your list will enjoy a jar of this ready-to-make cookie mix. All they'll need to do is add butter, an egg, and vanilla for a delicious batch of homemade treats.

prep: 8 min.

¾	cup firmly packed light brown sugar
½	cup granulated sugar
½	cup raisins
½	cup chopped pecans
1¾	cups uncooked regular oats
1	cup all-purpose flour
1	teaspoon baking soda
½	teaspoon salt

Layer first 5 ingredients in order given in a 1-quart wide-mouth jar, packing down each layer. Combine flour, soda, and salt. Layer mixture over oats in jar.

Directions for Gift Card: Empty cookie mix into a large bowl; stir well. Add ¾ cup softened butter, 1 lightly beaten egg, and 1 teaspoon vanilla extract, stirring until completely blended. (You may need to finish mixing with your hands.)

Shape into 1-inch balls. Place 2 inches apart on parchment-lined or lightly greased baking sheets. Bake at 350° for 13 to 14 minutes or until edges are lightly browned. Cool 1 minute on baking sheets; remove to wire racks to cool completely. Yield: 4½ dozen.

Oatmeal-Raisin-Nut Cookie Mix in a Jar

Spicy Chocolate Crackles

prep: 16 min.   cook: 9 min.

1   (18.25-ounce) package devil's food
      cake mix
⅓   cup vegetable oil
2   large eggs, lightly beaten
1   tablespoon ground ginger
½   teaspoon pepper
1   tablespoon water
¾   cup semisweet chocolate
      mini-morsels
¼   cup sugar

Combine first 6 ingredients in a large bowl, stirring until smooth. Stir in chocolate mini-morsels.

Shape dough into 1-inch balls; roll in sugar to coat. Place balls 2 inches apart on lightly greased baking sheets.

Bake at 375° for 9 minutes. Cool 2 to 3 minutes on baking sheets; remove to wire racks to cool completely. Yield: 4 dozen.

Chocolate Chip Pie Mix

prep: 7 min.

1   cup sugar
½   cup all-purpose flour
1   cup (6 ounces) semisweet chocolate
      morsels
½   cup flaked coconut
½   cup chopped pecans

Spicy Chocolate Crackles

Stir together sugar and flour; seal in a zip-top plastic bag. Place chocolate morsels, coconut, and pecans in another zip-top plastic bag; seal. Place both bags in a decorative gift container. Yield: 1 (2-bag) gift.

Directions for Gift Card: Combine ¼ cup melted butter, dry ingredient packet, and 2 large eggs; stir until dry ingredients are moistened. Stir in chocolate packet. Spoon into an unbaked 9-inch pastry shell. Bake at 350° for 35 to 40 minutes. Yield: 1 (9-inch) pie.

Lemon-Poppy Seed Cakes

Bake and deliver these gift loaves in reusable aluminum loafpans. You can find the pans at most grocery stores.

prep: 14 min. cook: 40 min. other: 10 min.

1 (18.25-ounce) package lemon cake mix without pudding
1 (3.4-ounce) package lemon instant pudding mix
1 cup water
½ cup vegetable oil
4 large eggs
½ cup chopped pecans
1 tablespoon poppy seeds
2 tablespoons sugar
½ cup lemon juice

Combine first 5 ingredients in a large mixing bowl; beat at medium speed with an electric mixer until blended. Stir in pecans and poppy seeds. Pour batter into 3 (8- x 2½-inch) greased reusable aluminum loafpans.

Bake at 325° for 40 minutes or until a wooden pick inserted in center comes out clean, shielding edges with aluminum foil after 30 minutes. Cool in pans on wire racks 10 minutes.

Combine sugar and lemon juice; brush over cakes. Cool completely on wire racks. Chill up to 1 week, or freeze up to 3 months. Yield: 3 loaves.

gift breads

Package homemade cakes and breads in lightweight recyclable aluminum pans available at most supermarkets. Wrap a pan with a large linen napkin. Or place in a gift bag, and tie with ribbon.

Chocolate-Almond Spread

prep: 5 min. cook: 11 min.

2 cups (12 ounces) semisweet chocolate morsels
⅓ cup light corn syrup
⅓ cup whipping cream
½ cup chopped almonds, toasted
1 teaspoon almond extract

Combine first 3 ingredients in top of a double boiler; bring water to a boil. Reduce heat to low, and cook until chocolate melts, stirring occasionally. Remove from heat; stir in almonds and almond extract.

Spoon evenly into 2 (1-cup) gift containers. Store in refrigerator up to 2 weeks. Yield: about 2 cups.

❄ **Directions for Gift Card:** Store Chocolate-Almond Spread in refrigerator up to 2 weeks. Serve with cookies, croissants, or fruit.

Praline Liqueur

Suggest to the recipient to pour this liqueur into coffee, or drizzle it over baked apples or a slice of pound cake.

prep: 9 min. cook: 13 min. other: 2 weeks

2 cups packed dark brown sugar
1 cup granulated sugar
2½ cups water
4 cups pecan pieces, lightly toasted
2 vanilla beans, split lengthwise
4 cups vodka

Combine first 3 ingredients in a medium saucepan, and cook over medium-high heat until sugars dissolve. Bring to a boil; reduce heat, and simmer 5 minutes. Place pecans and vanilla beans in a 1-gallon jar. Pour hot mixture into jar;

cool. Add vodka; stir well. Cover tightly, and store jar in a dark place at room temperature at least 2 weeks. Shake jar gently once daily.

Pour mixture through a wire-mesh strainer lined with 2 layers of cheesecloth into a bowl, discarding solids. Pour mixture through a wire-mesh strainer lined with a coffee filter into a bowl. Change filter often. (Mixture will drip slowly.) Pour mixture into jars; cover tightly. Store in a cool dark place. Yield: 4½ cups.

Mocha Latte Syrup

This syrup looks rich and tempting in a resealable glass jar with festive ribbon tied at the neck. Add colorful beads for extra charm.

prep: 4 min. cook: 7 min.

¾ cup sugar
⅓ cup unsweetened cocoa
¼ cup instant espresso or dark roast instant coffee
½ teaspoon ground cinnamon
½ cup water
2 tablespoons vanilla extract

Combine first 4 ingredients in a medium saucepan. Whisk in water, and bring to a boil over medium heat. Boil 1 minute, stirring often. Remove from heat; stir in 2 tablespoons vanilla. Refrigerate up to 2 weeks. Yield: 1¼ cups.

❄ **Directions for Gift Card:** Store in refrigerator up to 2 weeks. To prepare Mocha Latte Beverage, spoon 1 tablespoon Mocha Latte Syrup into a coffee cup; stir in ¾ cup hot milk.

Mocha Latte Syrup

Serve warm over Ice Cream

Maple-Pecan Ice Cream Topping

Easy to reheat in the microwave, this topping adds a new level of pleasure to a bowl of ice cream.

prep: 8 min.   cook: 8 min.

¾ cup firmly packed brown sugar
¼ cup water
3 tablespoons maple syrup
2 tablespoons butter or margarine
½ cup chopped pecans, toasted
¼ cup whipping cream

Combine brown sugar, water, and maple syrup in a medium saucepan. Attach a candy thermometer to pan, making sure thermometer does not touch bottom of pan. Stirring constantly, cook over medium heat 6 to 8 minutes or until thermometer registers 234° (soft ball stage). Remove from heat, and stir in butter. Cool.

Stir in pecans and whipping cream. Store in an airtight container in refrigerator up to 3 weeks. For gift-giving, pour mixture into a syrup pourer. Look for syrup pourers at any kitchen store. Yield: about 3 cups topping.

Directions for Gift Card: Store in refrigerator up to 3 weeks. Remove decoration and metal lid from syrup container, cover with plastic wrap, and microwave at HIGH (100% power) for 1 minute. Remove plastic wrap, and pour.

top it off

Top off decorative jars of homemade dessert sauces with colored raffia bows. Attach a homemade gift tag and a spoon to each. Look for small spoons at flea markets and tag sales.

Hot Fudge Ice Cream Topping

Hot Fudge Ice Cream Topping

Presents from the kitchen mean something special for you, too: freedom from last-minute shopping. For a gourmet treat, tuck a jar of this topping into a basket with an ice cream scoop.

prep: 3 min.   cook: 17 min.

2 (1-ounce) semisweet chocolate
    baking squares
¾ cup sugar
1 cup evaporated milk
2 tablespoons butter or margarine
1 teaspoon vanilla extract

Melt chocolate in a heavy saucepan over low heat. Stir in sugar until smooth. Gradually add milk, stirring until smooth. Bring to a boil over medium heat, stirring constantly.

Boil, stirring constantly, 6 minutes. Remove from heat; stir in butter and vanilla. Store in refrigerator up to 3 weeks. Serve warm over ice cream. Yield: 1½ cups.

Fabulous Fudge Sauce

The title of this thick, rich fudge sauce tells all—except maybe how quick and easy it is to make.

editor's favorite • quick & easy
prep: 5 min.   cook: 12 min.

2 cups (12 ounces) semisweet
    chocolate morsels
1 (14-ounce) can sweetened
    condensed milk
1 cup miniature marshmallows
½ cup milk
1 teaspoon vanilla extract

Combine all ingredients in a medium saucepan, and cook over medium-low heat until chocolate morsels and marshmallows melt, stirring occasionally. Serve warm over ice cream. Store in refrigerator up to 1 week. Yield: 3¼ cups.

Quick Caramel Sauce

prep: 3 min.   cook: 5 min.

1 (12-ounce) jar caramel topping
1 tablespoon butter or margarine
2 tablespoons bourbon (optional)

Combine caramel topping and butter in a small saucepan; cook over medium heat, stirring constantly, until butter melts and sauce is thoroughly heated. Remove from heat, and stir in bourbon, if desired. Cool slightly. Store in refrigerator up to 1 week. Yield: 1 cup.

no-recipe "recipes"

Here are a dozen really quick, really easy ideas to turn to for fast meals any time of year.

Fruit in a Flash

Fruit in a Flash

Purchase containers of precut fruits (found in the produce section of most grocery stores), or buy your favorite cut fruits by the pound at the salad bar. Add a tangy-sweet dressing for a quick and refreshing salad.

Dressed-Up Cream Cheese

Spoon about ⅔ cup whole-berry cranberry sauce over an 8-ounce block of cream cheese. Serve with crackers or gingersnaps.

Grilled Chicken and Poppy Seed Salad

Toss together torn romaine lettuce and chilled grilled chicken strips from the grocery store. Top with halved grapes, diced celery, and sliced almonds. Drizzle with bottled poppy seed dressing.

Dressed-Up Cream Cheese

Grilled Greek Chicken Salad

Grilled Greek Chicken Salad

Toss together torn romaine lettuce and chilled grilled chicken strips from the grocery store. Top with chopped tomato, sliced cucumber, feta cheese, and sliced ripe olives. Toss with bottled Greek dressing. Grind peppercorns over the top, if desired.

Three-Bean Salad Savvy

For an instant marinated salad, drain and mix 1 can green beans, 1 can lima beans, and 1 can kidney beans; toss with bottled vinaigrette. Chill salad until ready to serve. Garnish with sliced cherry tomatoes.

Turkey 'n' Slaw Wraps

For each wrap, place strips of smoked turkey breast on an 8-inch flour tortilla; top with preshredded cabbage, and drizzle with Ranch-style dressing. Tightly roll, and cut in half to serve.

Three-Bean Salad Savvy

◄ Barbecue Quesadillas

For each quesadilla, heat about ¼ cup barbecue meat with sauce (refrigerated or from your favorite barbecue joint). Spoon on half of a 6-inch flour tortilla; sprinkle with shredded Mexican four-cheese blend and a little minced fresh cilantro. Fold tortillas in half, pressing gently to seal. Grill in hot oil in a large skillet or on a griddle, turning to brown both sides. Cut into wedges. Serve with additional barbecue sauce and sour cream, if desired.

Fast Fajitas ▷

For an instant fiesta, heat and serve 1 package frozen fajita chicken or steak. (Some packages come with chopped vegetables and tortillas.) Serve with purchased guacamole, shredded lettuce, chopped tomatoes, and sour cream.

Beef-and-Cheese Rollups

Spread 2 tablespoons garlic-and-herb spreadable cheese over 1 side of an 8-inch flour tortilla; top with 2 curly leaf lettuce leaves and about ¼ pound thinly sliced deli roast beef, leaving a ½-inch border around the edges. Roll up the tortilla tightly. Cut in half, and serve immediately; or wrap in plastic wrap, and chill up to 8 hours.

Barbecue Quesadillas

Fast Fajitas

Cheesecake Sampler

◄ Cheesecake Sampler

Slice a purchased New York-style cheese-cake, and top with such favorite flavors as:
- **Orange Cheesecake:** Brush orange marmalade evenly over slice. Arrange sliced candied orange segments over top.
- **Walnut Cheesecake:** Spoon walnuts-in-syrup ice cream topping over slice.
- **Raspberry Cheesecake:** Brush melted seedless raspberry jam over slice. Arrange fresh raspberries on top; brush lightly with additional melted jam.
- **Holly Topping:** Pipe green cake decorating gel in the shape of holly leaves over slice. Add red candy-coated chocolate-covered peanut "berries."

Dipped and Drizzled Desserts ►

Garnish cookies or fruits with melted chocolate. To melt chocolate, seal ½ cup chocolate or vanilla morsels in a zip-top freezer bag. Dip bag in very hot water 2 to 3 minutes or until chocolate melts. Dip cookies and fruits in chocolate in the bag; or snip a tiny hole in 1 corner of the bag, and drizzle chocolate over the cookies and fruits. Dry on wax paper-lined trays.

Turtle Dessert in a Flash

Place 8 ice cream sandwiches in a 13- x 9-inch dish. Spread a 12-ounce jar caramel sauce over sandwiches. Sprinkle with toasted, chopped pecans. Top with 8 more ice cream sandwiches. Spread a 12-ounce container frozen whipped topping (thawed) over sandwiches. Sprinkle with more pecans. Cover and freeze at least 1 hour. Let stand 5 minutes before serving; cut into squares. Drizzle with warm hot fudge sauce.

Dipped and Drizzled Desserts

entertaining made easy

These helpful tips will get your holiday season off to a smooth start.

Party-Planning Timetable

Organization is the secret to easy entertaining. Keep this timetable handy to stay on track with your plans.

A month ahead:

• Set a date and time.
• Make out your guest list.
• Plan your menu, and review recipes. Make it easy on yourself. Choose recipes you can prepare ahead, and serve as many room-temperature dishes as possible.
• Make a grocery list of nonperishables that you can buy ahead and another of last-minute items.

3 weeks ahead:

• Mail your invitations—holidays schedules fill quickly!
• Organize in advance. Plan your table settings, serving dishes, and decorations. Borrow or buy, if needed.

2 weeks ahead:

• Shop for specialty items, such as wine, crackers, and cheeses.
• If convenience is most important to you, buy paper napkins and plastic wineglasses, plates, and utensils. Don't forget to check your supply of kitchen garbage bags.

1 week ahead:

• Gather a stack of favorite CDs, and place them near the player. Ask your spouse or a close friend to be in charge of the music.
• Shop for nonperishable items.
• Plan a timetable for recipes you can prepare ahead.

1 or 2 days ahead:

• Clean your house. If you're too busy, think about hiring a cleaning crew or delegate specific chores to family members.
• Create a centerpiece. Buy fresh flowers or greenery, and put them in vases; or set out a few pots of seasonal bulbs in bloom. An arrangement of candles and holiday ornaments looks lovely and lasts throughout the season.
• Arrange furniture to maximize seating. Consider using different rooms for different courses.
• Set up a beverage station near the kitchen so it will be convenient to replenish ice and glassware.
• Set out the linens and decorations, and plan exactly where you'll place each dish. Arrange plates, utensils, and serving dishes in logical order for guests to serve themselves without backtracking. Make sure that each dish has a serving utensil.
• Shop for perishable items.
• Prepare recipes according to your plan.

The big day:

• Start the evening with an empty dishwasher.
• Open wine before guests arrive. Briefly chill white wine. Prepare coffee for brewing, but wait until dinner plates are cleared to brew it. Have a sugar substitute on hand.
• Make last-minute preparations to food, and arrange in serving dishes.
• Plan to serve appetizers in the kitchen, where guests tend to gather initially.
• Pretend you're a guest, and walk through your front door. Think about coat storage and traffic flow—not only around the buffet table but also throughout your house.

Party Essentials

Stock a closet with essential items you'll need for holiday entertaining, and you'll be halfway there.

Centerpieces: Use a pretty container, such as a tureen, as the base for a centerpiece. In a pinch, fill a glass trifle dish with fruits for an easy, last-minute centerpiece.

Fabric and ribbons: Purchase a few yards of fabrics in holiday hues to swirl loosely down the center of the table. There's no need to hem the edges; just turn them under. Use coordinating ribbons as napkin rings.

Votive candleholders: Collect these by the dozen, and you'll have enough to spread a Christmassy glow all through the house—on the dining table, along the mantel, and in the guest bath.

Serving pieces: For casual entertaining, use baskets for easy cleanup. Line with colorful holiday napkins or tea towels. Large bowls make entertaining easy because you don't have to refill them very often. White serving pieces are good choices; they complement various food items and coordinate well with predominantly white dinner plates.

Beverages: You'll need an ice bucket and tongs. Wine carafes make attractive serving pitchers. A large coffeepot makes it easy to accommodate a group. Consider purchasing a pot jointly with a neighbor; then you can take turns using it.

One Oven Solutions

Here are some tips for making one oven work when you're cooking for a crowd.

Use electric heating plates to keep made-ahead dishes warm and ready to serve.

Include in your menu cold or room-temperature salads or marinated vegetables that don't require oven time.

Serve cold sliced ham as your entrée, and concentrate on making the other dishes warm and spectacular.

Smoke or fry a turkey. This frees up your oven for side dishes and dessert.

Enlist family members to bring dishes that have already been cooked. Reheat them briefly in the microwave, and finish in the oven just to crisp toppings.

Keep in mind that a roasted turkey stays hot under aluminum foil for up to 45 minutes. This allows you time to bake those last-minute side dishes.

buffet basics

small group

Arrange food on a sideboard if you're entertaining a small group that will be seated for dinner. Set the dinner table with napkins, flatware, breads, and beverages.

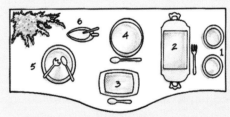

1. dinner plates
2. entrée
3. vegetable
4. vegetable
5. salad
6. sauce or salad dressing

Sideboard

medium-size group

A single round table can serve as a buffet for groups too large for a seated dinner. Place napkins and flatware on the buffet. For lots of guests, group two or more tables together or scatter them throughout for easy access.

1. dinner forks and napkins
2. dinner plates
3. entrée
4. vegetable
5. salad
6. salt and pepper shakers
7. bread

Round Table

large gathering

A dining table or freestanding buffet with space for two serving lines allows good traffic flow for a large group of guests.

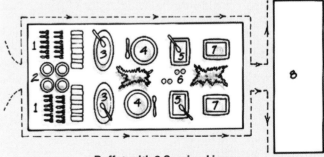

Buffet with 2 Serving Lines

1. dinner forks and napkins   2. dinner plates   3. entrée
4. vegetable   5. salad   6. salt and pepper shakers   7. bread
8. beverages

tabletop extras

Adding simple embellishments shows your creativity and makes your table even more festive. Here are a few ideas to try.

◄ Chair Decoration

Hang a paper cone filled with goodies from the back of a dining chair. To make a cone, cut a rectangle from construction paper. Roll the paper into a loose cone; trim the top with scissors to make a straight edge. Secure with double-sided tape. To line the cone, repeat to make a cone from contrasting paper; insert and hold together with double-sided tape. For the handle, punch a hole on each side of the cone opening, thread a ribbon through the holes, and knot the ribbon ends on the outside of the cone. If desired, punch holes and lace ribbon along the top of the cone.

Greenery Charger ►

Here's a fresh idea for a charger: Hot-glue sprigs of greenery and berries around the edges of a cardboard cake round (check with the grocery-store bakery for cake round). Before gluing on greenery, spray-paint the cardboard, if desired; let dry. The greenery stays fresh for several days, so the chargers can be enjoyed as a fragrant part of your dining room decorations.

◄ Place-Card Holder

Push a piece of craft foam into a small terra-cotta pot. Take a fairly straight twig, and push it into the craft-foam base. With a craft knife, cut a hole equal to the size of the twig in the bottom of an artificial pear. Insert the twig into the pear. With a craft knife, cut a slit in the back of the pear, just behind the stem, to hold a paper place card. Fill the top of the pot with moss, and glue leaves and berries on top of the moss. Tie bows around the trunk and stem, using desired ribbons.

◄ Napkin Ties

Fold napkins, accordian style. Tie ribbons around each napkin to act as holders. Choose ribbons that complement your table's color scheme.

Quick Fruit Centerpiece

To create this quick-and-easy centerpiece,
fill a large bowl with florist foam. Use
florist picks to secure bright red apples
and greenery in the foam around the edges
of the bowl. Set a small bowl in the center
of the large bowl and on top of the florist
foam. Stack apples in the small bowl, and
fill in with greenery and berry sprigs.

gift list

Use the lines on this page to note gift ideas and to keep track of gift-giving.

name	gift idea/gift	sent/delivered

make-ahead planner

Plan ahead for homemade food gifts, using the lines below.

September

Example: Jambalaya Mix, page 252 ....

....

....

....

....

....

....

....

....

....

....

October

Example: Bean-Pasta Soup Mix, page 255 ....

....

....

....

....

....

....

....

....

....

....

November

Example: Hot Cocoa Mix, page 246 ....

....

....

....

....

....

....

....

....

....

....

December

Example: Pepper Pecans, page 250 ....

....

....

....

....

....

....

....

....

....

....

family favorites

Keep a list of your most enjoyed holiday recipes as a handy reminder for next year's celebrations.

recipe	source/page	remarks

memory makers

Use this page to make note of everything you want to repeat (or try) next season.

Best Gift Ideas

....
....
....
....
....
....
....
....
....
....
....

Successful Decorating Ideas

....
....
....
....
....
....
....
....
....
....
....

Annual Holiday Events to Attend

....
....
....
....
....
....
....
....
....
....
....

Traditions to Keep

....
....
....
....
....
....
....
....
....
....
....

metric equivalents

The recipes that appear in this cookbook use the standard United States method for measuring liquid and dry or solid ingredients (teaspoons, tablespoons, and cups). The information on this chart is provided to help cooks outside the United States successfully use these recipes. All equivalents are approximate.

Metric Equivalents for Different Types of Ingredients

A standard cup measure of a dry or solid ingredient will vary in weight depending on the type of ingredient. A standard cup of liquid is the same volume for any type of liquid. Use the following chart when converting standard cup measures to grams (weight) or milliliters (volume).

Standard Cup	Fine Powder (ex. flour)	Grain (ex. rice)	Granular (ex. sugar)	Liquid Solids (ex. butter)	Liquid (ex. milk)
1	140 g	150 g	190 g	200 g	240 ml
¾	105 g	113 g	143 g	150 g	180 ml
⅔	93 g	100 g	125 g	133 g	160 ml
½	70 g	75 g	95 g	100 g	120 ml
⅓	47 g	50 g	63 g	67 g	80 ml
¼	35 g	38 g	48 g	50 g	60 ml
⅛	18 g	19 g	24 g	25 g	30 ml

Useful Equivalents for Liquid Ingredients by Volume

¼ tsp	=						1 ml	
½ tsp	=						2 ml	
1 tsp	=						5 ml	
3 tsp	=	1 tbls			= ½ fl oz	=	15 ml	
	=	2 tbls	= ⅛ cup	=	1 fl oz	=	30 ml	
	=	4 tbls	= ¼ cup	=	2 fl oz	=	60 ml	
	=	5⅓ tbls	= ⅓ cup	=	3 fl oz	=	80 ml	
	=	8 tbls	= ½ cup	=	4 fl oz	=	120 ml	
	=	10⅔ tbls	= ⅔ cup	=	5 fl oz	=	160 ml	
	=	12 tbls	= ¾ cup	=	6 fl oz	=	180 ml	
	=	16 tbls	= 1 cup	=	8 fl oz	=	240 ml	
	=	1 pt	= 2 cups	=	16 fl oz	=	480 ml	
	=	1 qt	= 4 cups	=	32 fl oz	=	960 ml	
					33 fl oz	=	1000 ml	= 1 l

Useful Equivalents for Dry Ingredients by Weight

To convert ounces to grams, multiply the number of ounces by 30.

1 oz	=	1/16 lb	=	30 g
4 oz	=	¼ lb	=	120 g
8 oz	=	½ lb	=	240 g
12 oz	=	¾ lb	=	360 g
16 oz	=	1 lb	=	480 g

Useful Equivalents for Length

To convert inches to centimeters, multiply the number of inches by 2.5.

1 in			= 2.5 cm	
6 in	= ½ ft		= 15 cm	
12 in	= 1 ft		= 30 cm	
36 in	= 3 ft	= 1 yd	= 90 cm	
40 in			= 100 cm	= 1 m

Useful Equivalents for Cooking/Oven Temperatures

	Fahrenheit	Celsius	Gas Mark
Freeze Water	32° F	0° C	
Room Temperature	68° F	20° C	
Boil Water	212° F	100° C	
Bake	325° F	160° C	3
	350° F	180° C	4
	375° F	190° C	5
	400° F	200° C	6
	425° F	220° C	7
	450° F	230° C	8
Broil			Grill

index